This book's contributors are leaders in reshaping and pushing the boundaries of traditional psychological theories to deliver healing frameworks, perspectives, and interventions to human trafficking victims, survivors, and providers. The contributors offer the full gamut of views to inform the psychological perspective, with chapters covering the crucial historical, social, clinical, organizational, and developmental issues that concern human trafficking, making it a gem of a book to teach and train all students interested in engaging this population.

— **Paola M. Contreras,** Associate Professor, William James College, Newton, MA; Member of the APA's Task Force on the Trafficking of Women and Girls

Providing psychological services to those who've experienced human trafficking is complex, especially since their needs are great and constantly changing. This is one of the most useful books for every psychologist to have on their reference shelf, precisely because it deals with human trafficking from a variety of theoretical frameworks in organizational, social, forensic, and clinical psychology.

— **Lenore E. Walker, EdD,** Professor Emerita, Nova Southeastern University College of Psychology, Davie, FL; Coauthor of *Handbook of Sex Trafficking: Feminist Transnational Perspectives*

An essential read for anyone who cares about human trafficking. Reaching out to researchers, practitioners, educators, policy makers, and activists, Dryjanska, Hopper, and Stoklosa have assembled an impressive roster of experts from diverse fields of psychology to bring new perspectives on a wealth of topics from prevention to intervention. Absorbing this book enriched my understanding of trafficking and made me want to get back to work with survivors.

— **Mary Crawford, PhD,** Professor Emerita, University of Connecticut, Storrs, CT; Author of *Sex Trafficking in South Asia*

PSYCHOLOGICAL PERSPECTIVES ON HUMAN TRAFFICKING

PSYCHOLOGICAL PERSPECTIVES ON HUMAN TRAFFICKING

Theory, Research, Prevention, and Intervention

Laura Dryjanska,	
Elizabeth K. Hopper,	
and Hanni Stoklosa	Editors

AMERICAN PSYCHOLOGICAL ASSOCIATION

Published by
American Psychological Association
750 First Street, NE
Washington, DC 20002
https://www.apa.org

Order Department
https://www.apa.org/pubs/books
order@apa.org

Typeset in Charter and Interstate by Circle Graphics, Inc., Reisterstown, MD

Printer: Gasch Printing, Odenton, MD
Cover Designer: Craig Davidson for Civic Design, Minneapolis, MN

Library of Congress Cataloging-in-Publication Data

Names: Dryjanska, Laura, editor. | American Psychological Association.
Title: Psychological perspectives on human trafficking : theory, research,
    prevention, and intervention / [Editors] Laura Dryjanska, Elizabeth K.
    Hopper, and Hanni Stoklosa.
Description: Washington, DC : American Psychological Association, [2024] |
    Includes bibliographical references and index.
Identifiers: LCCN 2023017763 (print) | LCCN 2023017764 (ebook) |
    ISBN 9781433838705 (paperback) | ISBN 9781433838712 (ebook)
Subjects: LCSH: Human trafficking--Psychological aspects. |
    Social psychology. | Post-traumatic stress disorder.
Classification: LCC HQ281 .P79 2024 (print) | LCC HQ281 (ebook) |
    DDC 362.88/51--dc23/eng/20230426
LC record available at https://lccn.loc.gov/2023017763
LC ebook record available at https://lccn.loc.gov/2023017764

https://doi.org/10.1037/0000379-000

Printed in the United States of America

10 9 8 7 6 5 4 3 2 1

Contents

Contributors

Lujain Alhajji, MD, Department of Psychiatry and Behavioral Sciences, University of Miami Leonard M. Miller School of Medicine, Miami, FL, United States

Robert Blanton, PhD, Department of Political Science and Public Administration, University of Alabama at Birmingham, Birmingham, AL, United States

Gregory J. Bott, PhD, Department of Information Systems, Statistics, and Management Science, University of Alabama, Tuscaloosa, AL, United States

Thema Bryant, PhD, Graduate School of Education and Psychology, Pepperdine University, Los Angeles, CA, United States

Jessa Dillow Crisp, MA, Denver Seminary, Littleton, CO, United States

Laura Dryjanska, PhD, Department of Psychology, Asbury University, Wilmore, KY, United States; Cardinal Stefan Wyszyński University, Warsaw, Poland

Nickolas K. Freeman, PhD, Department of Information Systems, Statistics, and Management Science, University of Alabama, Tuscaloosa, AL, United States

Barbara G. Friedman, PhD, Hussman School of Journalism and Media, University of North Carolina at Chapel Hill, Chapel Hill, NC, United States

Elizabeth K. Hopper, PhD, National Center on Child Trafficking; Justice Resource Institute, Boston, MA, United States

Deidre Hussey, PsyD, Baystate Family Advocacy Center, Springfield, MA; Department of Psychiatry, University of Massachusetts Chan Medical School—Baystate Regional Campus, Springfield, MA, United States

Becca C. Johnson, PhD, AIM-Agape International Mission, Roseville, CA; Engedi Refuge, Lynden, WA, United States

Burcu B. Keskin, PhD, Department of Information Systems, Statistics, and Management Science, University of Alabama, Tuscaloosa, AL, United States

Kelly Kinnish, PhD, National Center on Child Trafficking, Georgia State University, Atlanta, GA, United States

Cassandra Ma, PsyD, Reclaim 13, Lombard, IL, United States

Dominique A. Malebranche, PhD, Graduate School of Education and Psychology, Pepperdine University, Los Angeles, CA, United States

Maura J. Mills, PhD, Department of Management, University of Alabama, Tuscaloosa, AL, United States

Vanessa Padilla, MD, Department of Psychiatry and Behavioral Sciences, University of Miami Leonard M. Miller School of Medicine, Miami, FL, United States

JoNell Efantis Potter, PhD, Department of Obstetrics, Gynecology and Reproductive Sciences, University of Miami Leonard M. Miller School of Medicine, Miami, FL, United States

Nancy Sidun, PsyD, independent practice, Honolulu, HI, United States

Hanni Stoklosa, MD, MPH, HEAL Trafficking, Long Beach, CA; Department of Emergency Medicine, Harvard Medical School, Boston, MA, United States

Leanne M. Tortez, PhD, Department of Organizational and Leadership Psychology, William James College, Newton, MA, United States

Jessica Wozniak, PsyD, Department of Psychiatry, Baystate Health; University of Massachusetts Chan Medical School—Baystate Regional Campus, Springfield, MA, United States

Foreword

When I became aware of human trafficking in the early 2000s, I was astonished to learn how minimal were the efforts of psychologists and the discipline of psychology to address this grave human rights violation. I made it my passion and mission to raise awareness of human trafficking in psychology. I initially started presenting about human trafficking at the American Psychological Association (APA) annual convention and have continued to raise awareness. As this is a global problem, I approached the leadership of APA's Division 52 (International Psychology) to start a task force on human trafficking. Recognizing that all fields of psychology need to be involved, in 2011, APA created a systemwide Task Force on Human Trafficking of Women and Girls. I cochaired that task force, and our APA report made specific recommendations for research, practice, education and training, public policy, and public awareness—pivotal roles for psychologists. This APA task force report was the impetus for future and significant work that APA and its divisions have undertaken to counter human trafficking. In 2017, the APA Council adopted the Resolution on Human Trafficking in the United States, especially for women and girls. Each APA division has made meaningful contributions to tackle this devastating human rights violation. This book, published by APA, is the latest example of APA's commitment to understanding how psychology can play a pivotal role in combating the trafficking of humans. Each author is a committed and highly knowledgeable expert on their area of human trafficking. One rarely sees such a selection of stellar work in this arena.

Thema Bryant, APA's 2023 president, who cares profoundly and is highly dedicated to this issue, coauthored with Dominique Malebranche a critical chapter in this book on abolitionist psychology and human trafficking. I have been familiar with Dr. Bryant and Dr. Malebranche's work; I have presented with both authors and collaborated with Dr. Bryant on several projects addressing human trafficking. Our first endeavor was a video on human trafficking sponsored by APA's Division 35 (Society for the Psychology of Women) and coproduced by Thema. Dr. Bryant also cowrote a powerful chapter, "Cultural Oppression and Human Trafficking: Exploring the Role of Racism and Ethnic Bias," in a book I coedited, *A Feminist Perspective on Human Trafficking of Women and Girls* (2018). She is a brilliant scholar on trauma and racism and has authored numerous foundational books on trauma. Elizabeth (Elise) Hopper, one of the coeditors of this book, has written an outstanding chapter on the prevention of trafficking. She also contributed a chapter, "Trauma-Informed Psychological Assessment of Trafficking Survivors," for the human trafficking book I coedited. Her scholarly work on complex trauma, trauma-informed care, homelessness, and human trafficking bears witness to her understanding of the complexity of human trafficking. Elise and Kelly Kinnish, codirectors of the National Center on Child Trafficking, have also written two pivotal chapters in this book, one on the psychological impacts of labor and sex trafficking and the other on trauma-informed interventions with survivors. I have also had the opportunity to work closely with Laura Dryjanska and Cassandra Ma this past year on putting together a unique symposium for APA's annual convention on often overlooked aspects of human trafficking. I am pleased to see Ma's critical work on the frequently disregarded developmental aspects of trafficked child survivors included in this book. Knowing Ma before she launched her much-needed and valued long-term, trauma-informed residential treatment facility and being on their advisory board, I had the opportunity to witness her incredible impact on survivors and see her expertise reflected in her chapter, "Developmental Approaches to Child Trafficking." All the contributors to this book have worked directly with human trafficking survivors within various service organizations, with many authors researching and teaching this subject at academic institutions. For example, Dr. Hanni Stoklosa, one of the coeditors, is the cofounder and chief medical officer of Health, Education, Advocacy, Linkage (HEAL) Trafficking. I can comfortably attest to the extraordinary contributions of each author and the coeditors. This book captures major frameworks to understand the intricacies of human trafficking, including a much-neglected area, labor trafficking.

The authors and coeditors of the present book are stellar scholars, clinicians, and researchers. They have created a much-needed and sought-after collection of what different fields of psychology (e.g., social, clinical, positive psychology, industrial or organization psychology, developmental) can bring to the issue of human trafficking. All authors bring their unique lens and knowledge about human trafficking to their chapters. This book, *Psychological Perspectives on Human Trafficking: Theory, Research, Prevention, and Intervention*, offers a unique and essential voice to this grave human rights violation. It truly advances the knowledge of how psychology can assist survivors of trafficking and ultimately eliminate human trafficking. I anticipate that this book will become a classic and mandatory reading for all psychologists and other mental health professionals who want to understand human trafficking from a psychological lens.

Nancy M. Sidun, PsyD, ABPP, ATR
Clinical Psychologist, Scholar, Writer
Past Cochair, American Psychological Association Task Force
on Trafficking of Women and Girls
Coeditor of *A Feminist Perspective on Human Trafficking of Women
and Girls: Characteristics, Commonalities and Complexities*

PSYCHOLOGICAL PERSPECTIVES ON HUMAN TRAFFICKING

INTRODUCTION

Psychological Perspectives on Human Trafficking

LAURA DRYJANSKA, ELIZABETH K. HOPPER, AND HANNI STOKLOSA

German philosopher Rudolph Goclenuis, who first put the term "psychology" in writing, once said, "Add pride to the world, contributing your part unconditionally." We offer this volume in that spirit of contribution as a joint effort to introduce and explore the topic of human trafficking through the lens of psychology.

The United Nations Protocol to Prevent, Suppress, and Punish Trafficking in Persons (2000), also known as the Palermo Protocol, was the first legally binding instrument with an internationally recognized definition of human trafficking. Article 3 defines *trafficking* as

> the recruitment, transportation, transfer, harbouring or receipt of persons, by means of the threat or use of force or other forms of coercion, of abduction, of fraud, of deception, of the abuse of power or of a position of vulnerability or of the giving or receiving of payments or benefits to achieve the consent of a person having control over another person, for the purpose of exploitation. Exploitation shall include, at a minimum, the exploitation of the prostitution of others or other forms of sexual exploitation, forced labour or services, slavery or practices similar to slavery, servitude or the removal of organs. (p. 213)

https://doi.org/10.1037/0000379-001

Psychological Perspectives on Human Trafficking: Theory, Research, Prevention, and Intervention, L. Dryjanska, E. K. Hopper, and H. Stoklosa (Editors)

Although the protocol emphasizes the role of force, threat, or coercion in trafficking generally, it clarifies that these elements do not need to be present in trafficking children. While estimates of trafficking are fraught due to methodological and practical issues, estimates indicate that 27.6 million people are trafficked globally (International Labour Organization, 2022).

The essence of the crime of trafficking is controlling one human being for the profit of another. Over the last century, psychology has been advancing our understanding of, and response to, other forms of interpersonal violence, including domestic violence and child abuse. As a result, society has cultivated a more sophisticated understanding of the causes and impacts of interpersonal violence, generated improved strategies to mitigate interpersonal violence, and developed more efficacious interventions and treatments. Our hope is that this volume advances psychology's conversation about and solutions toward ending human trafficking.

This book synthesizes current psychological scholarship and translates theory into practice. Throughout, this volume emphasizes social determinants of human trafficking such as poverty, race, and gender. This book acknowledges the limited empirical research on the subject in terms of the exploitation of boys and men, as well as transgender, gender nonconfirming, and intersex people in human trafficking. The authors also address the lack of literature on labor trafficking and immigrant groups that are impacted. Psychological frameworks may vary by cultural contexts, and it is important to acknowledge the value of cross-cultural sharing of information, perspectives, and potential solutions (Darley & Dölemeyer, 2020).

While this volume addresses the issue of human trafficking through a variety of psychological perspectives, not all areas of psychology are included, and the potential contribution of other areas of psychology (e.g., school psychology, forensic psychology, cognitive psychology, health psychology) should be explored. Further, we do not thoroughly explore all areas of human trafficking, such as the psychology of forced marriage, forced criminality, or organ trafficking. Our language choices in this book are intentional. As much as possible, we use person-centered language. We reserve the term *victim* to refer to those currently experiencing the crime of trafficking and those actively engaged in the criminal justice system (e.g., as a "victim witness"). We use the term *survivor* to recognize the challenge of facing difficult or traumatic circumstances often involved in trafficking. However, we recognize the right of each person to choose language that best fits their perception of their own experience and identity. Furthermore, we do not use the term *prostitution*, given its legal repercussions, but rather refer to engagement in commercial sex acts. Given the conflation with chattel slavery, where possible the authors avoid the term "modern-day slavery."

The editors of the volume embody cooperation between different sub-fields of psychology as well as multidisciplinary collaboration. Alongside authors who specialize in diverse areas of psychology and are involved in antitrafficking theory, research, policy, and practice, we hope to stimulate a reflection on the role of psychology when it comes to labor and sex trafficking. In addition to contributions from each of the authors, the editors wish to thank Dr. Nancy M. Sidun for her foreword, which sets the stage for the volume, as well as the reviewers for providing helpful comments and suggestions.

In Chapter 1, Elizabeth K. Hopper presents overarching theoretical perspectives on the psychology of human trafficking, explaining how a socio-ecological framework can be used to develop primary, secondary, and tertiary prevention initiatives to combat human trafficking. This chapter frames the text as a whole by exploring societal, community, relational, and individual factors associated with human trafficking and discussing various approaches to moderate risk and promote resilience.

Chapter 2, by Thema Bryant and Dominique A. Malebranche, explores human trafficking among marginalized communities, using the theoretical orientation of liberation psychology that allows for an intersectional, justice-oriented framework. The authors focus on racism or ethnic bias, classism or caste systems, sexism or patriarchy, and heterosexism, highlighting the role of abolitionist psychologists—liberation psychologists who actively work to abolish human trafficking in practice, research, consultation, or advocacy.

Given the relative overemphasis on sex trafficking in comparison with labor trafficking in the field, Lujain Alhajji, JoNell Efantis Potter, and Vanessa Padilla concentrate an exclusive chapter (Chapter 3) on the latter form of exploitation. The authors define labor trafficking and describe its occurrence within specific industries, including agriculture and animal husbandry; domestic work; hospitality, restaurant, and food services; illicit massage, health, and beauty businesses; fisheries, traveling sales crews; and bars, strip clubs, and cantinas. They discuss indicators of labor trafficking and screening tools that may be helpful to psychologists and other professionals who come into contact with potential persons impacted by trafficking, especially considering the fact that many victims do not self-identify as such.

The volume then moves on to explore human trafficking from the perspective of diverse subfields of psychology, beginning with a chapter on developmental psychology and child trafficking by Cassandra Ma. In Chapter 4, Ma demonstrates how different developmental periods in childhood relate to vulnerability and impacts, taking into account various forms of exploitation such as child labor, child soldiers, child sex trafficking, and child marriage.

In Chapter 5, Barbara G. Friedman discusses human trafficking through the lenses of media psychology, exploring the issue of how the news frames human trafficking and highlighting the potential role of psychologists as experts who can influence public perception through framing media coverage of the topic. In particular, psychologists can offer context that frames the issue in terms of broader themes, moving the issue of trafficking beyond the immediate event or individual parties. In this way, they can place it into broader societal context, reducing victim blaming and promoting more active engagement from the general public in addressing the issue.

Social psychology may provide useful insights on human trafficking in terms of the social self-concept, cognitive processes, and biases when perceiving others, including people who have been impacted by human trafficking, as well as perpetrators. Chapter 6, by Laura Dryjanska, demonstrates that social psychology has much to offer in terms of understanding how trafficking survivors process information, perceive themselves and are perceived by others. In particular, the substantial body of research unveils some of the mechanisms behind cognitive processes and decision making in general.

Next, in Chapter 7, Maura J. Mills, Leanne M. Tortez, Robert Blanton, Burcu B. Keskin, Gregory J. Bott, and Nickolas K. Freeman discuss how industrial and organizational psychology can play a critical role in prediction and prevention of human trafficking, as well as in training employees to recognize signs of human trafficking in their workplaces. On a broader scale, it can also help improve understanding of some of the ways in which organizations can respond to trafficking both proactively and reactively in regard to tangential issues such as supply chain considerations as well as data collection and analysis.

A volume on psychology of human trafficking would not be complete without chapters written by clinical psychologists. Hopper and Kelly Kinnish explore clinical psychological perspectives on the traumatic nature of human trafficking and its impacts on survivors' biological, emotional, cognitive, and behavioral functioning (Chapter 8). Trauma and violence impacts are typically compounded by conditions of coercive control and emotional and relational harm, resulting in significant symptoms of posttraumatic stress and complex trauma symptoms; depression, anxiety, and suicidal ideation; substance use problems; and other deleterious mental health outcomes discussed in this chapter.

Furthermore, in Chapter 9, Kinnish and Hopper discuss current approaches to clinical intervention with trafficking survivors, emphasizing evidence-based treatments targeting some of the primary mental health impacts of trafficking, as well as addressing adjunctive treatments and promising practices. The authors address engagement and the therapeutic alliance, trauma-informed psychological assessment and treatment planning, and a variety of treatment approaches, including individual, group, and family interventions. They also highlight recommendations for further development in trauma-informed intervention with human trafficking survivors.

In Chapter 10, Jessa Dillow Crisp and Becca C. Johnson utilize the lens of positive psychology to demonstrate how the inner resilience and strength of individuals impacted by human trafficking can be supported and cultivated by multidisciplinary individuals and systems that interact with each survivor, fostering greater external and internal stability. Opportunities to facilitate resilience and posttraumatic growth are described as key factors in helping those who have experienced trafficking to move beyond victimization into a place of surviving and then thriving, by accomplishing individualized goals and nurturing a desired future identity.

Finally, in line with the social-ecological model introduced in the first chapter, this volume's final chapter, by Jessica Wozniak and Deidre Hussey, features a multidisciplinary approach to supporting and treating survivors of human trafficking. As members of a multidisciplinary team, psychologists can help improve methods for identifying trafficking survivors and can promote the development and utilization of evidence-based services and programs for human trafficking survivors through practice, consultation, training and education, research and program evaluation, and policy and prevention promotion.

The primary goal of this book is to use a variety of applied psychological frameworks—including developmental, social, industrial and organizational, clinical, and positive psychology, as well as multidisciplinary approaches—to better understand human trafficking and its impacts, guiding strategies for change. It is intended to be a resource not only for psychologists, social workers, and mental health clinicians but also for a broader audience of practitioners, researchers, administrators, and advocates to enrich psychological perspectives on human trafficking, enhancing trauma-informed multidisciplinary responses to human trafficking and those who are impacted.

REFERENCES

Darley, M., & Dölemeyer, A. (2020). Caring for victims of human trafficking: Staging and bridging cultural differences in Germany and France. *Sociologus*, *70*(1), 19–38. https://doi.org/10.3790/soc.70.1.19

International Labour Organization. (2022). *Forced labour, modern slavery and human trafficking*. https://www.ilo.org/global/topics/forced-labour/lang--en/index.htm

United Nations. (2000). *Protocol to prevent, suppress and punish trafficking in persons, especially women and children, supplementing the United Nations Convention Against Transnational Organized Crime*. https://treaties.un.org/Pages/ViewDetails.aspx?src=IND&mtdsg_no=XVIII-12-a&chapter=18&clang=_en

1

HUMAN TRAFFICKING PREVENTION

Using a Socioecological Framework to Moderate Risk and Promote Protective Factors

ELIZABETH K. HOPPER

In order to confront a problem, it is crucial to understand it. Many fields of psychology—including community, social, clinical, counseling, developmental, school, and industrial and organizational psychology, among others—can contribute insights into the circumstances and dynamics that make individuals and communities vulnerable to human trafficking, as well as protective factors that decrease risk. These insights establish the groundwork for primary prevention efforts that proactively address risk, secondary prevention programs that guide identification and early response to incidents of human trafficking, and tertiary prevention responses that aim to reduce the incidence of recidivism and revictimization and mitigate its long-term impacts.

Psychologist Urie Bronfenbrenner first developed the concept of a "socioecological model" in the late 1970s to describe how individuals affect, and are shaped by, a complex network of social influences and layered environmental contexts (Bronfenbrenner, 1979). Individuals are affected by both their immediate environments (e.g., families, schools, work settings, communities) and the larger social contexts within which these environments are embedded. Scientists are learning more about how social determinants of health—including social, economic, environmental, and structural

https://doi.org/10.1037/0000379-002
Psychological Perspectives on Human Trafficking: Theory, Research, Prevention, and Intervention, L. Dryjanska, E. K. Hopper, and H. Stoklosa (Editors)

disparities—contribute to intergroup differences in life experiences and health and mental health outcomes (Centers for Disease Control and Prevention, 2021), including human trafficking (Robichaux & Torres, 2022). Because of this, when examining the driving forces behind human trafficking, it is important to not only identify individual risk factors but also to look "upstream" to relational, community, and its larger societal underpinnings (American Psychological Association, 2014). Unequal allocation of resources and power (including societal attention and regard) across the lines of race, class, gender identity, sexual orientation, and other dimensions of individual and group identity, creates unique vulnerabilities to labor and sex trafficking. Societal biases have led to the division of groups of people into resource-rich or resource-poor neighborhoods, with a ripple effect that plays out in family dynamics and individual psychologies. A young child who is the product of a multigenerational family history marked by oppression, racism, and poverty enters the world at a disadvantage (Chetty et al., 2020), which can be exacerbated by additional layers of adversity. They may grow up in a community that is impacted by limited resources and repeated episodes of violence. Maybe the child is raised by an overwhelmed single parent who is often absent due to work obligations at a low-paying job, and there is not enough food in the cupboards. Even without the direct experience of abuse, this child's day-to-day life is marked by deprivation, isolation, and fear.

As found in the adverse childhood experiences (ACEs) studies, these types of early developmental risk factors can unfold into layers of negative sequelae over time, from high-risk behaviors to a host of mental, social and physical health issues (Felitti et al., 1998). Because the child described above is growing up with inadequate nutrition, lack of adult supervision, and chronic secondary trauma exposure, focusing and learning in school are likely to be difficult. Maybe their learning difficulties are exacerbated by a neurodevelopmental disorder such as attention-deficit/hyperactivity disorder (ADHD), a learning disability, autism, or an intellectual disability. Teachers and family members might become frustrated with the child's emotional and behavioral issues. Furthermore, the child may be rejected or bullied by peers due to aspects of their behavior or physical appearance such as their skin color, weight, or other physical differences. Lacking nurturance and support, with limited experiences of success, the child may begin to feel ashamed and worthless, entering a cycle of escalating challenges associated with a host of negative outcomes.

Additional vulnerabilities could be added to this example that further alter this child's outcomes. Maybe the child is a girl who is entering puberty early and gaining unwanted attention from older males. Or perhaps the child, assigned as a biological male at birth, has a more traditionally feminine presentation and is the target of escalating bullying and abuse. Consider the additional challenges and risks if they are a recent immigrant who does not speak English. How might their trajectory be different if they have an older, admired relative who is gang-affiliated or a caregiver with a substance use disorder? To effectively engage in antitrafficking work, including prevention, professionals must consider the complex interplay between individual, relational, community, and societal factors that contribute to conditions of human trafficking.

BUYERS, FACILITATORS, SURVIVORS, AND VICTIM-OFFENDER INTERSECTIONALITY

Before exploring these risk and protective factors further, it is important to identify the range of people who may be involved in human trafficking. This is a complicated task because there is no single profile of a buyer or consumer, a facilitator of human trafficking, or a trafficking survivor.[1] Individuals in these roles are not bound within the lines of race, color, national origin, disability, religion, age, gender, sexual orientation, gender identity, socioeconomic status, education level, or citizenship status. Instead, research is needed to identify psychological dynamics that are relevant for these different groups, as well as within-group variability in these psychological considerations.

The demand for human trafficking involves members of the general public who are buyers of goods and services whose supply chain involves trafficking, as well as owners and executives within businesses or enterprises that directly or indirectly involve it. Some consumers lack awareness of human trafficking in general and its relevance to themselves and their own practices, while others disregard the effects of exploitation. Businesses may also either inadvertently or intentionally prioritize profit margins over human rights. Although there is an absence of research into the psychological motivations of consumers in situations of labor trafficking, a psychological analysis of consumerism highlighted the effects of advertising, consumption, materialism, and a capitalistic economic system on child development and its negative effects on later personal, social, and ecological well-being (Kasser & Kanner,

---

[1]The terms included here are used due to brevity and are reflective of terminology in the cited literature. However, it is important to acknowledge the importance of person-first and identity-first language (e.g., "a person impacted by trafficking"), as well as the right of the person to select language that is most consistent with their own identity (e.g., while some people who have been impacted are comfortable with the term "victim," others identify with the term "survivors," while others do not identify with either of these terms).

2004). Psychology's exploration of consumer culture is an untapped area (Kasser & Kanner, 2004) that likely has relevance for human trafficking prevention on a global scale.

In contrast, more research has examined the purchase of commercial sex. Scholars have identified a number of psychological viewpoints that may motivate or justify the behavior of buyers of commercial sex, including the perception of sex as a commodity, normalized beliefs about the commercial sexual industry (e.g., the perception that buyers are just "guys being guys" and that prostitution is a victimless crime), the desire for sexual gratification, interest in diversifying sexual interests or in atypical (and, in some cases, societally objectionable) sexual practices, perceived romantic inadequacy, lack of an available partner, the desire for sexual contact without emotional connection, and the desire for power and control (Alves & Cavalhieri, 2021; Westerhoff, 2012). Research has identified a link between the purchasing of sex and key indicators of aggression against women (Alves & Cavalhieri, 2021; Farley et al., 2017).

Facilitators of human trafficking enable a scheme that derives financial benefit from exploiting victims. This group includes recruiters, managers, bosses, and others who organize, implement, and profit from human trafficking. Although they are also contributors to demand, buyers of commercial sex from minors are increasingly considered to be perpetrators of human trafficking, with legal precedent (Nichols & Heil, 2017). Because the bulk of the literature related to human trafficking focuses on people impacted by trafficking, little is known to date about the characteristics and motivations of facilitators of human trafficking (Sidun, 2018).

Further complicating research on this issue, the qualities and motives of facilitators of various forms of exploitation are likely to differ considerably. For instance, a family who brings a nanny of a perceived lower social status into their home, holds her documents, and promises to pay later may be influenced by their sociocultural perspective of group hierarchies and motivated by financial savings. A farm supervisor who requires migrant laborers to work long hours with no breaks, a lack of safety equipment, and little pay may be prompted to exploit the workers due to pressure from the crew boss or farm owner to meet benchmarks and a fear of repercussions, such as losing their job. In contrast, along with characteristics common to perpetrators of child abuse, addiction-related factors (e.g., cravings, withdrawal) may be the immediate impetus for a parent who provides sexual access to their child in exchange for drugs. Beyond the motivation for financial gain, a trafficker who belittles and beats the people they are commercially sexually exploiting may be spurred by aggressive impulses, along with a desire for control that stems from some of the same early adversities faced by victims. Reyes (2016) suggested that facilitators of labor and sex trafficking use a range of social psychological justifications for trafficking, including distortion (framing trafficking situations under more acceptable terms, such as concealing or disregarding indentured servitude that occurs under the pretense of an "internship" or cultural exchange visa program), rationalization (using faulty logic, including the belief that providing an unscrupulous "work opportunity" is preferable to the alternative of unemployment, or the idea that exploitative behavior is acceptable because "everyone does it"), social comparisons (comparing themselves favorably to more violent or abusive traffickers), blame shifting (accusing others or conditions outside of their control of forcing them to engage in trafficking behaviors), and dehumanization (viewing others as inferior and deserving of exploitation; see Chapter 6, this volume, for more on social psychology). Research is needed to investigate these theories and to explore diversity in the psychological processes of facilitators of different forms of labor and sex trafficking.

The majority of psychological research on human trafficking to date has focused on people who have been impacted, often referred to as "survivors" (see the previous discussion of inclusive language). Survivors of human trafficking are individuals who have been compelled or coerced into providing labor or services, including commercial sex acts, or minors who have been exploited for commercial sex, regardless of whether any force, fraud, or coercion was used. A strong body of research is available examining historical, contextual, and personal risk factors for trafficking-related victimization, coercive and abusive experiences during trafficking, and trauma-related effects (Hopper, 2017a; Hopper & Gonzalez, 2018; Ibrahim et al., 2019; Kiss, Pocock, et al., 2015a, 2015b; Kiss, Yun, et al., 2015; Kiss & Zimmerman, 2019; Nodzenski et al., 2020; Ottisova et al., 2016, 2018; Palines et al., 2020; Sprang & Cole, 2018; Swaner et al., 2016; Twis et al., 2022; see Chapter 8, this volume, for a review of trafficking experiences and psychological effects). There is a growing body of literature on issues faced by marginalized, underidentified, and/or underserved groups affected by trafficking and exploitation, including people from different racial or ethnic minority groups (Bryant-Davis & Gobin, 2019; Bryant-Davis & Tummala-Narra, 2018; Ortega et al., 2022), boys and men (Hebert, 2016), individuals who identify as LGBTQ+ (Hogan & Roe-Sepowitz, 2020), people with intellectual or developmental disabilities (Franchino-Olsen et al., 2020; Reid, 2018), and others (see Chapter 2 on trafficking marginalized communities). Psychology has also begun to explore the effectiveness of posttrafficking social and psychological interventions in reducing the severity and chronicity of trauma-related sequelae, including the risk of revictimization (Hopper, 2017c; Hopper et al., 2018; Kinnish et al., 2020; Powell et al., 2018; Salami et al., 2018; see Chapter 9, this volume, for a discussion of psychological intervention with individuals and families impacted by trafficking).

The distinctions between buyers, facilitators, and survivors are not always clear. A currently underresearched area is victim–offender intersectionality, the phenomenon of trafficking survivors who have engaged in conduct that violates trafficking-related laws. In some cases, victims may be explicitly coerced into this behavior. For instance, a person who is being labor trafficked within a gang may be threatened with physical harm if they do not recruit another person into the gang. In other cases, it may be protective, such as when a young person who is being commercially sexually exploited brings a friend to "work" a bachelor party because they are scared to go alone. Some trafficking networks are organized to allow for "upward social mobility" as trafficking victims move into enforcement roles. The term "bottom" was created and perpetuated by traffickers to refer to victim–offenders who are offered increased status or other benefits in order to perform roles such as recruitment, training, oversight, or facilitation of transactions involving other trafficking victims, thus protecting the trafficker from criminal justice repercussions. Since trafficking victims in this and similar situations may be charged as trafficking offenders, psychological frameworks are needed to explore and clarify the phenomenon of victim–offender intersectionality, contributing to new policies that address this unique group (Shared Hope International & the Villanova Law Institute To Address Commercial Sexual Exploitation, 2020).

RISK FACTORS FOR HUMAN TRAFFICKING

Although anyone can be a consumer, facilitator, or victim of human trafficking, the literature has highlighted a number of risk factors (American Psychological Association, 2014; Hopper, 2017c; Malebranche et al., 2020). A socioecological framework can be used to identify societal, community, relational, and individual risk factors for human trafficking (see Figure 1.1). Exploration of these risk factors can lead to prevention efforts to minimize threats to human freedom, dignity, and self-determination.

Societal Risk Factors

Societal risk factors are aspects of economic, political, and sociocultural systems that create conditions conducive to human trafficking. Globalization and systemic inequalities, economic insecurity, and cultural and social oppression are several societal factors that contribute to the incidence of human trafficking.

FIGURE 1.1. Socioecological Risk and Protective Factors Related to Human Trafficking

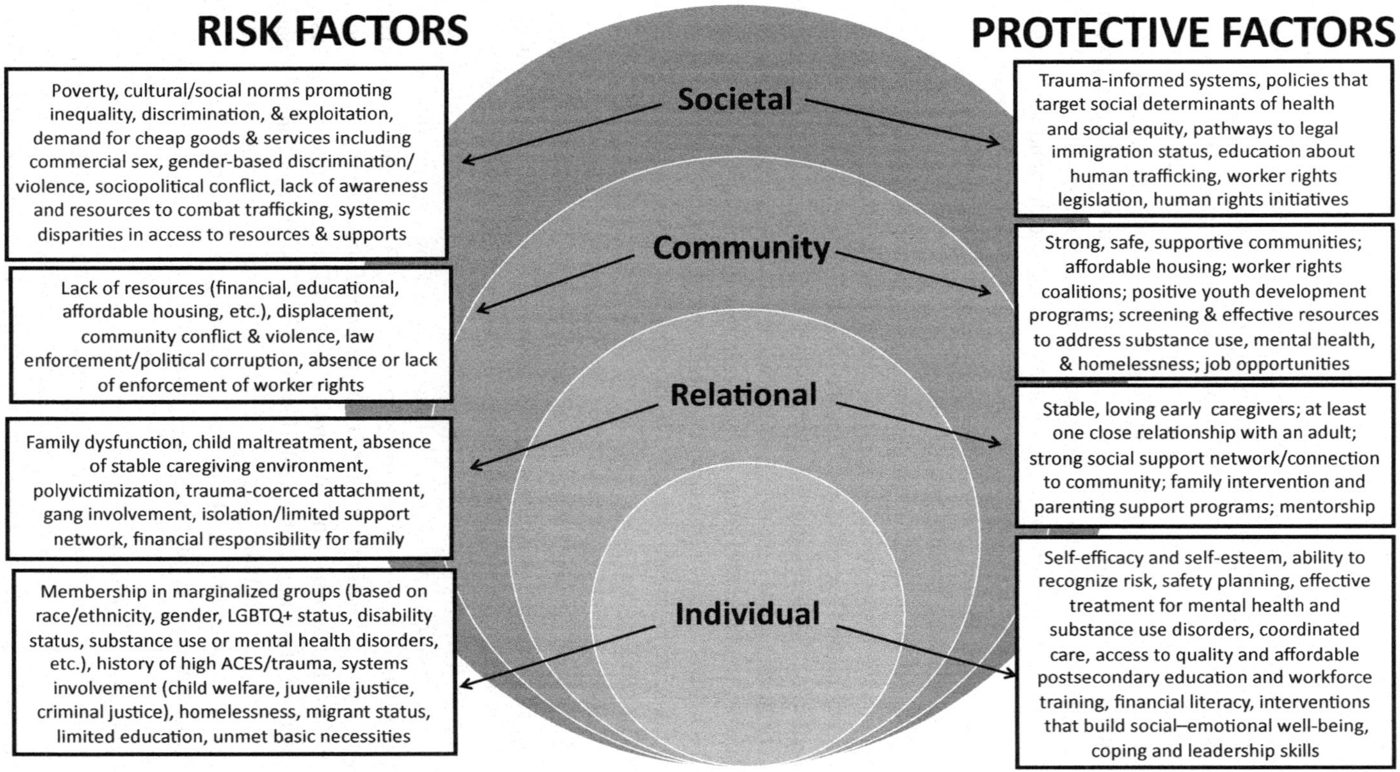

PROTECTIVE FACTORS

Societal

Trauma-informed systems, policies that target social determinants of health and social equity, pathways to legal immigration status, education about human trafficking, worker rights legislation, human rights initiatives

Community

Strong, safe, supportive communities; affordable housing; worker rights coalitions; positive youth development programs; screening & effective resources to address substance use, mental health, & homelessness; job opportunities

Relational

Stable, loving early caregivers; at least one close relationship with an adult; strong social support network/connection to community; family intervention and parenting support programs; mentorship

Individual

Self-efficacy and self-esteem, ability to recognize risk, safety planning, effective treatment for mental health and substance use disorders, coordinated care, access to quality and affordable postsecondary education and workforce training, financial literacy, interventions that build social–emotional well-being, coping and leadership skills

RISK FACTORS

Societal

Poverty, cultural/social norms promoting inequality, discrimination, & exploitation, demand for cheap goods & services including commercial sex, gender-based discrimination/ violence, sociopolitical conflict, lack of awareness and resources to combat trafficking, systemic disparities in access to resources & supports

Community

Lack of resources (financial, educational, affordable housing, etc.), displacement, community conflict & violence, law enforcement/political corruption, absence or lack of enforcement of worker rights

Relational

Family dysfunction, child maltreatment, absence of stable caregiving environment, polyvictimization, trauma-coerced attachment, gang involvement, isolation/limited support network, financial responsibility for family

Individual

Membership in marginalized groups (based on race/ethnicity, gender, LGBTQ+ status, disability status, substance use or mental health disorders, etc.), history of high ACES/trauma, systems involvement (child welfare, juvenile justice, criminal justice), homelessness, migrant status, limited education, unmet basic necessities

Globalization and Social Inequities

The global economy is so vast that many of the goods and services consumed today have been affected by human trafficking at some point along the supply chain (Zimmerman & Kiss, 2017). Globalization has increased competition among suppliers, spurring demand for inexpensive products and low-cost labor, often involving worker exploitation and leading to the underground economy of human trafficking (Aronowitz & Koning, 2014). Labor trafficking crosses a wide range of industries, including agriculture, child and elder care, housekeeping, construction, manufacturing, hospitality, mining, fishing, forestry, transportation, and other sectors. All of these industries have been influenced by globalization and the demand for inexpensive goods and services. Similarly, sex trafficking is responsive to the demand for low-cost sexual "goods" (e.g., pornography) and "services" (e.g., escort services, exotic dancing, prostitution).

Globalization has prompted an increasing migration of people from lower resource to higher resource regions, creating further vulnerabilities to human trafficking and exploitation. (Jones et al., 2007; Schwarz et al., 2019). The technological developments, particularly in transportation and communication, that have occurred hand in hand with globalization have created new methods for recruiting and exploiting individuals (O'Brien & Li, 2020; Quek, 2017), and the anonymity of technology such as the internet and the darknet have created obstacles to primary and secondary prevention (Reid & Fox, 2020).

Labor trafficking is supported by structural factors such as income inequalities, standard labor recruitment practices involving extortion and exploitation, and inequities in the power of corporations and businesses that diminish the rights and power of workers (Kiss & Zimmerman, 2019). Structural inequalities can normalize discriminatory treatment of different groups, masking awareness of human trafficking and interfering with the equitable allocation of resources to combat it. For instance, a comparative analysis of five countries found that, despite efforts to implement labor protections for transnational migrants, these workers continue to face systemic discrimination and rights violations based on "strikingly common patterns of structural inequality, exploitative behavior and weakness in institutional design" across a range of countries with varying economies, migration patterns, and legal systems (Faraday, 2021).

Economic Insecurity

Poverty and economic insecurity form a leading societal risk factor for human trafficking (Schwarz et al., 2019). As suggested in Maslow's (1943) hierarchy of needs, physiological necessities (e.g., food, water, shelter, rest) are humans' most primitive needs, eclipsing even the desire for safety. When people have unmet basic physiological needs, the drive for survival can lead them to take risks to improve their life situation that they otherwise might be unwilling to take. A young single mother who cannot support her family leaves her toddler with loved ones and travels alone to another country where she does not know anyone, for a promising job opportunity. A man who has lost his job and was evicted provides the deed to his family's land as collateral to cover exorbitant fees from an employment agency. A transgender adolescent who has run away from home moves in with an older man whom they just met that day. Facilitators of trafficking may take advantage of these basic survival needs as a means of coercion (Schwarz et al., 2019). In parallel, facilitators of human trafficking may be similarly motivated by economic insecurity and limited opportunities.

Cultural and Social Oppression
Cultural and social norms, the often unspoken rules or expectations of behavior within specific groups, can contribute to the risk of human trafficking. The devaluation and exploitation of other human beings is interwoven with cultural and social oppression, including racism, sexism, classism, and ethnic bias (Bryant-Davis & Tummala-Narra, 2018; Malebranche et al., 2020; see Chapter 2, this volume, for further exploration of human trafficking in marginalized communities). Because people who are marginalized and systematically oppressed typically have fewer opportunities for education, employment, and advancement, they face greater pressure to migrate or to take other risks to seek out opportunities, leading to an increased likelihood of being targeted for exploitation. The structural racism embedded within criminal justice, social services, health care, mental health, and other systems creates barriers for marginalized groups to access help, leaving members of these groups both underidentified and underserved (Bryant-Davis & Gobin, 2019; Bryant-Davis & Tummala-Narra, 2018; Ortega et al., 2022; Polaris Project, 2020; Stumblingbear-Riddle et al., 2019).

In communities where girls are perceived as being less valuable than boys, they may be seen as an economic burden to the family. Girls' futures may be sacrificed to pay for the education of male children in the family, and they may be sold into marriage or placed with or sold to other families to provide domestic work (Gacinya, 2020; International Organization for Migration [IOM], 2021). Lack of access to education and the inability to inherit property leads to further marginalization and disempowerment of women and girls. Societal acceptance of arranged marriage, dowries, domestic violence, and child marriage increase the vulnerability of women and children to exploitation and abuse. In some cultures, social standing and family reputation is contingent on a girl or woman's sexual "purity," with societal rejection or honor-based violence being used to control behavior within the family and community. Patriarchal social pressures can lead to girls and women being trafficked and then blamed or shamed upon their return, increasing the risk of revictimization (Gacinya, 2020; IOM, 2021). Sociocultural expectations that boys and men should be powerful or dominant may lead to greater acceptance of aggression and controlling behaviors in boys and men, with more traditionally masculine gender role ideologies being linked to perpetration of violence (Santana et al., 2006).

The misconception that males cannot be victims of human trafficking is promoted by traditional views of masculinity, with associated stereotypes of females as victims and males as perpetrators (Hebert, 2016). Males may differ from females in their experience of violence and coercion during trafficking (Stöckl et al., 2021), but they show similar trauma-related impacts (Iglesias-Rios et al., 2018; Pocock et al., 2016). Boys and men face unique barriers to help seeking in situations of human trafficking that may exacerbate some trauma-related effects, such as shame. Communities that hold more traditional gender roles may view the display of emotions as feminine or "weak" and may particularly discourage emotional expression and vulnerability in boys and men. Similarly, fear of judgment regarding actual or perceived sexual orientation can create further barriers to help seeking in boys and men. The lack of gender-specific antitrafficking education and resources for males creates yet another challenge to primary and secondary prevention of the trafficking of boys and men (Bykerk, 2022).

People who are transgender, nonbinary, or gender nonconforming and those who are nonheterosexual, have a heightened risk of exploitation and trafficking due to factors such as discrimination, exposure to gender-based violence, and social and economic marginalization (Grant et al., 2011; Hogan & Roe-Sepowitz, 2020; Stotzer, 2009). At the same time, limited attention has been devoted to identification and care of trafficked individuals who are not cisgendered or not heterosexual, particularly when discrimination is compounded across multiple aspects of identity (e.g., transgender migrants; Franco et al., 2022).

Cultural and social oppression can influence a person's self-perception and the perception of others. Cultural belief systems associated with power differentials are often instilled at an early age (e.g., beliefs that a young person should always demonstrate respect for elders, that a wife should be deferential to her husband, or that certain groups belong to a lower social status than others), increasing vulnerability to exploitation. When the surrounding community conveys the message that a person is of low worth or value, that person may perceive themselves as "less than." Human trafficking capitalizes on this perception, dehumanizing people and treating them as objects that can be bought and sold. This process leaves victims vulnerable to being targeted in the first place and creates barriers to help seeking and exiting the trafficking situation. Similarly, buyers and facilitators of human trafficking may use cultural and social norms to justify the exploitation. Investigators working on group-based child exploitation cases in the United Kingdom suggested that "othering" victims based on gender (e.g., misogynistic attitudes) or other intergroup differences (such as being from a different community) allows perpetrators to distance themselves from their victims, reducing internal constraints against trafficking (United Kingdom Home Office, 2021).

Community Risk Factors

Communities are groups of people that share identity-forming characteristics, including people that live in the same neighborhood, work together, or share the same norms, values, and beliefs. High levels of violence, limited resources and lack of opportunities for growth, and normalization of exploitation are community risk factors for trafficking. Alienation or displacement from community and its associated natural supports can also exacerbate the risk of trafficking.

Conflict, Low Resources, and Limited Opportunities

Communities that are shaped by conflict, corruption, economic disparities, and other forms of inequality may be particularly vulnerable to being influenced by human trafficking. Limited opportunities for growth and advancement, including lack of access to education, job skills, and employment, are risk factors for both victims and facilitators of human trafficking. Civil conflict and war can contribute to these conditions, as can community violence and trauma (Nelson et al., 2004).

Facilitation of labor or sex trafficking may provide status and influence for some individuals who live in communities impacted by poverty and violence, have a history of disenfranchisement and disrupted family environments, and/or experience limited opportunities in licit employment. In a sociological study of risk examining "lower echelon pimps" in a low-resource community (Harlem, New York), participants characterized themselves as "being respected," "being the boss," and "having an empire," finding power within illicit sectors that they were otherwise unable to access (Ruf, 2015).

Displacement and Migration

Individuals facing displacement, including refugees, asylees, migrant workers, undocumented immigrants, and unaccompanied minors are at risk of trafficking due to the lack of a support network and lack of familiarity with the laws, language, or customs of their destination. Many members of these groups have experienced chronic or repeated stress and trauma, leading them to flee their homes and communities. Immigrants face numerous challenges to mental health, including: the migration process, acculturation, employment problems, trauma, and discrimination and racism (American Psychological Association, 2012; Carvalho e Silva & Bucher-Maluschke, 2018). Migrant workers may be charged exorbitant fees by recruitment agencies in their home countries to obtain employment, frequently going into debt in order to seek employment opportunities. They may sign contracts in their home countries with these recruitment agencies, only to find that the contract is not upheld, or may be required to sign disadvantageous, exploitative, and unlawful contracts. When they reach their destination, identification documents and payment may be withheld, and workers find themselves dependent on their employers for shelter, food, clothing, and transportation (Dryjanska et al., 2022). They may be subjected to physical and/or sexual abuse. From a psychological perspective, trafficking victims who travelled from other countries for better opportunities may struggle with a strong sense of shame for failing to be "successful" or to provide for their families back home, increasing their vulnerability to being trapped in conditions of exploitation (American Psychological Association, 2012; Latham-Sprinkle et al., 2019).

Unstable Living Conditions and Absence of a Secure Caregiving Environment

The lack of a stable home and the absence of a secure caregiving environment are risk factors for both labor trafficking and the commercial sexual exploitation of children (Franchino-Olsen, 2021; Greenbaum et al., 2022). In some societies, impoverished families entrust their children to more affluent relatives, neighbors, or others. Parents may sell or trade their children in order to improve the family's economic prospects or in the hopes that their children will escape chronic poverty and have access to greater opportunities. Whether for altruistic reasons or financial incentives, this practice of "fostering out" increases the child's vulnerability to exploitation and trafficking (Bales, 2005). Housing instability or homelessness creates vulnerability to exploitation and trafficking due to unmet daily needs and the lack of a consistent safe environment. A 10-city study of youth experiencing homelessness found that nearly one in five of these young people had experienced human trafficking, with many reporting commercial sexual exploitation. Notably, over 40% of the young people who experienced trafficking (8% of the total sample) endorsed labor trafficking, with the majority being instances of forced drug dealing (Murphy, 2016). Adults facing housing instability or homelessness are also vulnerable to trafficking due to the lack of a consistent safe environment and unmet daily needs, with over one third of participants in a study of young adults experiencing homelessness reporting they were exposed to human trafficking (Hogan & Roe-Sepowitz, 2020).

Children in the child welfare and juvenile justice systems frequently lack a consistent caregiving environment as they are moved from placement to placement, heightening their risk of exploitation. In a study of child welfare-involved minors in Florida, children with allegations of trafficking exposure were twice as likely to have experienced out of home placements, five times as likely to have experienced congregate care, and ten times as likely to have run away from placements (Gibbs et al., 2018). Juvenile justice system-involved youth are also disproportionately affected by trafficking and are vulnerable to retrafficking due to elopement (Nichols et al., 2022). A study of trafficked youth in Washington state identified common multisystem involvement for these young people, with early and frequent contact with the child welfare system, multiple disruptions in their living situation, numerous instances of running away, and multiple episodes of juvenile detention (Pullmann et al., 2020). Individuals within the criminal justice or immigration systems are vulnerable to experiencing labor or sex trafficking within correctional (Kelly & McNamara, 2018; Polaris Project, 2020) and detention facilities (Chen & Gill, 2015), as well as being at risk of being recruited for trafficking upon release (Kelly & McNamara, 2018).

Community Normalization of Exploitation
The normalization of abuse and exploitation within communities and groups can sanction and promote human trafficking. For instance, the exploitation of migrant workers is so common that complaints may be dismissed or disparaged, and family members may encourage acceptance of exploitative working conditions due to the lack of alternatives (Palumbo, 2017). Similarly, in neighborhoods where commercial sex is prevalent, selling sex at an early age is accepted and sometimes even expected (Cecchet & Thoburn, 2014). Some subcultures have unique group dynamics, language, and rules that enable trafficking to occur. For instance, gangs create a subculture of expected behaviors that are enforced within the group, frequently through threats and violence (Frank & Terwilliger, 2015). Gang involvement is a risk factor for both labor trafficking (often through coerced transportation or sales of narcotics; Greenbaum et al., 2022) and sex trafficking (Roe-Sepowitz, 2019).

"The Game" or "the Life" refers to a subculture within the commercial sex industry with a hierarchy of authority and within-group language that defines rules to ensure compliance and creates perceived bonds within the group (e.g., referring to the exploiter as "Daddy" and other victims as a "wife-in-law"). In group-based child exploitation rings, perpetrators normalize and actively encourage abusive and exploitative behavior within the network (United Kingdom Home Office, 2021). The development of the internet, and particularly the darknet, has created virtual communities that further normalize and enable abuse and exploitation (Reid & Fox, 2020).

Relational Risk Factors

Because trafficking is a form of interpersonal abuse, prior interpersonal trauma and a lack of interpersonal supports can create increased vulnerability to trafficking. Relational risk factors, such as coercive interpersonal dynamics and the normalization of violence within relationships, may be particularly common in situations of trauma-coerced attachment and family-facilitated trafficking.

Child Maltreatment and Polyvictimization

Prior victimization has been identified as a key risk factor for sex trafficking (Franchino-Olsen, 2021; Reid et al., 2017), as well as labor trafficking (De Vries & Farrell, 2018). There is a strong link between trafficking and earlier child maltreatment, including child sexual abuse, physical abuse, emotional abuse, emotional and physical neglect, and family violence, with estimates of around a quarter to over half of survivors reporting exposure to earlier violence or abuse (Franchino-Olsen, 2021; Hopper, 2017a; Hopper & Gonzalez, 2018; Kiss, Yun, et al., 2015; Oram et al., 2012, 2016; Puigvert et al., 2021; Reid et al., 2017; Roe-Sepowitz, 2012).

Children who grow up in conflictual, rejecting, violent, abusive, and/or neglectful homes may run away or become involved in the child welfare or juvenile justice systems, leading to instability and a lack of a consistent caregiving environment (Franchino-Olsen, 2021). Further, the absence of early dependable, attuned, and loving relationships increases susceptibility to the grooming and victimization associated with later exploitative relationships, including traffickers who pose as romantic figures, caregivers, or both (Hopper, 2017a). Early physical, sexual, and/or psychological abuse may negatively affect a person's sense of self-worth (Flynn et al., 2014), contributing to negative cognitive schemas that can be exploited by traffickers such as the belief that "I don't deserve anything better." Childhood maltreatment can create associations for the child between love, control, and violence and can normalize the experience of interpersonal abuse (American Psychological Association, 2014; Craven et al., 2006; Reid, 2011; Reid et al., 2017). Thus, early exposure to interpersonal violence and abuse could be a risk factor for both victims and facilitators of human trafficking.

Polyvictimization—the experience of multiple forms of victimization— is common among people impacted by human trafficking (Hopper, 2017a; Reid et al., 2017). This type of cumulative trauma during formative developmental periods may have more severe biopsychosocial impacts than exposure to specific trauma types alone (Ford & Delker, 2018). Research has highlighted some of the compounded psychological effects of trafficking for people who have experienced multiple forms of victimization (Beksinska et al., 2021; Choi et al., 2009; De Vries & Farrell, 2018; Hopper, 2017a; Ottisova et al., 2016; see Chapter 8, this volume, for a further review).

Inadequate Support System

Individuals who lack a consistent, supportive relational network may be at increased risk for trafficking. Isolation or alienation from others may occur for many reasons, including separation from loved ones; rejection by others due to discrimination or disability; illness, incapacity, or death of loved ones; family dissolution; or other reasons. Grief and loss leave individuals psychologically vulnerable, compounding the lack of material and emotional support associated with isolation. Traffickers often physically and socially separate victims from supports; they may also create conditions in which victims are surrounded by peers who are unable to provide true social support because they are aligned with the trafficker or are themselves being coerced (Hagan et al., 2021).

Trauma-Coerced Attachment

Facilitators of human trafficking use many methods to psychologically coerce victims into conditions of trafficking, and one of the most insidious is the use of the relationship to manipulate another person (Casassa et al., 2022; Hopper, 2017a; Reid et al., 2013). Trauma-coerced attachment (also referred to as "trauma bonding" or "Stockholm syndrome") involves cycles of intermittent reinforcement, alternated with punishments, that affect the victim's worldview and sense of self and create a strong emotional connection to, and dependency on, the abuser (Chambers et al., 2022). Traffickers may utilize abusive control dynamics similar to the elements of power and control used by perpetrators of other forms of abuse, such as domestic violence, including extensive nonphysical methods of coercion (Hopper & Hidalgo, 2006). They exploit power imbalances based on differences in gender, financial resources, cultural factors, familiarity with surroundings, individual vulnerabilities (e.g., substance use disorders, disabilities, mental health concerns), and other disparities. Traffickers may isolate the victim from others and monopolize their attention, even when they are not physically present (e.g., calling frequently, monitoring activities, tracking location). Threats, degradation, demonstrations of omnipotence (e.g., claiming powerful alliances with law enforcement, immigration officials, violent offenders, or deities), and enforcement of trivial demands are designed to create or exaggerate power differentials. Extreme work demands (e.g., excessive work hours without days off, physically demanding or unsafe work, working through the night) can lead to exhaustion or debility, lowering a person's defenses. A victim's attempts to please the perpetrator may be difficult to extinguish due to intermittent reinforcement with money, gifts, or words of praise or affection ("occasional indulgences"), even when these rewards are alternated with extreme threats and violent attacks (Baldwin et al., 2015). Trauma-coerced attachment may lead survivors to minimize their experiences of abuse and exploitation, which creates barriers to exiting and increases the risk of revictimization (Baldwin et al., 2015; Chambers et al., 2022; Hopper & Hidalgo, 2006). Instances where a survivor returns to the perpetrator after exiting are common in trafficking situations and should be anticipated and addressed in secondary prevention efforts (Casassa et al., 2022; United States Department of State, 2020).

Family-Facilitated Trafficking
At the intersection of child maltreatment and trauma-coerced attachment, familial trafficking occurs when caregivers or family members facilitate the labor or sex trafficking of their family member or dependent, often a child or a relative with a specific vulnerability such as a disability. Family-facilitated trafficking typically involves complicated attachment relationships (Reid et al., 2015). For instance, a young person might be grateful to their family member who has provided them with food and a place to live in the United States, despite the fact that this person is controlling their working conditions and collecting all of their earnings. Children who experience family-facilitated minor sex trafficking often have extensive maltreatment histories, with a high severity of abuse and multiple forms of child maltreatment, including the widespread practice of being trafficked for illicit drugs (Sprang & Cole, 2018). Because of the often chronic nature of this type of trauma, emotional numbing and dissociation are common responses (Cole et al., 2016). All of the youth in one study examining familial sex trafficking of minors reported clinical levels of depression, anxiety, and posttraumatic stress disorder, and over half reported suicide attempts (Sprang & Cole, 2018). In family-facilitated trafficking, a person's reactions toward the perpetrator may be

further complicated by other members of the family. The victim may be urged toward secrecy, keeping things "within the family," and particularly discouraged from seeking help from law enforcement or other systemic sources of support. Even when such cases are reported, they are less likely to be founded or substantiated than when the reported perpetrator is not a family member (Edwards et al., 2022), exacerbating mistrust and deterring further help-seeking behaviors.

Individual Risk Factors

Because of its focus on the human psyche, psychology has perhaps the strongest contribution to exploring individual risk factors that contribute to human trafficking. Individual differences that increase vulnerability to trafficking include trauma-related and other mental health conditions, substance use problems, disabilities, and methods of coping with adversity, among others. Because of societal stigma, these individual risk factors may be associated with ostracization and alienation from protective relationships and systems. They may also compromise a person's ability to accurately assess risk, communicate clearly and assertively, engage in effective problem solving, and seek help when needed (Franchino-Olsen, 2021; Hopper, 2017b; Nichols & Heil, 2022; Reid et al., 2018).

Mental Health

Compared with other at-risk youth, trafficked minors have been found to have higher rates of a range of mental health diagnoses, including attention-deficit/hyperactivity disorder, bipolar disorder, posttraumatic stress disorder, depression, anxiety, conduct disorder, oppositional defiant disorder, and psychosis (Palines et al., 2020). There is frequent comorbidity of mental health conditions among adult survivors of sex and labor trafficking as well (Ottisova et al., 2016). Severe mental illness in trafficked adults is associated with a greater likelihood of compulsory inpatient psychiatric admissions, longer inpatient stays, and high levels of abuse before and after trafficking (Oram et al., 2015).

Although psychiatric problems may be the result of biological factors, many psychological symptoms can be linked to trauma exposure, including pre-trafficking and trafficking-related trauma. While trauma-related responses such as emotional numbing and dissociation can be protective against overwhelming emotions experienced during and after trafficking, these and other psychiatric symptoms can also interfere with help seeking and may increase the risk of coerced cooffending (see the earlier section on victim–offender intersectionality), delayed or inaccurate reporting, perceived ambivalence, and ongoing or revictimization (Franchino-Olsen, 2021; United States Department of State, 2020; see Chapter 8, this volume, for a review of psychological impacts of human trafficking).

Substance Use

Problem substance use is associated with a range of risk factors related to health and safety, including an increased risk of exploitation (Franchino-Olsen, 2021) or other victimization. Traffickers may exploit individuals' existing substance use disorders to coerce them into conditions of trafficking, utilizing substances as a "bargaining chip" to groom potential victims or to later ensure compliance (Hopper, 2017b; Langton et al., 2022). Individuals with substance use disorders may encounter disruptions in education or work, housing instability or homelessness, involvement in unhealthy or violent relationships, conflicts with legal systems, and substance-related health concerns. Due to stigma, people with substance use disorders who have experienced trafficking may not be recognized as victims and often face barriers to accessing services and effective trauma-informed treatment. Because of this, substance use relapse and retrafficking are common (Hopper, 2017b). Trafficking victims with substance use disorders are at increased risk of arrest and conviction for drug- and trafficking-related charges (e.g., prostitution), leading to a persistent cycle of retraumatization involving substance use, incarceration, exploitation and other forms of revictimization, and the lack of effective intervention (Marburger & Pickover, 2020).

Disabilities

People with disabilities experience disproportionately high rates of sexual victimization and are at increased risk for sex and labor trafficking (Franchino-Olsen et al., 2020; Reid, 2018). Disabilities include physical (e.g., impairments in vision, hearing, or mobility), mental (e.g., severe mental illness), cognitive (e.g., intellectual disability, traumatic brain injuries), or developmental (e.g., attention-deficit/hyperactivity disorder, learning disabilities, autism, Down syndrome) conditions that impair, interfere with, or limit a person's ability to participate in some typical daily activities and interactions. Reliance on caretakers can normalize unequal power dynamics for individuals who require regular assistance. Traffickers may take advantage of the loneliness and isolation of people with disabilities who have experienced interpersonal oppression, including social rejection and bullying (Nichols & Heil, 2022). Individuals with disabilities can face barriers to employment, increasing financial insecurity and vulnerability to exploitation. Because of challenges in understanding social nuance, these people may be more vulnerable to psychological coercion and may not understand what is happening during sexual abuse, assault, or trafficking. They may have communication challenges and can face social discrimination and alienation, creating barriers to help seeking (Nichols & Heil, 2022; Reid et al., 2018).

Coping

Individual differences in coping with adversity may also increase vulnerability to trafficking. While some people are risk averse, others are willing to tolerate them to improve disadvantageous circumstances such as financial destitution or feeling alone and unloved. These people may cope with desperate circumstances through illusions of control (Thompson, 1999) and a strong focus on successful outcomes. For instance, a mother whose children are facing starvation may convince herself that she will be able to keep herself safe while improving the family's financial situation if she accepts a job offer involving migration, even in the face of strong warning signs of danger. Traffickers may groom their victims by taking advantage of existing adversity and cultivating victims' hope, sense of agency, and willingness to take risks to access potential opportunities (Polaris Project, 2021).

PROMOTING PROTECTIVE FACTORS AGAINST HUMAN TRAFFICKING

Beyond identifying and confronting risk factors, effective primary, secondary, and tertiary prevention efforts must highlight resilience and promote protective factors. As with risk factors, factors that protect against human trafficking can be explored through a socioecological framework, including societal, community, relational, and individual protective factors (see Figure 1.1). With the support of the American Psychological Association's Division 27 (Society for Community Research and Action), the Research-to-Policy Collaboration developed a policy brief that highlighted the importance of using data-driven, community-based strategies in prevention work related to human trafficking. This brief recommends the use of multiple concurrent evidence-based approaches, tailored to the specific vulnerabilities and needs of individuals and communities, applied in a variety of levels and settings, and rigorously evaluated to assess effects (Long et al., 2018). Further research is needed on human trafficking, its impacts, and the development and evaluation of prevention and intervention programs—all areas where psychology can contribute.

Societal Protective Factors

Some aspects of economic, political, and sociocultural systems may be protective against human trafficking. Societies can work to promote social and economic equity across systems (e.g., immigration, child welfare and juvenile justice, criminal justice, legislation and regulatory governance) and can build more trauma-informed systems to prevent and respond to trauma. Educational efforts across societal systems can support primary, secondary, and tertiary prevention of human trafficking through awareness and behavior change initiatives.

Social and Economic Equity

Social and economic disparities directly and indirectly affect health and well-being. Legislation and policies that support economic and social equity (based on factors such as race, class, and gender) target "upstream" social determinants of health, bolstering protective factors against human trafficking and supporting overall population health (Robichaux & Torres, 2022). Policy analysis is crucial to address social disparities across a wide range of systems, including: criminal justice and juvenile justice, immigration, labor regulation, child welfare, health care, mental health, substance use, housing, public assistance, education, transportation, and others. Psychologists can inform and advise policy makers and government agencies on risk and protective factors, psychological impacts of trafficking, and legislation and policies that support trafficking prevention and intervention. Tailoring prevention efforts within different systems and targeting prevention initiatives to the unique needs of specific at-risk groups may increase the effect of antitrafficking efforts (Long et al., 2018). For instance, protective factors may be built into immigration, child welfare and juvenile justice, and criminal justice systems that address the unique needs of specific at-risk groups.

Equity within immigration systems. To promote protective factors within immigration systems, psychology must examine psychological processes associated with migration and address immigration-related challenges in ways that engage members of society, foster the health and well-being of migrants, and provide collective benefits to the community (Dovidio & Esses, 2001). Because immigration status is commonly used as a method of coercion in human trafficking (Owens et al., 2014), addressing immigration loopholes that create opportunities for exploitation and developing pathways to legal immigration status may decrease this vulnerability for migrants. Immigration policies that increase migrants' awareness of human rights, worker rights, human trafficking, and available legal protections may also be protective against human trafficking. Psychologists may function as advocates with policy makers, law enforcement officials, social service administrators, and court personnel in addressing immigration-related challenges. For example, psychologists or other mental health experts may provide education for judges, attorneys, and juries on the psychological issues involved in migration, psychological coercion and traumatic stress in human trafficking, and the drawbacks of looking for a stereotypical "good witness" in situations involving human trafficking (American Psychological Association, 2012, 2014). Psychologists, sociologists, social workers, and public health experts have a potential role in conducting outcome research on social protection intervention approaches that address structural inequities such as transparent labor recruitment methods, trafficking-informed labor immigration legislation, and worker-driven social responsibility reporting (Kiss & Zimmerman, 2019).

Equity within child welfare and juvenile justice systems. Because of the heightened risk of exploitation and trafficking for children in the child welfare and juvenile justice systems, it is imperative that these systems incorporate protective factors against trafficking. Single episode training on human trafficking is not adequate to maintain knowledge and influence behavior over time; instead, systematic training and guidance is needed within these systems to support the ability of child serving professionals to recognize and respond to situations of both sex and labor trafficking (Kenny et al., 2019; Shared Hope International, 2021). Nichols et al. (2022) highlighted the importance of nonputative interventions with minors in the juvenile justice system who engage in repeated runaway behaviors and experience retrafficking. Some of these measures include increasing children's access to trauma-informed mental health and substance use treatment; increasing safety planning measures such as regularly conducting risk assessments and providing information about resources such as drop-in centers and health care; streamlining hotline procedures for concerned caregivers; and developing specialized foster family placements with caregivers who are trained in the impacts of trauma, the dynamics of human trafficking, and understanding and managing high-risk behaviors.

Equity within criminal justice systems. Recruitment and exploitation also occur within the criminal justice system. Legislative efforts may be used to investigate labor programs within prisons, jails, and immigration detention facilities, ensuring that they are truly voluntary and are free from coercion or force (Polaris Project, 2020). Criminal justice policy reform is also needed to address sex trafficking recruitment and exploitation within correctional facilities. Mental health clinicians (including forensic, counseling, or clinical psychologists; social workers; or counselors) may lead educational primary or secondary prevention programs to increase awareness of exploitation and human trafficking in these settings. Increased safety procedures related to bail and commissary services may also be protective against incidents of trafficking. Postprison reentry services are needed to support the transition back into the community and to access employment, decreasing vulnerability to trafficking postrelease (Kelly & McNamara, 2018).

Regulatory systems to protect workers' rights. Well-organized and enforced regulatory systems can help to protect workers against exploitative labor conditions (Littenberg & Baldwin, 2017). In wealthier countries, including the United States, worker protection laws have included pay requirements, limits on work time, health and safety protections, the right to organize, parental leave benefits, Social Security benefits, and more. Further attention should be paid to challenges in the protections of these rights and identification of gaps in workers' rights. For instance, domestic workers and agricultural workers are two groups that are particularly likely to be omitted from many labor protections in the United States beginning with their exclusion from the U.S. Fair Labor Standards Act in 1935. In poorer countries, despite International Labour Organization (ILO) conventions (2022), workers may have few protections and regularly experience exploitative working conditions. Industrial and organizational psychology (see Chapter 7) has a potential role in evaluating the effectiveness and impacts of various regulatory systems on worker exploitation and human trafficking.

Trauma-Informed Systems

One of the most significant current contributions of psychology to systems reform involves the promotion of trauma-informed systems. A wide variety of systems—from schools to social services networks, to health care organizations and criminal justice systems—have served trauma-impacted individuals, including survivors of labor and sex trafficking, without adequately recognizing or responding to the effects of traumatic stress. Over the past few decades, there has been increasing awareness of the wide-ranging impacts of trauma and the importance of trauma-informed care. This approach is a paradigm shift that incorporates key principles about trauma into the culture of the organization, agency, or system. Trauma-informed systems understand the widespread influence of trauma and recognize the signs and symptoms of trauma in those served, as well as in families and staff members. These systems integrate knowledge about trauma into policies, procedures, and practices in order to resist retraumatization and understand potential paths of recovery from trauma (Substance Abuse and Mental Health Services Administration, 2014). Trauma-informed frameworks are particularly important for at-risk and trafficked individuals who have experienced chronic or cumulative patterns of victimization, in order to deter revictimization and reduce the severity of long-term impacts (tertiary prevention) of human trafficking (Hopper, 2017c). Psychological research can support trauma-informed systems by describing the traumatic nature of human trafficking, identifying its trauma-related effects, generating knowledge that influences trauma-informed legislation and policy, and guiding "best practices" for trauma-informed service delivery for survivors of human trafficking (Scott et al., 2019). For instance, psychological research might be used to develop an increased understanding of the implications of trauma-coerced attachment in trafficking within different systems (e.g., criminal and juvenile justice, child welfare, immigration, health care, and social service systems), leading to specific trauma-informed policies and practices for addressing barriers to exiting and responding to anticipated returns to an exploiter (Casassa et al., 2022).

Systems-Level Educational Initiatives

Sociocultural norms and belief systems that promote equality, diversity, and inclusion are protective against interpersonal exploitation (Greenbaum et al., 2018). Psychology can guide public awareness campaigns, with broad dissemination of prosocial messages that are protective against human trafficking, ranging from sociocultural messages that promote equality, diversity, and inclusion (e.g., social change movements such as Black Lives Matter and the #MeToo movement; antibullying campaigns such as #BeKind and #SeeMe; and awareness events such as Mental Health Awareness Month, Autism Awareness Month, and Pride Week), to public education that focuses specifically on human trafficking (see Chapter 5 on psychologists as frame sponsors in media coverage of human trafficking).

Educational prevention initiatives include general awareness campaigns, spending shift campaigns, and reporting campaigns. General awareness antitrafficking campaigns aim to increase the general public's knowledge of human trafficking and to combat common myths about trafficking. Spending-shift campaigns encourage consumers to abstain from buying goods produced or services delivered under unfair and harmful conditions, including goods and services involving child labor, coerced or forced labor, and commercial sexual exploitation. For consumers and businesses that profit indirectly from human trafficking in the supply chain, changing existing practices has considerable costs in terms of time, money, and resources. Industrial and organizational psychology can be used to understand and influence consumer behavior and to support organizations in modifying business processes that are an impetus for human trafficking (see Chapter 7 for more on industrial and organizational psychology's role in antitrafficking). Reporting campaigns encourage administrators, employees, consumers, or other members of the general public to report observations of potentially exploitative conditions (Cyrus & Vogel, 2017).

Although educational campaigns are a cornerstone of current prevention efforts, evaluations of these initiatives have been broadly lacking (Cyrus & Vogel, 2017). Psychological research is needed to evaluate the utility of education-based demand reduction campaigns and to modify these efforts to increase effectiveness, including monitoring and evaluating the effectiveness of intervention strategies over time and across subpopulations (Cyrus & Vogel, 2017; Kiss & Zimmerman, 2019). In addition, while educational campaigns are strongly emphasized within trafficking prevention, it is important to keep in mind that this approach is just one element of a larger, more comprehensive prevention strategy.

Community-Level Protective Factors

Strengthening social institutions and social safety nets are community-level efforts that can build community "safeness," an important element of trafficking prevention (Alpert & Chin, 2017). Through its focus on the functioning of communities and the relationship between the individual and the community, community psychology can support the development of robust community-level programs that build safety, stability, and health in the neighborhoods and settings where people live, work, and play. Community-level prevention strategies require coordinated collective action across local agencies and institutions such as schools, social services programs, law enforcement agencies, housing programs, health care settings, and so on.

Community Safety and Cohesion

Programs that support community cohesion and incorporate crime and violence prevention work to cultivate safer, more integrated communities. Living in a well-integrated supportive community offers some protection against trafficking and exploitation, as neighbors watch out for and support each other. Community engagement operates not only as a protective factor against experiencing trauma but also as an important element in the healing process following trauma exposure (Schultz et al., 2016).

Economic Stability and Growth Opportunities

Community strategies to stimulate economic development, equity, and stability are also protective, leading to opportunities for licit employment and advancement. Initiatives that support economic health in a community include job training and employment programs, accessible child care for working parents, micro loans for small business development, and programs that help people pay for food, health care, housing, and education. Programs that promote economic development for survivors, such as job training and supported employment, are elements of secondary prevention (Office of Justice Programs, 2022).

Educational Opportunities

The availability of strong educational opportunities and supports for children, adolescents, and adults can increase community resilience. Educational opportunities include literacy, early childhood education, linguistic education (e.g., English as a second language classes), vocational training, and higher education. School psychology may help to guide trafficking prevention efforts in schools, including initiatives such as training staff in trafficking-related risk factors and indicators; offering specialized human trafficking curriculum or incorporating trafficking prevention messages into standard educational curricula; providing education about online safety, safe dating, and healthy relationships; and offering mentoring to students. Other protective factors within schools and other learning environments include social–emotional skills education, enrichment programs, and afterschool programs (National Center on Safe Supportive Learning Environments, 2022).

Social Services and Health Care

Effective multisector collaboration and integrated social services can create a safety net for at-risk individuals (Schwarz et al., 2019). Access to basic necessities, such as stable housing and food security, can eliminate vulnerabilities that could be utilized as coercive factors by traffickers. Social services programs may be developed for specific at-risk populations. For instance, many transitional-age youth lose access to vital safety nets when they reach the age of majority, particularly youth transitioning out of foster care or juvenile detention facilities, youth who have run away from home or dropped out of school, and youth with disabilities. Prevention efforts may establish policies that expand services and supports for this population, developing skills and longer term healthy relationships and creating more gradual processes of moving to self-sufficiency. Educational trafficking prevention programs may also be embedded within existing programs for transitional-age youth (Shared Hope International, 2021). As another example, immigrants without valid documentation are vulnerable to exploitation and often lack access to integrated social services, creating further vulnerabilities. Comprehensive services programs for at-risk immigrants and victims of international human trafficking may support primary and secondary prevention (Davy, 2015; Potocky, 2010), and further development and evaluation of such programs is needed to determine effectiveness (Davy, 2016).

A related community-level protective factor is the availability of high-quality health care and equitable service delivery from health care providers who are well-versed in human trafficking and effective antitrafficking responses (Greenbaum et al., 2018). Collaborative multidisciplinary professional networks can be used to increase awareness and skills through training and resource sharing (e.g., HEAL Trafficking, 2023). While mental health disorders can exacerbate vulnerability to trafficking, access to evidence-based, trauma-informed mental health treatment may support primary and secondary prevention of human trafficking (Greenbaum et al., 2018; Hopper, 2017c). Because of the common use of substances as a means of coercion into conditions of trafficking, a barrier to exiting, and a vulnerability to reexploitation, access to integrated, trauma-informed substance use treatment may be another important protective factor (Hopper, 2017b).

Community Empowerment Models

Social psychology (see Chapter 6) underscores the impacts of marginalization within and between groups and highlights the importance of empowerment in its resolution. Human trafficking inherently involves depersonalizing and disempowering processes, and systems working to combat human trafficking can unwittingly repeat elements of disenfranchisement. Despite the fact that survivors have the most direct knowledge of the experience of trafficking and have been most centrally affected, they have historically not been a central part of establishing a solution. Worker-driven social responsibility, an approach that has its basis in human rights, places workers at the center of developing and enforcing solutions to the problem of human trafficking, involving worker-led efforts to promote the rights of workers within global supply chains (Bowersox, 2022). Psychology can contribute to understanding the psychological impacts of such social movements, including how labor movements contribute to psychological change, personal growth, and social acceleration (Carriere, 2020).

Community empowerment models use a grassroots approach to galvanize marginalized and economically disadvantaged groups to collectively identify priorities and demand their rights. For instance, research with vulnerable communities in India found that a community empowerment initiative was effective at combatting labor trafficking, leading to increased community empowerment, infrastructure, access to education, health care, work (having a job card) and government services, decreased household debt, increased food security, and improvement in labor conditions (Gausman et al., 2016).

In addition to addressing issues with underlying structural policies, community psychologists and macro-level social workers can collaborate with community partners to advocate for, develop, and evaluate these types of community programs.

Relational Protective Factors

Advantageous Childhood Experiences

While marginalization, displacement, alienation, and isolation are all risk factors, interpersonal connectedness is a key protective factor against human trafficking. As opposed to ACEs, advantageous childhood experiences (counter-ACEs)—such as early positive experiences and supportive relationships—have been shown to promote healthy relationships, health, and well-being in adulthood (Crandall et al., 2019). The presence of a safe, supportive, and stable caregiving environment in childhood provides the foundation for later self-esteem, coping, and interpersonal skills (Blaustein & Kinniburgh, 2018)—all protective factors against exploitation and abuse. Antitrafficking prevention efforts may focus on promoting these counter-ACEs, including interpersonal connection in childhood, school engagement, familial warmth, extrafamilial support, and instrumental support (e.g., tangible supports from other people; Crandall et al., 2019).

Caregiver/Family Education and Support

Family supports such as caregiver consultation and parenting guidance can offer assistance to stressed families, bolstering caregiver affect regulation, attachment, and attunement with the child (Blaustein & Kinniburgh, 2018). Psychological support and psychoeducation for caregivers and family members may address risk factors such as cultural factors (e.g., acculturation differences; gender stereotypes; stigma regarding gender identity, sexuality, or other individual differences; and victim-blaming attitudes) that create familial conflict and lead to alienation from family members as potential sources of support (Greenbaum, 2020). Foster parents and preadoptive and adoptive parents need training in trauma, human trafficking, and trauma-informed caregiving prior to placement, as well as ongoing support after placement (Nichols et al., 2022). In terms of secondary and tertiary prevention, family reunification, support of safe family members, and family counseling have been identified as important contributors to the healing process (Cecchet & Thoburn, 2014; Gibbs et al., 2015; Greenbaum, 2020). With adequate family engagement and relational safety, family, couples, or parent–child dyadic intervention can support effective communication and conflict management, promoting positive family relationships (Hopper, 2017c).

Strong Social Support Networks

A strong support network that comprises healthy relationships is another relational protective factor. Because individuals who are at risk of, or who have experienced, trafficking may struggle with issues related to trust, intimacy, assertiveness, and boundary setting, support in the development of healthy romantic partnerships, friendships, and work relationships is key for both primary and secondary prevention (Hopper, 2017c). For youth who are estranged from their family of origin and have been moved from placement to placement within the child welfare or juvenile justice systems, identifying a consistent, predictable, supportive relationship with an adult is essential, whether that be a family member, mentor, teacher, or therapist. In fact, one study found that homeless youth with a supportive adult in their lives were less likely to be trafficked than those without such a support (Chisolm-Straker et al., 2018). A qualitative study of survivors of domestic minor sex trafficking found that survivors perceived interpersonal relationships as being central in their lives, not only a risk factor but also in providing protection and fostering resiliency over the trafficking experiences (O'Brien, 2018). Case management can assist at-risk and trafficked individuals in expanding their social support networks, and programs (e.g., group therapies, survivor mentorship programs, and survivor leader initiatives) that bring together those with similar lived experiences of trafficking or exploitation can foster a sense of interpersonal connectedness (Hopper, 2017c).

Individual-Level Protective Factors

While marginalization, displacement, alienation, and isolation are all risk factors, interpersonal connectedness is a key protective factor against human trafficking. Positive early relationships cultivate and strengthen later well-being and can be bolstered by providing support and resources to caregivers and family members. Strong social support networks offer emotional and tangible support that is protective against interpersonal exploitation and abuse.

Individual Awareness

The ability to recognize healthy versus unhealthy situations, including knowledge about labor and sex trafficking and common coercive strategies, is a standard element of many educational prevention programs for at-risk populations. Most premigration trafficking prevention programming is based on the concept that migrants lack adequate information to keep them safe from exploitation (Zimmerman et al., 2015). Increased awareness of workers' rights, immigration laws and legal protections, common trafficking schemes, and available resources may be protective against labor exploitation for some at-risk groups, such as migrant workers and domestic workers (Fukushima, 2019). Similarly, educational programs focusing on prevention of sex trafficking often focus on increasing awareness of sexual exploitation, developing self-esteem, understanding the link between substance abuse and exploitation, promoting healthy relationships, learning about sexual health, and developing skills for finding help (Rothman et al., 2021).

When educational and awareness initiatives targeting at-risk individuals are not solidly grounded in contextual evidence, they may cause unintended harms. For instance, a program evaluation was conducted on a large-scale community-based awareness initiative that aimed to prevent the labor trafficking of women by promoting women's autonomy and by encouraging "safe migration practices" and assertion of migrant worker rights. This evaluation suggested that inexperienced field workers led some women to expect abstract rights and supports (e.g., rights related to compensation or time off, assistance with repatriation) that they did not experience during negative migration experiences, resulting in adverse emotional and financial consequences to these women (Blanchet et al., 2018). Thus, it is important to develop and evaluate concrete, evidence-based awareness initiatives tailored to the unique needs of particular groups. For example, the My Life My Choice curriculum is an educational prevention program tailored to the specific needs of youth who are at risk of commercial sexual exploitation, which was codeveloped and is coled by professionals with lived experience. Program evaluation of this prevention curriculum found that participants who completed the program had increased awareness about trafficking and its harms, were more likely to have given help or information about exploitation to a friend, reported fewer episodes of sexually explicit behavior, and were less likely to report dating abuse (Rothman et al., 2021). Prevention curricula tailored for specific at-risk groups is needed, including developmentally grounded sex education and healthy relationships curriculum for individuals with intellectual or developmental disabilities (Nichols & Heil, 2022); programming for male youth who are at-risk for involvement in commercial sexual exploitation as victims, buyers, or exploiters (Fitzgerald et al., 2021); and prevention programs for migrant and domestic workers that are grounded in concrete, factual knowledge of situations faced by migrants in particular contexts (Blanchet et al., 2018).

Access to Resources

Even when community resources are generally available, attention must be paid to accessibility at the individual level. Feelings of disenfranchisement are common and impede health care access behaviors and health services engagement (Price et al., 2021). Individual-level supports, such as trauma-informed case management and advocacy, can increase accessibility to resources described under community protective factors above, including community connectedness and safety, economic stability, educational opportunities, and social services and quality health care (Jain et al., 2022; Pesso, 2014).

Life Skills and Emotional Health and Well-Being

Because facilitators of human trafficking may target vulnerable individuals with lagging skills, individual-level prevention efforts may include instruction and support in the development of a range of life skills. Educational achievement, job skills, and stable employment with sustainable wages may decrease vulnerability to exploitation. Daily living skills such as self-care, household management, economic empowerment, and financial literacy may also be protective. The World Health Organization (WHO) breaks down life skills into three major areas: (a) critical thinking and decision-making skills (e.g., information gathering, decision making, problem solving skills), (b) interpersonal and communication skills (e.g., verbal and nonverbal communication, active listening, communicating thoughts and feelings, assertiveness, conflict negotiation, boundary-setting, empathy, respect, and teamwork), and (c) coping and self-management skills (e.g., self-efficacy and the belief in one's ability to affect change and make a difference in the future, self-esteem and the belief that one's life has value, self-awareness, the ability to set goals, personal beliefs or sense of meaning, stress management, time management, impulse control, and affect regulation skills; WHO, 2003). Developing skills in each of these areas is protective against risk in many areas, including risk of exploitation and human trafficking (Tsai et al., 2021).

Positive psychology focuses on the development of strengths, resiliency, and empowerment (see Chapter 10), all of which contribute to primary, secondary, and tertiary prevention. Survivor leadership can cultivate empowerment that supports secondary prevention against reexploitation. Social work and psychology play an important role in the development of life skills training programs that are tailored to the needs of survivors of human trafficking (Tsai et al., 2021), as well as promoting evidence-based, trauma-informed, developmentally appropriate, and culturally responsive mental and behavioral health care that supports emotional health and well-being (Hopper, 2017c; see Chapter 9, this volume, for further information on psychological interventions).

Integration of Individual Protective Factors With Contextual Factors

Even when individual level prevention initiatives are grounded in a strong evidence base and tailored to specific groups (Davy, 2016), they should be one component of a multilevel approach to prevention. There is likely to be limited benefit from initiatives that focus solely on raising awareness and individual-level risks and behaviors, without concurrently addressing upstream societal, community, and relational factors that contribute to trafficking (Kiss & Zimmerman, 2019; Zimmerman et al., 2015). Thus, an integrated, multilevel evidence-based approach to the prevention of human trafficking is key to sustained change.

CONCLUSION AND RECOMMENDATIONS

Psychology can be used to build a better understanding of the catalysts of human trafficking, providing a framework for prevention efforts at societal, community, relational, and individual levels. Primary prevention is dependent on addressing social and economic disparities based on factors such as race, ethnicity, class, gender, and sexuality. This may include cultivating cultural and social norms that value equality, diversity, and inclusion and creating trauma-informed systems that are committed to the equitable treatment of different populations. Prevention initiatives may work to decrease inequities in the systems that engage specific at-risk groups, such as child welfare and juvenile justice systems that intersect with trauma-impacted youth and families; immigration systems that focus on migrants and displaced persons; and social services and health care systems that engage with individuals affected by poverty, homelessness, mental health, and substance use concerns. The current knowledge base on risk and protective factors should guide specific policies and practices that decrease the risk of human trafficking or reexploitation. Further research is needed into the role of educational prevention initiatives and the effects of trafficking-related legislation and policy.

Trafficking prevention should include initiatives to develop safe, economically stable, empowered communities with adequate access to resources such as education and health care and opportunities for growth and advancement for community members. Partnerships between community psychology and public health may be created to explore community-related impacts of trafficking and to study the effectiveness of community-level prevention efforts. Cross-discipline antitrafficking professionals should receive advanced training in complex psychological processes that contribute to human trafficking to inform their organizational practices. Funding is needed to support community development and empowerment programs.

Prevention at the relational level involves supporting families, building healthy parent–child relationships, and strengthening social support networks.

Acknowledgment of the often devastating effects of trauma and active efforts to combat childhood trauma and interpersonal violence are essential in decreasing relational risk factors. Mental health practitioners can intervene in cycles of intergenerational transmission of trauma by supporting trauma-impacted parents and caregivers. Social psychological research can guide the development of programs to strengthen social support networks for at-risk groups.

At the individual level, prevention efforts target increased awareness among at-risk individuals about issues related to human trafficking, including human rights, worker rights and protections, healthy relationships, common trafficking schemes, relevant legislation, and community-based resources. Individual-level protections also include psychosocial programs that promote personal strengths, resiliency factors, and life skills that are protective against human trafficking. Psychological contributions include research that elucidates the impacts of trauma and complex trauma; development of mental health treatments to lessen the long-term effects of trauma and reduce revictimization; and establishment of an evidence base to support effective interventions.

Prevention is the foundation of the antitrafficking movement, including efforts to decrease long-term sequelae, to decrease the incidence of revictimization, and to moderate risk and promote protective factors before trafficking even occurs. A well-integrated, evidence-based approach to prevention across societal, community, relational, and individual levels is needed, with rigorous evaluation of prevention initiatives to ensure that resources are best allocated to combat human trafficking.

REFERENCES

Alpert, E. J., & Chin, S. E. (2017). Human trafficking: Perspectives on prevention. In M. Chisolm-Straker & H. Stoklosa (Eds.), *Human trafficking is a public health issue* (pp. 379–400). Springer. https://doi.org/10.1007/978-3-319-47824-1_22

Alves, C. D., & Cavalhieri, K. E. (2021). "Mongering is a weird life sometimes": Discourse analysis of a sex buyer online community. *Violence Against Women, 27*(9), 1448–1474.

American Psychological Association. (2012). *Crossroads: The psychology of immigration in the new century.* http://www.apa.org/topics/immigration/report.aspx

American Psychological Association. (2014). *Report of the Task Force on Trafficking of Women and Girls.* https://www.apa.org/pi/women/programs/trafficking/report.aspx

Aronowitz, A. A., & Koning, A. D. (2014). Understanding human trafficking as a market system: Addressing the demand side of trafficking for sexual exploitation. *Relations Internationales, 85*(3), 669–696.

Baldwin, S. B., Fehrenbacher, A. E., & Eisenman, D. P. (2015). Psychological coercion in human trafficking: An application of Biderman's framework. *Qualitative Health Research, 25*(9), 1171–1181. https://doi.org/10.1177/1049732314557087

Bales, K. (2005). *Understanding global slavery: A reader.* University of California Press.

Beksinska, A., Jama, Z., Kabuti, R., Kungu, M., Babu, H., Nyariki, E., Shah, P., Nyabuto, C., Okumu, M., Mahero, A., Ngurukiri, P., Irungu, E., Adhiambo, W., Muthoga, P., Kaul, R., Seeley, J., Beattie, T. S., Weiss, H. A., Kimani, J., & the Maisha Fiti Study Champions. (2021). Prevalence and correlates of common mental health problems and recent suicidal thoughts and behaviours among female sex workers in Nairobi, Kenya. *BMC Psychiatry, 21*(1), 503. https://doi.org/10.1186/s12888-021-03515-5

Blanchet, T., Biswas, H., Zaman, A., & Lucky, M. A. (2018). *From risks to rights: Evaluation of a training programme for women aspiring to migrate for work.* SANEM Publications. https://www.lshtm.ac.uk/files/swift-bangaldesh-evaluation-report-2018.pdf

Blaustein, M. E., & Kinniburgh, K. M. (2018). *Treating traumatic stress in children and adolescents: How to foster resilience through attachment, self-regulation, and competency.* Guilford Press.

Bowersox, Z. (2022). Union density and human trafficking: Can organized labor discourage trafficking? *Journal of Human Trafficking,* 1–14. https://doi.org/10.1080/23322705.2022.2073095

Bronfenbrenner, U. (1979). *The ecology of human development: Experiments by nature and design.* Harvard University Press.

Bryant-Davis, T., & Gobin, R. L. (2019). Still, we rise: Psychotherapy for African American girls and women exiting sex trafficking. *Women & Therapy, 42*(3–4), 385–405. https://doi.org/10.1080/02703149.2019.1622902

Bryant-Davis, T., & Tummala-Narra, P. (2018). Cultural oppression and human trafficking: Exploring the role of racism and ethnic bias. In N. M. Sidun & D. L. Hume (Eds.), *A feminist perspective on human trafficking of women and girls: Characteristics, commonalities and complexities* (pp. 146–163). Routledge/Taylor & Francis Group.

Bykerk, E. (2022). *The silenced minority: Sex trafficking of males.* Human Trafficking Institute. https://traffickinginstitute.org/the-silenced-minority/

Carriere, K. R. (2020). Workers' rights are human rights: Organizing the psychology of labor movements. *Current Opinion in Psychology, 35,* 60–64. https://doi.org/10.1016/j.copsyc.2020.03.009

Carvalho e Silva, J., & Bucher-Maluschke, J. S. N. F. (2018). Psychology of forced displacement and migration: A systematic review of the scientific literature. *Estudos de Psicologia, 35*(2), 127–136. https://doi.org/10.1590/1982-02752018000200002

Casassa, K., Knight, L., & Mengo, C. (2022). Trauma bonding perspectives from service providers and survivors of sex trafficking: A scoping review. *Trauma, Violence & Abuse, 23*(3), 969–984. https://doi.org/10.1177/1524838020985542

Cecchet, S. J., & Thoburn, J. (2014). The psychological experience of child and adolescent sex trafficking in the United States: Trauma and resilience in survivors. *Psychological Trauma: Theory, Research, Practice, and Policy, 6*(5), 482–493. https://doi.org/10.1037/a0035763

Centers for Disease Control and Prevention. (2021). *About social determinants of health.* https://www.cdc.gov/socialdeterminants/index.htm

Chambers, R., Gibson, M., Chaffin, S., Takagi, T., Nguyen, N., & Mears-Clark, T. (2022). Trauma-coerced attachment and complex PTSD: Informed care for survivors of human trafficking. *Journal of Human Trafficking,* 1–10. https://doi.org/10.1080/23322705.2021.2012386

Chen, A., & Gill, J. (2015). Unaccompanied children and the US immigration system: Challenges and reforms. *Journal of International Affairs, 68*(2), 115.

Chetty, R., Hendren, N., Jones, M. R., & Porter, S. R. (2020, May). Race and economic opportunity in the United States: An intergenerational perspective. *The Quarterly Journal of Economics, 135*(2), 711–783. https://doi.org/10.1093/qje/qjz042

Chisolm-Straker, M., Sze, J., Einbond, J., White, J., & Stoklosa, H. (2018). A supportive adult may be the difference in homeless youth not being trafficked. *Children and Youth Services Review, 91*(C), 115–120. https://doi.org/10.1016/j.childyouth.2018.06.003

Choi, H., Klein, C., Shin, M. S., & Lee, H. J. (2009). Posttraumatic stress disorder (PTSD) and disorders of extreme stress (DESNOS) symptoms following prostitution and childhood abuse. *Violence Against Women, 15*(8), 933–951. https://doi.org/10.1177/1077801209335493

Cole, J., Sprang, G., Lee, R., & Cohen, J. (2016). The trauma of commercial sexual exploitation of youth: A comparison of CSE victims to sexual abuse victims in a clinical sample. *Journal of Interpersonal Violence, 31*(1), 122–146. https://doi.org/10.1177/0886260514555133

Crandall, A., Miller, J. R., Cheung, A., Novilla, L. K., Glade, R., Novilla, M. L. B., Magnusson, B. M., Leavitt, B. L., Barnes, M. D., & Hanson, C. L. (2019). ACEs and counter-ACEs: How positive and negative childhood experiences influence adult health. *Child Abuse & Neglect, 96*, 104089. https://doi.org/10.1016/j.chiabu.2019.104089

Craven, S., Brown, S., & Gilchrist, E. (2006). Sexual grooming of children: Review of literature and theoretical considerations. *Journal of Sexual Aggression, 12*(3), 287–299. https://doi.org/10.1080/13552600601069414

Cyrus, N., & Vogel, D. (2017). *Learning from demand-side campaigns against trafficking in human beings: Evaluation as knowledge-generator and project-improver.* https://www.researchgate.net/publication/318494415_Learning_from_Demand-Side_Campaigns_against_Trafficking_in_Human_Beings_Evaluation_as_Knowledge-Generator_and_Project-Improver

Davy, D. (2015). Understanding the support needs of human-trafficking victims: A review of three human-trafficking program evaluations. *Journal of Human Trafficking, 1*(4), 318–337. https://doi.org/10.1080/23322705.2015.1090865

Davy, D. (2016). Anti–human trafficking interventions: How do we know if they are working? *The American Journal of Evaluation, 37*(4), 486–504. https://doi.org/10.1177/1098214016630615

De Vries, I., & Farrell, A. (2018). Labor trafficking victimizations: Repeat victimization and polyvictimization. *Psychology of Violence, 8*(5), 630–638. https://doi.org/10.1037/vio0000149

Dovidio, J. F., & Esses, V. M. (2001). Immigrants and immigration: Advancing the psychological perspective. *Journal of Social Issues, 57*(3), 378–387. https://doi.org/10.1111/0022-4537.00219

Dryjanska, L., Sanchez, J. N., & Parke, J. (2022). Forced migration, modern slavery, and the evil of shattered dreams. In L. Dryjanska & G. Pacifici (Eds.), *Evil in the modern world* (pp. 83–100). Springer. https://doi.org/10.1007/978-3-030-91888-0_6

Edwards, E. E., Middleton, J. S., & Cole, J. (2022). Family-controlled trafficking in the United States: Victim characteristics, system response, and case outcomes. *Journal of Human Trafficking*, 1–19. https://doi.org/10.1080/23322705.2022.2039866

Faraday, F. (2021). *The empowerment of migrant workers in a precarious situation: An overview.* Global Knowledge Partnership on Migration and Development (KNOMAD). https://www.knomad.org/sites/default/files/2021-12/KNOMAD%20 Working%20Paper%2039-Empowerment%20of%20Worker-Dec%202021.pdf

Farley, M., Golding, J. M., Matthews, E. S., Malamuth, N. M., & Jarrett, L. (2017). Comparing sex buyers with men who do not buy sex: New data on prostitution and trafficking. *Journal of Interpersonal Violence, 32*(23), 3601–3625. https://doi.org/ 10.1177/0886260515600874

Felitti, M. D., Anda, R. F., Nordenberg, M. D., Williamson, D. F., Spitz, A. M., Edwards, V., Koss, M. P., & Marks, J. S. et al. (1998). Relationship of childhood abuse and household dysfunction to many of the leading causes of death in adults: The adverse childhood experiences (ACE) study. *American Journal of Preventative Medicine, 14*(4), 245–258. https://doi.org/10.1016/s0749-3797(98)00017-8

Fitzgerald, M., Owens, T., Moore, J., Goldberg, A., Lowenhaupt, E., & Barron, C. (2021). Development of a multi-session curriculum addressing domestic minor sex trafficking for high-risk male youth. *Journal of Child Sexual Abuse, 30*(6), 667–683. https://doi.org/10.1080/10538712.2021.1937427

Flynn, M., Cicchetti, D., & Rogosch, F. (2014). The prospective contribution of childhood maltreatment to low self-worth, low relationship quality, and symptomatology across adolescence: A developmental-organizational perspective. *Developmental Psychology, 50*(9), 2165–2175. https://doi.org/10.1037/a0037162

Ford, J. D., & Delker, B. C. (2018). Polyvictimization in childhood and its adverse impacts across the lifespan: Introduction to the special issue. *Journal of Trauma & Dissociation, 19*(3), 275–288. https://doi.org/10.1080/15299732.2018.1440479

Franchino-Olsen, H. (2021). Vulnerabilities relevant for commercial sexual exploitation of children/domestic minor sex trafficking: A systematic review of risk factors. *Trauma, Violence & Abuse, 22*(1), 99–111. https://doi.org/10.1177/1524838018821956

Franchino-Olsen, H., Silverstein, H. A., Kahn, N. F., & Martin, S. L. (2020). Minor sex trafficking of girls with disabilities. *International Journal of Human Rights in Healthcare, 13*(2), 97–108. https://doi.org/10.1108/IJHRH-07-2019-0055

Franco, D., Sunkel, M., & Sherman, P. (2022). Social work with transgender survivors of human trafficking: Implications for practice. *Journal of Human Rights and Social Work, 7*(2), 118–127. https://doi.org/10.1007/s41134-021-00200-1

Frank, M. J., & Terwilliger, G. Z. (2015). Gang-controlled sex trafficking. *Virginia Journal of Criminal Law, 3*(2), 342.

Fukushima, A. I. (2019). *Migrant crossings: Witnessing human trafficking in the U.S.* Stanford University Press.

Gacinya, J. (2020). Gender inequality as the determinant of human trafficking in Rwanda. *Sexuality, Gender & Policy, 3*(1), 70–84. https://doi.org/10.1002/sgp2.12018

Gausman, J., Chernoff, M., Duger, A., Bhabha, J., & Chu, H. (2016). *When we raise our voice: The challenge of eradicating labor exploitation.* Freedom Fund. https:// freedomfund.org/wp-content/uploads/FINAL-When-We-Raise-Our-Voice-.pdf

Gibbs, D. A., Henninger, A. M., Tueller, S. J., & Kluckman, M. N. (2018). Human trafficking and the child welfare population in Florida. *Children and Youth Services Review, 88*, 1–10. https://doi.org/10.1016/j.childyouth.2018.02.045

Gibbs, D. A., Walters, J. L. H., Lutnick, A., Miller, S., & Kluckman, M. (2015). Services to domestic minor victims of sex trafficking: Opportunities for engagement and support. *Children and Youth Services Review, 54*, 1–7. https://doi.org/10.1016/j.childyouth.2015.04.003

Grant, J. M., Mottet, L. A., Tanis, J. J., & Min, D. (2011). *Transgender discrimination survey*. National Center for Transgender Equality and National Gay and Lesbian Task Force. https://cancer-network.org/wp-content/uploads/2017/02/National_Transgender_Discrimination_Survey_Report_on_health_and_health_care.pdf

Greenbaum, J. (2020). Child labor and sex trafficking. In J. H. Coverdale, M. R. Gordon, & P. T. Nguyen (Eds.), *Human trafficking: A treatment guide for mental health professionals*, 169–192. American Psychiatric Association.

Greenbaum, J., Sprang, G., Recknor, F., Harper, N. S., & Titchen, K. (2022). Labor trafficking of children and youth in the United States: A scoping review. *Child Abuse & Neglect, 131*, 105694. https://doi.org/10.1016/j.chiabu.2022.105694

Greenbaum, V. J., Titchen, K., Walker-Descartes, I., Feifer, A., Rood, C. J., & Fong, H. F. (2018). Multi-level prevention of human trafficking: The role of health care professionals. *Preventive Medicine, 114*, 164–167. https://doi.org/10.1016/j.ypmed.2018.07.006

Hagan, E., Raghavan, C., & Doychak, K. (2021). Functional isolation: Understanding isolation in trafficking survivors. *Sexual Abuse, 33*(2), 176–199. https://doi.org/10.1177/1079063219889059

HEAL Trafficking. (2023). *Health education advocacy linkage: Because human trafficking is a health issue*. https://healtrafficking.org/

Hebert, L. A. (2016). Always victimizers, never victims: Engaging men and boys in human trafficking scholarship. *Journal of Human Trafficking, 2*(4), 281–296. https://doi.org/10.1080/23322705.2016.1144165

Hogan, K. A., & Roe-Sepowitz, D. (2020). LGBTQ+ homeless young adults and sex trafficking vulnerability. *Journal of Human Trafficking, 9*(1), 63–78.

Hopper, E. K. (2017a). Polyvictimization and developmental trauma adaptations in sex trafficked youth. *Journal of Child & Adolescent Trauma, 10*(2), 161–173. https://doi.org/10.1007/s40653-016-0114-z

Hopper, E. K. (2017b). Trauma-informed treatment of substance use disorders in trafficking survivors. In M. Chisolm-Straker & H. Stocklosa (Eds.), *Human trafficking is a public health issue: A paradigm expansion in the United States* (pp. 211–230). Springer International Publishing. https://doi.org/10.1007/978-3-319-47824-1_12

Hopper, E. K. (2017c). The Multimodal Social Ecological (MSE) approach: A trauma-informed framework for supporting trafficking survivors' psychosocial health. In M. Chisolm-Straker & H. Stocklosa (Eds.), *Human trafficking is a public health issue: A paradigm expansion in the United States* (pp. 153–184). Springer International Publishing. https://doi.org/10.1007/978-3-319-47824-1_10

Hopper, E. K., Azar, N., Bhattacharyya, S., Malebranche, D. A., & Brennan, K. E. (2018). STARS experiential group intervention: A complex trauma treatment approach for survivors of human trafficking. *Journal of Evidence-Informed Social Work, 15*(2), 215–241. https://doi.org/10.1080/23761407.2018.1455616

Hopper, E. K., & Gonzalez, L. D. (2018). A comparison of psychological symptoms in survivors of sex and labor trafficking. *Behavioral Medicine, 44*(3), 177–188. https://doi.org/10.1080/08964289.2018.1432551

Hopper, E. K., & Hidalgo, J. (2006). Invisible chains: Psychological coercion of human trafficking victims. *Intercultural Human Rights Law Review, 1*, 185–209.

Ibrahim, A., Abdalla, S. M., Jafer, M., Abdelgadir, J., & de Vries, N. (2019). Child labor and health: A systematic literature review of the impacts of child labor on child's health in low- and middle-income countries. *Journal of Public Health*, *41*(1), 18–26. https://doi.org/10.1093/pubmed/fdy018

Iglesias-Rios, L., Harlow, S. D., Burgard, S. A., Kiss, L., & Zimmerman, C. (2018). Mental health, violence and psychological coercion among female and male trafficking survivors in the greater Mekong sub-region: A cross-sectional study. *BMC Psychology*, *6*(1), 56. https://doi.org/10.1186/s40359-018-0269-5

International Labour Organisation. (2022). *Introduction to international labour standards: Conventions and recommendations.* https://www.ilo.org/global/standards/introduction-to-international-labour-standards/conventions-and-recommendations/lang--en/index.htm

International Organization for Migration. (2021). *The tradition of toil: The interplay of social norms and stigma in relation to human trafficking in Indonesia.*

Jain, J., Bennett, M., Bailey, M. D., Liaou, D., Kaltiso, S. O., Greenbaum, J., Williams, K., Gordon, M. R., Torres, M. I. M., Nguyen, P. T., Coverdale, J. H., Williams, V., Hari, C., Rodriguez, S., Salami, T., & Potter, J. E. (2022). Creating a collaborative trauma-informed interdisciplinary citywide victim services model focused on health care for survivors of human trafficking. *Public Health Reports*, *137*(Suppl. 1), 30S–37S. https://doi.org/10.1177/00333549211059833

Jones, L., Engstrom, D. W., Hilliard, T., & Diaz, M. (2007). Globalization and human trafficking. *Journal of Sociology and Social Welfare*, *34*(2), 107–122.

Kasser, T., & Kanner, A. D. (Eds.). (2004). *Psychology and consumer culture: The struggle for a good life in a materialistic world.* American Psychological Association. https://doi.org/10.1037/10658-000

Kelly, A., & McNamara, M.-L. (2018, June 29). America's outcasts: The women trapped in a cruel cycle of exploitation. *The Guardian.* https://www.theguardian.com/global-development/2018/jun/29/americas-outcasts-women-trapped-in-cruel-cycle-of-exploitation

Kenny, M. C., Helpingstine, C., Long, H., Perez, L., & Harrington, M. C. (2019). Increasing child serving professionals' awareness and understanding of the commercial sexual exploitation of children. *Journal of Child Sexual Abuse*, *28*(4), 417–434. https://doi.org/10.1080/10538712.2018.1563264

Kinnish, K., McCarty, C., Tiwari, A., Osborne, M., Glasheen, T., Franchot, K. K., Kramer, C., & Self-Brown, S. (2020). Featured counter-trafficking program: Project intersect. *Child Abuse & Neglect*, *100*, 104132. https://doi.org/10.1016/j.chiabu.2019.104132

Kiss, L., Pocock, N. S., Naisanguansri, V., Suos, S., Dickson, B., Thuy, D., Koehler, J., Sirisup, K., Pongrungsee, N., Nguyen, V. A., Borland, R., Dhavan, P., & Zimmerman, C. (2015). Health of men, women, and children in post-trafficking services in Cambodia, Thailand, and Vietnam: An observational cross-sectional study. *The Lancet: Global Health*, *3*(3), e154–e161. https://doi.org/10.1016/S2214-109X(15)70016-1

Kiss, L., Yun, K., Pocock, N., & Zimmerman, C. (2015). Exploitation, violence, and suicide risk among child and adolescent survivors of human trafficking in the Greater Mekong Subregion. *JAMA Pediatrics*, *169*(9), e152278. https://doi.org/10.1001/jamapediatrics.2015.2278

Kiss, L., & Zimmerman, C. (2019). Human trafficking and labor exploitation: Toward identifying, implementing, and evaluating effective responses. *PLOS Medicine, 16*(1), e1002740. https://doi.org/10.1371/journal.pmed.1002740

Langton, L., Planty, M. G., Banks, D., Witwer, A. R., Woods, D., Vermeer, M. J. D., & Jackson, B. A. (2022). *Sex trafficking and substance use: Identifying high-priority needs within the criminal justice system.* RAND Corporation. https://www.rand.org/pubs/research_reports/RRA108-13.html

Latham-Sprinkle, J., David, F., Bryant, K., & Larsen, J. (2019). *Migrants and their vulnerability to human trafficking, modern slavery and forced labour.* International Organisation for Migration. https://publications.iom.int/system/files/pdf/migrants_and_their_vulnerability.pdf

Littenberg, N., & Baldwin, S. (2017). The ignored exploitation: Labor trafficking in the United States. In M. Chisolm-Straker & H. Stoklosa (Eds.), *Human trafficking is a public health issue* (pp. 67–91). Springer. https://doi.org/10.1007/978-3-319-47824-1_5

Long, E., Reid, J., McLeigh, J., Stoklosa, H., Felix, E., & Scott, T. (2018). *Preventing human trafficking using data-driven, community-based strategies.* https://www.communitypsychology.com/preventing-human-trafficking/

Malebranche, D. A., Hopper, E. K., & Corey, E. (2020). Sex and labor trafficking: Trauma-informed themes toward a social justice approach. In R. Geffner, J. W. White, L. K. Hamberger, A. Rosenbaum, V. Vaughan-Eden, & V. I. Vieth (Eds.), *Handbook of interpersonal violence and abuse across the lifespan* (pp. 1–28). Springer. https://doi.org/10.1007/978-3-319-62122-7_43-1

Marburger, K., & Pickover, S. A. (2020). A comprehensive perspective on treating victims of human trafficking. *The Professional Counselor, 10*(1), 13–24. https://doi.org/10.15241/km.10.1.13

Maslow, A. H. (1943). A theory of human motivation. *Psychological Review, 50*(4), 370–396. https://doi.org/10.1037/h0054346

Murphy, L. T. (2016). *Labor and sex trafficking among homeless youth: A ten-city study.* Loyola University. https://www.covenanthouse.org/sites/default/files/inline-files/Loyola%20Multi-City%20Executive%20Summary%20FINAL.pdf

National Center on Safe Supportive Learning Environments. (2022). *Preventing child trafficking at the school level.* https://safesupportivelearning.ed.gov/human-trafficking-americas-schools/preventing-child-trafficking-at-the-school-level

Nelson, S., Guthrie, J., & Coffey, P. S. (2004). *Literature review and analysis related to human trafficking in post-conflict situations.* United States Agency for International Development. https://pdf.usaid.gov/pdf_docs/PNACY689.pdf

Nichols, A. J., Gerassi, L. B., Gilbert, K., & Taylor, E. (2022). Provider challenges in responding to retrafficking of juvenile justice-involved domestic minor sex trafficking survivors. *Child Abuse & Neglect, 126*, 105521. https://doi.org/10.1016/j.chiabu.2022.105521

Nichols, A. J., & Heil, E. (2017). Prosecuting buyers in human trafficking cases: An analysis of the implications of United States v. Jungers and United States v. Bonestroo. *Dignity: A Journal of Analysis of Exploitation and Violence, 2*(4, 2), 1–16.

Nichols, A. J., & Heil, E. (2022). Human trafficking of people with a disability: An analysis of state and federal cases. *Dignity: A Journal of Analysis of Exploitation and Violence, 7*(1), 1.

Nodzenski, M., Kiss, L., Pocock, N. S., Stoeckl, H., Zimmerman, C., & Buller, A. M. (2020). Post-trafficking stressors: The influence of hopes, fears and expectations on the mental health of young trafficking survivors in the Greater Mekong Subregion. *Child Abuse & Neglect*, *100*, 104067. https://doi.org/10.1016/j.chiabu.2019.104067

O'Brien, J. E. (2018). "Sometimes, somebody just needs somebody—anybody—to care": The power of interpersonal relationships in the lives of domestic minor sex trafficking survivors. *Child Abuse & Neglect*, *81*, 1–11. https://doi.org/10.1016/j.chiabu.2018.04.010

O'Brien, J. E., & Li, W. (2020). The role of the internet in the grooming, exploitation, and exit of United States domestic minor sex trafficking victims. *Journal of Children and Media*, *14*(2), 187–203. https://doi.org/10.1080/17482798.2019.1688668

Office of Justice Programs. (2022, January). *Partnerships and pathways to economic opportunity for survivors of trafficking: A guide.* https://www.ojp.gov/library/publications/partnerships-and-pathways-economic-opportunity-survivors-trafficking-guide

Oram, S., Abas, M., Bick, D., Boyle, A., French, R., Jakobowitz, S., Khondoker, M., Stanley, N., Trevillion, K., Howard, L., & Zimmerman, C. (2016). Human trafficking and health: A survey of male and female survivors in England. *American Journal of Public Health*, *106*(6), 1073–1078. https://doi.org/10.2105/AJPH.2016.303095

Oram, S., Khondoker, M., Abas, M., Broadbent, M., & Howard, L. M. (2015). Characteristics of trafficked adults and children with severe mental illness: A historical cohort study. *The Lancet. Psychiatry*, *2*(12), 1084–1091. https://doi.org/10.1016/S2215-0366(15)00290-4

Oram, S., Stöckl, H., Busza, J., Howard, L. M., & Zimmerman, C. (2012). Prevalence and risk of violence and the physical, mental, and sexual health problems associated with human trafficking: Systematic review. *PLOS Medicine*, *9*(5), e1001224. https://doi.org/10.1371/journal.pmed.1001224

Ortega, J., Gordon, M., Gordon-Achebe, K., & Robitz, R. (2022). Survivors of human trafficking. In S. H. Koh, G. G. Mejia, & H. M. Gould (Eds.), *Diversity in action* (pp. 33–56). Springer. https://doi.org/10.1007/978-3-030-85401-0_3

Ottisova, L., Hemmings, S., Howard, L. M., Zimmerman, C., & Oram, S. (2016). Prevalence and risk of violence and the mental, physical and sexual health problems associated with human trafficking: An updated systematic review. *Epidemiology and Psychiatric Sciences*, *25*(4), 317–341. https://doi.org/10.1017/S2045796016000135

Ottisova, L., Smith, P., & Oram, S. (2018). Psychological consequences of human trafficking: Complex posttraumatic stress disorder in trafficked children. *Behavioral Medicine*, *44*(3), 234–241. https://doi.org/10.1080/08964289.2018.1432555

Owens, C., Dank, M., Farrell, A., Breaux, J., Banuelos, I., & Pfeffer, R. McDevitt, J. (2014). *Understanding the organization, operation, and victimization process of labor trafficking in the United States.* The Urban Institute. https://www.immigrationresearch.org/system/files/413249-Labor-Trafficking-in-the-United-States.pdf

Palines, P. A., Rabbitt, A. L., Pan, A. Y., Nugent, M. L., & Ehrman, W. G. (2020). Comparing mental health disorders among sex trafficked children and three groups of youth at high-risk for trafficking: A dual retrospective cohort and scoping review. *Child Abuse & Neglect*, *100*, 104196. https://doi.org/10.1016/j.chiabu.2019.104196

Palumbo, L. (2017). Exploiting for care: Trafficking and abuse in domestic work in Italy. *Journal of Immigrant & Refugee Studies, 15*(2), 171–186. https://doi.org/10.1080/15562948.2017.1305473

Pesso, L. (2014). Supporting human trafficking survivor resiliency through comprehensive case management. In L. Simich & L. Andermann (Eds.), *Refuge and resilience: International perspectives on migration* (Vol. 7, pp. 195–209). Springer. https://doi.org/10.1007/978-94-007-7923-5_13

Pocock, N. S., Kiss, L., Oram, S., & Zimmerman, C. (2016). Labour trafficking among men and boys in the Greater Mekong Subregion: Exploitation, violence, occupational health risks and injuries. *PLOS ONE, 11*(12), e0168500. https://doi.org/10.1371/journal.pone.0168500

Polaris Project. (2020). *The Latino face of human trafficking and exploitation in the United States.* https://polarisproject.org/wp-content/uploads/2020/04/EXECUTIVE-SUMMARY-The-Latino-Face-of-Human-Trafficking-and-Exploitation-in-the-United-States.pdf

Polaris Project. (2021, February). *Love and trafficking: How traffickers groom & control their victims.* https://polarisproject.org/blog/2021/02/love-and-trafficking-how-traffickers-groom-control-their-victims/

Potocky, M. (2010). Effectiveness of services for victims of international human trafficking: An exploratory evaluation. *Journal of Immigrant & Refugee Studies, 8*(4), 359–385. https://doi.org/10.1080/15562948.2010.522462

Powell, C., Asbill, M., Louis, E., & Stoklosa, H. (2018). Identifying gaps in human trafficking mental health service provision. *Journal of Human Trafficking, 4*(3), 256–269. https://doi.org/10.1080/23322705.2017.1362936

Price, K., Nelson, B. D., & Macias-Konstantopoulos, W. L. (2021). Understanding health care access disparities among human trafficking survivors: Profiles of health care experiences, access, and engagement. *Journal of Interpersonal Violence, 36*(21–22), NP11780–NP11799. https://doi.org/10.1177/0886260519889934

Pullmann, M. D., Roberts, N. A., Parker, E. M., Mangiaracina, K. J., Briner, L. R., Silverman, M., & Becker, J. R. (2020). Residential instability, running away, and juvenile detention characterizes commercially sexually exploited youth involved in Washington State's child welfare system. *Child Abuse & Neglect, 102.* https://doi:10.1016/j.chiabu.2020.104423

Puigvert, L., Duque, E., Merodio, G., & Melgar, P. (2021). A systematic review of family and social relationships: Implications for sex trafficking recruitment and victimisation. *Families, Relationships and Societies, 11*(4), 534–550. https://doi.org/10.1332/204674321X16358719475186

Quek, K. (2017). Globalization and sex trafficking. In A. Farazmand (Ed.), *Global encyclopedia of public administration, public policy, and governance* (pp. 1–9). Springer. https://doi.org/10.1007/978-3-319-31816-5_1315-1

Reid, J. A. (2011). An exploratory model of girls' vulnerability to commercial sexual exploitation in prostitution. *Child Maltreatment, 16*(2), 146–157. https://doi.org/10.1177/1077559511404700

Reid, J. A. (2018). Sex trafficking of girls with intellectual disabilities: An exploratory mixed methods study. *Sexual Abuse, 30*(2), 107–131. https://doi.org/10.1177/1079063216630981

Reid, J. A., Baglivio, M. T., Piquero, A. R., Greenwald, M. A., & Epps, N. (2017). Human trafficking of minors and childhood adversity in Florida. *American Journal of Public Health, 107*(2), 306–311. https://doi.org/10.2105/AJPH.2016.303564

Reid, J., & Fox, B. (2020). Human trafficking and the darknet. In B. Fox, J. A. Reid, & T. Masys (Eds.), *Science informed policing* (pp. 77–96). Springer. https://doi.org/10.1007/978-3-030-41287-6_5

Reid, J. A., Haskell, R. A., Dillahunt-Aspillaga, C., & Thor, J. A. (2013). Contemporary review of empirical and clinical studies of trauma bonding in violent or exploitative relationships. *International Journal of Psychological Research, 8*(1), 37–73.

Reid, J. A., Huard, J., & Haskell, R. A. (2015). Family-facilitated juvenile sex trafficking. *Journal of Crime and Justice, 38*(3), 361–376. https://doi.org/10.1080/0735648X.2014.967965

Reid, J. A., Strauss, J., & Haskell, R. A. (2018). Clinical practice with commercially sexually exploited girls with intellectual disabilities. In A. J. Nichols, T. Edmond, & E. C. Heil (Eds.), *Social work practice with survivors of sex trafficking and commercial sexual exploitation* (pp. 218–238). Columbia University Press. https://doi.org/10.7312/nich18092-012

Reyes, C. (2016, January 18). *Justifying human trafficking: The mind of a trafficker.* End Slavery Now. http://www.endslaverynow.org/blog/articles/justifying-human-trafficking-the-mind-of-a-trafficker

Robichaux, K., & Torres, M. I. M. (2022). The role of social determinants in caring for trafficked patients: A public health perspective on human trafficking. *Bulletin of the Menninger Clinic, 86*(Suppl. A), 8–17. https://doi.org/10.1521/bumc.2022.86.suppA.8

Roe-Sepowitz, D. E. (2012). Juvenile entry into prostitution: The role of emotional abuse. *Violence Against Women, 18*(5), 562–579. https://doi.org/10.1177/1077801212453140

Roe-Sepowitz, D. E. (2019). A six-year analysis of sex traffickers of minors: Exploring characteristics and sex trafficking patterns. *Journal of Human Behavior in the Social Environment, 29*(5), 608–629. https://doi.org/10.1080/10911359.2019.1575315

Rothman, E. F., Farrell, A., Paruk, J., Bright, K., Bair-Merritt, M., & Preis, S. R. (2021). Evaluation of a multi-session group designed to prevent commercial sexual exploitation of minors: The "My Life My Choice" curriculum. *Journal of Interpersonal Violence, 36*(19–20), 9143–9166. https://doi.org/10.1177/0886260519865972

Ruf, A. H. (2015). *Pimps of Harlem: Talk of labor and the sociology of risk* [Doctoral dissertation, City University of New York]. CUNY Academic Works. https://academicworks.cuny.edu/gc_etds/1115

Salami, T., Gordon, M., Coverdale, J., & Nguyen, P. T. (2018). What therapies are favored in the treatment of the psychological sequelae of trauma in human trafficking victims? *Journal of Psychiatric Practice, 24*(2), 87–96. https://doi.org/10.1097/PRA.0000000000000288

Santana, M. C., Raj, A., Decker, M. R., La Marche, A., & Silverman, J. G. (2006). Masculine gender roles associated with increased sexual risk and intimate partner violence perpetration among young adult men. *Journal of Urban Health, 83*(4), 575–585. https://doi.org/10.1007/s11524-006-9061-6

Schultz, K., Cattaneo, L. B., Sabina, C., Brunner, L., Jackson, S., & Serrata, J. V. (2016). Key roles of community connectedness in healing from trauma. *Psychology of Violence, 6*(1), 42–48. https://doi.org/10.1037/vio0000025

Schwarz, C., Alvord, D., Daley, D., Ramaswamy, M., Rauscher, E., & Britton, H. (2019). The trafficking continuum: Service providers' perspectives on vulnerability, exploitation, and trafficking. *Affilia, 34*(1), 116–132. https://doi.org/10.1177/0886109918803648

Scott, J. T., Ingram, A. M., Nemer, S. L., & Crowley, D. M. (2019). Evidence-based human trafficking policy: Opportunities to invest in trauma-informed strategies. *American Journal of Community Psychology, 64*(3–4), 348–358. https://doi.org/10.1002/ajcp.12394

Shared Hope International. (2021, November). *Report cards on child and youth sex trafficking* [Issue Briefs]. https://reportcards.sharedhope.org/issue-briefs/

Shared Hope International & the Villanova Law Institute to Address Commercial Sexual Exploitation. (2020, January). *Responding to sex trafficking victim-offender intersectionality: A guide for criminal justice stakeholders.* https://sharedhope.org/wp-content/uploads/2020/01/SH_Responding-to-Sex-Trafficking-Victim-Offender-Intersectionality2020_FINAL.pdf

Sidun, N. M. (2018). Traffickers: Who are they? In L. Walker, G. Gaviria, & K. Gopal (Eds.), *Handbook of sex trafficking: Feminist transnational perspectives* (pp. 99–109). Springer Nature Switzerland AG. https://doi.org/10.1007/978-3-319-73621-1_11

Sprang, G., & Cole, J. (2018). Familial sex trafficking of minors: Trafficking conditions, clinical presentation, and system involvement. *Journal of Family Violence, 33*(3), 185–195. https://doi.org/10.1007/s10896-018-9950-y

Stöckl, H., Fabbri, C., Cook, H., Galez-Davis, C., Grant, N., Lo, Y. A., Kiss, L., & Zimmerman, C. (2021). Human trafficking and violence: Findings from the largest global dataset of trafficking survivors. *Journal of Migration and Health, 16*(4). https://doi.org/10.1016/j.jmh.2021.100073

Stotzer, R. L. (2009). Violence against transgender people: A review of United States data. *Aggression and Violent Behavior, 14*(3), 170–179. https://doi.org/10.1016/j.avb.2009.01.006

Stumblingbear-Riddle, G. P., Burlew, A. K., Gaztambide, D., Madore, M. R., Neville, H., & Joseph, G. (2019). Standing with our American Indian and Alaska Native women, girls, and two-spirit people: Exploring the impact of and resources for survivors of human trafficking. *Journal of Indigenous Research, 7*(1).

Substance Abuse and Mental Health Services Administration. (2014). *SAMHSA's concept of trauma and guidance for a trauma-informed approach.* https://store.samhsa.gov/sites/default/files/d7/priv/sma14-4884.pdf

Swaner, R., Labriola, M., Rempel, M., Walker, A., & Spadafore, J. (2016). *Youth involvement in the sex trade: A national study.* Center for Court Innovation. https://www.ojp.gov/pdffiles1/ojjdp/grants/249952.pdf

Thompson, S. C. (1999). Illusions of control: How we overestimate our personal influence. *Current Directions in Psychological Science, 8*(6), 187–190.

Tsai, L. C., Ubaldo, J., & Sun, P. (2021). Adapting a life skills training program for survivors of human trafficking. *Journal of Modern Slavery, 6*(1), 52.

Twis, M. K., Gillespie, L., & Greenwood, D. (2022). An analysis of romantic partnership dynamics in domestic minor sex trafficking case files. *Journal of Interpersonal Violence, 37*(7–8), NP5394–NP5418.

United Kingdom Home Office. (2021). *Group based child sexual exploitation characteristics of offending.* https://www.gov.uk/government/publications/group-based-child-sexual-exploitation-characteristics-of-offending/group-based-child-sexual-exploitation-characteristics-of-offending-accessible-version

United States Department of State. (2020). *Trauma bonding in human trafficking.* https://www.state.gov/wp-content/uploads/2020/10/TIP_Factsheet-Trauma-Bonding-in-Human-Trafficking-508.pdf

Westerhoff, N. (2012, October 1). Why do men buy sex? *Scientific American.* https://doi.org/10.1038/scientificamericanbrain0512-60

World Health Organization. (2003). *Skills for health skills-based health education including life skills: An important component of a child-friendly/health-promoting school.* https://apps.who.int/iris/bitstream/handle/10665/42818/924159103X.pdf?sequence=1&isAllowed=y

Zimmerman, C., & Kiss, L. (2017). Human trafficking and exploitation: A global health concern. *PLOS Medicine, 14*(11), e1002437. https://doi.org/10.1371/journal.pmed.1002437

Zimmerman, C., McAlpine, A., & Kiss, L. (2015). *Safer labour migration and community-based prevention of exploitation: The state of the evidence for programming.* The Freedom Fund and London School of Hygiene and Tropical Medicine.

2

EXPLORING HUMAN TRAFFICKING OF MARGINALIZED COMMUNITIES THROUGH THE LENS OF LIBERATION PSYCHOLOGY

THEMA BRYANT AND DOMINIQUE A. MALEBRANCHE

The U.S. Department of State's Office to Monitor and Combat Trafficking of Persons (2021) issued an acknowledgment of the impact of systemic racism on human trafficking, noting that people of color are often left more vulnerable to exploitation and are less protected by antitrafficking initiatives. The minimal attention given to the intersectional systems of oppression that create and perpetuate human trafficking hinders progress in abolishing it (Malebranche et al., 2020). Intersectional, justice-oriented frameworks are needed to inform prevention and intervention strategies that can create the systemic change needed to eradicate human trafficking (Vollinger, 2021). According to Crenshaw (2005), *intersectionality* is the possession of multiple marginalized identities, which can create unique risk and vulnerabilities to labor and sexual exploitation. Exploitation is rooted in dehumanization, which is the systematic disregard of persons, including trafficking victims, presenting them as unworthy of compassion or care (Bloom, 2018; Viloria, 1999).

Liberation psychology, originating from Latin America, is one theoretical orientation that calls for attention to systemic oppression and the application of psychological science and practice to dismantle oppression with the

https://doi.org/10.1037/0000379-003
Psychological Perspectives on Human Trafficking: Theory, Research, Prevention, and Intervention, L. Dryjanska, E. K. Hopper, and H. Stoklosa (Editors)

intention of promoting holistic liberation for all people (Martín-Baró, 1994). While scholarship has grown in the documentation of the individual psychological consequences of human trafficking, less research has analyzed the interlocking webs of oppression that both promote and protect the trade of human beings. Whether addressing human trafficking for labor or for sexual exploitation, disenfranchised persons overwhelmingly face the greatest risk of human trafficking (Bryant-Davis & Tummala-Narra, 2017). The lives and bodies of oppressed peoples in the past and present have been treated as disposable—not simply by individuals but also by institutions, systems, and governments (Rajan & Bryant-Davis, 2021). This chapter first provides a brief overview of liberation psychology and then describes the intersection of oppression and human trafficking in the lives of those marginalized by race or ethnicity, socioeconomic status, gender, and sexuality. The authors also provide recommendations for psychologists to engage in professional actions to disrupt systems of oppression that perpetuate human trafficking. The aim of these recommendations is the promotion of holistic liberation, which includes the body, mind, emotions, social networks, political empowerment, and cultural heritage of marginalized persons.

LIBERATION PSYCHOLOGY

Liberation psychology, founded by Latin American social psychologist and priest Ignacio Martin-Baro, is rooted in the premise that psychological health is political and psychology can either play a central role in maintaining oppression or uplifting liberation (Comas-Díaz & Torres-Rivera, 2020). Martin-Baro argued that this choice is between continuing the status quo of centering people of European descent as the model of humanity and therefore promoting biases or beginning to make it a priority to attend to marginalized communities locally and globally (Barratt, 2011). Working in opposition to Western psychology, which is often decontextualized and ahistorical, liberation psychology works toward healing and empowering marginalized communities, which necessitates a psychological framework that is contextualized, systemic, historical, and sociopolitical (Comas-Díaz & Torres-Rivera, 2020). Falling under the umbrella of decolonizing psychology, or the active disruption of systemic oppression and the engaged attending to the experience and contributions of Indigenous peoples, liberation psychology meets these aims in theory and application (Yakushko, 2021).

Liberation psychology mandates attending to the psychology of the marginalized as documented, framed, and studied by historically marginalized and excluded psychologists (Burton & Guzzo, 2020). When Western psychologists study people and frame the Western experience and vantage point as neutral, the field inherently frames marginalized and excluded persons as pathological, deficient, and abnormal. By challenging notions of neutrality and centering culturally attuned psychologists and lay people, psychologists liberate psychology and the people they aim to empower. Liberation psychologists attend not only to the cultural identity of the individual but also the impact of political and economic forces on their lives (Thompson, 2019).

This type of psychology also attends to the internalization of oppression, which through distorted meaning making manifests itself as shame and guilt. Liberation-oriented practitioners address structural oppression, memory, and internalized oppression while countering it with strength, resilience, faith, and hope (Torres Rivera, 2020). To embody liberation, psychologists must shift away from trafficking interventions, prevention programs, and research that ignore context, as attending to the culture, identity, and systems affecting survivors' lives is critical to the development of responsive, culturally attuned interventions. Liberation-oriented psychologists take consciousness raising and active engagement seriously within themselves, clients or participants, and the greater public to counter the narratives in the media and other systems that deflect attention away from poverty, oppression, and dehumanization, often gravitating toward centering the pathology of the individual (Burton & Guzzo, 2020).

LIBERATION PSYCHOLOGY AND HUMAN TRAFFICKING: AN ETHICAL MANDATE

Survivors of labor trafficking, exploitation for criminal activity, and sex trafficking face negative consequences to their physical and mental health as a result of the multiple forms trauma they have faced (Clay-Warner et al., 2021). Psychologists need to adopt an antioppression, decolonizing framework to address human trafficking to fulfill the guidelines of the American Psychological Association (APA; 2017) to attend to cultural context, including power, privilege, inequities, disparities, and oppression. Analyzing and addressing human trafficking as merely a psychological wound in need of recovery and prevention is inadequate. Psychologists, whether they are practitioners, researchers, consultants, or advocates, need to attend to the sociopolitical interlocking webs of oppression in which human trafficking flourishes (Twis & Preble, 2020). Psychologists, who are committed to human rights and dignity, need to apply their science to the dismantling of individual and institutional factors that promote and sustain the selling of marginalized human beings; those factors include oppression in all of its forms (Vejar & Quach, 2013). Liberation psychologists who address human trafficking, referred to as "abolitionist psychologists" in this chapter, attend to oppression and work to counter it as an integral component of their ethical responsibility in service of the public in general and those most vulnerable to human trafficking and other forms of degradation.

Additionally, research can be a site for resistance to foster social change. Hardesty and Gunn (2019) argued that research, particularly qualitative research, can be a political tool that rejects notions of scientific neutrality and instead builds on the power of voice and representation for marginalized persons. Abolitionist psychological researchers can evaluate wraparound programs, which provide housing, therapy, education, jobs training, and health care to determine not only effectiveness in decreasing psychological distress but also effectiveness in addressing economic and educational needs of trafficking survivors.

This chapter focuses on racism and ethnic bias, classism and caste systems, sexism and patriarchy, and heterosexism. While risk factors and recommendations are addressed for each type of oppression, awareness of intersectionality is vital, as many trafficking survivors hold multiple marginalized identities such as queer, impoverished, adolescent girls of color (Cho et al., 2013).

THE INTERSECTION OF OPPRESSION AND HUMAN TRAFFICKING

It is important to develop a sociopolitical analysis to understand root causes and implications of human trafficking across various sociocultural experiences. In the following subsections, we describe the intersections of oppression and human trafficking in the lives of those historically and contemporarily marginalized. For the sake of this chapter, this analysis will explore race and ethnicity, socioeconomic status, gender, and sexuality.

Race, Racism, Ethnic Bias, and Xenophobia

To understand the realities of risk for human trafficking, psychologists must understand that race itself is not the source of vulnerability. Nothing inherent to the variable race predisposes people to be at risk for human trafficking. Racism, ethnic bias, and xenophobia are the actual factors that increase risk for human trafficking (Bryant-Davis & Tummala-Narra, 2017). The racial hierarchy that values White bodies over those of people of color is at the root of the racial disparities in human trafficking, both in labor and in sexual exploitation (United Nations, 2001). Racism and ethnic biases are the prejudicial attitudes that those who benefit from racism use to justify discriminatory behavior, including both their actions and inaction (Dovidio & Gaertner, 2004). Globally, racism in conjunction with colonialism and neocolonialism have resulted in nations that are predominately White, and wealthier exploiting nations predominated by the global majority, people of color (Tummala-Narra et al., 2011). The pathways that connect racism and ethnic bias to human trafficking include stereotypes, barriers to resource access, prior abuse, colonialism, and poverty (Bryant-Davis & Tummala-Narra, 2017). Regarding sex trafficking, the term "ethnosexuality," as coined by Joanne Nagel, draws attention to the ways sex and sexuality are socially influenced by stereotypes rooted in race, racism, and nationality, which promote and justify sexual violence against women and girls of color (Chong, 2014). Even more prevalent than sex trafficking is labor trafficking, which disproportionately affects people of color and people living in poverty, and yet labor trafficking is routinely overlooked in U.S.-based anti-trafficking efforts (Littenberg & Baldwin, 2017). While most dialogue regarding human trafficking centers captivating stories of sexual degradation, across the United States and globally, human beings, largely immigrants from impoverished majority non-White countries, that contend with biased immigration policies, are forced to labor in diverse fields, including agriculture, factories, construction, and domestic work in exploitive conditions (Brennan, 2014).

In terms of labor trafficking, undocumented people of color are more vulnerable to traffickers and are more likely to face detection, detention, and deportation, which increases the risk for labor trafficking and exploitation without legal protection (Brennan, 2014). Forced labor of all types—including agricultural, domestic, and construction work—occurs in a national and global context in which a racial hierarchy leaves people of color, including migrants of color, at increased risk (Brennan, 2014; Bryant-Davis et al., 2009).

In the United States, among domestic sex trafficking victims, 40% were found to be Black and 24% were found to be Latinx, demonstrating a higher risk of sexual exploitation for people of color and particularly girls and women of color (Banks & Kyckelhahn, 2011). In South Dakota, while Native American people represent only 8% of the population, Native American women comprise 40% of trafficking victims (Ferguson, 2016). In Nebraska, based on several months of data collection from online advertisements for adult and youth in commercial sex, Black people only comprise 5% of the population yet represent 50% of the persons offered for or offering sexual acts; the researchers estimated that 15% of Black women in commercial sex in Nebraska are at high risk of exploitation in conditions that would qualify for human trafficking (Price & Clark, 2017) and in Cook County, Illinois, which is 41.6% White, 25.6% Latino, and 22.6% Black, 66% of sex trafficking victims between 2012 and 2016 were Black women (Cook County Sheriff's Office, 2017). The racial disparities in sex trafficking also emerge in data with child survivors of sex trafficking. In King County, Washington, 52% of all child sex trafficking victims are Black, and 84% of youth victims are female, though Black girls only constitute 1.1% of the general population (Richey, 2017). In Multnomah County, Oregon, 27% of child sex trafficking victims are Black, though Black people comprise less than 6% of the population and in Louisiana, 49% of child sex trafficking victims are Black girls, though Black girls comprise only 19% of Louisiana's youth population (Carey & Teplitsky, 2013; Louisiana Department of Children and Family Services, 2018). Simultaneously, an overwhelming majority of buyers of commercial sex are White men, approximately 80% (Demand Abolition, 2022; Martin et al., 2017; Richey, 2017). A 5-year systematic review of online arrest records indicated that men (75.4%) and Black people (71%) were most likely to be arrested in the United States for sex trafficking of minors; it should be noted that race was reported in only 51.6% of the records (Roe-Sepowitz, 2019). The U.S. Department of State (2021) also acknowledged that racial biases regarding who is seen as a trafficker and who is seen as a victim have left racially marginalized persons more likely to be targeted for arrest and racially marginalized victims criminalized and underserved. Trafficking strategies that emerged based on case reviews and interviews with victim service providers include utilizing boyfriend or lover scripts, ruses involving debt bondage, friendship or faux family scripts, threats of forced abortion or to take away children, and coerced co-offending (Reid, 2016).

Internationally, the sexualization, objectification, and dehumanization of people of color have also resulted in a sexual exploitation tourism industry in which primarily White Americans and Europeans travel to nations predominately consisting of people of color, such as Thailand, to purchase sex with people of color (Vejar & Quach, 2013). Additionally, colonialism and globalization have paved the way for exploitation of the labor of the global majority, who are people of color (Bryant-Davis et al., 2009). Government instability and lack of infrastructure for monitoring, safety, and justice also increase the risk for the exploitation (Jani, 2017). Globally, anti-Black racism translates to devaluating people of African descent in particular such that it is less expensive to purchase sex with an African person than a European person (Bryant-Davis et al., 2009). Fetishism and erotization of people of color, which manifest as stereotypes of people of color (including children of color) as being hypersexual, immoral, animalistic, and unrapable, also put a high demand on the global majority for both domestic servitude and commercial sexual exploitation (Alvarez & Alessi, 2012; Hua & Tjiu, 2019; Rajan & Bryant-Davis, 2021).

Racism and xenophobia shape the immigration laws in the United States and European countries, making it more difficult for people of the global majority to immigrate legally; therefore, desperate migrants become vulnerable to smugglers who are in fact human traffickers (Peña-Sullivan, 2020). In the context of a lack of legal migration options, traffickers promise safe passage and even use false promises of opportunities; they use deception, threats, and violence to control trafficking victims who lack documentation and, in some cases, lack English literacy, support networks, financial resources, and/or knowledge of applicable trafficking laws (Vejar & Quach, 2013). In exploring the experiences of undocumented Latinx communities, Peña-Sullivan (2020) named the realities of premigration trauma, acculturative stress, discrimination, as well as stigma due to the undocumented person's status within the United States, which cumulatively serve to heighten risk and vulnerability to exploitation and distress. Additionally, one in 10 Black people in the United States are immigrants, and Black immigrants are disproportionately subjected to immigration enforcement (Vera Institute of Justice, 2021). Nations that are predominately the global majority, people of color, have also faced increased tampering, governmental manipulation, and illegal arms trading from wealthy nations, which increases instability and thus impedes the ability of the nations to protect their citizens (Bryant-Davis et al., 2009).

The risk posed by racism, ethnic bias, and xenophobia is present not only in human trafficking that crosses borders but also in trafficking within the borders of developed nations (De la Cruz & Gomez, 2011). Domestically within the United States and Europe, persons who are from the global majority and yet live with the realities of marginalization are at the highest risk of human trafficking ranging from farm laborers to those engaging in commercial sex (Rajan & Bryant-Davis, 2021). In terms of domestic sex trafficking, Black girls face the highest risk in the United States (Bryant-Davis & Gobin, 2019). Racism resulting in barriers to educational and economic empowerment plays a role, and so does racism in the criminal justice system and media (Martin & Rud, 2007). Trafficking victims of the global majority, people of color, receive less media attention and face more blame and criminalization than White victims face (Rajan & Bryant-Davis, 2021). When people of color are attended to in the media reports of human trafficking, the terminology "modern day slavery" usually ignores the ongoing consequences of the enslavement of Black people, solely and falsely presents the West as liberators and abolitionist for the vulnerable, and promotes carceral solutions that creates additional barriers for persons of color (Beutin, 2018).

Social Class, Classism, and Caste Systems

Impoverished, exploited nations have more economically disenfranchised residents who live with limited vocational, educational, or economic opportunities. These people are more vulnerable to human traffickers (Bryant-Davis et al., 2009). The societal trauma of poverty, including lack of resources and discriminatory treatment toward those who lack resources, increases the risk of human trafficking. Being from an impoverished family and/or being from an impoverished nation increases one's risk for human trafficking in all its forms (Adejumo, 2008). Child trafficking for labor and sex is rooted in familial poverty, debt, lack of agency, and force by employers, recruiters, and property owners (Basu & Chau, 2007).

The risk factor of poverty and race for human trafficking, in both labor and sex, is pervasive across the globe, and these factors often are heightened by denial of laborers' right to organize (Bryant-Davis & Tummala-Narra, 2017; Littenberg & Baldwin, 2017). In Ethiopia, along with political instability and gender discrimination, poverty and economic problems are push factors, while the need or desire for cheap labor is a pull factor (Beck et al., 2017). Poverty is also a major factor affecting human trafficking on the Texas–Mexico border (Brooks, 2018). Rajan (2015), based on a qualitative study in India, found that the caste system and poverty greatly contributed to vulnerability to labor and sex trafficking. Dalla et al. (2020) found from their interviews that for certain castes in India, child sex trafficking is normative and expected, with girls being routinely selected by the family to carry the weight of the families' financial burdens until they age out and are no longer receiving paying consumers, and then a younger girl in the family is selected to take her place. In terms of labor trafficking, reproductive exploitation is another aspect of labor trafficking facing impoverished women including not only coerced surrogacy but also organ trafficking including trafficking of women to obtain human milk (Steele & Hernandez-Salazar, 2020).

Gender, Sexism, and Transphobia

Cultural norms of patriarchy and gender inequality are important factors in considering how assigning greater power, status, and access to men intersects with other systems of oppression to contribute to risk factors of human trafficking. The focus of trafficking research, social services and public awareness have highlighted the disproportionate effect of sex trafficking on women and girls (APA, 2014; Crawford, 2017) as primary victims of human trafficking. However, a lack of a gendered approach and an imbalance of research and public attention creates a false narrative of a stereotypical "perfect victim" that can only be a young woman and undermines the ability to correctly identify men and nonbinary individuals as trafficking victims with unique needs (Holger-Ambrose et al., 2013). These harmful implications of cis heteropatriarchy support discrimination against transgender, gender nonconforming, and intersex (TGNCI) individuals and promote a hypersexualized and hypermasculine culture that makes victimization of men and boys invisible, creating barriers for self and societal identification (Barron & Frost, 2018).

While societal normalization of violence against women, sexualization and objectification put women and girls at an increased risk for commercial sexual exploitation (Watts & Zimmerman, 2002), gender norms support demand for domestic servitude, and gender-based systemic oppression and discrimination supports marginalization and violence against TGNCI individuals (Williamson & Flood, 2021). These same power dynamics also minimize men and boys as victims of trafficking (Barron & Frost, 2018). According to the United Nations' General Embassy policy forum, Inter-Agency Coordination Group Against Trafficking in Persons (2017), male victims represent 82% of trafficking for organ removal, while a United Kingdom-based study identified boys and men as substantially more likely to have been trafficked for labor (Cockbain & Bowers, 2019). Historically, unequal access to care and legal rights, as well as structural economic barriers, have produced vulnerable conditions for non-dominant gender identifying individuals to receive adequate support (Grant et al., 2011) and make decisions regarding their own body (Rose & Hartmann, 2018). When considering vulnerabilities to human trafficking, it is necessary for psychologists to contextualize the role of systemic gender discrimination in risk disparities.

Trends of international trafficking demonstrate conditions of gender-based economic inequality that limit choices and opportunities for women, transgender and nonbinary individuals and produce increased risk for exploitation. In source countries, or economically developing nations where trafficking originates, women often work longer hours than men; globally, women work twice as much unpaid labor than men (World Bank, 2014). These economic vulnerabilities also support recruitment for trafficking. Women, and TGNCI individuals, are often coerced into human trafficking with deceptive employment offers to Western, or destination, countries with a strong demand for domestic labor. Meanwhile, literature has supported men as primary drivers in perpetuating demand for sex trafficking (Farley et al., 2017; Hunt, 2013).

Transphobia also plays a role in TGNCI individuals' experience of economic inequality based on gender. In a survey, transgender and gender nonconforming individuals reported discrimination due to rejected gender identity in seeking employment and job promotion (James et al., 2016). They were three times more likely to be unemployed and more than twice as likely to live in vulnerable conditions of poverty. Globally, transwomen in disparate cultural groups have also reported various forms of harassment and discrimination as well as limited opportunities in home countries where institutional structures and family norms explicitly and more strongly demonstrated favoritism toward boys (Malebranche et al., 2017). Intersecting cultural factors, such as abusive discrimination against TGNCI in their home countries, can also increase vulnerability to more extreme violence with fewer protections as a victim of trafficking. Normalized sexist and transphobic conditions create a lack of safe place and well-being for girls and TGNCI youth and promote internalization of their victimization and disposability of their bodies.

Sexuality, Heterosexism, and Homophobic Bias

Systems of homophobic bias and discrimination have created environmental conditions that negatively affect resources and support for nonheterosexual people, making these youth more vulnerable to exploitation. It is important that psychologists consider the impact of oppression in the trafficking vulnerability of those who identify as lesbian, gay, bisexual, transgender, queer or questioning, and other (LGBTQ+). While transgender experiences are generally discussed in the literature amongst lesbian, gay, and bisexual individuals, it is important to note that gender nuances specifically relevant to transgender and gender nonconforming populations are discussed in the previous section, while the remainder of this part will focus on the intersections of sexuality. Research continues to demonstrate that LGBTQ+ people are disproportionately represented among trafficked individuals in the United States (Choi, 2015; Martinez & Kelle, 2013; Twis & Preble, 2020). Sexuality has been used by traffickers and exploited by "johns" to take advantage of vulnerabilities resulting from systemic, relational, and individual risk factors. Particularly, socioecological factors related to systemic discrimination, homophobic bias, internalized oppression, and lack of safe community and expression not only function as explicit factors of risk and vulnerability for LGBTQ+ people, but they also contribute to the misidentification, neglect, and criminalization of LGBTQ+ trafficked youth (Martinez & Kelle, 2013). Until 1973, homosexuality was considered a mental health disorder (Kirby, 2003) and was stigmatized within psychology training and literature by cis hetero-sexual psychological professionals. To date, some states and nations still crim-inalize homosexuality and same-sex sexual behaviors. These societal norms have negatively influenced systemic discrimination and government sanc-tioned harassment that contribute to experiences of harm and violence for LGBTQ+ youth and create barriers for them to disclose experiences of sexual and other forms of abuse and exploitation (Martinez & Kelle, 2013; Peters et al., 2017). Examples of discrimination continue to be present in today's institutions.

LGBTQ+ individuals face significant challenges in obtaining safe health-, education-, and justice-related services due to discrimination (Durso & Gates, 2012); these organizational structures that should be supportive end up con-tributing to their victimization through system-level marginalization (Martinez & Kelle, 2013). For example, inadequate medical training and preparation for meeting the unique needs of this population result in unmet medical (e.g., Mahdi et al., 2014) and psychological (e.g., Rutherford et al., 2012) needs for LGBTQ+ individuals. In addition, homophobic bias against LGBTQ+ people from those in authority can express prejudices that threaten their safety. For instance, LGBTQ+ communities have reported a history of police harassment, verbal abuse, profiling, entrapment, neglect, and physical assault (Dank et al., 2015; Rutherford et al., 2012). Given this reality of targeted harm, LGBTQ+ youth who are trafficked are unlikely to view law enforcement as a viable source of aid.

Homophobic bias can also influence spiritual health systems and encour-age familial maltreatment that threatens the safety of LGBTQ+ youth. Xian and colleagues (2017) discussed how homophobic interpretations of reli-gious principles may result in *spiritual wounding,* which is developed from noncontextual religious doctrinal interpretation that harms individuals through internalizing a spiritual condemnation or injuring their spiritual core by defy-ing the entire religion. The impact on self-worth through the experiences of rejection and abandonment can increase vulnerability to exploitation, as indi-viduals seek acceptance and belonging outside of the familial and religious homes (Xian et al., 2017), leaving them at higher risk for being trafficked (Baker, 2018).

While some self-identified LGBTQ+ youth become unhoused due to dis-criminatory factors (Hogan & Roe-Sepowitz, 2020; Morton et al., 2017) or experiences of abuse by a household member (Xian et al., 2017), others have been shown to leave their home due to being trafficked by a family member (Covenant House, 2013; Romero et al., 2020). Traffickers often take advantage of initial vulnerability of homelessness by recruiting youth who independently sell sex for housing, resources, and basic needs (Williamson & Flood, 2021; Xian et al., 2017). While trading sex for survival is commonly discussed in the literature (Dank et al., 2015), abolitionist psychologists must apply a critical lens in understanding how the term *survival sex* can contribute negative implications for sex trafficked LGBTQ+ youth in coordinated services (e.g., misidentification among service providers, health professionals, and law enforcement). For example, it is important to understand a distinction between empowerment in the language that survivors may use to describe their experiences, while also recognizing the financial and systemic barriers to accessing safe resources. Abolitionist psychologists must be careful not to assume false agency of victimized youth, given their use of language, and contextualize behaviors in limited choices and circumstances (Xian et al., 2017). In addition, traffickers exploit sexual orientation status to reinforce oppression, prejudice, and inequality (Countryman-Roswurm, 2015) and use these vulnerabilities as methods of coercion. This is exemplified in circumstances where traffickers loiter outside of shelters, inform youth that shelters are full, and offer a place to stay, exploiting the unhoused status of youth (Covenant House, 2013). Traffickers have also been noted to manipulate vulnerabilities to make fraudulent promises to introduce LGBTQ+ youth to accepting communities and a sense of belonging (Hogan & Roe-Sepowitz, 2020).

RECOMMENDATIONS FOR ABOLITIONIST PSYCHOLOGISTS

A review of the literature from the framework of liberation psychology leads to several recommendations for abolitionist psychologists. Table 2.1 provides concrete strategies for applying psychological science to the liberation of those most vulnerable to labor and sex trafficking. As researchers, advocates, practitioners, educators, and consultants, psychologists can play an important role in eradicating human trafficking by attending to the systems in which trafficking occurs.

CONCLUSION

Given that dimensions of difference and dominance intersect with each other to produce vulnerable populations, an intersectional justice approach is needed to address, prevent, and abolish systems of oppression that support human trafficking. A liberation psychology framework is needed for abolitionist

TABLE 2.1. Recommendations for Abolitionist Psychologists

Themes	Practice	Research	Policy/Advocacy	Consultation
Attend to and engage context (sociopolitical and socioeconomic)	Practice liberation psychology: problematize oppression; attend to dehumanization rooted in human trafficking and oppression; denaturalization, as the opposite action to normalization; consciousness-raising and deconstructing dominant messages in lived experiences; deideologizing through examining and reconstructing cultural norms of harm	Engage with emancipatory approaches to research as a transformative change agent (e.g., participatory action research, community-based participatory research)	Address economic inequities and discrimination in organizational practices, service provision, dissemination of resources, and policy	Practice denaturalization and question the normalization of discrimination and oppression in organizational policies and practices
Reflexivity of psychologist	Address internal biases through mental health providers' reflexivity (self-awareness) as an ethical responsibility in alignment with APA recommended guidelines for multicultural practice	Examine self-as-researcher and address internal biases	Challenge normative education and training in human trafficking policy to expose intersectional sources of domination	Address inequity, bias, and power dynamics in non-profit, governmental, public, private, and other institutional settings in hiring, advancement, retention, workload, and sense of safety and belonging for people of color
Center survivors' experiences (not only experiences of trafficking, but also experiences of oppression)	Include historical and contemporary societal trauma of oppression in assessment questions, case conceptualization, and treatment planning	Prioritize community engagement and shared knowledge between researchers and survivor's lived experiences	Develop and evaluate alternatives to criminal justice system's role in prevention of entry and rehabilitation	Center survivor voices and lived experiences in training, implementation and dissemination in public and private sectors

(continues)

TABLE 2.1. Recommendations for Abolitionist Psychologists (Continued)

Themes	Practice	Research	Policy/Advocacy	Consultation
Adopt liberation psychology principles	Support clients to resist systems of oppression, while practicing antioppression as practitioners	Identify dimensions of systemic marginalization and challenge power dynamics in the research process	Cross-collaborate with survivor leaders and survivor mentors to deconstruct and repair institutional systems that impact vulnerability to human trafficking	Incorporate a critical liberatory perspective to trauma-informed approaches in organizational change that address root causes of unequal and unsafe conditions for vulnerable populations
Adopt holistic collaborative framework	Encourage a holistic understanding of one's embodied experience and internalizations of oppression	Prioritize program evaluation research in collaboration with survivor leaders	Mobilize conscientization, or critical consciousness	Target power dynamics in environments rather than emphasizing individual and survivor behaviors
Remain open to innovation of systems and application of indigenous psychological approaches	Incorporate cultural somatic, body-based, trauma sensitive somatic interventions, and empowerment tools that foster reclaiming survivor agency, protecting and honoring human rights, and uprooting oppressive beliefs regarding the marginalized body as a site for exploitation and violence	Reorient existing research agendas that fail to center voices of those most impacted by violence and exploitation	Increase education and training on the impact of poverty and other systems of oppression in human trafficking policy	Incorporate survivor voices and experiences to inform new ideas, technologies, and approaches that advance the empowerment of at-risk individuals within various systems and institutions

Adopt intersectional, social justice framework	Address barriers to economic and educational resources	Incorporate intersectional frameworks to comprehend and address the lives of persons who are multiply marginalized (e.g., address binaries)	Engage in interdisciplinary practices in writing, advocating for, and monitoring policy and multisector teams and interventions to attend to psychological factors and socioeconomic factors	Advocate for adoption of antiracist and antioppressive policies across public and private settings including psychological departments, counseling centers, research labs, and governmental agencies
Honor multiple ways of knowing (e.g., Indigenous ways of knowing and knowledge based on lived experience of survivors)	Integrate and/or collaborate with practitioners who utilize Indigenous pathways of healing	Utilize qualitative methodologies to amplify voices of marginalized persons, apply critical understanding of political and social oppression, and inform the collective work of macrosystem change	Support peer-to peer survivor-facilitated support groups or mentorship relationships	Incorporate multiple ways of knowing, understanding, and being in antitrafficking program development, training, implementation, and dissemination
Actively participate in and encourage resistance/advocacy skills and awareness raising/consciousness raising of larger community	Promote resistance strategies instead of solely coping strategies to assist development of strategies to address, confront, and dismantle systems of oppression within individual and institutions	Disseminate findings beyond persons who access academic publications to non-academics with the aim of informing policy and raising the consciousness of community members	Build and maintain cross-collaborative relationships within advocacy and community-based agencies serving victims and/or promoting antiviolence and trafficking to support community outreach	Support consultees in capacity building for community engagement and accountability

psychologists to productively shift practice, research, advocate, and organize initiatives for human trafficking by understanding the interaction of systems of domination based on race, class, gender, and sexual orientation. These primary domains of identity also overlap with ethnicity and immigration status, as well as mental and physical disability and religion, that can be further explored in other systems of domination through an intersectional liberation-oriented lens. Principles of liberation psychology used to address root causes of human trafficking must include (a) problematizing oppression, (b) deconstructing and dismantling dominant social messages, (c) subverting cultural norms of dehumanization, (d) interrupting internalizations of targeted discrimination, and (e) raising consciousness to address inequity in systems that are meant to support the safety and wellness of individuals intersecting societal margins (Comas-Díaz & Torres-Rivera, 2020; Tate et al., 2013).

We need to examine historical and contemporary conditioning resulting in beliefs that bodies of those most marginalized are disposable, correspondingly leading to increased vulnerability to violence and exploitation. Abolitionist psychologists are called to disrupt norms of dominance, center historically marginalized voices, and collaborate with those with lived experience of human trafficking. Psychologists who fail to incorporate a critically informed lens of risk factors and related recommendations for addressing the intersections of oppression and human trafficking miss an opportunity to engage productive and sustainable efforts across multilevel systems.

REFERENCES

Adejumo, G. (2008). Psychosocial predictors of involvement of women as victims of trafficking in persons in South West Nigeria. *Gender & Behaviour, 6*(1), 1480–1493. https://doi.org/10.4314/gab.v6i1.23370

Alvarez, M. B., & Alessi, E. J. (2012). Human trafficking is more than sex trafficking and prostitution: Implications for social work. *Affilia: Journal of Women & Social Work, 27*(2), 142–152. https://doi.org/10.1177/0886109912443

American Psychological Association. (2014). *Report of the Task Force on Trafficking of Women and Girls*. https://www.apa.org/pi/women/programs/trafficking

American Psychological Association. (2017). *Multicultural guidelines: An ecological approach to context, identity, and intersectionality*. http://www.apa.org/about/policy/multicultural-guidelines.pdf

Baker, C. N. (2018). *Fighting the US youth sex trade: Gender, race, and politics*. Cambridge University Press. https://doi.org/10.1017/9781108225045

Banks, D., & Kyckelhahn, D. (2011, April). *Characteristics of suspected human trafficking incidents, 2008–2010*. Bureau of Justice Statistics. https://bjs.ojp.gov/content/pub/pdf/cshti0810.pdf

Barratt, B. B. (2011). Ignacio Martín Baró's "Writings for a liberation psychology." *Psychoanalytic Psychotherapy in South Africa, 19*(2), 121–134.

Barron, I. M., & Frost, C. (2018). Men, boys, and LGBTQ: Invisible victims of human trafficking. In L. Walker, G. Gaviria, & K. Gopal (Eds.), *Handbook of sex trafficking* (pp. 73–84). Springer. https://doi.org/10.1007/978-3-319-73621-1_8

Basu, A. K., & Chau, N. H. (2007). An exploration of the worst forms of child labor: Is redemption a viable option? In K. A. Appiah & M. Bunzl (Eds.), *Buying freedom: The ethics and economics of slave redemption* (pp. 37–76). Princeton University Press. https://doi.org/10.1515/9780691186405-005

Beck, D. C., Choi, K. R., Munro-Kramer, M. L., & Lori, J. R. (2017). Human trafficking in Ethiopia: A scoping review to identify gaps in service delivery, research, and policy. *Trauma, Violence & Abuse, 18*(5), 532–543. https://doi.org/10.1177/1524838016641670

Beutin, L. P. (2018). *Trafficking in anti-Blackness: The political stakes of "modern day slavery" discourse in global campaigns to end human trafficking* [Doctoral dissertation, University of Pennsylvania]. Scholarly Commons. https://repository.upenn.edu/edissertations/2922/

Bloom, S. (2018). The sanctuary model and sex trafficking: Creating moral systems to counteract exploitation and dehumanization. In A. J. Nichols, T. Edmond, & E. C. Heil (Eds.), *Social work practice with survivors of sex trafficking and commercial sexual exploitation* (pp. 242–273). Columbia University Press. https://doi.org/10.7312/nich18092-013

Brennan, D. (2014). *Life interrupted: Trafficking into forced labor in the United States.* Duke University Press.

Brooks, S. H. (2018). *Convergence of modern-day slavery with poverty, drugs, and conflict in vulnerable populations: Training rural public health workers to promote human trafficking awareness* [Doctoral dissertation, Columbia University]. Academic Commons. https://academiccommons.columbia.edu/doi/10.7916/D8W6837K

Bryant-Davis, T., & Gobin, R. L. (2019). Still we rise: Psychotherapy for African American girls and women exiting sex trafficking. *Women & Therapy, 42*(3–4), 385–405. https://doi.org/10.1080/02703149.2019.1622902

Bryant-Davis, T., Tillman, S., Marks, A., & Smith, K. (2009). Millennium abolitionists: Addressing the sexual trafficking of African women. *Beliefs and Values, 1*(1), 69–78. https://doi.org/10.1891/1942-0617.1.1.69

Bryant-Davis, T., & Tummala-Narra, P. (2017). Cultural oppression and human trafficking: Exploring the role of racism and ethnic bias. *Women & Therapy, 40*(1–2), 152–169. https://doi.org/10.1080/02703149.2016.1210964

Burton, M., & Guzzo, R. (2020). Liberation psychology: Origins and development. In L. Comas-Díaz & E. Torres Rivera (Eds.), *Liberation psychology: Theory, method, practice, and social justice* (pp. 17–40). American Psychological Association. https://doi.org/10.1037/0000198-002

Carey, C., & Teplitsky, L. (2013). *Memo regarding the commercial sexual exploitation of children (CSEC) in the Portland metro area.* U.S. Department of Justice. https://www.justice.gov/sites/default/files/usao-or/legacy/2013/10/29/the_csec_report.pdf

Cho, S., Crenshaw, K. W., & McCall, L. (2013). Toward a field of intersectionality studies: Theory, applications, and praxis. *Signs, 38*(4), 785–810. https://doi.org/10.1086/669608

Choi, K. R. (2015). Risk factors for domestic minor sex trafficking in the United States: A literature review. *Journal of Forensic Nursing, 11*(2), 66–76. https://doi.org/10.1097/JFN.0000000000000072

Chong, N. G. (2014). Human trafficking and sex industry: Does ethnicity and race matter? *Journal of Intercultural Studies, 35*(2), 196–213. https://doi.org/10.1080/07256868.2014.885413

Clay-Warner, J., Edgemon, T. G., Okech, D., & Anarfi, J. K. (2021). Violence predicts physical health consequences of human trafficking: Findings from a longitudinal study of labor trafficking in Ghana. *Social Science & Medicine, 279*, 113970. https://doi.org/10.1016/j.socscimed.2021.113970

Cockbain, E., & Bowers, K. (2019). Human trafficking for sex, labour and domestic servitude: How do key trafficking types compare and what are their predictors? *Crime, Law, and Social Change, 72*(1), 9–34. https://doi.org/10.1007/s10611-019-09836-7

Comas-Díaz, L., & Torres-Rivera, E. (Eds.). (2020). *Liberation psychology: Theory, method, practice, and social justice.* American Psychological Association. https://doi.org/10.1037/0000198-000

Cook County Sheriff's Office. (2017). *Buyers and sellers: A window into sex trafficking.*

Countryman-Roswurm, K. (2015). Rise, unite, support: Doing "no harm" in the anti-trafficking movement. *Slavery Today, 2*(1), 1–22. https://slavefreetoday.org/journal_of_modern_slavery/v2i1a2_Rise_Unite_Support_Doing_No_Harm_in_the_AntiTrafficking_Movement_countryman_roswurm.pdf

Covenant House. (2013). *Homelessness, survival sex and human trafficking: As experienced by the youth of Covenant House New York.* https://humantraffickinghotline.org/en/resources/homelessness-survival-sex-and-human-trafficking-experienced-youth-covenant-house-new-york

Crawford, M. (2017). International sex trafficking. *Women & Therapy, 40*(1–2), 101–122. https://doi.org/10.1080/02703149.2016.1206784

Crenshaw, K. (2005). Mapping the margins: Intersectionality, identity politics, and violence against women of color (1994). In R. K. Bergen, J. L. Edleson, & C. M. Renzetti (Eds.), *Violence against women: Classic papers* (pp. 282–313). Pearson Education New Zealand.

Dalla, R. L., Panchal, T. J., Erwin, S., Peter, J., Roselius, K., Ranjan, R., Mischra, M., & Sahu, S. (2020). Structural vulnerabilities, personal agency, and caste: An exploration of child sex trafficking in rural India. *Violence and Victims, 35*(3), 307–330. https://doi.org/10.1891/VV-D-19-00048

Dank, M., Yahner, J., Madden, K., Bañuelos, I., Yu, L., Ritchie, A., Mora, M., & Conner, B. M. (2015). *Surviving the streets of New York: Experiences of LGBTQ youth, YMSM, and YWSW engaged in survival sex.* https://www.urban.org/research/publication/surviving-streets-new-york-experiences-lgbtq-youth-ymsm-and-ywsw-engaged-survival-sex

De la Cruz, M., & Gomez, C. (2011). Ending oppression. Building solidarity. Creating community solutions. In C.-I. Chen, J. Dulani, & L. L. Piepzna-Samarasinha (Eds.), *The revolution starts at home: Confronting intimate violence within activist communities* (pp. 25–56). South End Press.

Deer, S. (2010). Relocation revisited: Sex trafficking of Native women in the United States. *William Mitchell Law Review, 36*(2), 621–683.

Demand Abolition. (2022). *Facts about men who buy sex.* https://www.demandabolition.org/research/facts-men-buy-sex/

Dovidio, J. F., & Gaertner, S. L. (2004). Aversive racism. In M. P. Zanna (Ed.), *Advances in experimental social psychology* (Vol. 36, pp. 1–52). Elsevier Academic Press.

Durso, L. E., & Gates, G. J. (2012). *Serving our youth: Findings from a national survey of services providers working with lesbian, gay, bisexual and transgender youth who are homeless or at risk of becoming homeless.* UCLA Williams Institute. https://escholarship.org/uc/item/80x75033

Farley, M., Schuckman, E., Golding, J. M., Houser, K., Jarrett, L., Qualliotine, P., & Decker, M. (2017). Comparing sex buyers with men who don't buy sex: New data on prostitution and trafficking. *Journal of Interpersonal Violence, 32*(23), 3601–3625.

Ferguson, D. (2016). Law enforcement, Native communities focus on sex trafficking prevention training. *Argus Leader.* https://www.argusleader.com/story/news/crime/2016/08/27/law-enforcement-native-communities-focus-sex-trafficking-prevention-training/89273822/

Grant, J. M., Mottet, L. A., Tanis, J., Harrison, J., Herman, J. L., & Keisling, M. (2011). *Injustice at every turn: A report of the National Transgender Discrimination Survey.* National Center for Transgender Equality and National Gay and Lesbian Task Force.

Hardesty, M., & Gunn, A. J. (2019). Survival sex and trafficked women: The politics of re-presenting and speaking about others in anti-oppressive qualitative research. *Qualitative Social Work: Research and Practice, 18*(3), 493–513. https://doi.org/10.1177/1473325017746481

Hogan, K. A., & Roe-Sepowitz, D. (2020). LGBTQ+ homeless young adults and sex trafficking vulnerability. *Journal of Human Trafficking, 9*(1), 63–78.

Holger-Ambrose, B., Langmade, C., Edinburgh, L. D., & Saewyc, E. (2013). The illusions and juxtapositions of commercial sexual exploitation among youth: Identifying effective street-outreach strategies. *Journal of Child Sexual Abuse, 22*(3), 326–340. https://doi.org/10.1080/10538712.2013.737443

Hua, J., & Tjiu, J. (2019). Transnational feminist perspectives on human trafficking: Centering structures, institutions, and subjects. In L. H. Collins, S. Machizawa, & J. K. Rice (Eds.), *Transnational psychology of women: Expanding international and intersectional approaches* (pp. 211–228). American Psychological Association. https://doi.org/10.1037/0000148-010

Hunt, S. (2013). Deconstructing demand: The driving force of sex trafficking. *The Brown Journal of World Affairs, 19*(2), 225–241.

James, S. E., Herman, J. L., Rankin, S., Keisling, M., Mottet, L., & Anafi, M. (2016). *The report of the 2015 U.S. transgender survey.* National Center for Transgender Equality. https://transequality.org/sites/default/files/docs/usts/USTS-Full-Report-Dec17.pdf

Jani, J. S. (2017). Reunification is not enough: Assessing the needs of unaccompanied migrant youth. *Families in Society, 98*(2), 127–136. https://doi.org/10.1606/1044-3894.2017.98.18

Kirby, M. (2003). The 1973 deletion of homosexuality as a psychiatric disorder: 30 years on. *Australian & New Zealand Journal of Psychiatry, 37*(6), 674–677.

Littenberg, N., & Baldwin, S. (2017). The ignored exploitation: Labor trafficking in the United States. In M. Chisolm-Straker & H. Stoklosa (Eds.), *Human trafficking is a public health issue.* Springer. https://doi.org/10.1007/978-3-319-47824-1_5

Louisiana Department of Children and Family Services. (2018). *Human trafficking, trafficking of children for sexual purposes and commercial sexual exploitation: Annual report.* https://www.dcfs.louisiana.gov/page/508

Mahdi, I., Jevertson, J., Schrader, R., Nelson, A., & Ramos, M. M. (2014). Survey of new Mexico school health professionals regarding preparedness to support sexual minority students. *The Journal of School Health, 84*(1), 18–24. https://doi.org/10.1111/josh.12116

Malebranche, D. A., Hopper, E. K., & Corey, E. (2020). Sex and labor trafficking: Trauma-informed themes toward a social justice approach. In R. Geffner, V. Vieth, V. Faughan-Eden, A. Rosenbaum, L. K. Hamberger, & J. White (Eds.), *Handbook for interpersonal violence across the lifespan* (pp. 1–28). Springer Science. https://doi.org/10.1007/978-3-319-62122-7_43-1

Malebranche, D. A., Rajan, I., & Sidun, N. (2017, November). *Cultural considerations in work with survivors of human trafficking: Lessons from four disparate groups* [Panel presentation]. International Society for Traumatic Stress Studies 33rd Annual Meeting, Chicago, IL, United States.

Martin, L., Melander, C., Karnik, H., & Nakamura, C. (2017). *Mapping demand: Sex buyers in the state of Minnesota.* University of Minnesota. https://conservancy.umn.edu/bitstream/handle/11299/226520/MappingtheDemand-ExecutiveSummary%20FINAL%20July%2028%202017.pdf?sequence=1&isAllowed=y

Martin, L., & Rud, J. (2007). *Prostitution research report: Data sharing to establish best practices for women in prostitution.* Prostitution Project, Hennepin County [Minnesota] Corrections and the Folwell Center.

Martín-Baró, I. (1994). *Writings for a liberation psychology* (A. Aron & S. Corne, Trans. & Eds.). Harvard University Press.

Martinez, O., & Kelle, G. (2013). Sex trafficking of LGBT individuals: A call for service provision, research, and action. *The International Law News, 42*(4), 21–24.

Morton, M. H., Dworsky, A., & Samuels, G. M. (2017). *Missed opportunities: Youth homelessness in America: National estimates.* Voices of Youth Count. https://voicesofyouthcount.org/wp-content/uploads/2017/11/VoYC-National-Estimates-Brief-Chapin-Hall-2017.pdf

Peña-Sullivan, L. (2020). The "wrong kind" of immigrants: Pre-migration trauma and acculturative stress among the undocumented Latinx community. *Clinical Social Work Journal, 48*(4), 351–359. https://doi.org/10.1007/s10615-019-00741-z

Peters, J. W., Becher, J., & Hirschfeld, D. J. (2017, February 22). Trump rescinds rules on bathrooms for transgender students. *The New York Times.* https://www.nytimes.com/2017/02/22/us/politics/devos-sessions-transgender-students-rights.html

Price, C. N., & Clark, T. D. (2017). *Nebraska's commercial sex market.* Omaha Women's Fund. https://ordnebraska.com/wp-content/uploads/2017/04/Nebraskas-Commercial-Sex-Market-Report-FINAL.pdf

Rajan, I. (2015). *Speaking self out of darkness: The lived experience of sex trafficking survivors in Kolkata, India* (Order no. 3619411) [Doctoral dissertation, Pacifica Graduate Institute]. ProQuest Dissertations & Theses Global.

Rajan, I., & Bryant-Davis, T. (2021). An examination of racial minority immigrants and the trauma of human trafficking. In P. Tummala-Narra (Ed.), *Trauma and racial minority immigrants: Turmoil, uncertainty, and resistance* (pp. 165–183). American Psychological Association. https://doi.org/10.1037/0000214-010

Reid, J. A. (2016). Entrapment and enmeshment schemes used by sex traffickers. *Sexual Abuse: Journal of Research and Treatment, 28*(6), 491–511. https://doi.org/10.1177/1079063214544334

Richey, V. (2017, May 30). *Reducing demand for the commercial sexual exploitation of minors in your community* [Webinar]. Office of Juvenile Justice and Delinquency Prevention. https://ojjdp.ojp.gov/media/video/25801

Roe-Sepowitz, D. (2019). A six-year analysis of sex traffickers of minors: Exploring characteristics and sex trafficking patterns. *Journal of Human Behavior in the Social Environment, 29*(5), 608–629.

Romero, A. P., Goldberg, S. K., & Vasquez, L. A. (2020). *LGBT people and housing affordability, discrimination, and homelessness.* UCLA School of Law, Williams Institute. https://williamsinstitute.law.ucla.edu/publications/lgbt-housing-instability/

Rose, S. J., & Hartmann, H. (2018). *Still a man's labor market: The slowly narrowing gender wage gap.* Institute for Women's Policy Research. https://iwpr.org/wp-content/uploads/2020/08/C474_IWPR-Still-a-Mans-Labor-Market-update-2018-2.pdf

Rutherford, K., McIntyre, J., Daley, A., & Ross, L. E. (2012). Development of expertise in mental health service provision for lesbian, gay, bisexual and transgender communities. *Medical Education, 46*(9), 903–913. https://doi.org/10.1111/j.1365-2923.2012.04272.x

Steele, S. L., & Hernandez-Salazar, E. E. (2020). A very lucrative liquid: The emerging trade in human milk as a form of reproductive exploitation and violence against women. *International Journal of Human Rights in Healthcare, 13*(2), 171–183. https://doi.org/10.1108/IJHRH-07-2019-0058

Tate, K. A., Rivera, E. T., Brown, E., & Skaistis, L. (2013). Foundations for liberation: Social justice, liberation psychology, and counseling. *Revista Interamericana de Psicología/Interamerican Journal of Psychology, 47*(3), 373–382.

Thompson, C. E. F. (2019). *A psychology of liberation and peace: For the greater good.* Palgrave Macmillan. https://doi.org/10.1007/978-3-030-13597-3

Torres Rivera, E. (2020). Concepts of liberation psychology. In L. Comas-Díaz & E. Torres Rivera (Eds.), *Liberation psychology: Theory, method, practice, and social justice* (pp. 41–51). American Psychological Association. https://doi.org/10.1037/0000198-003

Tummala-Narra, P., Saleem, R., Dale, S., Claudius, M., Gomez, C., & Narain, N. (2011). *Report on trafficking of women and girls.* American Psychological Association Division 35 Special Committee on Violence Against Women and Girls. http://www.apadivisions.org/division-35/news-events/trafficking-report.pdf

Twis, M. K., & Preble, K. (2020). Intersectional standpoint methodology: Toward theory-driven participatory research on human trafficking. *Violence and Victims, 35*(3), 418–439. https://doi.org/10.1891/VV-D-18-00208

United Nations. (2001, August 31–September 7). *The race dimensions of trafficking in persons—Especially women and children* [Press kit]. World Conference Against Racism, Racial Discrimination, Xenophobia and Related Intolerance, Durban, South Africa. https://www.un.org/WCAR/e-kit/issues.htm

United Nations General Assembly, Inter-Agency Coordination Group against Trafficking in Persons. (2017, September). *The gender dimensions of human trafficking* (Issue Brief No. 4). https://icat.un.org/sites/g/files/tmzbdl461/files/publications/icat-ib-04-v.1.pdf

United States Department of State. (2021). *Acknowledging historical and ongoing harm: The connections between systemic racism and human trafficking.* https://www.state.gov/acknowledging-historical-and-ongoing-harm-the-connections-between-systemic-racism-and-human-trafficking/

Vejar, C. M., & Quach, A. S. (2013). Sex slavery in Thailand. *Social Development Issues: Alternative Approaches to Global Human Needs, 35*(2), 105–123.

Vera Institute of Justice. (2021). *Detention of immigrants.* https://www.vera.org/ending-mass-incarceration/reducing-incarceration/detention-of-immigrants

Viloria, M. D. G. (1999). *From exclusion to compassion: An interdisciplinary study of sexual trafficking among Filipinas* (Order no. 9930054) [Doctoral dissertation, Fuller Theological Seminary]. ProQuest Dissertations & Theses Global.

Vollinger, L. (2021). Concretizing intersectional research methods: Incorporating social justice and action into United States sex trafficking research. *Journal of Human Behavior in the Social Environment, 31*(5), 599–625. https://doi.org/10.1080/10911359.2020.1799902

Watts, C., & Zimmerman, C. (2002). Violence against women: Global scope and magnitude. *The Lancet, 359*(9313), 1232–1237. https://doi.org/10.1016/S0140-6736(02)08221-1

Williamson, E., & Flood, A. (2021). Systemic and structural roots of child sex trafficking: The role of gender, race, and sexual orientation in disproportionate victimization. In M. Chisolm-Straker & K. Chon (Eds.), *The historical roots of human trafficking* (pp. 191–216). Springer. https://doi.org/10.1007/978-3-030-70675-3_11

World Bank. (2014). *Gender at work.* http://www.worldbank.org/content/dam/Worldbank/document/Gender/GenderAtWork_web.pdf

Xian, K., Chock, S., & Dwiggins, D. (2017). LGBTQ youth and vulnerability to sex trafficking. In M. Chisolm-Straker & H. Stoklosa (Eds.), *Human trafficking is a public health issue: A paradigm expansion in the United States* (pp. 141–152). Springer. https://doi.org/10.1007/978-3-319-47824-1_9

Yakushko, O. (2021). On the dangers of transnational influences of western psychology: Decolonizing international perspectives on women and therapy. *Women & Therapy, 44*(1–2), 193–211. https://doi.org/10.1080/02703149.2020.1776018

3

LABOR TRAFFICKING

A Mental Health Perspective

LUJAIN ALHAJJI, JONELL EFANTIS POTTER, AND
VANESSA PADILLA

CASE VIGNETTE

Marie, a 17-year-old Haitian girl, travels to the United States with her stepfather to work as a live-in housekeeper for a wealthy family.[1] Her stepfather
assures her mother back in Haiti that Marie will complete her schooling in the
United States and be well taken care of in her employer's large household.
Marie's passport is taken away upon arrival, and her cell phone is confiscated, in order to not "distract her from her work duties." She is forbidden to
contact her family members. The employer forces Marie to work from 7 a.m.
to 11 p.m. with no breaks. She now owes her employer $10,000 in recruit-
ment and employment fees. Marie is not paid for her work, and she relies on
her employer to supply her with food and personal hygiene products. Her
employer threatens her and her stepfather with deportation if she tries to
leave. Marie does not recognize that she is trafficked due to trafficker abuse,
manipulation, and poor understanding of labor laws and legal rights.

---

[1] All case study material in this chapter is fictional, uses composites, or has been
disguised by changing names and altering or removing identifying information to
preserve client confidentiality.

https://doi.org/10.1037/0000379-004

*Psychological Perspectives on Human Trafficking: Theory, Research, Prevention, and
Intervention*, L. Dryjanska, E. K. Hopper, and H. Stoklosa (Editors)

DEFINING LABOR TRAFFICKING

Labor trafficking is recruiting, harboring, transporting, providing, or obtaining a person for labor or services, through the use of force, fraud, or coercion for the purpose of subjection to involuntary servitude, peonage, debt bondage, or slavery. Labor trafficking is an underreported and overlooked global health issue. In 2021, the International Labour Organization (ILO) estimated that approximately 49.6 million people are trafficked worldwide, with 27.6 million trapped in forced labor and 22 million people forced into marriage (ILO et al., 2022). Of those persons, 17.3 million were trafficked in the private sector, 3.9 million in the government or state authorities sector and 6.3 million in forced sex industries. Women and girls comprised 6 million of those in forced labor, and children represented 3.3 million of those affected by forced labor. From 2007 to 2021, the U.S. National Human Trafficking Hotline received more than 5,000 reports about potential labor trafficking cases involving domestic servitude, agriculture, food and restaurant work, traveling sales crews, and health and beauty service industries (Polaris, 2021c). In June 2021, the U.S. Bureau of International Labor Affairs (2020) identified 156 goods from 77 countries made by forced and child labor. In 2014, the American Psychological Association Task Force on Trafficking of Women and Girls published a report to provide guidelines, awareness, research, and education on human trafficking. Psychologists have been called to join efforts to identify and eradicate human trafficking by recognizing signs, building trust with survivors, providing safety plans, and seeking educational training (American Psychological Association, 2014).

EFFECTS OF LABOR EXPLOITATION

Labor exploitation occurs when employers unfairly profit from their workers. The legal term *labor violations* occurs when an employer violates federal, state, or local laws, such as work conditions violations or improper wages payments. People experience labor law violations through labor exploitation, including wage theft, tip theft, debt bondage, extensive work hours, or unsafe work environments. Labor trafficking occurs when people are compelled to perform labor through the use of force, fraud, or coercion. Many trafficked workers live in their workplace or in degraded, unsuitable housing conditions with limited ability to leave the premises, no work contract, and little or no access to their earnings. If they receive a work contract, trafficked individuals often cannot negotiate its terms, change it, or read it (Zimmerman

& Kiss, 2017). Restriction of freedom, longer durations of trafficking, and detention in transit or destination countries may affect mental health and have independently predicted anxiety and depression in a sample of Ethiopian trafficking returnees (Gezie et al., 2018). Violence and coercion have been associated with increased anxiety, depression, and posttraumatic stress disorder (PTSD) in survivors of human trafficking (Iglesias-Rios et al., 2018).

LABOR TRAFFICKING: A CYCLE OF VULNERABILITY AND EXPLOITATION

Globalization, industrialization, economic pressures, low wages, war, conflict, and poor law enforcement have increased migration and forced labor (ILO et al., 2022; Rose et al., 2021). Multiple elements influence labor trafficking, including individual, community, institutional, national, global, socioeconomic, legal, political, and legislative. Some business models promote exploitative practices by relying on disposable labor, unmonitored supply chains, intermediaries with limited surveillance, and poor controls from government agencies. Weakening labor governance and protections may increase labor exploitation (Zimmerman & Kiss, 2017). Increased internal and cross-border migration may be impacted by climate change effects on labor practices and production, humanitarian crises (e.g., war, armed conflicts), environmental disasters (e.g., hurricanes, earthquakes), organized crime and gang violence, poor social support, and market-driven soil fatigue (Zimmerman et al., 2016). Labor inspections do not frequently occur within industries and are unlikely to assess for trafficked workers (Zimmerman & Kiss, 2017).

Vulnerability refers to the inherent, environmental, or contextual factors increasing the susceptibility of an individual to be trafficked (United Nations Office on Drugs and Crime, 2013). Labor traffickers profit from exploiting these vulnerabilities. They use physical, emotional, sexual, or financial abuse, such as debt bondage, restriction of movement, forced drug use, starvation, isolation, manipulation, threats, and degradation, to continue the cycle of exploitation (Coverdale et al., 2016). Traffickers may appeal to religious or cultural beliefs and relationship dynamics to coerce individuals into labor exploitation. Historical and ongoing oppression, generational trauma, racial, ethnic, and gender discrimination are elements that fuel community-wide susceptibility to human trafficking (U.S. Department of State, 2021).

Individual factors that may trap individuals in an exploitation cycle and increase the vulnerability to labor trafficking include migration, low socioeconomic backgrounds, economic deprivation, cognitive and mental health disabilities, substance use disorders, and lack of shelter (Dank et al., 2021). Language barriers, lack of legal status, disability, and illness can make people more vulnerable to coercion and control. Studies in the U.S. Midwest metropolitan areas have identified factors increasing the risk of human trafficking, such as the presence of high poverty, violence, widespread substance use, a weak education system, increased numbers of homeless and runaway children, and large immigrant populations (Koegler et al., 2019; Stickle, 2021).

TIED WORK VISAS AND LABOR EXPLOITATION

The U.S. H-2A visa guest worker program allows U.S. employers or agents who fulfill regulatory requirements to sponsor foreign nationals for temporary or seasonal agricultural jobs. With the expansion of the H-2A temporary visa program, its misuse and labor trafficking cases have grown (U.S. Department of State, 2021). Trafficked persons seldom exercise their legal entitlements or assert labor rights, especially when bound to employers through migration sponsorship programs and tied work visa programs.

Over 5 years, the National Human Trafficking Hotline identified more than 3,200 trafficked H-2A visa holders (Polaris, 2021b). The H-2A program structure can enable fraud and coercion by controlling legal visa status through the sponsoring employer. Employers in these low-wage industries will rely on the frequent flow of vulnerable workers without improving their wages or work conditions. Many H-2A visa workers come from Indigenous, impoverished, or low-literacy communities. Trafficked workers are frequently charged with unlawful large sums of recruitment fees and indebted to the labor contractor before even arriving in the United States. Despite holding valid work visas, trafficked workers are often threatened with deportation if they leave their jobs, sent to work in isolated and undisclosed locations, stripped of their passports, and forced to work beyond the validity of their visa permit. During the COVID-19 pandemic, approximately one third of H-2A visa holders have complained about being denied access to medical care (Polaris, 2021a). An effort toward potential solutions through H2-A visa program regulations has been much needed in order to protect vulnerable workers.

In January 2020, the U.S. Department of Labor announced new regulations prohibiting shifting employment costs and added the Joint Liability Standard, which makes joint employers equally responsible for complying with worker protection laws. Advocacy efforts have aimed to increase oversight and enforcement of labor workers' protections, restructure the H-2A program to allow guest workers to fairly seek other employment opportunities, expand the H-2A program to year-round work, and increase workers' access to health care services (Polaris, 2021b).

CHARACTERISTICS OF LABOR TRAFFICKING INDUSTRIES

Common industries involved in labor trafficking include agriculture and animal husbandry, domestic workers, hospitality, restaurants and food services, illicit massage businesses, health and beauty businesses, fisheries, construction, traveling selling crews, as well as bars, strip clubs, and cantinas. Traffickers can discreetly maneuver persons into these industries, while other workers and customers do not recognize the signs of labor trafficking.

Manipulative labor traffickers recruiting techniques include false promises of a better life, economic support via direct cash payments, and travel, career, or educational opportunities. They recruit through print media, online and social media advertisements, direct in-person hires, award schemes, competitions, and contests. Extensive psychological consequences, primarily mediated by chronic stress, may affect survivors of labor trafficking due to psychological tactics such as dehumanization, instilling false fears over worst-case scenarios, fostering distrust in others, controlling movement, and threatening victims (Baldwin et al., 2015).

Among trafficked farmworkers, psychological consequences may arise from isolation during seasonal, temporary work in remote rural areas, hindering access to any support system (Mora et al., 2016). They often suffer from depression, anxiety, and alcohol misuse due to overcrowding, harassment, poor housing, and working conditions (Lambar & Thomas, 2019). Isolation, immigration status, financial issues, absence of work contracts, and lack of legal protections also place domestic workers at risk of labor trafficking, stress, and psychological abuse (Polaris, 2019a). Women trafficked in illicit massage and beauty businesses face high levels of abuse that takes an emotional toll. Indicators of potential trafficking in illicit massage and beauty businesses include significantly low prices, workers appearing distressed if not given a tip, living on the business premises, hidden entryways, covered windows, and advertisements placed on pornographic websites (Polaris, 2018). Trafficked men and boys in the fisheries industry are vulnerable to abuse, violence, physical isolation, and harsh working environments (Mackay et al., 2020). A systematic review of trafficked seafarers and fishers from the Greater Mekong Subregion reported the following symptoms: anger, anxiety, suicidal thoughts, substance misuse, guilt, shame, and memory loss (Pocock et al., 2018). Predeparture mental health screening, reduced work hours, decreased offsite duty tours, and increased time off could positively impact workers' mental health in the fisheries industry (Pocock et al., 2018). Trafficked salespersons often face abuse and coercion and are left in unfamiliar and undisclosed locations, devoid of belongings and identification (Polaris, 2019b).

Numerous organizations (e.g., United Farm Workers) educate farmworkers on their legal rights and protections from labor exploitation and advocate for industries to take accountability for their practices. Supporting legislation for a domestic workers' bill of rights, enforcing labor violations, imposing mandatory education for employers, and promoting antitrafficking awareness campaigns may help lower the rates of labor trafficking. Psychologists can play a meaningful role in advocacy through raising awareness in the community, building knowledge about migration, and supporting bills restricting labor violations. They can educate industries on the trauma and psychological consequences of trafficking and offer direct clinical services to industry-specific trafficked persons.

INDICATORS OF LABOR TRAFFICKING

Identifying trafficked persons within a health care setting can be challenging (see Figure 3.1; Hemmings et al., 2016). Psychologists face many obstacles, including high work volume, time constraints, and misconceptions of human trafficking. Mental health providers seldom receive education on human trafficking. Provider-specific barriers to identifying trafficked persons include lack of education and awareness on human trafficking, absence of a human trafficking response protocol, dearth of private areas to conduct assessments safely, and limited training or expertise in trauma-informed care (Coverdale et al., 2016). Barriers in the mental health care system may include discomfort or cultural stigma against mental health care, unavailability of trauma-informed care providers, limited affordable mental health care options, and logistical difficulties (Hopper & Gonzalez, 2018). Patient-specific barriers include experiencing distrust, shame, guilt, fear of criminalization or deportation, trauma bonding, financial constraints, and lack of awareness that their situation violates human rights (Coverdale et al., 2020).

While looking for potential general indicators of labor trafficking (i.e., red flags) can help identify labor trafficking, approaching the patient in a trauma-informed manner, and listening to their story, provides a better understanding of their trafficking history. Nevertheless, it can be helpful

FIGURE 3.1. Barriers to Identifying Trafficked Persons by Health Care Systems, Providers, and Trafficked Persons

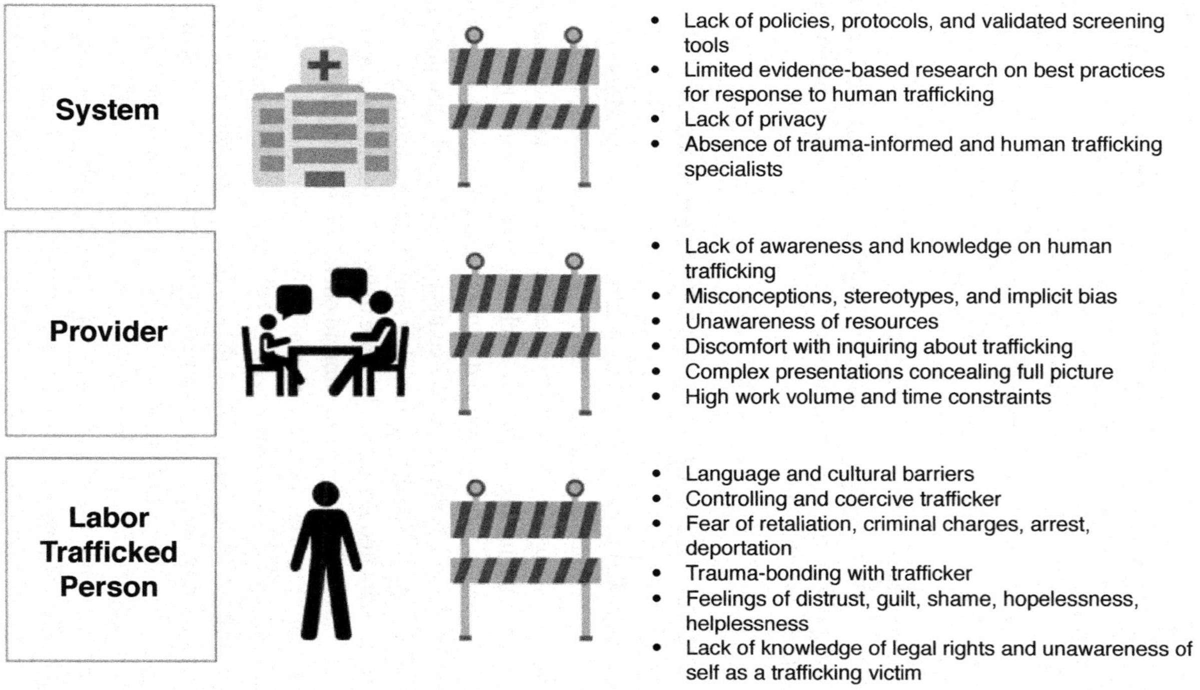

System

- Lack of policies, protocols, and validated screening tools
- Limited evidence-based research on best practices for response to human trafficking
- Lack of privacy
- Absence of trauma-informed and human trafficking specialists

Provider

- Lack of awareness and knowledge on human trafficking
- Misconceptions, stereotypes, and implicit bias
- Unawareness of resources
- Discomfort with inquiring about trafficking
- Complex presentations concealing full picture
- High work volume and time constraints

Labor Trafficked Person

- Language and cultural barriers
- Controlling and coercive trafficker
- Fear of retaliation, criminal charges, arrest, deportation
- Trauma-bonding with trafficker
- Feelings of distrust, guilt, shame, hopelessness, helplessness
- Lack of knowledge of legal rights and unawareness of self as a trafficking victim

EXHIBIT 3.1. Potential Indicators of Labor Trafficking in a Health Care Setting

Has been abused at work or threatened with harm by an employer or supervisor.
Is not allowed to take adequate breaks, food, or water while at work.
Is not provided with adequate personal protective equipment for hazardous work.
Was recruited for different work than they are currently doing.
Is required to live in housing provided by an employer or at their place of work.
Has a debt to the employer or recruiter that they cannot pay off.
Is isolated from family, and fears harm to family if they quit.
Has been hired for a different job based on false promises.

Note. Data from National Human Trafficking Resource Center (2018).

for psychologists to recognize that the presence of several indicators should prompt a comprehensive evaluation of labor trafficking (see Exhibit 3.1). The ILO (2012) provides an opportunity to further explore potential indicators of labor trafficking.

PHYSICAL SEQUELAE OF LABOR TRAFFICKING

Labor-trafficked persons face many health risks (Turner-Moss et al., 2014). Trafficking victims rarely receive health care, social services, legal services, or financial compensation for work-related injuries, especially disability-related lost future earning after exiting trafficking (Zimmerman & Kiss, 2017). One U.S. retrospective study estimated that approximately 68% of patients who were victimized by trafficking had contact with a health care provider while actively being trafficked, while another similar American study among female survivors estimated the rate to be close to 88% (Chisolm-Straker et al., 2016; Lederer & Wetzel, 2014). In an effort to effectively quantify data and estimate health care services rendered to trafficked persons, unique *International Classification of Diseases* (11th ed., 2018), Clinical Modification codes are available for data collection on adult or child forced labor or sexual exploitation, either confirmed or suspected. These billing codes may be used in addition to other existing codes for abuse, neglect, and other maltreatment (Kerr & Bryant, 2022; World Health Organization, 2018, 2023).

Unfortunately, seeking medical care is often delayed or not sought for labor-trafficked persons unless it hinders their ability to work (Ronda-Pérez & Moen, 2017). Most research studies focus on the immediate acute health consequences after exiting trafficking, leaving long-term health issues difficult to define (Zimmerman & Kiss, 2017). Persons forced to work in physical labor may experience overuse injuries, such as tendonitis, muscle strains, and sprains (Ronda-Pérez & Moen, 2017). Those forced to work outdoors or in enclosed work areas may present with hyper- or hypothermia. Industries requiring the use of chemicals may expose trafficked persons to chemical inhalation or intoxication. The use of heavy machinery and lack of protective equipment may lead to acute traumatic injuries, including amputations, falls, traumatic brain injuries, hearing loss, burns, cuts, and fractures. The harmful health risks as a result of child labor include malnourishment, stunted growth, blunt trauma, fractures, lack of immunizations, and reproductive and dental problems (Greenbaum, 2021). Lack of nutritious meals may lead to chronic malnutrition and nutritional deficiencies. Living in overcrowded and unsanitary places increases the risk for infectious diseases (Coverdale et al., 2020) among migrant workers and labor-trafficked persons engaging in survival sex (Langmagne et al., 2021).

MENTAL HEALTH SEQUELAE OF LABOR TRAFFICKING

Risk factors for developing mental health issues include a history of childhood abuse, violence before and during trafficking, restricted freedom, poor living and working conditions while trafficked, limited social support, and unmet social needs following escaping trafficking (Hossain et al., 2010). Mental illness may further exacerbate the cycle of exploitation by social isolation, marginalization, and financial insecurity (Oram et al., 2012). Survivors of all forms of human trafficking commonly report symptoms of anxiety, depression, insomnia, nightmares, chronic fatigue, and disordered eating (Gordon et al., 2018; Ottisova et al., 2016). Mental health disorders arising as a consequence of labor trafficking are enduring. They include substance use disorders, depressive and anxiety disorders, PTSD, and somatic symptom disorders (Ottisova et al., 2016).

Human trafficking may exacerbate chronic mental illnesses, including bipolar disorder or psychotic disorders (Gordon et al., 2018). Acute symptoms such as psychosis, delirium, mania, or agitation can interfere with accurately identifying and disclosing trafficking. If the suspicion for human trafficking is high, a resurvey by mental health providers is indicated once acute symptoms are stabilized (Nguyen et al., 2017).

One study demonstrated that trafficked adults were more likely to have an involuntary psychiatric admission and a longer inpatient stay than non-trafficked persons (Oram et al., 2015). Another study sampling trafficked adults, the majority of whom were women, who received mental health care posttrafficking found that 33% of participants had a history of self-harm before receiving mental health services, and 25% further self-harmed while receiving care (Borschmann et al., 2017). A U.S. study found 43% of sampled labor-trafficked survivors experienced suicidal ideation (Hopper & Gonzalez, 2018). A review of case records of labor-trafficked men and women in the United Kingdom revealed that 57% reported at least one PTSD symptom (Turner-Moss et al., 2014). Psychologists need to prioritize labor-trafficked patients' safety and ensure an ongoing suicide risk assessment of current psychosocial stressors, physical health, and mental health symptoms.

The heterogeneity in the rate of psychiatric symptoms and diagnoses among trafficked survivors was confirmed in a systematic review, possibly secondary to different trafficking circumstances, predisposing factors, and study samples (Ottisova et al., 2016). A study in Nepal comparing types of trafficking found that all sex-trafficked women met criteria for depression, and 29.6% met criteria for PTSD, compared with labor-trafficked women, of whom 80.8% met criteria for depression and 7.5% for PTSD (Tsutsumi et al., 2008). A large study on Ethiopian trafficking returnees demonstrated that violence was associated with anxiety and PTSD (Gezie et al., 2018). A U.S.-based study examining mental health consequences of a mixed-sample of labor of sex trafficking survivors found no difference in the rates of depression or PTSD based on the type of trafficking. However, it revealed that survivors of labor trafficking were more likely to experience depression without other psychiatric comorbidities than survivors of sex trafficking, who were more likely to experience comorbid PTSD and depression (Hopper & Gonzalez, 2018). Persons trafficked for longer than 6 months have higher levels of depression and anxiety compared with those trafficked for less than 3 months (Oram et al., 2012). Traffickers may coerce victims into drugs or alcohol use; however, some may start to use substances to cope with their mental health symptoms, trafficking situation, or aftermath (Le, 2014).

LABOR TRAFFICKING IN MEN AND LGBTQIA+ PERSONS

Traditional gender norms and expectations of men and boys being strong and self-sufficient can help elucidate their underrecognition as trafficked (Greenbaum, 2021). Men may be less likely to report being "victims" of trafficking and may be reluctant to return home after escaping trafficking due to feelings of shame and worries about family disappointment (Omole, 2016; Zimmerman & Kiss, 2017). Findings from research on trafficked men can help dispel the misconception that only men are traffickers and can help shape health policies to provide and advocate for mental health services for trafficked men (Omole, 2016). Many labor-trafficked men endorse one or more symptoms of depression, anxiety, or PTSD, with reports of physical violence, threats, and being locked in a room (Kiss et al., 2015). A study sampling men established in mental health care indicated that 21% were diagnosed with depression, 37% with schizophrenia and related psychoses, and 26% with PTSD and adjustment disorders (Oram et al., 2012). A sample of labor-trafficked men in Florida, originating from the Philippines, Guatemala, Haiti, Romania, and Thailand, revealed a prevalence of approximately 23% for anxiety and 15% for depressive symptoms (Omole, 2016).

Little is known about the risk of labor trafficking among LGBTQIA+ individuals. Homeless LGBTQIA+ youth are at significant risk for human trafficking. One Atlanta-based survey on homeless youth found that 6.5% of respondents identified as transgender, and 27.5% identified as gay, lesbian, or bisexual, with 29.3% of all respondents reporting experiencing labor trafficking (Wright et al., 2021). Psychologists can provide their at-risk LGBTQIA+ youth patients with resources and support to prevent them from engaging in high-risk behavior (Greenbaum, 2021).

CHILD LABOR TRAFFICKING

Child labor trafficking occurs when a person engages a child under 18 in forced labor through intimidation, fraud, or coercion. It takes place in various industries, the military, and paramilitary regimes. One study found that 19% of homeless youth in shelters have been trafficked, with 43% trafficked for labor and 18% trafficked for both sex and labor (Mostajabian et al., 2019). Another study examining a similar population in 10 cities identified that 9% of cisgender boys experienced labor trafficking (Murphy, 2016).

Risk factors for child labor trafficking include male gender, unaccompanied minors, and prior involvement in child welfare services (Letsie et al., 2021). Exposure to traumatic experiences in childhood also increases vulnerability to child labor trafficking, and subsequent cycles of reentering trafficking (Chambers et al., 2022; Hopper & Gonzalez, 2018). Traffickers utilize psychological violence against labor-trafficked children and youth, including threats of harm to themselves or their families, starvation, threats of deportation, and restrictions of outside contact (Letsie et al., 2021). Physical and sexual violence are common tactics to perpetuate labor youth exploitation (Letsie et al., 2021; Ottisova et al., 2018). Labor-trafficked youth often fall into a cycle of exiting and returning to their traffickers before finally exiting, especially if they have been trafficked by a family member or a trusted individual (Chambers et al., 2022; Greenbaum, 2021; Murphy, 2016).

Trafficked children may present to a health care setting alone, with a peer, acquaintance, employer, parent, or relative who may not be related (Greenbaum, 2021). Health care providers often fail to identify labor-trafficked children (Greenbaum, 2021). Studies of child labor trafficking reveal significant mental health consequences, including PTSD, anxiety, depression, adjustment disorders, conduct disorders, and increased vulnerability to future violence (Greenbaum, 2021; Oram et al., 2012; Ottisova et al., 2018). A sample of labor- and sex-trafficked children with PTSD revealed symptoms related to affect regulation, self-perception, somatic symptoms, and interpersonal relationships (Ottisova, Smith, & Oram, 2018). Foreign-born trafficked children face additional barriers to receiving care, including ethnicity and nationality stigma, language barriers, lack of provider knowledge on cultural beliefs and norms, and dearth of translated written material (Albright et al., 2020). Given all the potential challenges faced by these children, a call to action is important to promote their safety and well-being.

Psychologists need to prioritize comprehensive safety assessments for children and adolescents, as many youth survivors attempt suicide even after establishing care with mental health services (Ottisova et al., 2018). Like other forms of child abuse, psychologists need to follow mandatory reporting laws if they have a reasonable degree of concern for child labor trafficking (Greenbaum, 2021). Mandatory reporting can incorporate trauma-informed strategies by providing the patient with a choice of whether or not they want to be involved in the reporting process and protecting them from trafficker retaliation (Greenbaum, 2021). Psychologists should create a safe environment for labor-trafficked children by separating them from their companions before their assessment, establishing privacy and safety, maintaining transparency, minimizing retraumatization, asking focused questions to provide adequate mental health care, and utilizing a calm, nonjudgmental approach (Greenbaum, 2021). A trauma-informed multidisciplinary approach in mental health treatment of labor-trafficked minors is critical in ensuring diagnostic clarity, identifying risks for future harm, advocating for trauma-sensitive care, and creating an individualized comprehensive mental health care plan (Albright et al., 2020; Greenbaum, 2021; Letsie et al., 2021; Ottisova et al., 2018). Creating collaborative relationships with child advocacy groups and other mental health centers can help streamline referrals to services (Greenbaum, 2021). Psychologists can educate and collaborate with entry-point services to mental health care for trafficked youth, including emergency medicine, primary care, and social services (Ottisova et al., 2018).

LABOR TRAFFICKING AND THE COVID-19 PANDEMIC

The COVID-19 pandemic significantly impacted persons vulnerable to human trafficking. Measures to limit the virus spread, including "shelter in place" orders, social distancing, and lockdowns, led to separation from loved ones, isolation, movement restrictions, school and business closures, and financial, housing, and job losses. These changes challenged the identification of trafficked persons and affected the ability of health care, legal and social services professionals to provide essential services. Pandemic-related stress has likely increased children's risk for trafficking through worsening pre-existing mental health issues, increased exposure to violence, and increased online and social media use (Greenbaum, 2021).

Reports of labor-trafficked persons in the agricultural and farming industry have increased, as these workers were deemed "essential" during the pandemic (Polaris, 2021a). The National Human Trafficking Hotline labor trafficking reports of temporary H-2A work visa holders doubled after placing "shelter in place" orders. At the same time, labor trafficking reports within the hospitality industry decreased due to the COVID-19 restrictions. The Wage and Hour Division shifted to conducting virtual investigations, limiting in-person interactions with vulnerable persons. The National Health Resource Center on Domestic Violence has provided a guideline on addressing human trafficking through telehealth (available at https://www.futureswithoutviolence.org; National Health Resource Center on Domestic Violence, 2020). During telehealth encounters, psychologists can screen for signs of violence, abuse, overbearing companions, and other unsafe situations (Greenbaum et al., 2020). Psychologists can offer telehealth services with the continued provision of patient safety, support, psychoeducation, and referrals.

CULTURAL ASPECTS OF LABOR TRAFFICKING

Poverty, cultural and gender identity, sexual preference, and racial and language disparities increase the vulnerability to human trafficking. Cultural stigma against mental illness may prevent a trafficked person from seeking mental health services. Cultural interpretation of gender roles, gender identity, sexuality, emotional expression, spirituality, social determinants of health, views of life stressors, and trauma can affect how patients describe their situation during a clinical encounter (Greenbaum, 2021). The psychological evaluation of a trafficked person needs to incorporate the patient's own culturally normative framework as a lens.

A culturally responsive approach allows understanding the complex dynamics of human trafficking, as culture can influence the individual's response and interpretation of trauma. Therapeutic modalities and interventions, such as narrative exposure therapy and group cognitive behavior therapy, have been implemented in a culturally competent approach (Coverdale et al., 2020). Psychologists need to recognize cultural idioms of distress and help-seeking behaviors and understand culturally influenced communication styles, including body language, eye contact, and expression of positive and negative emotions (Greenbaum, 2021).

Language barriers may represent one of the most significant vulnerabilities for individuals at risk of labor trafficking. Language interpreters and advocates are essential in educating the community about the risks, legal rights, and available resources (Hemmings et al., 2016). Language interpreters involved in the care of trafficking survivors should be skilled, neutral, unbiased, and trustworthy and should recognize facial and body language and nonverbal cues. Interpreters should also help trafficked persons navigate the justice system (The Office for Victims of Crime Training and Technical Assistance Center, n.d.). Community leaders may volunteer to provide translated short, concise, educational materials to peers, emphasizing worker's rights, employer's responsibilities, and contact information to connect with language advocates. Interpreters should recognize any misunderstandings due to language or cultural differences while providing the victims with a space to voice their needs and concerns to gain confidence and independence from the trafficker (Lederer & Wetzel, 2014).

It is necessary to accommodate services to trafficked persons with physical, emotional, or cognitive disabilities, including comfortable and easy access for those with mobility impairments, availability of assistive devices for those with sensory impairments, and additional time for adaptive communication for those with cognitive impairments. Health care providers must offer effective communication such as audible information to visually impaired persons or sign language services to deaf or hard-of-hearing persons (Office for Victims of Crime Training and Technical Assistance Center, n.d.).

One of the goals of psychotherapy should be to help trafficked persons reintegrate into supportive and safe communities (Okech et al., 2018). Matching the trafficked person with a survivor leader outreach can help with the engagement of the trafficked person in care. The approach should be person centered, considering the benefits from a supportive church, spiritual or religious leader, prayer, acupuncture, traditional medicine, music, art, dance, or family and community engagement (Coverdale et al., 2020). Connecting trafficked persons with specific agencies, for example, domestic workers' rights agencies, can assist with the continued education on legal rights and connect with peer survivors (Hopper, 2017a).

ASSESSING AND ADDRESSING MENTAL HEALTH NEEDS OF LABOR-TRAFFICKED PERSONS

In 2016, less than 1% of hospitals in the United States had an established response protocol for human trafficking (Stoklosa et al., 2017). A survey of 400 participants conducted by the American Hospital Association found that 54% of participating hospitals did not have a human trafficking response program (Stoklosa & Askew, 2021). Human trafficking is a public health issue yet remains poorly understood and insufficiently taught (Coverdale et al., 2016; Greenbaum, 2021). Additional research on the ideal response protocol, teaching curricula, validated screening tools, and online training platforms for health care providers and health systems is needed. Available resources to help health care providers identify trafficked persons include SOAR (Stop, Observe, Ask, Response), HEAL (Health, Education, Advocacy, Linkage), and Polaris (https://www.polarisproject.org). The PEARR (Provide Privacy, Educate, Ask, Respect and Respond) tool assists health care providers in providing trauma-informed care to persons with suspected trafficking and focuses on providing universal education before screening for trafficking (Dignity Health, 2019). Universal education involves providing a nonjudgmental summary of abuse, trafficking, violence effects on health and well-being, and local and national resources (Dignity Health, 2019). The goal of human trafficking inquiry should not be for the purpose of disclosure—as it can retraumatize a person who may not be ready to disclose—but rather it should be used to evaluate the need for services and inform the trafficked person of available resources (see Exhibit 3.2). Trafficked persons or at-risk persons should feel comfortable sharing their concerns and experiences.

Pretrafficking and posttrafficking symptoms such as depression, anxiety, PTSD, and psychosis can influence mental health treatment outcomes (Hopper, 2017b). Mental health treatment strategies for trafficked persons are adopted from protocols used for other trauma groups (Gordon et al., 2018). General recommendations for psychologists include utilizing an integrated, person-centered, culturally humble, and trauma-informed care approach (Coverdale et al., 2016; Hopper, 2017b). Ensuring safety is the most critical initial step to help any trauma victim. Psychologists aid in building trust, establishing a solid therapeutic alliance, and fostering a holding environment for trafficking survivors. Treatment implementation can be challenging for both psychologists and trafficked persons, but it is crucial to work together to provide

EXHIBIT 3.2. Suggested Screening Questions for Suspected Labor Trafficking That Can Be Utilized in the "Ask" Section of the PEARR Tool

How did you feel about where you worked?

How did you feel about your employer/supervisor/crew leader/ or another controller?

Did you feel that you were paid fairly at this job?

What were your normal work hours? How many hours did you have to work each day?

What happened if you worked fewer hours or took breaks?

Did anyone ever threaten you if you indicated you did not want to work the expected hours?

Did you have to live in housing provided by the controller? What were the housing conditions?

Did you have to pay a fee to the controller in order to stay in this housing?

Did the controller ever promise to secure, renew, or pay for your legal documents or visa?

What were your weekly/monthly expenses to the controller?

Did the controller provide transportation to the worksite? What did this look like?

Note. Data from National Human Trafficking Resource Center (2014).

the appropriate tools to overcome trauma sequelae. Processing trauma requires professional psychological help to alleviate the emotional pain and suffering. Initial psychological evaluations should be tailored to identify current mental health needs, vulnerabilities, psychological and medical history, and ongoing psychosocial stressors (Iqbal et al., 2021). Trust, attachment, interpersonal challenges, current psychological state, stigma and marginalization, socioeconomic barriers to care, support network, and mental health provider competence are some factors for psychologists to consider when providing mental health services (Coverdale et al., 2020). Psychologists need to be aware of their professional limitations when providing care to trafficked persons, including building competence in working with labor-trafficked persons, taking time to build alliance with the patient, adhering to up to date evidence-based practice, and addressing secondary traumatic stress. Secondary traumatic stress needs to be identified when present as it requires additional professional supervision to address burnout and maintain personal well-being (Coverdale et al., 2020). Psychologists need to protect documentation of sensitive information and be cognizant of other persons with potential access to the patient records, such as traffickers, guardians, and those involved in legal proceedings (Greenbaum, 2021).

Psychotherapy can assist labor-trafficked persons in building trust, fostering self-empowerment, and gaining self-esteem. Providing continuity of care is essential in maintaining trafficked persons' mental well-being (Okech et al., 2018). Multiple trauma-focused psychotherapy modalities are effective for trafficked persons, including cognitive processing therapy, prolonged exposure therapy, imaginal exposure therapy, and eye movement desensitization and reprocessing therapy, especially for those suffering from depressive disorder, anxiety disorders, PTSD, and dissociative symptoms. Motivational interviewing can help those with substance use disorders (Iqbal et al., 2021).

Building connections with the patients while promoting an open, safe environment for recovery and maintaining trust and confidentiality will help to create a trusting relationship to foster empowerment and resilience in the trafficked person. Collaborating with survivors has growing evidence as best practice in human trafficking screening, protocols, and guidelines (Miller et al., 2020). Psychologists can assist labor trafficking survivors with overcoming their vulnerabilities by connecting them to survivor advocates, support groups, continuing education, job training, antitrafficking case management, and family reunification efforts (Iqbal et al., 2021). Understanding each survivor's story is essential in developing an individualized, person-centered, and strength-focused treatment plan. Psychologists can contact the National Human Trafficking Hotline to clarify reporting requirements that vary from state to state within the United States, obtain referrals for trafficked persons, and help trafficked persons connect to resources.

The role of a mental health provider extends beyond the direct interaction with the trafficked person to include advocacy and linkage (Alhajji et al., 2021; see Exhibit 3.3). Mental health practitioners, including psychologists, should collaborate with policy makers to create broader awareness and more effective responses to the violence and mental health consequences of labor trafficking (Rose et al., 2021). Psychologists can act as the core of

EXHIBIT 3.3. Antitrafficking Advocacy Roles for Mental Health Providers

Educating colleagues, trainees, and students about human trafficking.
Creating antitrafficking protocols within their system or workplace.
Establishing multidisciplinary, trauma-informed, integrated clinics for trafficked persons.
Promoting health care and social services for trafficking survivors.
Supporting policy and legislation changes to increase health care access for vulnerable groups.
Advocating for increased funding for trauma-informed mental health services.
Volunteering in antitrafficking organizations.
Including multilingual and inclusive flyers and resources for trafficking survivors in visible spaces within the provider's workplace.
Engaging in data collection and evidence-based scientific research on labor trafficking.
Collaborating with community members including law enforcement, child welfare services, survivor advocates, and social services to improve service provision.
Joining organizations, such as HEAL trafficking, to stay informed on best evidence-based practices for health care professionals.
Contacting legislators to prioritize legislation that protect survivors of human trafficking.

health care services and collaborate with community stakeholders such as legal services, housing, and vocational training (Iqbal et al., 2021).

CONCLUSION

Labor trafficking negatively impacts millions of persons every year. The ability of psychologists to intervene may be hindered by the complexity of recognizing labor trafficking victims and connecting them with available resources. Psychologists can create evidence-based educational materials and develop best practice guidelines with community members, law enforcement, the criminal justice system, social workers, school counselors, immigration and legal aid agencies, and political leaders. The goal of human trafficking inquiry should not be for the purpose of disclosure—as it can retraumatize a person who may not be ready to disclose—but it should rather evaluate the need for services and inform the trafficked person of available resources. Psychologists need universal access to educational training in trauma-sensitive care to avoid retraumatization, stigmatization, and adverse mental health consequences on labor-trafficked patients. When working with a labor-trafficked person, each therapist should utilize an integrated, person-centered, culturally humble, and trauma-informed care approach.

Labor-trafficked persons' medical and psychological needs require continuous monitoring and assessment. Psychologists should recognize the risk factors, stereotypes, misconceptions, and the cycle of labor exploitation to fully comprehend the challenges faced by trafficked persons. Further research is needed to validate screening tools for labor trafficking, especially for specific vulnerable populations such as minors, men, and the LGBTQIA+ community.

Efforts are needed on a larger global scale to create and reinforce anti-labor trafficking laws, policies, and reporting requirements. Psychologists can collaborate with local organizations to educate the community and increase outreach efforts. Engaging with persons with lived labor-trafficking experience can be a useful tool for clinicians to successfully help their patients. Psychologists can also work within their practicing health system to create human trafficking response protocols and provide education on human trafficking to other colleagues and staff.

REFERENCES

Albright, K., Greenbaum, J., Edwards, S. A., & Tsai, C. (2020). Systematic review of facilitators of, barriers to, and recommendations for healthcare services for child survivors of human trafficking globally. *Child Abuse & Neglect, 100,* 104289. https://doi.org/10.1016/j.chiabu.2019.104289

Alhajji, L., Hadjikyriakou, M., & Padilla, V. (2021, December). Psychiatrists' response to human trafficking. *The Psychiatric Times, 38*(12), 67–70.

American Psychological Association. (2014). *Report of the Task Force on Trafficking of Women and Girls.* https://www.apa.org/pi/women/programs/trafficking/report.pdf

Baldwin, S. B., Fehrenbacher, A. E., & Eisenman, D. P. (2015). Psychological coercion in human trafficking: An application of Biderman's framework. *Qualitative Health Research, 25*(9), 1171–1181. https://doi.org/10.1177/1049732314557087

Borschmann, R., Oram, S., Kinner, S. A., Dutta, R., Zimmerman, C., & Howard, L. M. (2017). Self-harm among adult victims of human trafficking who accessed secondary mental health services in England. *Psychiatric Services, 68*(2), 207–210. https://doi.org/10.1176/appi.ps.201500509

Chambers, R., Gibson, M., Chaffin, S., Takagi, T., Nguyen, N., & Mears-Clark, T. (2022). Trauma-coerced attachment and complex PTSD: Informed care for survivors of human trafficking. *Journal of Human Trafficking,* 1–10. https://doi.org/10.1080/23322705.2021.2012386

Chisolm-Straker, M., Baldwin, S., Gaïgbé-Togbé, B., Ndukwe, N., Johnson, P. N., & Richardson, L. D. (2016). Health care and human trafficking: We are seeing the unseen. *Journal of Health Care for the Poor and Underserved, 27*(3), 1220–1233. https://doi.org/10.1353/hpu.2016.0131

Coverdale, J., Beresin, E. V., Louie, A. K., Balon, R., & Roberts, L. W. (2016). Human trafficking and psychiatric education: A call to action. *Academic Psychiatry, 40*(1), 119–123. https://doi.org/10.1007/s40596-015-0462-2

Coverdale, J. H., Gordon, M. R., & Nguyen, P. T. (2020). *Human trafficking: A treatment guide for mental health professionals.* American Psychiatric Association.

Dank, M., Farrell, A., Zhang, S., Hughes, A., Abeyta, S., Fanarraga, I., Burke, C., & Solis, V. (2021). *An exploratory study of labor trafficking among U.S. citizen victims.* Office of Justice Programs. https://www.ojp.gov/pdffiles1/nij/grants/302157.pdf

Dignity Health. (2019). *Using the PEARR tool.* https://www.dignityhealth.org/content/dam/dignity-health/pdfs/pearrtoolm15nofield2019.pdf

Gezie, L. D., Yalew, A. W., Gete, Y. K., Azale, T., Brand, T., & Zeeb, H. (2018). Socioeconomic, trafficking exposures and mental health symptoms of human trafficking returnees in Ethiopia: Using a generalized structural equation modelling. *International Journal of Mental Health Systems, 12*(1), 62. https://doi.org/10.1186/s13033-018-0241-z

Gordon, M., Salami, T., Coverdale, J., & Nguyen, P. T. (2018). Psychiatry's role in the management of human trafficking victims: An integrated care approach. *Journal of Psychiatric Practice, 24*(2), 79–86. https://doi.org/10.1097/PRA.0000000000000287

Greenbaum, J. (2021). Child labor and sex trafficking. *Pediatrics in Review, 42*(12), 639–654. https://doi.org/10.1542/pir.2020-001396

Greenbaum, J., Stoklosa, H., & Murphy, L. (2020). The public health impact of coronavirus disease on human trafficking. *Frontiers in Public Health, 8,* 561184. https://doi.org/10.3389/fpubh.2020.561184

Hemmings, S., Jakobowitz, S., Abas, M., Bick, D., Howard, L. M., Stanley, N., Zimmerman, C., & Oram, S. (2016). Responding to the health needs of survivors of human trafficking: A systematic review. *BMC Health Services Research, 16*(1), 320. https://doi.org/10.1186/s12913-016-1538-8

Hopper, E. K. (2017a). The multimodal social ecological (MSE) approach: A trauma-informed framework for supporting trafficking survivors' psychosocial health.

In M. Chisolm-Straker & H. Stoklosa (Eds.), *Human trafficking is a public health issue* (pp. 153–183). Springer.

Hopper, E. K. (2017b). Trauma-informed psychological assessment of human trafficking Survivors. *Women & Therapy, 40*(1–2), 1–2, 12–30. https://doi.org/10.1080/02703149.2016.1205905

Hopper, E. K., & Gonzalez, L. D. (2018). A comparison of psychological symptoms in survivors of sex and labor trafficking. *Behavioral Medicine, 44*(3), 177–188. https://doi.org/10.1080/08964289.2018.1432551

Hossain, M., Zimmerman, C., Abas, M., Light, M., & Watts, C. (2010). The relationship of trauma to mental disorders among trafficked and sexually exploited girls and women. *American Journal of Public Health, 100*(12), 2442–2449. https://doi.org/10.2105/AJPH.2009.173229

Iglesias-Rios, L., Harlow, S. D., Burgard, S. A., Kiss, L., & Zimmerman, C. (2018). Mental health, violence and psychological coercion among female and male trafficking survivors in the greater Mekong sub-region: A cross-sectional study. *BMC Psychology, 6*(1), 56. https://doi.org/10.1186/s40359-018-0269-5

International Labour Organization. (2012, October 1). *ILO indicators of forced labour.* https://www.ilo.org/global/topics/forced-labour/publications/WCMS_203832/lang--en/index.htm

International Labour Organization, Walk Free, and International Organization for Migration. (2022). *Global estimates for modern slavery.* https://www.ilo.org/wcmsp5/groups/public/---ed_norm/---ipec/documents/publication/wcms_854733.pdf

Iqbal, S. Z., Salami, T., Reissinger, M. C., Masood, M. H., Ukrani, K., & Shah, A. A. (2021). The mental health clinician's role in advocacy for survivors of human trafficking: Treatment and management. *Psychiatric Annals, 51*(8), 373–377. https://doi.org/10.3928/00485713-20210707-02

Kerr, P. L., & Bryant, G. (2022). Use of ICD-10 Codes for human trafficking: Analysis of data from a large, multisite clinical database in the United States. *Public Health Reports, 137*(Suppl. 1), 83S–90S. https://doi.org/10.1177/00333549221095631

Kiss, L., Pocock, N. S., Naisanguansri, V., Suos, S., Dickson, B., Thuy, D., Koehler, J., Sirisup, K., Pongrungsee, N., Nguyen, V. A., Borland, R., Dhavan, P., & Zimmerman, C. (2015). Health of men, women, and children in post-trafficking services in Cambodia, Thailand, and Vietnam: An observational cross-sectional study. *The Lancet: Global Health, 3*(3), e154–e161. https://doi.org/10.1016/S2214-109X(15)70016-1

Koegler, E., Mohl, A., Preble, K., & Teti, M. (2019). Reports and victims of sex and labor trafficking in a major Midwest metropolitan area, 2008–2017. *Public Health Reports, 134*(4), 432–440. https://doi.org/10.1177/0033354919854479

Lambar, E. F., & Thomas, G. (2019). The health and well-being of North Carolina's farmworkers: The importance of inclusion, accessible services and personal connection. *North Carolina Medical Journal, 80*(2), 107–112. https://doi.org/10.18043/ncm.80.2.107

Langmagne, S., Tenkorang, E. Y., & Elabor-Idemudia, P. (2021). High HIV/AIDS prevalence in a suburban area in Ghana: A context analysis of its relationship to human trafficking. *Journal of Human Trafficking, 7*(2), 187–201. https://doi.org/10.1080/23322705.2019.1703092

Le, P. D. (2014). *Human trafficking and psychosocial well-being: A mixed-methods study of returned survivors of trafficking in Vietnam* [Doctoral dissertation, University of California Los Angeles]. eScholarship. https://escholarship.org/uc/item/3c5088hh

Lederer, L., & Wetzel, C. (2014). The health consequences of sex trafficking and their implications for identifying victims in healthcare facilities. *Annals of Health Law,* *23*(1), 61–91.

Letsie, N. C., Lul, B., & Roe-Sepowitz, D. (2021). An eight-year analysis of child labor trafficking cases in the United States: Exploring characteristics, and patterns of child labor trafficking. *Child Abuse & Neglect, 121,* 105265. https://doi.org/ 10.1016/j.chiabu.2021.105265

Mackay, M., Hardesty, B. D., & Wilcox, C. (2020). The intersection between illegal fishing, crimes at sea, and social well-being. *Frontiers in Marine Science, 7,* 589000. https://doi.org/10.3389/fmars.2020.589000

Miller, C. L., Chisolm-Straker, M., Duke, G., & Stoklosa, H. (2020). A framework for the development of healthcare provider education programs on human trafficking part three: Recommendations. *Journal of Human Trafficking, 6*(4), 425–434. https://doi.org/10.1080/23322705.2019.1635342

Mora, D. C., Quandt, S. A., Chen, H., & Arcury, T. A. (2016). Associations of poor housing with mental health among North Carolina Latino migrant farmworkers. *Journal of Agromedicine, 21*(4), 327–334. https://doi.org/10.1080/1059924X.2016.1211053

Mostajabian, S., Santa Maria, D., Wiemann, C., Newlin, E., & Bocchini, C. (2019). Identifying sexual and labor exploitation among sheltered youth experiencing homelessness: A comparison of screening methods. *International Journal of Environmental Research and Public Health, 16*(3), 363. https://doi.org/10.3390/ijerph16030363

Murphy, L. (2016). *Labor and sex trafficking among homeless youth: A ten-city study full report.* Covenant House. https://www.covenanthouse.org/sites/default/files/ inline-files/Loyola%20Multi-City%20Executive%20Summary%20FINAL.pdf

National Health Resource Center on Domestic Violence. (2020). *Telehealth, COVID-19, intimate partner violence, and human trafficking: Increasing safety for people surviving abuse.* Futures Without Violence. https://www.futureswithoutviolence.org/ wp-content/uploads/Telehealth-COVID-19-IPV-and-HT_Guide.pdf

National Human Trafficking Resource Center. (2014, October 4). *Comprehensive human trafficking assessment tool.* https://humantraffickinghotline.org/resources/ comprehensive-human-trafficking-assessment-tool

National Human Trafficking Resource Center. (2018, January 3). *What to look for in a healthcare setting.* National Human Trafficking Hotline. https:// humantraffickinghotline.org/resources/what-look-healthcare-setting

Nguyen, P. T., Coverdale, J. H., & Gordon, M. R. (2017). Identifying, treating, and advocating for human trafficking victims: A key role for psychiatric inpatient units. *General Hospital Psychiatry, 46,* 41–43. https://doi.org/10.1016/j.genhosppsych. 2017.02.006

Office for Victims of Crime Training and Technical Assistance Center. (n.d.). *Human trafficking task force e-guide.* https://www.ovcttac.gov/taskforceguide/

Okech, D., Hansen, N., Howard, W., Anarfi, J. K., & Burns, A. C. (2018). Social support, dysfunctional coping, and community reintegration as predictors of PTSD among human trafficking survivors. *Behavioral Medicine, 44*(3), 209–218. https://doi.org/ 10.1080/08964289.2018.1432553

Omole, C. (2016). *Human trafficking: The health of men forced into labor trafficking in the United States* [Doctoral dissertation, Walden University]. ScholarWorks. https://scholarworks.waldenu.edu/dissertations/1980/

Oram, S., Khondoker, M., Abas, M., Broadbent, M., & Howard, L. M. (2015). Characteristics of trafficked adults and children with severe mental illness: A historical cohort study. *The Lancet: Psychiatry, 2*(12), 1084–1091. https://doi.org/10.1016/S2215-0366(15)00290-4

Oram, S., Stöckl, H., Busza, J., Howard, L. M., & Zimmerman, C. (2012). Prevalence and risk of violence and the physical, mental, and sexual health problems associated with human trafficking: Systematic review. *PLOS Medicine, 9*(5), e1001224. https://doi.org/10.1371/journal.pmed.1001224

Ottisova, L., Hemmings, S., Howard, L. M., Zimmerman, C., & Oram, S. (2016). Prevalence and risk of violence and the mental, physical and sexual health problems associated with human trafficking: An updated systematic review. *Epidemiology and Psychiatric Sciences, 25*(4), 317–341. https://doi.org/10.1017/S2045796016000135

Ottisova, L., Smith, P., & Oram, S. (2018). Psychological consequences of human trafficking: Complex posttraumatic stress disorder in trafficked children. *Behavioral Medicine, 44*(3), 234–241. https://doi.org/10.1080/08964289.2018.1432555

Ottisova, L., Smith, P., Shetty, H., Stahl, D., Downs, J., & Oram, S. (2018). Psychological consequences of child trafficking: An historical cohort study of trafficked children in contact with secondary mental health services. *PLOS ONE, 13*(3), e0192321. https://doi.org/10.1371/journal.pone.0192321

Pocock, N. S., Nguyen, L. H., Lucero-Prisno III, D. E., Zimmerman, C., & Oram, S. (2018). Occupational, physical, sexual and mental health and violence among migrant and trafficked commercial fishers and seafarers from the Greater Mekong Subregion (GMS): Systematic review. *Global Health Research and Policy, 3*(1), 28. https://doi.org/10.1186/s41256-018-0083-x

Polaris. (2018, January). *Human trafficking in illicit massage businesses.* https://massagetherapy.nv.gov/uploadedFiles/massagetherapy.nv.gov/content/Resources/FullReportHumanTraffickinginIllicitMassageBusinesses.pdf

Polaris. (2019a, October 28). *Human trafficking at home: Labor trafficking of domestic workers.* https://polarisproject.org/resources/human-trafficking-at-home-labor-trafficking-of-domestic-workers/

Polaris. (2019b, December 20). *Knocking at your door: Labor trafficking on sales crews.* https://polarisproject.org/resources/knocking-at-your-door-labor-trafficking-on-sales-crews/

Polaris. (2021a, June 23). *Labor exploitation and trafficking of agricultural workers during the pandemic.* https://polarisproject.org/resources/labor-exploitation-and-trafficking-of-agricultural-workers-during-the-pandemic/

Polaris. (2021b). *Labor trafficking and H-2A visas: Employer essentials.* https://polarisproject.org/resources/essential-guide-for-h-2a-visa-sponsors/

Polaris. (2021c, October 25). *Polaris analysis of 2020 data from the National Human Trafficking Hotline.* https://polarisproject.org/2020-us-national-human-trafficking-hotline-statistics/

Ronda-Pérez, E., & Moen, B. E. (2017). Labour trafficking: Challenges and opportunities from an occupational health perspective. *PLOS Medicine, 14*(11), e1002440. https://doi.org/10.1371/journal.pmed.1002440

Rose, A. L., Howard, L. M., Zimmerman, C., & Oram, S. (2021). A cross-sectional comparison of the mental health of people trafficked to the UK for domestic servitude, for sexual exploitation and for labor exploitation. *Journal of Human Trafficking, 7*(3), 258–267.

Stickle, W. (2021). Human trafficking in the Midwest: A case study of St. Louis and the Bi-State area. *Journal of Human Trafficking, 7*(2), 238–240. https://doi.org/10.1080/23322705.2019.1675031

Stoklosa, H., & Askew, G. (2021). *Three steps every hospital can take to implement human trafficking prevention programs.* American Hospital Association. https://www.aha.org/news/blog/2021-07-01-headline-three-steps-every-hospital-can-take-implement-anti-human-trafficking

Stoklosa, H., Dawson, M. B., Williams-Oni, F., & Rothman, E. F. (2017). A Review of U.S. Health Care Institution protocols for the identification and treatment of victims of human trafficking. *Journal of Human Trafficking, 3*(2), 116–124. https://doi.org/10.1080/23322705.2016.1187965

Tsutsumi, A., Izutsu, T., Poudyal, A. K., Kato, S., & Marui, E. (2008). Mental health of female survivors of human trafficking in Nepal. *Social Science & Medicine (1982), 66*(8), 1841–1847.

Turner-Moss, E., Zimmerman, C., Howard, L. M., & Oram, S. (2014). Labour exploitation and health: A case series of men and women seeking post-trafficking services. *Journal of Immigrant and Minority Health, 16*(3), 473–480. https://doi.org/10.1007/s10903-013-9832-6

United Nations Office on Drugs and Crime. (2013). *Abuse of a position of vulnerability and other "means" within the definition of trafficking in persons.* https://www.unodc.org/documents/human-trafficking/2012/UNODC_2012_Issue_Paper_-_Abuse_of_a_Position_of_Vulnerability.pdf

United States Bureau of International Labor Affairs. (2020). *List of goods produced by child labor or forced Labor.* https://www.dol.gov/agencies/ilab/reports/child-labor/list-of-goods

United States Department of State. (2021, September 14). *2021 trafficking in persons report.* https://www.state.gov/reports/2021-trafficking-in-persons-report/

World Health Organization. (2018). *International classification of diseases* (11th ed.). https://icd.who.int/en

World Health Organization. (2023). *International statistical classification of diseases and related health problems (ICD).* https://www.who.int/standards/classifications/classification-of-diseases

Wright, E. R., LaBoy, A., Tsukerman, K., Forge, N., Ruel, E., Shelby, R., Higbee, M., Webb, Z., Turner-Harper, M., Darkwa, A., & Wallace, C. (2021). The prevalence and correlates of labor and sex trafficking in a community sample of youth experiencing homelessness in Metro-Atlanta. *Social Sciences, 10*(2), 32. https://doi.org/10.3390/socsci10020032

Zimmerman, C., & Kiss, L. (2017). Human trafficking and exploitation: A global health concern. *PLOS Medicine, 14*(11), e1002437. https://doi.org/10.1371/journal.pmed.1002437

Zimmerman, C., McAlpine, A., & Kiss, L. (2016, February). *Safer labour migration and community-based prevention of exploitation: The state of the evidence for programming.* Freedom Fund. https://freedomfund.org/wp-content/uploads/FF_SAFERMIGRATION_WEB.pdf

4 DEVELOPMENTAL APPROACH TO CHILD TRAFFICKING

CASSANDRA MA

Children comprise almost 12% of victims of human trafficking worldwide, almost evenly divided into labor trafficking versus sex trafficking (International Labour Organization [ILO] et al., 2022). The ILO defines *forced labor* as "all work or service which is exacted from any person under the menace of any penalty and for which the said person has not offered himself voluntarily" (ILO et al., 2022). The Trafficking Victims Protection Act (2000) defines *human trafficking* as consisting of one of two primary forms, sex and labor. It further distinguishes sex trafficking in that minors, those under 18, are considered victims of human trafficking, or sex trafficking, regardless of the elements of force, fraud, or coercion. Since that 2016 report, the number of victims involved in forced labor has increased by 2.7 million to 49.6million people, reflecting 27 million in forced labor and 22 million in forced marriage (ILO et al., 2022).

Trafficking beginning in childhood has a lifelong impact on the developmental path of the survivor. Trafficking is rarely the only traumatic experience in the victim's life (Hopper, 2017). The cumulative impact of trafficking and additional adverse childhood experiences markedly affects the life course,

https://doi.org/10.1037/0000379-005
Psychological Perspectives on Human Trafficking: Theory, Research, Prevention, and Intervention, L. Dryjanska, E. K. Hopper, and H. Stoklosa (Editors)

leaving victims vulnerable to lifelong health, psychological, and relational consequences (Hopper, 2017; Hopper & Gonzalez, 2018; Hunt et al., 2017). A developmental conceptualization of child trafficking considers the developmental level of the child victim and preexisting trauma to understand the psychological impact and vulnerabilities to revictimization. Child trafficking, in the context of child development and developmental trauma, contextualizes the effects of this distinctive complex trauma in the developing child's life.

This chapter's purpose is to view experiences of child trafficking and the traumatic sequelae through a developmental lens. Applying developmental concepts to child trafficking improves our understanding of the psychological impact of experiences child trafficking survivors endure. A comprehensive trauma-informed conceptualization of child trafficking is beneficial to inform clinical assessment and treatment of the child's developmental trajectory, identifying the specific vulnerabilities left by traumatic interruptions to the child's development.

DIFFERENT TYPES OF CHILD TRAFFICKING

Children are trafficked in multiple ways, each with different forms of exploiting their vulnerabilities. Child labor trafficking and child soldiers tend to fall under the commonly understood form of labor trafficking, whereas child sex trafficking and child marriages tend to connote sex trafficking. Despite these delineations, children who are exploited are often abused in more than one way during the course of trafficking.

Child Labor Trafficking

According to the ILO and the United Nations International Children's Emergency Fund's (UNICEF, 2022) report on global child labor trafficking, over 160 million children are engaged in child labor, with 79 million of those engaged in "hazardous work" (ILO, 2022). More boys than girls are involved in child labor trafficking (ILO & UNICEF, 2022). The distinction between child labor, which constitutes trafficking, and that which is culturally or legally sanctioned is complex. Not all forms of child labor constitute child labor trafficking. Children might help with "work" in the home, such as chores, or hold jobs after a certain age. Child trafficking requires the use of force, fraud, or coercion, but excessive and overt force are not often required to get children to comply due to their dependent status (Greenbaum et al.,

2022). In this respect, child labor trafficking may be more difficult to differentiate from child labor (Office of Juvenile Justice and Delinquency Prevention [OJJDP], 2016). The ILO's definition of *child labor* is "work that deprives children of their childhood, their potential and their dignity, and that is harmful to physical and mental development" (ILO, 2022). The broader definition is useful for understanding the impact of child labor trafficking on the developing child.

From a developmental perspective, school is the primary form of "work" for children. Developmentally appropriate work tasks fit the developmental abilities and capabilities of the child (e.g., they are strong enough, physical and gross motor skills match the task, in a time frame that children can tolerate). The developmental process involves a gradual transition of the "work" of school into labor that is applied to productivity and the identity of adulthood. Child labor trafficking involves tasks with demands beyond the abilities of the child and distorts the potential intrinsic motivation for "work." Marginalized children, particularly ones without adult protection, such as refugees and undocumented children, are at higher risk for trafficking (Greenbaum et al., 2022; OJJDP, 2016).

Traffickers exploit children in forced labor since they are easier to control than adults (Greenbaum et al., 2022), they can accomplish tasks requiring smaller sizes, and their options for protection and shelter are limited (UNICEF, 2022). Recruitment tactics of traffickers include primarily false promises, lies regarding the type of employment, and the offer of shelter (Bracy et al., 2021). Forced labor activities include farming, domestic servitude, fishing, and mining (ILO & UNICEF, 2021; OJJDP, 2016).

Child Soldiers

The term *child soldier* describes labor trafficking in that exploitation involves coerced indoctrination into a lifestyle of violence and harming others. Child soldiers are compelled to participate in violent warfare and forced to participate in the injuring and killing of others. Exposure to the realities of warfare and extreme violence results in severe trauma and personality changes that cause significant harm to the child's ability to integrate into society (Schauer & Elbert, 2010). Juveniles involved in gangs have been compared to child soldiers since the tactics of gangs are similar in the use of psychological coercion to engage younger members in perpetration of violence against others (OJJDP, 2016). The violence of juvenile gangs, however, is considered delinquent behavior, highlighting another complexity between the criminal and legal perspective versus the psychological and developmental perspective.

Child Sex Trafficking

Child sex trafficking is defined as a commercial sex act induced by force, fraud, or coercion, or when a person under 18 years of age is induced to perform such acts (Victims of Trafficking and Violence Protection Act, 2000). Victims of child sex trafficking experience high levels of trauma, resulting in post-traumatic stress disorder, depression, and anxiety. Furthermore, they experience these problems regardless of the elements of force, fraud, or coercion experienced in the course of their abuse (Hopper & Gonzalez, 2018; Hossain et al., 2010). Popular portrayals of child sex trafficking often misrepresent the experience of survivors—images of victims tied up and held in captivity do not reflect the day-to-day reality of most child sex trafficking victims. Instead, it typically involves psychological manipulation and relational grooming by traffickers. Traffickers prey upon the vulnerabilities of their victims to entice them into relationships that become exploitive; traffickers offer money, love and companionship, a sense of belonging, and more.

Child Marriage

Child marriage is defined as the marital union between a minor, under the age of 18, and an adult (UNICEF, 2022). Approximately two out of five victims in forced marriage were children, and over 90% of minors coerced into marriage were family members (ILO et al., 2022). Compelling a child to marry essentially legalizes sexual relationships that might be considered child abuse without the legal institution. Marriage prior to adulthood diminishes the opportunities for children to be children. It is directly correlated with lost educational advancement, which, in turn, affects future vocational potential and independence (UNICEF, 2022).

DEVELOPMENTAL IMPACT OF TRAFFICKING

Children are especially vulnerable to victimization due to their smaller stature and because they have not fully developed the base of knowledge, values, life skills, and self-regulatory capacities that provide the foundation for independent living. They are biologically wired to become attached to those whom they must rely upon during this vulnerable period. Initially, babies and young children depend upon parents and primary caregivers to learn these indirect lessons. Over time, the group of adults who influence the child's developmental trajectory widens to include teachers, coaches, and other adults in the child's day-to-day life. During adolescence, the child's values, morality, personality, identity, and more are reshaped through an interactive process between the child and her interpersonal world.

The younger the child, the greater dependence the child has upon caregivers. The dependency state of children necessitates caregiving and adult guidance to navigate the challenges of life as children develop to full maturity. Children are cognitively, emotionally, and physically less capable of defending themselves than adults. They depend directly upon adults to care for and protect them, which makes them susceptible to the plans of adult caregivers. Children without healthy adult attachments and protection are at the greatest risk for child trafficking and other forms of child maltreatment. The adult–child relationship involves dependency and a clear difference in power and abilities, yet the perceived meaning of exploitive relationships is different for a 6-year-old than it is for a 14-year-old.

Emotional Regulation and Coping

Child trafficking is best understood as interpersonal exploitation of childhood vulnerabilities. Infants and children depend upon adults, primarily caregivers, to learn to manage increasingly complex emotions and emotional distress through a process of coregulation (Paley & Hajal, 2022). In the absence of healthy caregiving and the formation of adult–child relationships marked by exploitation and abuse, children are left to contend with highly traumatic experiences without the coregulatory and psychological resources to do so.

The histories of child trafficking survivors often reflect multiple forms of pretrafficking adversity: homelessness, family conflict, substance abuse, domestic abuse, sexual, physical, and emotional abuse (Chambers et al., 2021; Cole et al., 2016; Crosland & Dunlap, 2015; Hopper, 2017; Tyler & Bersani, 2008). The psychological impact of child trafficking is reflected in problems with emotional regulation, depression, changes in interpersonal relationships, and posttraumatic stress disorder (Hopper & Gonzalez, 2018; Milojevich et al., 2020). Emotional dysregulation is associated with externalizing behaviors and involvement with the criminal justice system, with increased risk for *revictimization* beyond initial experiences of exploitation (Finklea et al., 2015; Greeson et al., 2019).

Trafficking impedes the child's ability to maintain their normal developmental pace. Abused children contending with psychological and physical trauma beyond their developmental capacities commonly struggle to acquire social, emotional, and academic skills that are on par with their peers. Attention problems, flashbacks, and emotional struggles are common trauma-related symptoms that interfere with successful completion of most developmental tasks of childhood.

Educational Development

Exploitation replaces educational experiences in the developmental path of trafficked children. Disrupted educational histories tend to be the rule rather than the exception among child trafficking survivors. Trafficked youth often have educational histories affected by their experiences during exploitation (e.g., they are taken out of school for exploitation, they associate with people not in school). As a result, most trafficked children and youth are behind their peers in educational level. Even when a child is no longer in the abusive environment, the impact of the trauma places additional challenges to normal development and makes integration with peers harder.

Inconsistencies in school attendance contribute to marginalization from peers and missed learning opportunities. Trafficked children report many unhappy and negative associations with school. Academic difficulties, lack of access to educational supports, peer problems (e.g., bullying), and exploitation in lieu of school are some of the reasons they often struggle with their education. In addition to academic and social problems (e.g., poor concentration, keeping up with age cohort, managing bullies), trafficking experiences replace formal education. Gaps in learning further impede the child's ability to remain integrated in a normative developmental path. Matriculating a 16-year-old who began to run when she was in the eighth grade with peers who are in their junior year of high school has complications not easily remedied by an individualized education plan. The loss of formal educational opportunities and guidance from healthy role models contributes to a child's vulnerability to adopting other perspectives and limits future potential roles and vocational choices.

Physical Development

Growing children learn how to use their bodies to accomplish physical tasks. Young athletes learn how to use their bodies in ways that lead to a heightened sense of physical competency. Child labor trafficking narrows the physical skills development to those required for the forced labor (e.g., housecleaning) just as child sex trafficking trains exploited youth to behave in ways that enhance their marketability (e.g., how to behave sexually, engage in sex acts), and this becomes a part of the child's identity. Over time, the child's repertoire of relationally shaped behaviors can further influence identity development as the their emerging skills are limited to physical and psychological survival (Berry et al., 2017). Coerced labor or sexual activity that exceeds the size and physical development of the child victim causes damage, sometimes irreparable, to the developing child's body.

Cognitive Development

Child trafficking survivors experience compounded relational trauma in which more than one perpetrator of abuse and/or exploitation function in a caregiving role, beginning with a parent or parents and shifting into a trafficker, if not the same person. Children learn from these experiences of polyvictimization that adults are not trustworthy and cause harm (Hopper, 2017). Clinicians have long observed that the child's worldview, including their view of self, evolves during adolescence and stabilizes as one approaches adulthood (Blos, 1966).

The knowledge base children possess at different ages affects the degree to which the perpetrator's reality is internalized. Young children are more easily manipulated due to their developing cognitive skills. They are vulnerable to cognitive rationalizations of adults for abusive dynamics.

"He told me it was my fault and I believed him."—13-year-old trafficking victim

Traffickers use this misattribution of locus of control and blame to maintain control of victims.

Worldview and Identity Formation

A child's sense of right and wrong, values, and belief systems are formed by the people in the immediate environment, and, in turn, shape behaviors and identity consistent with a developing worldview. Children look to adult caregivers for wisdom regarding how to manage interpersonal relationships and navigate life's difficulties in general. The developmental level of the child factors into how readily they will believe adult perpetrators' messages. Young children and preadolescent children are particularly impressionable and quickly adopt the belief systems, behaviors, emotional expressions, and thought patterns of adult caregivers. Younger children are more vulnerable to coercion and dehumanization and require more intensive treatments (Bruhns et al., 2018). The child's developmental level defines the extent of the trafficker's influence on the child's sense of interpersonal social power (Preble & Black, 2020). The child's preexisting worldview will affect the degree to which the adult perpetrator's value system is adopted.

> *M was 13 when she was first trafficked. Her trafficker made her go to the store to steal hygiene products when she needed them. Stealing felt morally wrong to her, but another girl, also trafficked with her, seemed to be able to steal more easily. She would comply in an effort to please her trafficker since she saw the other child receive praise for her ability to steal, but developed high anxiety at the idea of entering a store of shopping after trafficking ended.[1]*

The trauma of ongoing abuse by adults during childhood affects the child's perspectives and expectations of the adult world. Daily exposure to a worldview that condones exploitation of others and includes emotional, physical, or sexual abuse has further potential to shape the developing values of the child survivor (Lee et al., 2015; Stogsdill, 2019). In fact, a form of *criminal socialization* can occur when an attachment relationship forms with the perpetrator. Money, shelter, food, and other enticements (e.g., manicures, hair styling), presented as benefits, can be confusing to a child. Perpetrators, also, distort the meaning of these "gifts" to silence victims. To a child, the meaning of these inducements can be viewed as kindnesses by the perpetrator and can be distorted as a sign of willing participation. This developmental vulnerability explains, in part, the reason why many child sex trafficking survivors do not see themselves as victims.

Psychological Coercion

Relational trauma as a part of exploitation involves coercive tactics that amplify the dependent state of the child victim and the control of the abuser. Traffickers do not need to rely upon extreme, physically coercive measures and can, instead, use psychologically manipulative tactics to gain compliance of child victims.

> *Y was 9 when she ran away from home. Her mother never reported her as missing. So, at the age of 9 she was left to fend for herself. 9-year-olds are not able to get a job to make money to get food or shelter. When she was offered McDonald's by the man who would traffic her, he became her hero.*

Tactics include isolation, monopolization of perception, induced debility or exhaustion, threats, occasional indulgences, demonstration of omnipotence, degradation, and enforcement of trivial demands (Baldwin et al.,

---

[1]All case study material in this chapter is fictional, uses composites, or has been disguised by changing names and altering or removing identifying information to preserve client confidentiality.

2015). Trauma-coercive bonding with a criminal perpetrator is a unique aspect of child trafficking. These tactics isolate child victims, keeping them away from sources of support, and interfere with their developing sense of agency (Mumey et al., 2021). Psychological coercion tends to be less clearly definable and identifiable to children, especially to those who are still developing cognitive, relational, and emotional coping skills. Further, the attachment relationship formed through the pairing of a vulnerable child with less overtly offensive or harmful interactions creates a strong trauma bond often unrecognizable to the child victim (Chambers et al., 2021).

TOWARD A DEVELOPMENTAL CONCEPTUALIZATION OF TRAFFICKING TRAUMA

Childhood is a time of staggering growth in learning in all areas associated with becoming an adult—how to relate to others, how to manage emotions, how to behave in the world, how to solve problems, how to make choices, and more. A developmental trauma-informed model is necessary to comprehend the special vulnerabilities of children and the unique impact of child sex trafficking on children's developing psyche. The externalizing behaviors exhibited by trafficked youth, such as running away, oppositional behaviors, school problems, delinquency, mistrust of law enforcement are most compassionately understood through a developmental trauma lens. When these behaviors are understood in the context of a developmental understanding of child trafficking, interventions appropriate for healing the needs of the child can be implemented to restore a healthy life course.

A developmental profile of a survivor of child sex trafficking must include a full picture of the child's attachment history, including who provided protection and caretaking at times of increased vulnerability (such as when homeless). The developing psyches of child victims are shaped by trauma and missed developmental milestones, leading to developmental vulnerabilities that are exploited by adult perpetrators. Consideration of the developmental stage at which the child's exploitation began, and even other abusive experiences at the hands of adults, assists in the identification of lost opportunities and unmet needs that made the child vulnerable in the first place. An understanding of the broad developmental impact of child sex trafficking is critical to implementing interventions that will stop the cycle of victimization.

A developmental approach to child trafficking seeks to identify the vulnerable moments when perpetrators entered the child's internal world and subverted their values, their identity, and their worldview (Stogsdill, 2019). A clinical goal is to help the child learn to recognize the perpetrator's voice within the child's inner dialogue (Salter, 1995). When a pattern of relationships involving abuse is established during formative years the child's ability to recognize the danger signs is compromised. Further, the dependency state of the child victim makes the potential for leaving and gaining independence from abusive relationships more challenging.

A developmental evaluation of a child who has been a victim of child trafficking might also include a thorough history of the abusive and exploitive attachment relationships with adults. Child abuse found in the histories of child trafficking victims compounds the dynamics of complex trauma and the child's perspective of relationships with adults. Overcoming the damage to the child's ability to trust takes time, and they may be reluctant to depend on others anymore. A developmental approach to child trafficking must include a dynamic description of the nature of the relationship with the perpetrator(s). Identification of all coercive tactics that interfere with the child's development of a sense of agency can focus treatment goals to foster developmentally appropriate sources of agency.

A developmental approach to child sex trafficking recognizes the importance of clarifying and resolving identity issues for a child who has internalized a maladaptive view of self. Clinicians must negotiate a delicate balance in which adaptive living skills may be packaged with a nonprosocial identity. Developmental considerations are relevant in the conversations about trafficking as it has to do with "choice." This concept, in the context of child trafficking, is frequently introduced as a means of helping minors regain a sense of control over life choices. Providing choices, even limited choices, can increase the child's sense of agency but also can entrench learned skills into the child's identity. However, children are limited by their "choice" in relationships (Finkelhor, 2008). Choices must be consistent with the complexities of disparate developmental levels.

Any form of child sexual victimization results in a child who has developmental knowledge regarding sex that is disparate from other areas of development, requiring a more complex conceptualization of a child's developmental level. A 6-year-old child who has been exposed to adult sexual activity will have an advanced awareness of sex but still cannot be expected to make an informed choice about returning to a situation of continued sexual vulnerability. A developmental approach to child sex trafficking also targets all the areas in which the child may by lagging behind, including academic and life skills.

Child trafficking viewed through a developmental framework can guide clinicians in understanding the relevant psychological issues to design the most effective treatments. A developmental approach can be applied to adult survivors in the consideration of all relationships in the survivor's history helps to understand the outward presentation and to, hopefully, engender a more empathic response on the part of those who have the opportunity to be a part of the initial and long-term healing journey of survivors.

REFERENCES

Baldwin, S. B., Fehrenbacher, A. E., & Eisenman, D. P. (2015). Psychological coercion in Human trafficking: An application of Biderman's framework. *Qualitative Health Research, 25*(9), 1171–1181. https://doi.org/10.1177/1049732314557087

Berry, L. J., Tully, R. J., & Egan, V. (2017, October). A case study approach to reducing the risks child sexual exploitation (CSE). *Journal of Child Sexual Abuse, 26*(7), 769–784. https://doi.org/10.1080/10538712.2017.1360428

Blos, P. (1966). *On adolescence: A psychoanalytic perspective.* Free Press.

Bracy, L., Lul, B., & Roe-Sepowitz, D. (2021). A four-year analysis of labor trafficking cases in the United States: Exploring characteristics and labor trafficking patterns. *Journal of Human Trafficking, 7*(1), 35–52. https://doi.org/10.1080/23322705.2019.1638148

Bruhns, M. E., del Prado, A., Slezakova, J., Lapinski, A. J., Li, T., & Pizer, B. (2018). Survivors' perspectives on recovery from commercial sexual exploitation beginning in childhood. *The Counseling Psychologist,* 2018-05, *46*(4), 413–455.

Chambers, R., Gibson, M., Chaffin, S., Takagi, T., Nguyen, N., & Mears-Clark, T. (2021). Trauma-coerced attachment and complex PTSD: Informed care for survivors of human trafficking. *Journal of Human Trafficking,* 1–10. https://doi.org/10.1080/23322705.2021.2012386

Cole, J., Sprang, G., Lee, R., & Cohen, J. (2016). The trauma of commercial sexual exploitation of youth: A comparison of CSE victims to sexual abuse victims in a clinical sample. *Journal of Interpersonal Violence, 31*(1), 122–146.

Crosland, K., & Dunlap, G. (2015). Running away from foster care: What do we know and what do we do? *Journal of Child and Family Studies, 24,* 1697–1706.

Finkelhor, D. (2008). *Childhood victimization.* Oxford University Press. https://doi.org/10.1093/acprof:oso/9780195342857.001.0001

Finklea, K., Fernandes-Alcantara, A. L., & Siskin, A. (2015). *Sex trafficking of children in the United States: Overview and issues for Congress.* Congressional Research Service.

Greenbaum, J., Sprang, G., Recknor, F., Harper, N. S., & Titchen, K. (2022). Labor trafficking of children and youth in the United States: A scoping review. *Child Abuse & Neglect, 131*(September), 105694. https://doi.org/10.1016/j.chiabu.2022.105694

Greeson, J. K. P., Treglia, D., Wilfe, D. S., & Wasch, S. (2019). Prevalence and correlates of sex trafficking among homeless and runaway youths presenting for shelter services. *Social Work Research, 43*(2), 91–99.

Hopper, E. K. (2017). Polyvictimization and developmental trauma adaptations in sex trafficked youth. *Journal of Child & Adolescent Trauma, 10*(2), 161–173. https://doi.org/10.1007/s40653-016-0114-z

Hopper, E. K., & Gonzalez, L. D. (2018). A comparison of psychological symptoms in survivors of sex and labor trafficking. *Behavioral Medicine, 44*(3), 177–188. https://doi.org/10.1080/08964289.2018.1432551

Hossain, M., Zimmerman, C., Abas, M., Light, M., & Watts, C. (2010). The relationship of trauma to mental disorders among trafficked and sexually exploited girls and women. *American Journal of Public Health, 100*(12), 2442–2449. https://doi.org/10.2105/AJPH.2009.173229

Hunt, T. K. A., Slack, K. S., & Berger, L. M. (2017). Adverse childhood experiences and behavioral problems in middle childhood. *Child Abuse & Neglect, 67*, 391–402. https://doi.org/10.1016/j.chiabu.2016.11.005

International Labour Organization. (2022). *What is child labour.* https://www.ilo.org/ipec/facts/lang--en/index.htm

International Labour Organization, & United Nations International Children's Emergency Fund. (2021). *The role of social protection in the elimination of child labour.* https://www.ilo.org/wcmsp5/groups/public/---ed_norm/---ipec/documents/publication/wcms_845168.pdf

International Labour Organization, Walk Free Foundation, & International Organization for Migration. (2022). *Global estimates of modern slavery forced labour and forced marriage.* https://www.ilo.org/wcmsp5/groups/public/@ed_norm/@ipec/documents/publication/wcms_854733.pdf

Lee, J. O., Herrenkohl, T. I., Jung, H., Skinner, M. L., & Klika, J. B. (2015). Longitudinal examination of peer and partner influences on gender-specific pathways from child abuse to adult crime. *Child Abuse & Neglect, 47*, 83–93. https://doi.org/10.1016/j.chiabu.2015.07.012

Milojevich, H. M., Machlin, L., & Sheridan, M. A. (2020). Early adversity and children's emotion regulation: Differential roles of parent emotion regulation and adversity exposure. *Development and Psychopathology, 32*(5), 1788–1798. https://doi.org/10.1017/S0954579420001273

Mumey, A., Sardana, S., Richardson-Vejlgaard, R., & Akinsulure-Smith, A. M. (2021). Mental health needs of sex trafficking survivors in New York City: Reflections on exploitation, coping, and recovery. *Psychological Trauma: Theory, Research, Practice, and Policy, 13*(2), 185–192. https://doi.org/10.1037/tra0000603

Office of Juvenile Justice and Delinquency Prevention. (2016, December). *Child labor trafficking.* https://ojjdp.ojp.gov/model-programs-guide/literature-reviews/child_labor_trafficking.pdf

Paley, B., & Hajal, N. J. (2022). Conceptualizing emotion regulation and coregulation as family-level phenomena. *Clinical Child and Family Psychology Review, 25*(1), 19–43. https://doi.org/10.1007/s10567-022-00378-4

Preble, K. M. (2020). Under their "control": Perceptions of traffickers' power and coercion among international female trafficking survivors during exploitation. *Victims & Offenders, 14*(2), 199–221. https://doi.org/10.1080/15564886.2019.1567637

Preble, K. M., & Black, B. M. (2020). Influence of survivors' entrapment factors and Traffickers' characteristics on perceptions of interpersonal social power during exit. *Violence Against Women, 26*(1), 110–133. https://doi.org/10.1177/1077801219826742

Salter, A. C. (1995). *Transforming trauma: A guide to understanding and treating adult survivors of child sexual abuse.* SAGE.

Schauer, E., & Elbert, T. (2010). The psychological impact of child soldiering. In E. Martz (Ed.), *Trauma rehabilitation after war and conflict: Community and individual perspectives* (pp. 311–360). Springer Science + Business Media. https://doi.org/10.4135/9781452232102

Stogsdill, S. (2019). *The impact of childhood abuse on moral development.* Taylor University. https://pillars.taylor.edu/ovc-student/1

Tyler, K. A., & Bersani, B. (2008). A longitudinal study of early adolescent precursors to running away. *The Journal of Early Adolescence, 28*(2), 230–251. https://doi.org/10.1177/0272431607313592

United Nations International Children's Emergency Fund. (2022, August 26). *Child marriage.* https://www.unicef.org/protection/child-marriage

United States Department of State. (2022, August 26). *Understanding human trafficking.* https://www.state.gov/what-is-trafficking-in-persons/

Victims of Trafficking and Violence Protection Act, Pub. L. No. 106-386, 114 Stat. 1464. (2000). https://www.govinfo.gov/content/pkg/PLAW-106publ386/pdf/PLAW-106publ386.pdf

5

PSYCHOLOGISTS AS VITAL FRAME SPONSORS IN NEWS COVERAGE OF HUMAN TRAFFICKING

BARBARA G. FRIEDMAN

In a 2010 proclamation establishing the annual observance of National Slavery and Human Trafficking Prevention Month, President Barack Obama urged "all Americans to educate themselves about all forms of modern slavery and the signs and consequences of human trafficking" (Proclamation, 2010). Recognizing that psychologists had an important role in the fight against trafficking, the American Psychological Association (APA) formed the Task Force on Trafficking of Women and Girls in 2011. In its 2014 report, the task force wrote, "Public awareness and understanding of the crime of human trafficking and the dynamics of coercion and trauma are essential for the success of anti-trafficking efforts" (p. 55). They called on psychologists to address trafficking in "all professional capacities: research, education and training, advocacy and public policy, public awareness, and practice" (p. 4). Much of this work would require psychologists to work with and through the media.

When the APA founded its media psychology division (Division 46) earlier in 1987, its focus was on the appearance of *psychologists in the media* as expert sources. Since then, Division 46 efforts have been directed toward *psychology*

https://doi.org/10.1037/0000379-006
Psychological Perspectives on Human Trafficking: Theory, Research, Prevention, and Intervention, L. Dryjanska, E. K. Hopper, and H. Stoklosa (Editors)

as a basis for the study of media. Media psychology is "the scientific study of human behavior, thoughts, and feelings experienced in the context of media use and creation" (Dill, 2013, p. 6).

A current objective of the division, to "facilitate the interaction between psychology and media representatives to encourage a fair and accurate representation of the science and practice of psychology" (Society for Media Psychology and Technology, 2013), paired with current APA tips on preparing for a videoconference interview and "getting your message out on social media," reflect an ongoing interest in how psychologists communicate through media.

This chapter weds these two concerns: media influence research and how psychologists participate in media. It examines news frames, which derive their effects from psychological mechanisms (Lecheler & de Vreese, 2019), to scrutinize the ways that psychologists, as important mental health "educators, advocates, and researchers" (Greenbaum et al., 2018, p. 165) have participated in recent news coverage about human trafficking, and what they offer as news sources in comparison to other groups consulted about trafficking.

PSYCHOLOGY OF NEWS FRAMING

Although social media platforms have broadened who can participate in the information marketplace, news media remains a primary source for the public to learn about issues such as human trafficking (Liedke & Gottfried, 2022). However, news coverage in the United States and elsewhere has been criticized for misrepresenting or sensationalizing the issue and for causing additional harm to victims and survivors. Research has shown that news media tends to report about sex trafficking more than labor trafficking and about women and girl victims more than about men, boys, or LGBTQIA+ victims (Austin & Farrell, 2017). The media regularly conflate prostitution with human trafficking and stigmatize commercial sex; news coverage of "Super Bowl sex trafficking" offers a perennial example of this tendency (Albright & D'Adamo, 2017; Weitzer, 2018).

Framing as a conceptual approach to research is used in multiple disciplines, including psychology, for its attention to media influence and audience behavior, and it has "become ubiquitous in communication science research" (Lecheler & de Vreese, 2019, p. 8). Frames are "organizing principles that are socially shared and persistent over time, that work symbolically to meaningfully structure the social world" (Reese, 2001, p. 11). Research has repeatedly shown that the way that an issue is framed in the news influences how the public (including policy makers) comes to understand and act upon the issue

(Chong & Druckman, 2007; Gubitz et al., 2018, Hetey & Eberhardt, 2014). The theory of media framing and its effects are drawn from psychology and sociology, and views media discourse and public opinion as "parallel systems." As Gamson and Modigliani (1989) explained, "Media discourse is part of the process by which individuals construct meaning, and public opinion is part of the process by which journalists and other cultural entrepreneurs develop and crystallize meaning in public discourse" (p. 2). Frames are related to audiences' cognitive appraisal processes. By emphasizing some information in a story while minimizing or excluding other information, news frames can privilege certain perspectives or interpretations (Gamson & Modigliani, 1989). Emphasis framing effects are supported by three psychological mechanisms: the availability of frame-relevant beliefs; their accessibility when an issue is confronted; and applicability, the degree to which a frame-relevant belief is related to an issue and useful for addressing the issue (Chong & Druckman, 2007).

Framing in a news story is "manifested by the presence or absence of certain keywords, stock phrases, stereotyped images, sources of information, and sentences that provide thematically reinforcing clusters of facts or judgments" (Entman, 1993, p. 52). Through selection and salience, frames can define problems, diagnose causes, make moral judgments, and suggest remedies related to the issue being reported. Cumulative news coverage of human trafficking using a crime frame, for example, that reports police raids, sting operations in the name of antitrafficking work, might dispose audiences to support passage of stricter laws to punish traffickers as opposed to greater allocation of resources to expand victim services. Framing is "a 'kissing cousin' of agenda setting," the power of the news to influence the prominence of a topic on the public agenda (Bryant & Oliver, 2009, p. xii).

Put simply, news frames have powerful effects on how audiences interpret the news. When news stories include anecdotes, they may be especially persuasive in that they can elicit attachment to characters based on perceived similarity with the character, and the willingness to adopt a character's perspective (identification). Attachment amplifies characters' influence on an audience member's beliefs and attitudes (Broom et al., 2021; Cohen, 2006; Green, 2004). Further, identification and similarity may reduce an individual's psychological bias of invulnerability when a character is shown experiencing vulnerability. When an audience member feels a similar vulnerability, they may be more inclined toward attitudes and actions that will reduce the threat (Moyer-Gusé, 2008). The perception of vulnerability might also be related to victim blame. In their study of narrative persuasion, for example, Shafer and Looney (2018) found that participants exposed to a news story that framed an individual as being abducted and forced into trafficking reported greater perceived similarity to the kidnapped victim, increased vulnerability to becoming a victim of trafficking, and they blamed the victim less, in comparison with a story that framed someone as having been groomed into trafficking by a manipulative partner. Participants' feelings of vulnerability—that they could be abducted and forced into trafficking—were associated with increased support for victim services. The willingness to help was influenced by the way the news framed, and the participant understood, the trafficking victim's responsibility for her situation. "This increased efficacy," the authors cautioned, "should be weighed against the potential long-term harm of perpetuating the rescue or ideal victim frames" (Shafer & Looney, 2018, p. 12). In a study of prosocial responses to descriptions of trafficking, Silver et al. (2015) found that participants' just-world beliefs and attitudes toward commercial sex were predictors of empathy toward and willingness to help women who were described as either "prostitutes" or "having been trafficked."

In study of news coverage of interpersonal violence (IPV), an issue that has overlap with human trafficking, Carlyle et al. (2008) found that media portrayals of IPV were primarily reported as singular events absent the context necessary to make connections and formulate appropriate responses. For example, a typical IPV story reports that police were called to a residence following a 911 call about a domestic disturbance, with no additional context or follow-up reporting. In a subsequent study, Carlyle et al. (2014) found that exposure to a news story about an IPV incident that included context to lower perception of victim responsibility resulted in participants feeling increased sympathy for the victim, leading to affective perspective taking (thinking about what the victim might be feeling) and, ultimately, support for IPV prevention efforts.

News frames can be either episodic or thematic and can shape audience interpretation (Iyengar, 1991). Studies of news coverage of human trafficking have found that the issue is typically framed episodically—that is, event oriented and prompted by government action such as an arrest, an indictment, or a law passed (Gulati, 2011). Episodic framing, which reports concrete events and singular cases (Iyengar, 1991), provides news audiences with little opportunity to think about the issue as occurring in a broader, thematic context, such as poverty, education, racism, or immigration, or to consider solutions beyond the individual, for example. Some studies suggest that episodic framing may elicit more intensive emotional responses precisely because of its focus on individuals, and in this way, strengthen the framing effect (Lecheler & de Vreese, 2019, p. 39). An effective public health response to human trafficking, in which audiences engage with the complexity of the issue and feel compelled to engage in evidence-based helping behaviors, requires details and clarity that are missing in most news coverage of the issue.

Newsgathering routines are in part to blame, as they have limited journalists' abilities to convey the contexts necessary for audiences to understand how trafficking occurs, how it affects its victims, and survivors' emergent and long-term needs (Johnston et al., 2014; Sobel et al., 2019)—information that psychologists are well suited to provide. Sources, such as experts who journalists consult and quote to verify parts of a story, add credibility, or provide diverse views, are an essential part of the newsgathering routine. Sources are instrumental to the frame-building process of the news.

FRAME SPONSORS AND THEIR INFLUENCE IN THE NEWS

Sources can function as "frame sponsors" in that they have influence over how a topic is covered in the news (Wichgers et al., 2021), and thus how audiences come to understand and respond to an issue. Frame sponsors have reasons for orienting their perspectives in a particular way—groups arguing for or against a ballot measure decriminalizing commercial sex, for example, want to direct attention and action in specific ways—and may be similarly capable of "tuning the ears of journalists" to their agenda (Gamson & Modigliani, 1989, p. 6), particularly when they emphasize (and thus activate) familiar cultural frames (Van Gorp, 2007). In turn, journalists adopt socially shared category systems in their reporting that become "important tools for information processing" among their audiences (Tewksbury & Scheufele, 2009, p. 18). Sanford et al. (2016) found that elite news outlets' reporting about trafficking between 2012 and 2013 reinforced U.S. and United Nations policy agendas (then concerned primarily with sex trafficking) and minimized labor trafficking despite its ubiquity; the authors attributed this to an overreliance on government sources. Award-winning investigative reporting on labor trafficking in the seafood industry has illuminated the tangle of business and political interests that has stood in the way of meaningful progress toward combating severe forms of labor exploitation (Kelly, 2018). Caruana et al. (2021), in a search for studies in business and management of "modern slavery," found a "(non)field" (p. 253). These conditions inevitably impact news reporting about trafficking since they limit journalists' access to information and expertise.

The initial framing of an issue is more important than subsequent coverage, explained by the serial position effect, or specifically, the primacy effect, in which the information learned first is weighted more heavily than information learned later (Murdock, 1962). Hertog and McLeod (2001) noted that "when a topic is framed, its context is determined" (p. 147); "who speaks first" can impose boundaries for debate over important issues. A comparison of studies over time demonstrated the persistence of news coverage that frames trafficking as an issue that affects mostly women and girls and that involves forced commercial sex rather than forced labor or domestic servitude, despite labor trafficking being the dominant form of trafficking (Gulati, 2011; Johnston et al., 2014, 2015; Marchionni, 2012; Sanford et al., 2016). Likewise, when *The Lancet* erred by conflating smuggling with trafficking, Stoklosa and Baldwin (2017) were concerned with early impressions. "Health professionals are currently a tabula rasa regarding trafficking," they wrote. "How we educate them now forever imprints how they view trafficking going forward" (p. 1641).

As the news cycle progresses, however, news frames can and do shift (Bonilla & Mo, 2019; Sobel et al., 2019). The role of psychologists as educators, advocates, and researchers benefits from engagement with the media and, in turn, benefits the public. "As a discipline that explores the depth and breadth of human behavior," the 2014 APA task force report noted, "psychology is well positioned to study the multiple intrapsychic, developmental, interpersonal, relational, social, cultural, religious, educational, institutional, societal and economic issues that intersect to contribute to the phenomenon of trafficking" (p. 53).

LOCATING PSYCHOLOGISTS IN NEWS FRAMES OF TRAFFICKING

A study of news coverage of human trafficking is one way to understand how the issue has been framed recently, and, moreover, the role of psychologists as knowledgeable, and potentially influential, news sources. This section presents findings from a qualitative content analysis that used framing theory to examine U.S. print, broadcast, and web-based news coverage of human trafficking from January 1, 2019, to December 31, 2021, for the presence of mental health professionals with expertise about the dynamics of trafficking.

Sources in news coverage are presumed to have something at stake (Wichgers et al., 2021), although they may have varying levels of authority. Their contributions to the news are approached as sponsored frames with the *potential* to affect the ways that the public understands, talks about, and responds to the issue of human trafficking. The 2014 report of the APA Task Force on Trafficking of Women and Girls concluded with specific ideas about how mental health professionals could use their expertise to raise public awareness of trafficking. These recommendations are helpful for thinking about the contributions of sources in news coverage about trafficking. These guidelines address common myths about trafficking and its victims, increase awareness of both labor and sex trafficking, educate the public about common signs of trafficking to help identify potential victims in their communities, raise awareness about the vulnerability of certain communities (i.e., immigrants, refugee or asylees, homeless youth), and address the intersections between trafficking and other forms of violence (i.e., child abuse, intimate partner violence) and exploitation (i.e., labor exploitation violations). Given that limited awareness of human trafficking is a risk factor for human trafficking at the community and society levels (Greenbaum et al., 2018), frame sponsorship is important for its potential role in human trafficking prevention.

Stories for analysis were collected using ProQuest U.S. Newsstream, a database allowing full-text access to daily newspapers, broadcast news transcripts, and online news. The period under study, January 2019 through December 2021, included multiple high-profile stories that alleged trafficking, although it was not always centered in the narratives—for example, the arrest and death by suicide of financier and convicted sex offender Jeffrey Epstein; the search for, arrest, trial, and conviction of Epstein's accomplice, Ghislaine Maxwell; the arrest and trial of singer R. Kelly; the trial of the Nxivm "sex cult" leader Keith Raniere and his principals; the arrest of Lawrence Ray, who moved into his daughter's dorm at Sarah Lawrence College and subjected her friends to years of physical abuse and sexual exploitation, including forced commercial sex; and the arrest of New England Patriots owner Robert Kraft in a trafficking sting. The date range also includes a shooting rampage at three Atlanta-area spas by someone who claimed to have a "sex addiction"—some reporting presumed the spas were sites of trafficking— as well as references to U.S. Representative Matt Gaetz, the subject of a Justice Department investigation into child sex trafficking, and to debunked conspiracy theories about sex trafficking. These stories and others during the period were thought to offer copious opportunities for psychologists as experts to help explain trafficking to news audiences.

News items for analysis totaled 268. This does not represent all of the news coverage about human trafficking in the time period but rather the subset of stories about trafficking that also mention something about psychology.[1]

---

[1] An advanced broad search for the phrases "human trafficking" or "labor trafficking" or "sex trafficking" in news coverage during this period yielded 18,787 results. The number surely includes duplicates and other items that would be excluded from a similar study (i.e., reviews, calendar items) but suggests the dearth of mental health professionals cited in news about trafficking.

Two themes emerged: psychology as coercion (as in part of a trafficker's modus operandi) and psychology as consequences of exploitation (as in psychological trauma or posttraumatic stress disorder). These themes appeared primarily in stories that used episodic frames as well as in stories that used thematic frames.

FRAME SPONSORS AND SUBSTANCE

Consistent with the findings of previous studies about U.S. news coverage of trafficking, the stories here were dominated by sex trafficking (222 of 268 stories). Some stories about immigration were conspicuous for their lack of reference to labor trafficking and instead referred to "human trafficking and sex trafficking" as if they were two distinct forms of exploitation. Most of the stories came from newspapers and online news outlets; about a third of the stories appeared in broadcast format. As for sources, or potential frame sponsors, the news coverage attributed material to 956 human sources (Figure 5.1), and 220 document sources.

If the success of frame sponsors is measured by quantity, lawyers and judges triumphed; they accounted for about one in five sources in this study's news coverage of human trafficking. When politicians and law enforcement are added to that group, "official" sources to whom expertise or firsthand experience were attributed accounted for one out of three sources in this category. These sources appeared in all types of coverage: newspapers, broadcast news, and websites. However, if the success of frame sponsors is dependent on the substance of their contributions, mental health professionals were

FIGURE 5.1. Human Sources in News Coverage 2019–2021 (*N* = 956)

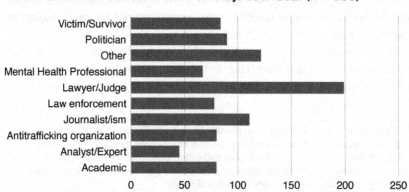

vital in that regard, although they appeared only once in 69 broadcast stories and accounted for just one in 14 sources overall.

Psychologists as Potential Frame Sponsors

Neither psychologists nor their research was among the most cited sources in 2019 to 2021 news coverage of trafficking that also mentioned psychology. However, when they did appear, they offered context that contributed to thematic frames—in other words, they moved the issue of trafficking beyond the immediate event or individual parties to place it into broader societal context and, as a potential effect, reduced victim blaming among their news audience. As sources, psychologists fulfilled and exceeded the APA's 2014 call for raising public awareness about the issue, as the exemplars in the following sections illustrate.

Power in Prominent Trafficking Cases

For example, in a 2020 *USA Today* story about Maxwell, who would later be found guilty of sex trafficking, a clinical psychologist and editor of an APA journal addressed public shock at the socialite's role in Epstein's abuse of minors, and made connections to other forms of abuse: "One of our psychological defenses against feeling vulnerable ourselves is to create this idea that it must take some kind of monster to commit sexual assault or any of these other types of sexual offenses" (Dastagir, 2020). Whereas most stories in the study period relied on lawyers or legal analysts to predict and explain the stages of trial, psychologists often appeared as expert witnesses to provide testimony about the processes that allowed their abuse to occur. For example, journalists covering Maxwell's trial for *The New York Times* and CNN quoted psychologists' testimony about "hindsight bias" (O'Brien, 2021), a social and cognitive psychology theory about the tendency to view past events as having been predictable (Bernstein et al., 2007), and about the grooming of minors for sexual abuse (Del Valle, 2021). Literal grooming was part of a *New York Times* essay about how Maxwell's poshness "could have beguiled those teenage girls of mostly modest backgrounds" and enabled Epstein's trafficking enterprise. A psychologist was cited in that piece, as well, and although the story used an individual (Maxwell) for its starting point as an episodic frame might do, the psychologist helped to make important connections between exploitation and class (Garelick, 2021).

In other stories about prominent and powerful figures accused of sex trafficking, psychologists offered expertise on the limits of sex offender registries in a story about the ways wealth and influence shielded Epstein from prosecution (Romero & Kulish, 2019); and in a story on singer R. Kelly's conviction, psychologists "shed light on the systemic silencing of Black girls and the power of celebrity influence" (Mitchell & Aviles, 2021). The last government witness in Kelly's trial was a psychologist who testified as an expert on abusive relationships. *USA Today* reported that the witness summarized "studies showing that many abusers systematically isolate, demean, subjugate, and spy on their victims as means of control" (Trepany, 2021).

In other news stories, the work of psychologists as it appeared in court filings or testimony was a source for journalists, including evaluations made of trafficking victims (Contrera, 2021; Vaughn, 2021) and accused predators (Swygart, 2019; Yates, 2019). In one case, a psychologist was the perpetrator, and journalists covered his sentencing (Brasch & Dixon, 2019).

Immigration and Trafficking

As potential frame sponsors, psychologists added much-needed depth to stories about trafficking and immigration at a time when record numbers of migrants sought to cross into the United States without authorization (Wong et al., 2021). Most immigration stories among the search results appeared in broadcast news, where commentators, along with their politician and law enforcement sources, worried about a "border crisis," "sex predators," and "thugs" (Arroyo, 2019). "America's open border with Mexico is allowing drug cartels and human traffickers to ply their trade with impunity," warned Tucker Carlson (2020) on his eponymous Fox News program. Frame building in these broadcast stories was unidirectional (Wichgers et al., 2021), with hosts and sources remarking on and repeating one another's comments. Stories were framed episodically and prompted by government action, as in a story about a visit to the border by Republican elected officials (Bream, 2021). Democrats also visited the border, and in an MSNBC story following President Joe Biden's comments about overcrowded facilities, the correspondent referred explicitly to framing: "The president framed this as a humanitarian issue" (Gamboah et al., 2021). No mental health professionals appeared as sources in the broadcast stories about trafficking and immigration analyzed for this study.

However, a *Washington Post* article, a part of a series, demonstrated the potential for differences in framing when mental health professionals did act as sources for newspaper stories about trafficking and immigration. In 2020, the *Post* reported reactions to the use of therapists' presumably confidential notes by U.S. Immigration and Customs Enforcement to detain or deport unaccompanied minors, including certified human trafficking victims. Multiple professional organizations, including the APA, submitted a joint letter to Congress, calling the practice "a violation of broadly accepted mental health ethical standards" and "'an affront to this country's basic principles' of civil rights protection," for example (Dreier, 2020). In this thematic story, psychologists linked trafficking to another social issue—immigration—and focused on the vulnerability rather than alleged criminality of refugee communities, whose trauma was compounded by using their disclosures to make "life and death" decisions about their status. The journalist's interviews with psychologists and use of related document sources provided context to a Honduran teenager's involvement with a feared criminal gang that forced him to sell drugs for them, a fact he disclosed to a therapist, which led to his detention (Dreier, 2020). The *Washington Post* reporter was recognized with multiple awards for this work (i.e., WashPostPR, 2021). Mental Health America, in honoring her with the 2020 Media Award, observed, "The story was the first to explore the kind of therapy migrant children are given in detention" (MHA National, 2020).

Conspiracy Theories About Trafficking
Psychologists were valuable news sources for understanding disinformation, another pressing issue during the study's time period. Here, their contributions were not about traffickers' coercive tactics and the psychological impacts on victims but rather the peddling and uptake of conspiratorial beliefs that continue to interfere with legitimate antitrafficking efforts. Four years after "Pizzagate," a far-right conspiracy theory alleging (without evidence) that Democrats were operating a child sex-trafficking ring out of a Washington, DC, pizza parlor (Kline, 2017), social media claims that retailer Wayfair was engaged in a bizarre scheme to traffic children resulted in a glut of calls to the National Human Trafficking Hotline, compromising legitimate efforts to fight trafficking (Roose, 2020). The nongovernmental organization responsible for operation of the hotline urged the public to "learn more about what human trafficking really looks like in most situations, and about how you can help fight trafficking in your own community" (Polaris, 2020). Disinformation is a topic at the juncture of media and psychology, and efforts to combat it benefit from the expertise of mental health professionals—partisan appropriation of trafficking is counterproductive to preventing trafficking and helping survivors. In the news coverage under study, psychologists were knowledgeable sources for understanding what makes individuals gravitate toward conspiracy theories, such as the ones undergirding claims that Wayfair was trafficking children inside their furniture (Spring, 2020). "For believers and followers, [conspiracy theories] provide a recreational pastime, a sense of belonging and even a new identity and mission in life," said a professor of psychiatry to the *New York Daily News* (Dillon, 2020). In another story, however, a social

psychologist said any comfort afforded by belief in conspiracy theories was short lived: "Over time, research finds, trading in conspiracies not only fails to satisfy our psychological needs, but also tends to worsen feelings of fear or helplessness" (Fisher, 2020). In a *New York Times* op-ed about religious leaders "trying to save their flocks from the lure of the online conspiracy theory," a psychologist (and evangelical Christian) said that White evangelicals' uncritical acceptance of conspiracy theories was about justifying their political beliefs (Posner, 2020).

If Not Mental Health Professionals, Then Who?

Psychologists, as mental health professionals, offered valuable context for understanding the issue of human trafficking, but mental health professionals were not among the top groups consulted for their expertise. What were some of the other groups journalists cited on the topic of the psychology of trafficking, and what might explain their presence as expert sources? What are the implications?

Lawyers and Judges

The most cited human sources in the news coverage on the topic of the psychology of trafficking were lawyers and judges. This finding is not entirely unexpected because the period for study, 2019 to 2021, coincided with several trafficking cases involving prominent (and, thus, newsworthy) figures. The reliance on sources within the criminal justice system is consistent with the United States' focus on carceral solutions to the problem of human trafficking, and discounting of trauma-informed approaches that focus on its root causes and the "empowerment of the oppressed rather than rescue and protection of women and girls" (Baker, 2015, p. 197).

An abundance of lawyers and judges can also result from news outlets' reliance on their court-beat or crime-beat reporters to cover these cases—lawyers and judges' quotes were available in situ, at way posts in the criminal justice system, tending toward more efficient episodic coverage as a result. For example, at the 2021 sentencing in a Wisconsin trafficking case, a reporter for the *Marshfield News Herald* quoted the judge, who called the case "'one of—no, the most heinous example' of abusive sex trafficking behavior she'd seen in her legal career" (Vielmetti, 2021, p. A3). This story is newsworthy for its unusualness but maintains focus on a singular instance of trafficking (Vielmetti, 2021). Routinized news coverage predisposes court- and crime-beat reporters toward these sources, as well as to the documents that lawyers and judges generate in their work.

News conferences, too, become part of a reporter's routine. Like in the story mentioned in the previous paragraph, they tend to result in episodic reporting. "This is a true predator," said the Suffolk County (New York) district attorney, neatly providing *Newsday* with both a news frame (crime) and provocative headline. At a news conference to announce a 10-count grand jury indictment against an alleged trafficker, the district attorney explained, "This is what traffickers do. They use a combination of psychological, emotional, financial, and physical torture to keep their victims in sex slavery" (Brodsky, 2020). In stories like this, the district attorney notes psychological coercion as part of a trafficker's modus operandi, but the story is limited to a breaking news event, the public announcement of criminal charges against one individual. As frame sponsors, lawyers and judges have a stake in framing the story as one of law and order.

Academics

Professors of law offered commentary on legal issues, and overall, academics did a better job of broadening the issue of trafficking, sponsoring thematic frames related to the causes of trafficking and advocating for vulnerable groups. A University of Chicago professor's quote recorded by a reporter covering a poverty summit for *La Raza* neatly summed up the story's thematic framing: "[Poverty] creates a ripple effect across a family and a community, rather than something that only happens to an individual." A study of the roots of poverty among Chicago's Latino community and its many impacts, also part of the *La Raza* story, noted that "human trafficking exists because poverty exists" (Cartagena, 2020).

In a *Tampa Bay Times* op-ed, a law school student who was also a foster and adoptive parent noted a similar "ripple effect" in the child welfare system. Along with a retired juvenile judge and an adolescent psychologist, the law student argued in favor of a pardon system for those who grew up in child welfare systems and were charged with crimes committed as a result of childhood trauma. The authors of the op-ed offered a comparison between their proposal and the affirmative defense mechanism made available in some states to trafficking victims accused of crimes (Sullivan et al., 2021). Psychologists have increasingly developed and participated in cross-disciplinary antitrafficking projects with law enforcement, the courts system, and academics, for example, but this role might be excluded from news coverage when it occurs beyond the journalist's view.

Academics sometimes tried to shift the news frame from one of sex trafficking exclusively to commercial sex and the possibility of decriminalization. An *Atlanta Journal-Constitution* columnist, in a story about Patriots owner

Kraft's arrest in a trafficking sting, cited a professor who "suggested we strip away our assumptions that sex is always attached to romantic relationships" (Staples, 2019). In a story after the Atlanta spa shootings, academics were sources for journalists on the history and impact of Asian American stereotypes, as well as the presence of Asian American women among low-wage service workers, a vulnerability "that can make Asian women, particularly immigrants, at risk of being forced into the sex trade by traffickers" (Contrera et al., 2021, p. A1).

Survivors

In earlier studies of news coverage of sex trafficking, survivors have been among the least represented sources (Johnston et al., 2014, 2015), and among survivors with direct experience as news subjects, some have described the harms inflicted by the resulting coverage (Sanders, 2018). Increasingly, survivor-led coalitions (i.e., National Survivor Network) have advocated for a trauma-informed approach to antitrafficking and, relatedly, more control over how their stories are told and by whom.

In this study, survivors appeared throughout the coverage—at about the same rate as academics and more often than psychologists, reflective of increased survivor leadership, networked activism, and of emergent spaces for storytelling. One survivor of online sexual abuse told *The Boston Globe* that survivors behind the #MeToo movement inspired her to speak publicly about her experience. "It was just so powerful to see the unity among women, the sense of being seen," she said. "The movement takes the stigma off of trauma." Survivors appeared as plaintiffs in high-profile cases (Matchan, 2020, p. R18), and in some instances, were celebrities themselves (Brown & Exposito, 2021).

Importantly, survivors as news sources sponsored thematic frames that delivered on nearly all of the APA's task force recommendations: They addressed common misconceptions and myths about trafficking victims; emphasized the fact that human trafficking occurs in all types of communities; and educated the public about common signs of trafficking, often disclosing the conditions that made them vulnerable to traffickers, such as deep insecurities, substance use disorders, and homelessness. In some news coverage, survivors chronicled the impact of their experiences and the need for ongoing care. "It's not like I just woke up and everything was better," one survivor told a reporter. "I still struggle with this" (Matchan, 2020, p. R18).

Additional sources included representatives of antitrafficking organizations, who appeared as sources about as often as academics and survivors. A category of "other" sources was less frequent and wide ranging, including family members of trafficking victims, who offered support for their loved ones (Weiser & Marcus, 2021), a house seller whose property became a shelter for trafficking victims (Pitts, 2019), and a customer of one of the Asian spas targeted in the 2021 mass shooting (Contrera et al., 2021), for example.

FRAME SPONSORSHIP REMAINS AN IMPORTANT ROLE FOR PSYCHOLOGISTS

U.S. news coverage of human trafficking increased exponentially following the 2000 passage of the Trafficking Victims Protection Act, which itself imposed and exported a criminal justice framework to fight trafficking (Baker, 2015; Bonilla & Mo, 2019; Gulati, 2011). If, as the primacy effect suggests, the initial framing of an issue is more important than subsequent coverage, psychologists likely missed the opportunity to shape public discourse and policy related to trafficking—the APA's task force issued their appeal 14 years later. But the news cycle goes on. While it is true that journalists must look for new stories to report, they must also find new angles with which to report about established issues. If journalists can resist the "gravitational pull" of their earliest routines (Sobel et al., 2019, p. 55), research suggests there are many themes and frames unexplored or underexplored. A 2018 special issue of the *Anti-Trafficking Review*, for example, focused on "life after trafficking," demonstrating in a series of research articles "the challenges and successes after trafficking that largely have unfolded off stage," out of the media spotlight (Brennan & Plambech, 2018, p. 1). Because news frames influence the ways that audiences think about an issue, and news sources are part of frame building, mental health professionals knowledgeable about reintegration processes could become vital frame sponsors for policies that provide comprehensive support for survivors after trafficking. Survivor experts would likewise be powerful frame sponsors in this regard.

Although mental health professionals were not the most-cited sources in this study of news coverage about human trafficking (despite the many opportunities presented by then-current events), "public awareness and understanding of the crime of human trafficking and the dynamics of coercion and trauma" *did* find their way into the news via other sources (APA, 2014, p. 55). Judges, lawyers, academics, law enforcement, journalists, and analysts were capable sources for communicating this essential information, particularly in print and online news—perhaps these groups have taken advantage of increasing opportunities to become educated on the fundamentals of human trafficking. "Official" sources such as lawyers, judges, and law enforcement are not likely to be displaced as sources for news coverage of human trafficking. They populate reporters' beat areas, making them familiar and, likely, accessible to journalists working on frequent, short deadlines. Because trafficking is a crime, journalists could possibly learn about the issue through law enforcement sources and, ultimately, frame their stories accordingly. If law enforcement focuses on sex trafficking, so will journalists. It should be noted, however, that reporters and their routine practices factor into a hierarchy of influences on news reporting; media ownership structures also can influence what stories are reported and how (Shoemaker & Reese, 2014).

Of course, there are many reasons why a psychologist (or survivor) might have reservations about acting as an expert news source. "When a psychologist gets a call from a reporter, the first response is often reluctance or even a fear to respond," remarked one practitioner from personal experience. "Most psychologists feel like they're approaching quicksand because the reporter's motives and reputation for fairness and accuracy are usually unknown" (McGarrah, 2009, p. 173). Avoiding ethical pitfalls requires clarifying details with a journalist about the reporting and editing processes—for example, will the source be shown their quotes before publication? When there are inaccuracies, how to request corrections? Journalists are trained to "humanize" their stories and so often ask psychologists to provide access to a survivor who can talk about their experiences. Psychologists, in turn, are concerned with confidentiality and harm to the survivor. Psychologist sources' willingness to explain their concerns with the reporting process could help to shake journalists out of their routines and improve coverage of trafficking by encouraging them to think of other ways to report about the issue.

Mental health professionals are among the best-situated groups to offer varied and more-nuanced ways of thinking about the issue of human trafficking. The APA's 2014 report of the Task Force on Trafficking of Women and Girls lists "connective tissue" that remains valuable for media engagement and audience understanding:

> As a discipline that explores the depth and breadth of human behavior, psychology is well positioned to study the multiple intrapsychic, developmental, interpersonal, relational, social, cultural, religious, educational, institutional, societal, and economic issues that intersect to contribute to the phenomenon of trafficking. (p. 53)

It is not always possible to know how certain psychologists come to the attention of journalists, although given the deadline-driven, resource-deprived nature of news, proximity and prominence are the likeliest explanations. Since mental health professionals appeared in coverage primarily as sources, rather than as authors of news, boosting their social media presence, promoting new research, and emphasizing specializations are recommended. A simple search of the psychologists quoted in these stories showed their widespread use of Twitter and LinkedIn. Journalists rarely have time or resources to attend scholarly conferences (only one story in this sample emerged from such an event), but these are ideal settings for media training by industry professionals. Trafficking is a public health issue; journalists (and, in turn, their audiences) would benefit from mental health professionals' perspectives on how and why this is. The APA's (2020) "how to work with media" guidelines offer helpful strategies for mental health professionals wanting to leverage their important roles as educators, advocates, researchers—and potential frame sponsors—on the urgent issue of human trafficking.

REFERENCES

Albright, E., & D'Adamo, K. (2017). The media and human trafficking: A discussion critique of the dominant narrative. In M. Chisholm-Straker & H. Stoklosa (Eds.), *Human trafficking is a public health issue: A paradigm expansion in the United States* (pp. 363–378). Springer. https://doi.org/10.1007/978-3-319-47824-1_21

American Psychological Association. (2014). *Report of the Task Force on Trafficking of Women and Girls.* https://www.apa.org/pi/women/programs/trafficking/report.pdf

American Psychological Association. (2020). *How to work with the media.* https://www.apa.org/pubs/authors/working-with-media

Arroyo, R. (Host). (2019, February 15). *Trump declares national emergency at border.* Fox News. https://www.proquest.com/other-sources/trump-declares-national-emergency-at-border-dems/docview/2182333944/se-2?accountid=14244

Austin, R., & Farrell, J. (2017). *Human trafficking and the media in the United States.* Oxford Research Encyclopedias.

Baker, C. (2015). An examination of some central debates on sex trafficking in research and public policy in the United States. *Journal of Human Trafficking, 1*(3), 191–208. https://doi.org/10.1080/23322705.2015.1023672

Bernstein, D. M., Atance, C., Meltzoff, A. N., & Loftus, G. R. (2007). Hindsight bias and developing theories of mind. *Child Development, 78*(4), 1374–1394. https://doi.org/10.1111/j.1467-8624.2007.01071.x

Bonilla, T., & Mo, C. H. (2019). The evolution of human trafficking messaging in the United States and its effect on public opinion. *Journal of Public Policy, 39*(2), 201–234. https://doi.org/10.1017/S0143814X18000107

Brasch, B., & Dixon, K. (2019, February 16). Abuse case: Child psychologist admits molesting girl. *The Atlanta Journal-Constitution*, B1.

Bream, S. (Anchor & Host). (2021, March 26). *Sen. Marsha Blackburn (R-TN) is being interviewed about border disorder.* Fox News@Night. https://www.proquest.com/docview/2506115572?accountid=14244

Brennan, D., & Plambech, S. (2018). Editorial—Moving forward: Life after trafficking. *Anti-Trafficking Review, 10*(10), 1–12.

Brodsky, R. (2020, December 3). DA: Trafficker a "predator." *Newsday*, 17.

Broom, T. W., Chavez, R. S., & Wagner, D. D. (2021). Becoming the King in the North: Identification with fictional characters is associated with greater self-other neural overlap. *Social Cognitive and Affective Neuroscience, 16*(6), 541–551. https://doi.org/10.1093/scan/nsab021

Brown, A., & Exposito, S. (2021, November 7). Onstage persona or dark reality? Marilyn Manson's accusers detail alleged abuse enabled by his artistic reputation. *Los Angeles Times*, A1.

Bryant, J., & Oliver, M. B. (Eds.). (2009). *Media effects: Advances in theory and research* (3rd ed.). Routledge. https://doi.org/10.4324/9780203877111

Carlson, T. (Host). (2020, January 6). *Lara Logan talks about the Mexico drug cartels*. Fox News. https://www.proquest.com/other-sources/american-dystopia-san-francisco-decline-more-u-s/docview/2334091466/se-2?accountid=14244

Carlyle, K. E., Orr, C., Savage, M. W., & Babin, E. A. (2014). News coverage of intimate partner violence: Impact on prosocial responses. *Media Psychology, 17*(4), 451–471. https://doi.org/10.1080/15213269.2014.931812

Carlyle, K. E., Slater, M. D., & Chakroff, J. L. (2008). Newspaper coverage of intimate partner violence: Skewing representations of risk. *Journal of Communication, 58*(1), 168–186. https://doi.org/10.1111/j.1460-2466.2007.00379.x

Cartagena, M. (2020, September 21). The harsh cycle of poverty for Chicago's Latina women. *La Raza*. https://laraza.com/2020/09/21/the-harsh-cycle-of-poverty-for-chicagos-latina-women/

Caruana, R., Crane, A., Gold, S., & LeBaron, G. (2021). Modern slavery in business: The sad and sorry state of a non-field. *Business & Society, 60*(2), 251–287. https://doi.org/10.1177/0007650320930417

Chong, D., & Druckman, J. N. (2007). Framing theory. *Annual Review of Political Science, 10*(1), 103–126. https://doi.org/10.1146/annurev.polisci.10.072805.103054

Cohen, J. (2006). Audience identification with media characters. In J. Bryant & P. Voderer (Eds.), *Psychology of entertainment* (pp. 183–198). Lawrence Erlbaum.

Contrera, J. (2021, June 8). State of Ohio vs. a sex-trafficked teenager. *The Washington Post*, A1.

Contrera, J., Jan, T., & MacMillan, D. (2021, March 20). Killings start discussions on sex work, exploitation. *The Washington Post*, A1.

Dastagir, A. E. (2020, July 14). Why the Ghislaine Maxwell case is so shocking to so many. *USA Today*. https://www.usatoday.com/story/news/nation/2020/07/14/ghislaine-maxwell-reminder-sex-abuse-transcends-gender-class/5422843002/

Del Valle, L. (2021, November 29). *Prosecution links Ghislaine Maxwell to Jeffrey Epstein while defense says she is being blamed for his actions*. CNN. https://www.cnn.com/2021/11/29/us/ghislaine-maxwell-trial-starts/index.html

Dill, K. E. (Ed.). (2013). *The Oxford handbook of media psychology*. Oxford University Press.

Dillon, N. (2020, September 6). The queasy cult that likes Trump crawls from shadows of the internet spouting cannibalism and pedophilia. *New York Daily News*, CS4.

Dreier, H. (2020, March 5). Bill would end practice of using migrant children's therapy notes against them. *The Washington Post*, A22. https://www.proquest.com/newspapers/bill-would-end-practice-using-migrant-childrens/docview/2370796613/se-2?accountid=14244

Entman, R. M. (1993). Framing: Toward clarification of a fractured paradigm. *Journal of Communication, 43*(4), 51–58. https://doi.org/10.1111/j.1460-2466.1993.tb01304.x

Fisher, M. (2020, April 9). The infectious danger of conspiracy theories. *The New York Times*, A10.

Gamboah, S., Shabad, R., & Gregorian, D. (2021, March 26). *Democrats, Republicans hold dueling border trips.* MSNBC. https://www.nbcnews.com/politics/congress/democrats-republicans-stage-dueling-trips-u-s-mexico-border-n1262144

Gamson, W., & Modigliani, A. (1989). Media discourse and public opinion on nuclear power: A constructionist approach. *American Journal of Sociology, 95*(1), 1–37. https://doi.org/10.1086/229213

Garelick, R. (2021, December 17). Ghislaine Maxwell always looked impeccable. That was the point. *The New York Times.* https://www.nytimes.com/2021/12/17/style/ghislaine-maxwell-fashion-trial.html

Green, M. (2004). Transportation into narrative worlds: The role of prior knowledge and perceived realism. *Discourse Processes, 38*(2), 247–266. https://doi.org/10.1207/s15326950dp3802_5

Greenbaum, V. J., Titchen, K., Walker-Descartes, I., Feifer, A., Rood, C. J., & Fong, H. F. (2018). Multi-level prevention of human trafficking: The role of health care professionals. *Preventive Medicine, 114,* 164–167. https://doi.org/10.1016/j.ypmed.2018.07.006

Gubitz, S. R., Klar, S., Robison, J., & Druckman, J. N. (2018). Political dynamics of framing. In T. N. Ridout (Ed.), *New directions in media and politics* (pp. 29–53). Routledge. https://doi.org/10.4324/9780203713020-3

Gulati, G. J. (2011). News frames and story triggers in the media's coverage of human trafficking. *Human Rights Review, 12*(3), 363–379. https://doi.org/10.1007/s12142-010-0184-5

Hertog, J. K., & McLeod, D. M. (2001). A multiperspectival approach to framing analysis: A field guide. In S. D. Reese, O. H. Gandy, Jr., & A. E. Grant (Eds.), *Framing public life: Perspectives on media and our understanding of the social world* (pp. 141–162). Routledge.

Hetey, R. C., & Eberhardt, J. L. (2014). Racial disparities in incarceration increase acceptance of punitive policies. *Psychological Science, 25*(10), 1949–1954. https://doi.org/10.1177/0956797614540307

Iyengar, S. (1991). *Is anyone responsible? How television frames political issues.* University of Chicago Press. https://doi.org/10.7208/chicago/9780226388533.001.0001

Johnston, A., Friedman, B., & Shafer, A. (2014). Framing the problem of sex trafficking: Whose problem? What remedy? *Feminist Media Studies, 14*(3), 419–436. https://doi.org/10.1080/14680777.2012.740492

Johnston, A., Friedman, B., & Sobel, M. (2015). Framing an emerging issue: How U.S. print and broadcast news media covered human trafficking, 2008–2012. *Journal of Human Trafficking, 1*(3), 235–254. https://doi.org/10.1080/23322705.2014.993876

Kelly, A. (2018, January 23). Thai seafood: Are the prawns on your plate still fished by slaves? *The Guardian.* https://www.theguardian.com/global-development/2018/jan/23/thai-seafood-industry-report-trafficking-rights-abuses

Kline, J. (2017). C. G. Jung and Norman Cohn explain Pizzagate: The archetypal dimension of a conspiracy theory. *Psychological Perspectives, 60*(2), 186–195. https://doi.org/10.1080/00332925.2017.1314699

Lecheler, S., & de Vreese, C. H. (2019). *News framing effects*. Routledge.

Liedke, J., & Gottfried, J. (2022, October 27). *U.S. adults under 30 now trust information from social media almost as much as from national news outlets*. Pew Research Center. https://www.pewresearch.org/fact-tank/2022/10/27/u-s-adults-under-30-now-trust-information-from-social-media-almost-as-much-as-from-national-news-outlets/

Marchionni, D. M. (2012). International human trafficking: An agenda-building analysis of the U.S. and British press. *The International Communication Gazette, 74*(2), 145–158. https://doi.org/10.1177/1748048511432600

Matchan, L. (2020, August 23). Speaking out to save others. *The Boston Globe*, R18.

McGarrah, N. A. (2009). Working with the media: Soaring professionally or sinking in quicksand? *Professional Psychology, Research and Practice, 40*(2), 172–180. https://doi.org/10.1037/a0015520

Mental Health America. (2020, June 24). *Mental Health America announces winners of 2020 awards*. https://www.mhanational.org/mental-health-america-announces-winners-2020-awards

Mitchell, T. S., & Aviles, G. (2021, October 12). *Advocates say an R. Kelly verdict "would not have happened" without campaigns for justice led by Black women*. Insider. https://www.insider.com/r-kelly-verdict-would-not-have-happened-without-black-women-2021-10

Moyer-Gusé, E. (2008). Toward a theory of entertainment persuasion: Explaining the persuasive effects of entertainment-education messages. *Communication Theory, 18*(3), 407–425. https://doi.org/10.1111/j.1468-2885.2008.00328.x

Murdock, B. B., Jr. (1962). The serial effect of free recall. *Journal of Experimental Psychology, 64*(5), 482–488. https://doi.org/10.1037/h0045106

O'Brien, R. D. (2021, December 20). What is hindsight bias and why does it matter in the Maxwell trial? *The New York Times*. https://www.nytimes.com/live/2021/12/20/nyregion/ghislaine-maxwell-trial

Pitts, J. M. (2019, July 21). Pioneering a path out of "the life." *Baltimore Sun*, A1.

Polaris. (2020, July 20). *Polaris statement on Wayfair sex trafficking claims*. https://polarisproject.org/press-releases/polaris-statement-on-wayfair-sex-trafficking-claims/

Posner, S. (2020, September 20). The evangelicals battling QAnon. *The New York Times*, SR8.

Proclamation No. 8621, National Slavery and Human Trafficking Prevention Month, 3 C.F.R. (December 22, 2010).

Reese, S. D. (2001). Prologue—Framing public life: A bridging model for media research. In S. D. Reese, O. H. Gandy, Jr., & A. E. Grant (Eds.), *Framing public life: Perspectives on media and our understanding of the social world* (pp. 7–31). Routledge. https://doi.org/10.4324/9781410605689-7

Romero, S., & Kulish, N. (2019, July 12). Sex offender in 2 states, but not in New Mexico. *The New York Times*, A1.

Roose, K. (2020, August 13). How conspiracists hijack anti-trafficking efforts. *The New York Times*, B1.

Sanders, S. (2018). What will be headlines when we die? Survivors as news stories and news sources. *Journal of Human Trafficking, 4*(1), 86–88. https://doi.org/10.1080/23322705.2018.1423449

Sanford, R., Martínez, D. E., & Weitzer, R. (2016). Framing human trafficking: A content analysis of recent U.S. newspaper articles. *Journal of Human Trafficking, 2*(2), 139–155. https://doi.org/10.1080/23322705.2015.1107341

Shafer, A., & Looney, B. (2018). Victim profiles: Direct and indirect effects of anecdotes and responsibility attribution on support for sex trafficking victims. *Journal of Human Trafficking, 4*(1), 21–34. https://doi.org/10.1080/23322705.2018.1423444

Shoemaker, P. J., & Reese, S. D. (2014). *Mediating the message in the 21st century: A media sociology perspective*. Routledge.

Silver, K. E., Karakurt, G., & Boysen, S. T. (2015). Predicting prosocial behavior toward sex-trafficked persons: The roles of empathy, belief in a just world, and attitudes toward prostitution. *Journal of Aggression, Maltreatment & Trauma, 24*(8), 932–954. https://doi.org/10.1080/10926771.2015.1070231

Sobel, M., Friedman, B., & Johnston, A. (2019). Sex trafficking as a news story: Evolving structure and reporting strategies. *Journal of Human Trafficking, 5*(1), 43–59. https://doi.org/10.1080/23322705.2017.1401426

Society for Media Psychology and Technology. (2013). *About us*. https://www.apadivisions.org/division-46/about

Spring, M. (2020, July 15). *Wayfair: The false conspiracy about a furniture firm and child trafficking*. BBC News. https://www.bbc.com/news/world-53416247

Staples, G. B. (2019, March 7). Why do rich men pay for sex when they can get it free? *The Atlanta Journal-Constitution*. https://www.ajc.com/lifestyles/why-rich-men-pay-for-sex-when-they-can-get-free/WEeX5HTpsa1WjGEXogeunN/

Stoklosa, H., & Baldwin, S. B. (2017). Health professional education on trafficking: The facts matter. *The Lancet, 390*(10103), 1641–1642. https://doi.org/10.1016/S0140-6736(17)32453-4

Sullivan, I., Solazzo, A., & Hawkins, B. P. (2021, January 31). It is foster kids who really deserve "pardoning." *Tampa Bay Times*. https://www.tampabay.com/opinion/2021/01/29/it-is-foster-kids-who-really-deserve-pardoning-column/

Swygart, J. (2019, October 9). Alleged rapist ruled incompetent to stand trial. *The Lima News*. https://www.proquest.com/newspapers/alleged-rapist-ruled-incompetent-stand-trial/docview/2303202440/se-2?accountid=14244

Tewksbury, D., & Scheufele, D. A. (2009). News framing theory and research. In J. Bryant & M. B. Oliver (Eds.), *Media effects: Advances in theory and research* (3rd ed., pp. 17–33). Routledge.

Trepany, C. (2021, September 7). R. Kelly's sex-trafficking trial: Everything that happened, up to the guilty verdict. *USA Today*. https://www.proquest.com/newspapers/r-kellys-sex-trafficking-trial-everything-that/docview/2569565162/se-2?accountid=14244

Van Gorp, B. (2007). The constructionist approach to framing: Bringing culture back in. *Journal of Communication, 57*(1), 60–78.

Vaughn, J. (2021, October 7). Zephi Trevino's lawyers are ready to take her case to the Supreme Court. *Dallas Observer*. https://www.dallasobserver.com/news/fight-for-zephi-trevino-heads-to-texas-supreme-court-12550548

Vielmetti, B. (2021, Oct. 5). Milwaukee pimp avoids life sentence, but will be 88 when he's released. *Marshfield News Herald*, A3.

WashPostPR. (2021, June 10). The Washington Post's Hannah Dreier awarded 2021 Livingston Award for national reporting. *The Washington Post.* https://www.washingtonpost.com/pr/2021/06/10/washington-posts-hannah-dreier-awarded-2021-livingston-award-national-reporting/

Weiser, B., & Marcus, E. (2021, March 1). She was seen as a victim in the Sarah Lawrence cult case. Now she's charged. *The New York Times.* https://www.nytimes.com/2021/03/01/nyregion/lawrence-ray-sarah-lawrence-cult.html

Weitzer, R. (2018). Resistance to sex work stigma. *Sexualities, 21*(5–6), 717–729. https://doi.org/10.1177/1363460716684509

Wichgers, L., Jacobs, L., & van Spanje, J. (2021). The battle of frame building: The reciprocal relationship between journalists and frame sponsors. *The International Journal of Press/Politics, 26*(3), 674–698. https://doi.org/10.1177/1940161220942760

Wong, T. K., De Roche, G., & Venzor, J. R. (2021, March 25). The migrant "surge" at the U.S. border is actually a predictable pattern. *The Washington Post.* https://www.washingtonpost.com/politics/2021/03/23/theres-no-migrant-surge-us-southern-border-heres-data/

Yates, R. (2019, March 16). Serial rapist is a predator, judge rules, calling it a "no brainer." *Morning Call*, A6.

6 SOCIAL PSYCHOLOGY OF HUMAN TRAFFICKING

LAURA DRYJANSKA

This chapter considers the insight that social psychology brings to human trafficking research and practice. It discusses the relevance of the social self-concept, cognitive processes, and biases when perceiving persons, particularly human trafficking survivors and perpetrators. The chapter also explains how stereotypes, prejudice, and discrimination can be especially devastating to human trafficking survivors, keeping them in bondage and providing justifications for inhumane treatment and refusal of dignity. It is worth noting some other relevant domains of social psychology would be helpful to explore in relation to human trafficking, for example, helping behavior and altruism.

Social psychology has been defined as "a branch of psychology dedicated to the study of how people think about, influence, and relate to each other" (Sutton & Douglas, 2020, p. 3) or, in other words, "the scientific study of the feelings, thoughts, and behaviors of individuals in social situations" (Gilovich et al., 2019, p. 5). These definitions certainly delineate a very broad field, likely to touch on multiple aspects of individual lives. The core areas of interest to social psychologists include the social dimension of the self-concept, social cognition (or how people perceive and think about others

https://doi.org/10.1037/0000379-007
Psychological Perspectives on Human Trafficking: Theory, Research, Prevention, and Intervention, L. Dryjanska, E. K. Hopper, and H. Stoklosa (Editors)

and situations), social attribution (or how people explain their own and others' behavior), attitudes, emotions, rationalization, communication, and persuasion, social influence, stereotypes, prejudice, and discrimination, group behavior, intergroup relations, as well as such topics as close relationships and interpersonal attraction, aggressive behavior, and altruism and cooperation. Some of the constructs mentioned, such as attitudes, emotions, and rationalization, may not seem intrinsically social. However, social psychologists consider the relevance of the context and interpersonal relations for developing and expressing attitudes and emotions. Cognitive processes such as rationalization are often based on social learning and other phenomena that occur as a result of interaction with other people and groups. Stereotypes, prejudice, and discrimination—that constitute a major field of study for social psychologists—also play a role in increasing vulnerability to trafficking. Certainly, additional areas of social psychology could be fruitful to explore in future work, which are not covered in the current chapter.

In the light of the fact that social psychology explores such numerous areas relevant to the lives of human beings in general, it seems to be a worthwhile effort to explore how social psychological findings can apply in situations of human trafficking. It is important to stress that what is presented in the chapter are the author's thoughts about how different concepts and areas of research from social psychology might be applied to better understand the phenomena. However, there is, as yet, little empirical work examining these processes with survivors or with perpetrators of trafficking. This field of psychology may offer insight into questions that arise when working with the survivors, such as why did they not leave their trafficker? How was the trafficker able to manipulate and persuade them? What is the impact of stereotypes, racism, and discrimination in trafficking situations? Why do bystanders not take action when witnessing a possible trafficking situation?

This chapter addresses some of these questions, uncovering possible social psychological dynamics present in human trafficking, in light of well-established research findings from this field of psychology. The organizational framework consists of the discussion of social psychological processes that might be involved in public perceptions of traffickers or of trafficking survivors; processes that might be involved with survivors in creating vulnerability, finding ways to cope, freeing themselves and rebuilding lives; as well as processes that might be involved explaining the behavior of traffickers. Further areas could be explored, for example, the bystander question, especially in the light of more research becoming available in this intersection of social psychology and human trafficking studies.

It seems worthwhile to note that theories in social psychology apply to individuals in general, including human trafficking survivors. In other words, there is no distinct, established field of social psychology of human trafficking. Rather, while recognizing and emphasizing cultural differences, social psychology typically assumes some "universals" of human nature. For example, all cultures have norms and standards of behavior, although such norms differ and are expressed in diverse ways across cultures.

SELF-CONCEPT OF INDIVIDUALS WHO HAVE EXPERIENCED HUMAN TRAFFICKING

Self-concept is an extensive area of research in social psychology. This section explores several approaches that may help us better understand its relevance in case of human trafficking.

How accurate is our self-knowledge? Given that majority of persons who have experienced human trafficking do not self-identify as such (Donahue et al., 2019), it may be beneficial to consider the accuracy of their beliefs about themselves. According to social psychologists, the complete set of such beliefs that make up one's self-concept is organized in self-schemas, cognitive structures that derive from past experiences and help people process self-relevant information, guiding how they believe they should feel, think, and act in specific situations (Markus, 1977). Typically, the sense of self originates from family and other socialization agents, situation, and culture. Psychological research suggests that individuals who have experienced human trafficking are from diverse backgrounds, and it is not uncommon that they come from dysfunctional families and have been socialized to violence and abuse since their childhood (Chu & Billings, 2020; Zimmerman et al., 2011). Neglect or abuse tend to impact survivors' beliefs about others' reactions to and appraisals of them, which are based on the social psychological premise that people come to know themselves by imagining what others think of them. Unsurprisingly, this may often result in low self-esteem, defined as the subjective sense of the self as intrinsically negative (Rosenberg et al., 1968). This is not to imply that all trafficking survivors necessarily have a low self-esteem; in fact, a study with victims in Nigeria has found that self-esteem level was a factor that varied and was likely to correlate with and determine posttraumatic stress disorder (Ezeakor & Okpala, 2020). This correlation with self-esteem may have important implications for practice in considering survivors' self-concept, their evaluation of self-worth, and the posttraumatic impact of complex traumatic experiences leading to and present during trafficking, while keeping in mind that generalizations do not apply to all.

Individuals who have experienced human trafficking are also likely perceive significant discrepancies between their actual self (how they see themselves in a given moment), ideal self (how they would like to see themselves), and ought self (how they think they ought to be, for example based on ideals of duty and responsibility to the trafficker). These three aspects of self-concept are at the heart of the self-discrepancy theory (Higgins, 1987), which focuses on how people perceive the discrepancies between their actual self, ideal self, and ought self and examines emotional responses to these discrepancies, such as frustration and annoyance. In terms of self-concept, which has been one of the core interests of social psychology, some trafficking survivors could experience a distorted view of self. Motivated to reduce the discrepancies, people often attempt to match their behavior with an ideal or ought self, thereby engaging in self-regulation (Higgins, 1987). At any stage of being trafficked, this can result in negative emotions and a high cognitive load, bearing in mind that each situation is unique and it is important to avoid generalizations. Just as an example, a possible scenario could be as follows: during grooming, the trafficker may prompt their victim's ideal self by promising prosperity (in case of labor trafficking) or a happy marriage (in case of sex trafficking). Motivated to reach the ideal self, these particular cases defined as a successful worker or a fulfilled wife and mother, the victim agrees to the trafficker's proposed course of action to achieve that status and reconcile their actual self with the ideal self. While being trafficked, a new expectation of an ought self enters the person's life, for example with the concept of meeting a daily quota. In labor trafficking, it may mean harvesting fruit on a farm for extremely long hours in order to gather a specific weight by the end of the day. In sex trafficking in street-based commercial sex, it may mean that a person is expected to be on the street and have sex with clients until they pay the total of $1,000 (or another amount set by the trafficker) per night, no matter how long that takes. In these examples, the ought self could thus be constructed by the trafficker and other exploited individuals who engage in self-regulation until they meet the daily quota. Failure to comply might involve physical punishment, as well as social psychological consequences related to the negative emotions of frustration and anxiety. However, the expectation of engaging in a specific self-presentation desired by the trafficker, especially in the case of exploitation in commercial sex, likely requires a lot of energy and resources. Self-monitoring or altering behavior to fit the specific demands of interaction with clients possibly means that a person cannot afford to show how they truly feel. It is important to stress that the aim of providing this example is not to create a picture of a person who is highly malleable and controllable, thinking what they are told to think. On the contrary, there is no unique scenario that would apply to persons who have been trafficked and their self-concept. The dynamics related to the actual, ideal, and ought self are very complex and depend on multiple factors. Some individuals who have been trafficked might buy into the trafficker's ought self and measure themselves against it, while others can subvert it. In addition, another scenario could include the "ought" self from a person's childhood, or the one rooter in their education or their own values coming into play and overriding what the trafficker is telling them.

Many survivors of trafficking speak of the experience of "dying on the inside" while having to smile and pretend that they enjoy what they are forced to do. In social psychology, this could be considered as an extreme example of ego depletion (Hagger et al., 2010), based on the notion that self-control and willpower to self-monitor are a finite resource that can be used up. This process can be taxing and impact one's judgment, for example, not allowing the victim of trafficking to have enough cognitive resources to even consider asking for help. The struggle with achieving a more accurate self-concept typically continues for years following the trafficking experience (Jowett et al., 2021; Lockyer & Koenig, 2020). While many persons self-handicap from time to time (Zuckerman & Tsai, 2005), for trafficking survivors to self-handicap at the courtroom or during a job interview can have severe consequences for their overall well-being. Social psychological consequences of trafficking for the self-concept are typically long-lasting, and survivors require years of individual therapy as well as a supportive community to help them overcome the distorted view of self (Marburger & Pickover, 2020).

EXPLAINING BEHAVIOR BY SOCIAL ATTRIBUTION

One of the aims of social psychology is to explain human behavior, especially when it seems irrational. Among the well-established theories, the theory of attribution stands out as a set of concepts that strive to explain how people assign causes to events and to understand the effects of such causal assessments.

In relation to human trafficking, it is helpful to understand the process of causal attribution when considering various explanations or justifications that bystanders offer when pondering the phenomenon. The common question is: "Why did they get involved in it in the first place?" Typically, the perception of how much control another person had over their actions is a very important factor in how they are being judged. If someone becomes a trafficking victim due to concrete external or situational circumstances, such as being kidnapped and physically forced into conditions of exploitation, the common tendency might be to judge them in a more positive way than victims who were coerced through more subtle methods (Cunningham & Cromer, 2016; Menaker & Franklin, 2015; Shin et al., 2022). This may have profound consequences for those who were (often erroneously) perceived to exercise a higher degree of control over their situation. The bystander can assume that a person had a choice, for example, because they knew the trafficker and engaged in risky behaviors such as drug and alcohol use, and, as a consequence, the bystander may choose not to call for help. In terms of law enforcement responses, trafficked persons might not receive help due to erroneous or biased perceptions. Such perceptions can also have negative consequences, especially when they are held by a therapist, service provider, jury member, or a prosecutor (Farrell et al., 2014).

Fundamental Attribution Error

Studies of social attribution reveal several common errors and biases, demonstrating that people often reason based on false premises. One of the most common such biases is the fundamental attribution error (Ross, 1977) or the failure to recognize the impact of situational influences on behavior while overemphasizing the importance of dispositions (personal character-istics). As discussed earlier, this may result in less compassion and under-standing for the trafficking victims. One of the causes of the fundamental attribution error considered by social psychologists has been the just world theory or the belief that people receive what they deserve in life (Lerner & Simmons, 1966). Silver et al. (2015) explained the theory by highlighting its main premise:

> People need and want to believe the world is a safe and fair place where everyone gets what they deserve. It is comforting to trust that people in an underprivileged state earned their circumstances, whereas it is unsettling to believe disadvantaged people are fortuitous victims of some social processes over which they have little personal control. (p. 935)

Some of reasons why the fundamental attribution error occurs are related to the perception of safety and control over one's circumstances, more common in cultures that value independence and autonomy (San Martin et al., 2019). Research on perception of victims of rape (Abrams et al., 2003) and domestic abuse (Summers & Feldman, 1984) showed that it seems common to derogate the victim or point out some likely flaws in their character or previous trans-gressions. These findings also apply in case of sex trafficking victims, as some studies demonstrated the impact of belief in a just world on structural attributions toward human trafficking (Digidiki et al., 2016) and prosocial behavior toward sex-trafficked persons (Silver et al., 2015). Digidiki and colleagues (2016) found that in Greece, belief in a just world theory was a significant predictor of attitudes toward the victim exclusively, demonstrating that the greater the perception of the world as a just place where everyone gets what one deserves, the greater the negative attitudes towards the victim. In a study with participants from the United States (Silver et al., 2015), just world belief, beliefs about prostitutes, and family values relating to commercial sex had direct effects on empathic concern; in turn, empathic concern had a direct effect on proactive behavior toward individuals who experienced human trafficking.

Actor–Observer Bias

Fundamental attribution error is just one example of the negative impact of inaccurate perceptions examined by social psychologists. What happens when we consider causes of our own behavior, rather than someone else's? In this case, social psychologists have identified another attribution error known as the actor–observer bias (S. R. Wilson et al., 1997) or the tendency to attribute one's own behavior to the situation and for observers to explain it in terms of personality traits. In other words, actors are more likely to see their own behavior as a result of circumstances, while external observers tend to focus on actor's dispositions. This phenomenon may be responsible for yet more significant discrepancies between how human trafficking survivors justify their own behavior compared with the law enforcement officials, for example. A significant portion of training for law enforcement or other curricula concentrates on perspective-taking techniques that allow the participants to see the world through the trafficking victim's eyes (Farboudi-Jahromi et al., 2022; Litam, 2019).

A person may believe that they were exploited in commercial sex or labor in slaverylike conditions because they were not good or smart enough to do anything else. If they have a particular attributional style, they may be prone to think that such condition is stable and internal, unlikely to change, and that could result in self-handicapping and reluctance to make an effort to leave "the life." The attributional style (or explanation of social situations) can be considered in the light of the accumulating evidence showing biased attributional processing in traumatized individuals (Seah & Berle, 2022). This may be related to depression, which is known to have an attributional style in which negative events in life are attributed to internal, global, and stable causes (Cole et al., 2008). In fact, trauma-focused cognitive behavior therapy challenges such overly pessimistic, self-defeating ways to explain events (Beck, 1993) and has been highly recommended for persons who experienced human trafficking (Hemmings et al., 2016). While there is no one-size-fits-all reply to why traffickers choose to exploit others, it is interesting to consider their motivations in the light of social attribution.

Qualitative research conducted by Brennan (2014) with individuals who experienced labor trafficking included some considerations of the justification that their exploiters employed. Most traffickers of migrants considered the slaverylike labor as a "normal" work, very similar to what a person would experience as "employed" in their home country. For example, exploitation in domestic servitude was perpetuated by a person of the same nationality as the migrant, justifying the inhumane conditions as still being "better" than in their country of origin (Brennan, 2014). Sometimes traffickers rationalize their behavior by emphasizing their similarities to the victim and alleged ability to understand their needs better than individuals in the host country. As Bales (2002) put it when considering the social psychology of human trafficking, "the psychology of a slave is mirrored by that of the slaveholder" (p. 87). In other words, it is essential to focus on the traffickers' mindset and circumstances in order to understand the phenomenon of human trafficking from a social psychological perspective.

However, some traffickers prey on the undocumented status of migrants and justify the exploitation by belittling the victim as someone who has already broken the law. Owens et al. (2014) interviewed alleged traffickers, concluding that they often step into the preexisting chain of exploitation and take advantage of vulnerable migrants due to their immigration status and smuggling debt. Portraying the person who experienced human trafficking as a criminal has also been described by Fukushima (2019) in the ghost case. Chinese American migrants were swindled out of their money and jewelry by a group of Chinese migrants. Social attribution theory is concerned with inferring the causes of events or behaviors. The defense attorneys of the Chinese migrants argued that they were trafficked to facilitate the scam and that the crimes were committed out of necessity, trying to point out that such necessity was the cause of behavior. Through this defense, the migrants would be transformed from "criminals" to "alleged victims of human trafficking" (attempting to change the attribution of blame), yet the criminal charges ultimately trumped the alleged victimization. Thus, by forcing their victims to commit illegal acts, traffickers can use social attribution of constructing the image of an individual as a criminal rather than someone whom they exploited. Furthermore, those who exploit others in labor trafficking can also see themselves as "helping" their victims and emphasize their dire circumstances even prior to being trafficked (Gallo et al., 2020).

The study by Raphael and Myers-Powell (2010), who interviewed 25 former pimps in Chicago, includes some excerpts that shed light on attributions made by traffickers, such as the following:

- "I would look for girls who needed sh—who would do whatever to come out of the messed-up homes and escape from their f—ed-up parents. I pulled these girls. Women who had been abused by some sucker and wanted better treatment and nice things"—the attribution in this quote, especially when referring to "better treatment and nice things" may be interpreted as the trafficker placing himself in a position of a person who provided "an improvement" in already very miserable life conditions of the victims;

- "Any player can tell when a girl has the look of desperation that you know she needs attention or love. It's something you start to have a sixth sense about"—in a similar way to the previous example, the trafficker points out to himself as someone who provides for the specific needs of attention and love, implying that by meeting those needs he is actually ameliorating the situation of the trafficked person;

- "I helped girls who no one else would. I picked up throwaways and runaways and dressed them up and taught them how to survive"—the attribution of a "helping" behavior to self, points out that according to the trafficker, the victims would have had nobody else to "enable" them to survive (p. 5).

It is striking that in terms of social attribution, traffickers frequently justify their actions by considering themselves as being people who "help" women and girls, which might minimize their negative view of self. However, traffickers seem to be keenly aware of the impact of circumstances, such as poverty, drug abuse, and sexual abuse history, when rationalizing their own actions due to the victims' backgrounds (Sidun, 2018).

Overall, social attribution influences how the law enforcement officers, court officials, social service and health care workers (among other sectors), traffickers, and survivors themselves explain the phenomenon of human trafficking. It also provides an interesting insight on various justifications of why human trafficking takes place across the globe. While not all social psychological findings have been considered as replicable in different cultures (for example, there is a pronounced difference between Asians' and Westerners' attention to context), the fundamental attribution error seems widespread in the world, in spite of being more pronounced for Westerners (Krull et al., 1999).

SOCIAL COGNITION BIASES AND STEREOTYPES

The majority of current social psychological studies of perception and stereotyping are rooted in the social cognition or the study of how people perceive, remember, and interpret information about themselves and others. These processes are not free from biases, which constitute a particular interest for social psychologists, and have a profound impact on virtually all social phenomena, including human trafficking.

One of the main premises for understanding social cognition biases is the distinction between automatic versus controlled processing, present in a number of social psychological theories known as dual process theories (Strack & Deutsch, 2015). Automatic processing is much more frequent and requires considerably less effort than controlled processing, or what we habitually consider as rational thinking and decision making. To be efficient, human beings have developed various cognitive shortcuts where much of mental processing takes place outside of one's awareness. This allows for cognitive multitasking: engaging in a more effortful, conscious processing while applying heuristics or rules of thumb that can be used to make less reliable judgments, which nevertheless give an accurate answer in most situations. Heuristics are also much more related to emotions. A social psychologist, Jonathan Haidt (2012), used a metaphor of an elephant (automatic processing) and a rider (controlled processing) to demonstrate the difference between these two types of processing information. He explained that "the mind is divided like a rider on an elephant and the rider's job is to control the elephant. The rider is our conscious reasoning. . . . The elephant is the other 99 percent of mental processes" (p. xv). Such a premise of social psychology, which may seem initially surprising, can provide useful insight into the pressing questions related to human trafficking, for example, a victim not leaving their situation or choosing to go back to the trafficker—to many, when thinking rationally such behavior makes no sense, but once they adopt the position that a large portion of human behavior is not rational, new venues open up to understanding the victim's actions.

Under usual circumstances, using both automatic and controlled processing seems to work quite well for most people, helping them filter a high volume of information, and function in the social world. However, individuals who have suffered from complex trauma, like human trafficking survivors, have likely developed their automatic processing under the conditions of ongoing stress, abuse, and imminent danger. This mechanism is discussed in more detail in Chapter 8, which delineates the indicators of posttraumatic stress disorder and complex trauma often resulting from human trafficking.

Negativity Bias

A common bias that may result in serious consequences on daily functioning of human trafficking survivors is the negativity bias. This bias consists of assigning more importance to negative than to positive information about people. Once negative information has been presented, and this influences the overall impression that is formed, it is difficult to defuse the negative information. This might be a reason why it is challenging for human trafficking survivors to make friends and trust others following their complex traumatic experiences. Everyone has some positive and negative traits, and especially once we begin to get to know a person better, we become aware of faults in their character. Unfortunately, possibly due to the negativity bias, such shortcomings are attached more weight, and, in turn, could make it harder for human trafficking survivors to develop meaningful relationships. While this may seem oversimplified, it brings into light a possible dynamic that considers nonrational thinking. However, the mistrust could perhaps be rational thinking based in experience, rather than a bias or heuristic, and no general claims can be made (Chou et al., 2022).

Projection

Projection stands out as a heuristic that made its way into social psychology from psychoanalysis and the writings of Freud. Since it is hard to know what other people are thinking or feeling, someone may attribute their own characteristics, such as attitudes or emotions, to others. Again, while this may work fairly well under regular circumstances, an individual who experienced human trafficking is likely to be disadvantaged by this bias. The distorted view of others may result from the survivor's own negative thoughts and emotions due to prior traumatic experiences (Bennett-Murphy, 2012). As a result, a trafficked person may be less likely to seek help or interpret other people's reactions as threatening or hostile.

Confirmation Bias

Projection may be paired with the confirmation bias (Klayman, 1995) or a tendency to notice or search for information that confirms one's beliefs, while ignoring information that disconfirms them. As Rinker and Lawler (2018) noted, confirmation bias "might be invoked to partially explain the intransigent beliefs one group holds about another and how new disconfirming information about the other group gets invalidated" (p. 155). For a human trafficking survivor, it is possible (in the light of risk factors) that people in their lives have somehow taken advantage of them or neglected them. Thus, their expectation might be that a new encounter would be aimed at further abuse. People with the history of complex trauma could seek and notice information that confirms their beliefs about others' manipulative or evil intent, also asking questions designed to confirm expectations. Again, this might create further barriers to building trust and developing healthy relationships. According to Goldenson et al. (2022), confirmation bias could also impact others involved in assisting trafficking survivors, for example, by leading judges to focus on information that confirms their preconceptions.

Compounded Impact of Social Cognition Biases

Aside from friendships and meaningful relationships with others, diverse social cognition biases can impair brief encounters that impact daily life. For example, a survivor who is looking for a job and participates in an interview, might perceive the interviewer as threatening or hostile. In some cases, in the light of the past experiences of abuse and complex trauma, it could become very difficult to engage in controlled social cognition while flooded by negative emotions that result from automatic processing. This might make functioning in the social world challenging for human trafficking survivors who carry a much heavier load related to how various biases color their perception.

It is noteworthy to emphasize that social cognition biases influence judgment of individuals in general—not only human trafficking survivors. These examples have concentrated on how daily functioning of the latter can be impaired, but another side of the coin is related to the stereotypical views of individuals who have been trafficked by others.

Stereotypes

Stereotypes can be seen as an example of a representativeness heuristic or a cognitive shortcut where people are placed in categories based on their similarity or resemblance to the category. Chapter 2 of this book discussed the negative impact of stereotypes in human trafficking in the light of liberation psychology. A stereotype can be positive or negative, largely true or entirely false. Based on categorization, it involves thinking about a person not as an individual, but as a member of a group, and projecting the beliefs about the group onto that person. Stereotypes are often "proliferated by the media and popular culture" (Raby & Chazal, 2022, p. 13), which also takes place when it comes to human trafficking perception (Rodríguez-López, 2018). In other words, "the mainstream media has predominantly presented trafficking narratives as sensationalist stories which detail specific experiences of physical and emotional suffering and use imagery and language designed to shock and invoke an emotional reaction" (Raby & Chazal, 2022, p. 17). Chapter 5 of this volume went into detail of how the process of stereotyping occurs, providing some recent examples.

Many labor trafficking victims do not fit the stereotypical view of human trafficking, especially widespread during the last decade, that emphasized exploitation of young women in commercial sex, abducted and held at gunpoint by a violent stranger, in line with an ideal victim paradigm (M. Wilson & O'Brien, 2016). Likely, this stereotype has become more outdated in the recent years, as recognition of forms of variance in forms of sex trafficking and the existence of labor and other forms of trafficking increases in various countries. Nevertheless, recent research continues to point out that stereotypes of this kind still exist in different countries, for example, the Russia (McCarthy, 2020), Portugal (Cunha et al., 2022), and Australia (Raby & Chazal, 2022). Contrary to the most diffused media portrayals, an older man or a boy who know the perpetrator quite well can be victims of human trafficking, for instance, by being forced to work on a farm or in a factory. Another example could be an older woman forced to beg on the streets, a middle-aged man who "sells" his kidney to provide for his family, or a young man who is forced to smuggle cocaine in his stomach in order to pay off an irrational debt. Such survivors might not to self-identify as human trafficking victims due to psychological and other factors; likewise, law enforcement or other individuals who come into contact with them often may not consider the possibility that they could be trafficked. The solution involves the deconstruction of stereotypes related to human trafficking and how it is perceived (Rodríguez-López, 2018), topics well researched by social psychologists. Otherwise, detecting human trafficking will continue to suffer from these stereotypical views and numerous victims who do not fit the prototypical characteristics of an ideal victim diffused by the media will continue to be overlooked (Christie, 1986). This also applies to the stereotypical, limited view of an ideal offender or ideal trafficker (Raby & Chazal, 2022).

Another way in which stereotypes fuel human trafficking is related to racism and ethnic bias. Traffickers employ the racist ideology to justify the demand for a particular "type" of laborer. Chapter 3 (this volume) gave some striking examples of how this may occur. Another good example of this phenomenon can be found in research conducted by Holmes (2007) with migrant workers at berry farms, bringing into attention what is hidden in U.S. agriculture. The author concluded that "the segregation of laboring bodies by perceived ethnicity and legality into a hierarchy produces correlated suffering, which reinforces stereotypical views" (p. 67).

Stereotypes need to be taken into account, recognized, understood, and actively refuted. For instance, businesses and organizations can play an active role in preventing and detecting human trafficking if employees are equipped with appropriate psychological knowledge. Mills et al. (2019) shared some examples of how employees in the hospitality and transportation industries and health care professionals, who have an increased likelihood of encountering trafficking victims, should be trained in recognizing signs and suspicious behaviors. In a similar way, Farboudi-Jahromi et al. (2022) also highlighted the importance of actively refuting stereotypes of human trafficking by those who work in lodging industry. If not made sensitive to their own biases and stereotypes, those who come in contact with human trafficking victims may miss such signs.

While stereotypes may include some positive elements, prejudice and discrimination constitute negative intergroup bias. Social psychologists define prejudice as an attitude or affective response toward a group and its individual member, thus focusing on judgment. For example, Logan et al. (2009) noted that in relation to human trafficking, the prejudice against migrants in the United States can have a negative impact on survivors who are not originally from the country. However, discrimination emphasizes behavior or an unfavorable treatment of individuals based on their membership in a particular group. Stereotypes, prejudice, and discrimination often go together. Much of social psychological research has been dedicated to stereotypes related to gender and race, as well as age, weight, physical and mental disability, and so on. It is worthwhile noting that trafficking survivors may be members of diverse stigmatized groups, sometimes also overlapping, which further increases their vulnerability.

Overall, it is noteworthy that cognitive biases and stereotypes, prejudice, and discrimination serve as a double-edged sword, affecting how traffickers, those who purchase commercial sex, bystanders, and survivors themselves perceive the phenomenon of trafficking and its victims. Often, various forms of prejudice and discrimination may occur together at the same time—for example, objectification can be related to dehumanization of trafficking survivors. Victims who are members of a stigmatized group may face additional challenges due to stereotype threat or the fear of confirming the stereotypes that others have about their group (Gerassi et al., 2019). Often, traffickers can manipulate others by using the stereotype threat and consistently reminding their victims of their lack of privilege. This coercive control may take place alongside criminal socialization, in some cases seen as factors that are intrinsic to the experience of human trafficking. As a result of such manipulation, as well as the influence of other bias and environment, cognitive processing may lead to further discrimination and self-handicapping. While it could be easier to correct for the biases present in controlled processing, implementing healthy changes in the automatic processing requires years of positive experiences and relationships in the climate of safety and trust.

CONCLUSION

Social psychology has much to offer in terms of understanding how trafficking survivors process information, perceive themselves, and are perceived by others. In particular, the substantial body of research unveils some of the mechanisms behind cognitive processes and decision making in general. As shown in the previous sections, understanding how people see themselves, process information, and are subject to some bias and errors may be useful when considering the disadvantages faced by human trafficking survivors.

This chapter has concentrated on areas of social psychology related to self, social attribution, and social cognition biases and stereotypes. Certainly, many other areas of interest of social psychologists could provide valuable insight on human trafficking (e.g., consideration of the bystander intervention and aggressive behavior). More research is needed on how the well-established social psychological principles affect human trafficking phenomena and various individuals involved in it: traffickers, sex and labor trafficking victims, individuals who purchase commercial sex, bystanders, providers of services, and others. Furthermore, various types of interventions should be informed by social psychological phenomena, which might provide or enrich the theoretical rationale for the implementation of specific techniques and solutions. Other chapters of this volume provide examples of diverse interventions, many of which could be discussed in the light of social psychology.

REFERENCES

Abrams, D., Viki, G. T., Masser, B., & Bohner, G. (2003). Perceptions of stranger and acquaintance rape: The role of benevolent and hostile sexism in victim blame and rape proclivity. *Journal of Personality and Social Psychology, 84*(1), 111–125. https://doi.org/10.1037/0022-3514.84.1.111

Bales, K. (2002). The social psychology of modern slavery. *Scientific American, 286*(4), 80–88. https://doi.org/10.1038/scientificamerican0402-80

Beck, A. T. (1993). Cognitive therapy: Past, present, and future. *Journal of Consulting and Clinical Psychology, 61*(2), 194–198. https://doi.org/10.1037/0022-006X.61.2.194

Bennett-Murphy, L. M. (2012). Haunted: Treatment of a child survivor of human trafficking. *Journal of Infant, Child, and Adolescent Psychotherapy, 11*(2), 133–148. https://doi.org/10.1080/15289168.2012.673413

Brennan, D. (2014). *Life interrupted: Trafficking into forced labor in the United States.* Duke University Press.

Chou, E. Y., Hsu, D. Y., & Myung, N. (2022). Once bitten, twice shy: The negative spillover effect of seeing betrayal of trust. *Journal of Experimental Psychology: Applied, 28*(2), 360–378. https://doi.org/10.1037/xap0000301

Christie, N. (1986). The ideal victim. In E. A. Fattah (Ed.), *From crime policy to victim policy: Reorienting the justice system* (pp. 17–30). Springer Link. https://doi.org/10.1007/978-1-349-08305-3_2

Chu, K., & Billings, J. (2020). Mental health experiences of sex trafficking victims in western countries: A qualitative study. *Journal of Human Trafficking, 8*(4), 1–23.

Cole, D. A., Ciesla, J. A., Dallaire, D. H., Jacquez, F. M., Pineda, A. Q., Lagrange, B., Truss, A. E., Folmer, A. S., Tilghman-Osborne, C., & Felton, J. W. (2008). Emergence of attributional style and its relation to depressive symptoms. *Journal of Abnormal Psychology, 117*(1), 16–31. https://doi.org/10.1037/0021-843X.117.1.16

Cunha, A., Gonçalves, M., & Matos, M. (2022). An assessment of Portuguese social professionals awareness of human trafficking. *European Journal of Social Work, 25*(3), 512–524. https://doi.org/10.1080/13691457.2021.1934413

Cunningham, K. C., & Cromer, L. D. (2016). Attitudes about human trafficking: Individual differences related to belief and victim blame. *Journal of Interpersonal Violence, 31*(2), 228–244. https://doi.org/10.1177/0886260514555369

Digidiki, V., Dikaiou, M., & Baka, A. (2016). Attitudes towards the victim and the client of sex trafficking in Greece: The influence of belief in a just world, structural attributions, previous experience, and attitudes towards prostitution. *Journal of Human Trafficking, 2*(4), 297–315. https://doi.org/10.1080/23322705.2016.1176385

Donahue, S., Schwien, M., & LaVallee, D. (2019). Educating emergency department staff on the identification and treatment of human trafficking victims. *Journal of Emergency Nursing, 45*(1), 16–23. https://doi.org/10.1016/j.jen.2018.03.021

Ezeakor, A. I., & Okpala, M. O. (2020). Posttraumatic stress disorder among trafficked victims, role of self-esteem, demographic factors and relevance of psychotherapy. *International Journal for Psychotherapy in Africa, 5*(1), 84–97.

Farboudi-Jahromi, M., Tasci, A. D. A., & Sönmez, S. (2022). Employees' helping behavior toward the victims of human trafficking in the lodging industry. *International Journal of Contemporary Hospitality Management.* https://doi.org/10.1108/IJCHM-04-2022-0454

Farrell, A., Owens, C., & McDevitt, J. (2014). New laws but few cases: Understanding the challenges to the investigation and prosecution of human trafficking cases. *Crime, Law, and Social Change, 61*(2), 139–168. https://doi.org/10.1007/s10611-013-9442-1

Fukushima, A. I. (2019). *Migrant crossings: Witnessing human trafficking in the U.S.* Stanford University Press.

Gallo, M., Konrad, R. A., & Thinyane, H. (2020). An epidemiological perspective on labor trafficking. *Journal of Human Trafficking, 8*(2), 1–22.

Gerassi, L., Fabbre, V., Howard, A., Edmond, T. E., & Nichols, A. (2019). How sex trading identities shape experiences of service provision: Insights from adult women with lived experiences and service providers. *Journal of Human Trafficking, 5*(1), 74–87. https://doi.org/10.1080/23322705.2018.1447198

Gilovich, T., Keltner, D., Chen, S., & Nisbett, R. (2019). *Social psychology* (5th ed.). W. W. Norton & Co.

Goldenson, J., Brodsky, S. L., & Perlin, M. L. (2022). Trauma-informed forensic mental health assessment: Practical implications, ethical tensions, and alignment with therapeutic jurisprudence principles. *Psychology, Public Policy, and Law, 28*(2), 226–239. https://doi.org/10.1037/law0000339

Hagger, M. S., Wood, C., Stiff, C., & Chatzisarantis, N. L. D. (2010). Ego depletion and the strength model of self-control: A meta-analysis. *Psychological Bulletin, 136*(4), 495–525. https://doi.org/10.1037/a0019486

Haidt, J. (2012). *The righteous mind: Why good people are divided by politics and religion.* Vintage.

Hemmings, S., Jakobowitz, S., Abas, M., Bick, D., Howard, L. M., Stanley, N., Zimmerman, C., & Oram, S. (2016). Responding to the health needs of survivors of human trafficking: A systematic review. *BMC Health Services Research, 16*(1), 320–328. https://doi.org/10.1186/s12913-016-1538-8

Higgins, E. T. (1987). Self-discrepancy: A theory relating self and affect. *Psychological Review, 94*(3), 319–340. https://doi.org/10.1037/0033-295X.94.3.319

Holmes, S. M. (2007). "Oaxacans like to work bent over": The naturalization of social suffering among berry farm workers. *International Migration, 45*(3), 39–68. https://doi.org/10.1111/j.1468-2435.2007.00410.x

Jowett, S., Argyriou, A., Scherrer, O., Karatzias, T., & Katona, C. (2021). Complex post-traumatic stress disorder in asylum seekers and victims of trafficking: Treatment considerations. *BJPsych Open, 7*(6), e181. https://doi.org/10.1192/bjo.2021.1007

Klayman, J. (1995). Varieties of confirmation bias. In B. H. Ross (Ed.), *Psychology of learning and motivation* (Vol. 32, pp. 385–418). Academic Press.

Krull, D. S., Loy, M. H. M., Lin, J., Wang, C. F., Chen, S., & Zhao, X. (1999). The fundamental attribution error: Correspondence bias in individualist and collectivist cultures. *Personality and Social Psychology Bulletin, 25*(10), 1208–1219. https://doi.org/10.1177/0146167299258003

Lerner, M. J., & Simmons, C. H. (1966). Observer's reaction to the "innocent victim": Compassion or rejection? *Journal of Personality and Social Psychology, 4*(2), 203–210. https://doi.org/10.1037/h0023562

Litam, S. D. A. (2019). She's just a prostitute: The effects of labels on counselor attitudes, empathy, and rape myth acceptance. *The Professional Counselor, 9*(4), 396–415. https://doi.org/10.15241/sdal.9.4.396

Lockyer, S., & Koenig, C. J. (2020). At the intersection of method and empowerment: Reflections from a pilot photovoice study with survivors of human trafficking. *Journal of Human Trafficking, 8*(4), 1–20.

Logan, T. K., Walker, R., & Hunt, G. (2009). Understanding human trafficking in the United States. *Trauma, Violence & Abuse, 10*(1), 3–30. https://doi.org/10.1177/1524838008327262

Marburger, K., & Pickover, S. (2020). A comprehensive perspective on treating victims of human trafficking. *The Professional Counselor, 10*(1), 13–24. https://doi.org/10.15241/km.10.1.13

Markus, H. (1977). Self-schemata and processing information about the self. *Journal of Personality and Social Psychology, 35*(2), 63–78. https://doi.org/10.1037/0022-3514.35.2.63

McCarthy, L. A. (2020). A gendered perspective on human trafficking perpetrators: evidence from Russia. *Journal of Human Trafficking, 6*(1), 79–94.

Menaker, T. A., & Franklin, C. A. (2015). Gendered violence and victim blame: Subject perceptions of blame and the appropriateness of services for survivors of domestic sex trafficking, sexual assault, and intimate partner violence. *Journal of Crime and Justice, 38*(3), 395–413. https://doi.org/10.1080/0735648X.2014.996321

Mills, M. J., Tortez, L. M., & Blanton, R. (2019). Moving beyond employees: Antitrafficking training as facilitating social change. *Industrial and Organizational Psychology: Perspectives on Science and Practice, 12*(1), 34–38. https://doi.org/10.1017/iop.2019.4

Owens, C., Dank, M., Breaux, J., Bañuelos, I., Farrell, A., Pfeffer, R., & McDevitt, J. (2014). *Understanding the organization, operation, and victimization process of labor trafficking in the United States.* Urban Institute.

Raby, K., & Chazal, N. (2022). The myth of the 'ideal offender': Challenging persistent human trafficking stereotypes through emerging Australian cases. *Anti-Trafficking Review, 18*(2022), 13–32. https://doi.org/10.14197/atr.201222182

Raphael, J., & Myers-Powell, B. (2010). *From victims to victimizers: Interviews with 25 ex-pimps in Chicago.* Schiller DuCanto & Fleck Family Law Center of DePaul University College of Law.

Rinker, J., & Lawler, J. (2018). Trauma as a collective disease and root cause of protracted social conflict. *Peace and Conflict, 24*(2), 150–164. https://doi.org/10.1037/pac0000311

Rodríguez-López, S. (2018). (De) constructing stereotypes: Media representations, social perceptions, and legal responses to human trafficking. *Journal of Human Trafficking, 4*(1), 61–72. https://doi.org/10.1080/23322705.2018.1423447

Rosenberg, S., Nelson, C., & Vivekananthan, P. S. (1968). A multidimensional approach to the structure of personality impressions. *Journal of Personality and Social Psychology, 9*(4), 283–294. https://doi.org/10.1037/h0026086

Ross, L. (1977). The intuitive psychologist and his shortcomings: Distortions in the attribution process. In L. Berkowitz (Ed.), *Advances in experimental social psychology* (Vol. 10, pp. 173–220). Academic Press. https://doi.org/10.1016/S0065-2601(08)60357-3

San Martin, A., Schug, J., & Maddux, W. W. (2019). Relational mobility and cultural differences in analytic and holistic thinking. *Journal of Personality and Social Psychology, 116*(4), 495–518. https://doi.org/10.1037/pspa0000142

Seah, R., & Berle, D. (2022). Negative attributions as a source of vulnerability for trauma-related shame and PTSD Symptoms. *Journal of Rational-Emotive & Cognitive-Behavior Therapy,* 1–16. https://doi.org/10.1007/s10942-022-00481-z

Shin, R. J., Oberlin, A. M., Rigby, F., & Chelmow, F. (2022). Educating physicians on sex trafficking: Who receives our empathy and whom do we blame? *Journal of Human Trafficking, 8*(3), 265–281. https://doi.org/10.1080/23322705.2020.1808776

Sidun, N. M. (2018). Traffickers: Who are they? In L. Walker, G. Gaviria, & K. Gopal (Eds.), *Handbook of sex trafficking* (pp. 99–109). Springer. https://doi.org/10.1007/978-3-319-73621-1_11

Silver, K. E., Karakurt, G., & Boysen, S. T. (2015). Predicting prosocial behavior toward sex-trafficked persons: The roles of empathy, belief in a just world, and attitudes toward prostitution. *Journal of Aggression, Maltreatment & Trauma,* *24*(8), 932–954. https://doi.org/10.1080/10926771.2015.1070231

Strack, F., & Deutsch, R. (2015). The duality of everyday life: Dual-process and dual system models in social psychology. In M. Mikulincer, P. R. Shaver, E. Borgida, & J. A. Bargh (Eds.), *APA handbook of personality and social psychology: Vol. 1. Attitudes and social cognition* (pp. 891–927). American Psychological Association. https://doi.org/10.1037/14341-028

Summers, G., & Feldman, N. S. (1984). Blaming the victim versus blaming the perpetrator: An attributional analysis of spouse abuse. *Journal of Social and Clinical Psychology,* *2*(4), 339–347. https://doi.org/10.1521/jscp.1984.2.4.339

Sutton, K., & Douglas, R. (2020). *Social psychology* (2nd ed.). McMillan International.

Wilson, M., & O'Brien, E. (2016). Constructing the ideal victim in the United States of America's annual trafficking in persons reports. *Crime, Law, and Social Change,* *65*(1–2), 29–45. https://doi.org/10.1007/s10611-015-9600-8

Wilson, S. R., Levine, K. J., Cruz, M. G., & Rao, N. (1997). Attribution complexity and actor-observer bias. *Journal of Social Behavior and Personality,* *12*(3), 709–726.

Zimmerman, C., Hossain, M., & Watts, C. (2011). Human trafficking and health: A conceptual model to inform policy, intervention and research. *Social Science & Medicine,* *73*(2), 327–335. https://doi.org/10.1016/j.socscimed.2011.05.028

Zuckerman, M., & Tsai, F. F. (2005). Costs of self-handicapping. *Journal of Personality,* *73*(2), 411–442. https://doi.org/10.1111/j.1467-6494.2005.00314.x

7

INDUSTRIAL AND ORGANIZATIONAL PSYCHOLOGY AND HUMAN TRAFFICKING

Harnessing the Potential for Proactivity, Prediction, and Prevention

MAURA J. MILLS, LEANNE M. TORTEZ, ROBERT BLANTON, BURCU B. KESKIN, GREGORY J. BOTT, AND NICKOLAS K. FREEMAN

Over the past 2 decades, human trafficking has become an increasing problem (Pourmokhtari, 2015). However, during that time, great strides have also been made in better understanding and implementing approaches to proactively prevent and intervene in instances of trafficking. Industrial and organizational (I/O) psychology represents a critical piece of that solution, given its focus on human behavior in regard to work. As such, it is inherently relevant to better understanding and curbing trafficking, as trafficking is often inextricably intertwined with workplaces and/or work itself. In this way, I/O psychology—and its socially conscious subfield of humanitarian work psychology (Carr et al., 2012)—can play a critical role in predicting and preventing trafficking as well as in training employees to recognize signs of human trafficking in their workplaces. On a broader scale, it can also help improve understanding of some of the ways in which organizations can respond to trafficking both proactively and reactively in regard to tangential issues such as supply chain considerations, as well as data collection and analysis. Importantly, while different trafficking types (labor trafficking, sex trafficking) have a number of central differences (Cockbain & Bowers, 2019), there

https://doi.org/10.1037/0000379-008
Psychological Perspectives on Human Trafficking: Theory, Research, Prevention, and Intervention, L. Dryjanska, E. K. Hopper, and H. Stoklosa (Editors)

are important commonalities in what I/O psychology can offer insofar as proactively responding to, predicting, and preventing trafficking at large.

ANTITRAFFICKING EMPLOYEE TRAINING

Arguably, the most directly relevant impact I/O psychology can have on the landscape of human trafficking is through informing improved training practices for employees. That is, I/O psychologists can play an important part in advising organizations regarding how best to craft programs and practices that educate and train employees on how to identify indicators of human trafficking, as well as providing accessible resources for responding to trafficking suspicions. These trainings come at a time when various industries, organizations, and even governments have increasingly recognized the need for antitrafficking training (Fukushima et al., 2021). This is particularly the case for certain industries in which employees are more likely to encounter trafficking victims, including health care, transportation, and hospitality. In the United States, a growing number of states now mandate (or are in the process of mandating), antitrafficking training for employees in such industries, as well as other relevant and public-facing industries, such as law enforcement (ECPAT-USA, 2019). Several of these mandates even allow for the possibility of criminal and civil liability for organizations and employees that knowingly allow trafficking to occur on their premises.

Importantly for the generalizability and cost-effectiveness of trainings, there are a number of commonalities across antitrafficking trainings, even across industries (Q. C. Miller et al., 2021; Mills et al., 2020). These include trainings focusing predominantly on an informational approach, aiming to give employees a general awareness of human trafficking. Such trainings have been produced by antitrafficking organizations (e.g., the Polaris Project) and government agencies (e.g., Department of Health and Human Services' SOAR training, Department of Homeland Security's Blue Campaign) and are often available for face-to-face (in-person) delivery as well as delivery via online modules. These training approaches certainly have some important benefits, including their relative accessibility, generalizability, and comparative cost-effectiveness (Mills et al., 2019).

I/O best practices would also suggest that industry-specific training is critical, particularly for employees working in those industries that are most likely to encounter human trafficking. Indeed, some key behavioral indicators of trafficking vary across industries and therefore necessitate specialized employee training. This includes indicators such as frequent entering or exiting of vehicles, suspicious use of restrooms, and uncertainty about travel details (*transportation*); unexplained repeat injuries, hovering companions, and lack of health insurance (*health care*); and large cash payments, guests without luggage, many visitors to the same hotel room, and/or requests for rooms near exits (*hospitality*). A number of organizations have adopted this industry-specific approach, including antitrafficking organizations like KnowTheChain, HEAL (Health, Education, Advocacy, Linkage) Trafficking, Truckers Against Trafficking, and In Our Backyard, the latter of which focuses on training convenience store workers. Other industries have also answered the call, including the health care industry, which now offers several antitrafficking training programs targeted toward health fields in particular. Many of these programs include, among other features, provision of tangible reference materials to employees (e.g., signage and pocket-sized reference cards with hotline information and key trafficking indicators).

Some companies and industries have gone further, and, in accordance with critical I/O principles, have moved beyond static informational modules and resources toward more simulation-based trainings (e.g., Stoklosa et al., 2017). The latter have the benefit of offering a more realistic environment, thereby closing the gap between the training and reality, and enhancing the validity— and likely effectiveness—of the training program. Indeed, research has consistently found that allowing individuals the opportunity to practice their reactions to stimuli in a simulated situation increases the likelihood that they will feel able to replicate those same behaviors when presented with the situation in reality (Grossman & Salas, 2011).

Given the sheer number of employees in the industries most commonly confronted with trafficking situations, it is important that organizations lean on I/O psychology for its expertise in pyramid approaches to training. Otherwise known as "train-the-trainer" approaches, these programs train a smaller number of organizational members (e.g., supervisors, human resources staff, other key personnel) in the content and key tenets of the training, and those individuals, in turn, train others in their organization (see Peck, 2021, for an example of a train-the-trainer approach to providing trafficking education to health care practitioners). This is often considered a relatively cost-effective and time-effective way to generate some level of in-house expertise in both relevant content and the training approaches, thereby enabling the training to be offered more frequently, including periodic training options (e.g., annual refreshers), and/or to new hires when they are onboarded into the organization.

Yet, as detailed by Mills et al. (2020), despite the increasing willingness of organizations to conduct trafficking trainings, some key I/O psychology principles have as yet been underutilized in developing these trainings and should be more heavily considered as the programs continue to be developed and refined. In particular, this includes best practices during the three main stages of training commonly referred to in I/O psychology: before the training, during the training, and after the training (see Mills et al., 2020 for a corresponding checklist for each stage).

Before the Training

Effective trainings are well planned. To determine specific training needs within an organization or agency, needs assessments (e.g., organizational analyses, task analyses, person analyses) should be conducted. Results of the needs assessment should serve as the basis for the design, delivery, and evaluation of the training. At a higher level, it is necessary to ensure that there is support for the training from leaders in the organization. Ideally, organizational leaders should invite employees to the training while communicating the importance of the training and its relevance to the organization's industry. Those developing the training should consult with experts (e.g., those with lived experience of trafficking, social service providers, legal experts, law enforcement, researchers) to ensure that the training is accurate, relevant, and up to date. Trafficking training in particular should also take into account the organization's locale and any relevant specifics, limitations, or unique circumstances in that regard. Likewise, it should account for the potential of such trainings to yield unintended negative consequences—such as arrest or deportation of potential trafficking victims. In an effort to guard against this, distinctions should be made, for example, between commercial sex and sex trafficking (Yale Global Health Justice Partnership, 2020), and the harms inherent in conflating the two (Schreter et al., 2007) should be covered as a core aspect of the training. Standards such as the HEAL Trafficking Curriculum Assessment Tool (C. Miller et al., 2019) and the U.S. Department of Health and Human Services' (n.d.) Core Competencies can provide helpful guidance for content in this regard. Alternatively, an organization may choose to outsource the training or pieces of the training to trafficking training experts. Regardless of which training method is used, developing specific goals of the training and being explicit about what trainees are expected to learn from the training at the outset is critical.

As the training is developed, it is important to ensure that it is applicable to employees at all levels of the organization. Aspects of the training should be modified as needed so that they are applicable to different positions, departments, and so on. For trafficking training in particular, it is also imperative that the training be approached sensitively, as some employees may find the material upsetting. To facilitate this, I/O psychologists may consider working with clinical and other trauma-informed psychologists, counselors, and social workers who can better speak to the potentially triggering nature of the material and can be available to speak with employees who find such material difficult.

Finally, in advance of the training, organizations must create a method for how the effectiveness of the training will be evaluated—an all-too-common oversight in organizational trainings. This includes identifying outcomes that should increase or improve as a result of participating in the training. For example, pre- and posttests assessing employees' knowledge of and attitudes about trafficking, or their acquired knowledge about how to respond, are useful measurement tools to serve this aim.

During the Training

Antitrafficking training, just like any job-based training, can vary by both content, as well as delivery method. At its core, however, it is important that the training include informational content to educate trainees on the basics of human trafficking. This includes clarifying what trafficking is (and distinguishing its types—e.g., labor, sex), its prevalence, common misconceptions, statistics, relevance to specific industries, and resources that trainees can access to learn more, as well as to respond to cases of suspected trafficking. Trainees should also be made aware of their state and local statutes around trafficking. Likewise, in the case of organizations and corporations operating internationally, trainees should also be made aware of antitrafficking resources in all countries in which the business operates or with which it does business.

Training best practices suggest using a variety of delivery methods if feasible, including, for example, online videos, in-person training, and guest speakers. As noted earlier, some antitrafficking trainings have included interactive simulations and workshops that involve role-play scenarios tailored to a specific industry (e.g., Stoklosa et al., 2017). Trainees can then practice identifying indicators of a potential trafficking situation—and responding accordingly—in a scenario that is highly similar to their own job role. For antitrafficking trainings not already run by survivor-led organizations or programs, such trainings may also invite a trafficking survivor(s) to be guest speakers in order to share their expertise (and their personal experience if they opt to do so), which can help increase personalization and intrinsic motivation to respond to cases of suspected trafficking, while simultaneously highlighting the survivor voice (Mills et al., 2019, 2020). However, organizations looking to incorporate this angle would do well to consult Freedom United's (n.d.) Survivor Alliance Pledge in an effort to ensure that their interactions with and expectations of trafficking survivors are optimally ethical and aboveboard, that is, that such training programs do not suffer the unforeseen consequence of improving the training at the expense of survivors' well-being.

After the Training

Upon conclusion of the training, feedback from trainees should be sought (e.g., via a brief survey). Organizations should consider asking trainees to provide feedback about their satisfaction with and perceived usefulness of the training, in addition to suggestions to improve the training for subsequent administrations. Trainees should also be provided with tangible resources they can refer to after the training as needed. These may include pocket reference cards that remind trainees of how to respond to possible trafficking, or visible signage in employee areas (e.g., in break rooms, restrooms, behind a hotel reception desk). These resources can help facilitate positive transfer of training (see Burke & Hutchins, 2007, for a review), as can the aforementioned organizational support of employees who take action in responding to cases of suspected trafficking. To assess the extent of long-term transfer of the knowledge and skills learned in training, organizations should also conduct follow-up surveys (e.g., at 1, 3, 6 months posttraining). As an additional benefit, follow-up surveys also serve to refresh employees' trafficking-related knowledge and reinforce the salience of the information. Finally, as trainings should be offered periodically, as opposed to one-time-only trainings, organizations would do well to proactively develop a plan for how often this training will be offered. Moreover, refresher content, such as a brief video or slide deck, should be always accessible to employees so that they can review basic information as needed.

Importantly, however, the unique sensitivity of the subject matter inherent in trafficking trainings means that not all training-related best practices from I/O psychology can be strictly adhered to when planning or carrying out a training (Mills et al., 2020). For example, I/O best practices suggest that trainings should be offered "just in time" so that employees are learning specific knowledge and skills directly before they are expected to use the information (Brandenburg & Ellinger, 2003). This type of training is typically recommended over a "just in case" type of training, which teaches knowledge and skills that employees *may* use in the future. These trainings are sometimes viewed as a relative waste of resources, since time is spent developing knowledge and skills that employees may never be called upon to use. Yet antitrafficking trainings are almost entirely just-in-case trainings because employees cannot know when they will encounter a possible trafficking situation. Thus, despite the downsides generally associated with just-in-case trainings, they are necessary in the case of trafficking training specifically. Further, the superseding benefits of antitrafficking trainings are unique insofar as their potential for harnessing employees' intrinsic desire to benefit humanity and contribute to a socially conscious cause (Mills et al., 2019; Ryff, 2018).

Also, unique to trafficking training programs are the challenges faced as a result of the inherently clandestine nature of trafficking (Furnham, 2016), thereby making it more difficult to evaluate the effectiveness of the program by traditional evaluation standards (Bates, 2004; Kirkpatrick, 1976; Powell et al., 2017). For example, while it is usually important that training programs define what "success" looks like, it is much harder to outline specific measurable indicators of success for antitrafficking educational and training programs. For example, a common misconception is that the number of trafficking victims identified is a reasonable metric of success. However, antitrafficking experts have emphasized that this is not an optimal metric such that it is not a survivor-centered goal. Rather, such experts emphasize that the more micro attitudinal and behavioral changes on the part of the learner (employee) are a more appropriate metric of training program success. More broadly, there also exist many context-specific constraints inherent in antitrafficking program evaluation, including measurement difficulties, limited publicly accessible data, unreliable data, anonymous data sources, and the covert nature of the populations involved (Mills et al., 2020), all of which likewise challenge traditional and "best practice" training program evaluation and require acceptance of more nontraditional measures of success (Bates, 2004; Kirkpatrick, 1976).

FACILITATING EMPLOYEES' FELT PSYCHOLOGICAL SAFETY IN RESPONDING

While the previously mentioned resources and training aspects are critical in ensuring employees have access to the information they need when they need it (e.g., after the training program has ended), it is equally as important that employees feel psychologically safe (Kahn, 1990; Newman et al., 2017) in responding to instances of trafficking. That is, regardless of how good the training itself is, it is essential that employees feel confident that taking action on a trafficking suspicion will not result in their identification by traffickers, nor in retaliation or a reprimand from their employing organization. Rather, employees must feel actively supported by their employer in responding to cases of suspected trafficking in the organization or place of business.

Whistleblower protections are particularly important for employees who are less likely to have ready access to legal protections, such as those in the agriculture industry (Wilkens, 2018). Nonetheless, many of the policy examples we see occur in more traditional organizations. Hewlett-Packard (HP), for example, has an anonymous grievance reporting channel available to not only HP employees but also to its suppliers and customers, ensuring that everybody affiliated with the company either directly or indirectly has a mechanism whereby they can report suspected violations of worker rights. In a similar spirit, Marriott recently implemented nonretaliation policies for any employee completing their Marriott Incident Reporting Application (Marriott International, 2021).

SUPPLY CHAINS AND CIRCUIT BEHAVIOR OF TRAFFICKING NETWORKS

Another broader way that the strengths of I/O psychology can help in the fight against human trafficking is by looking to the businesses and industries involved in traffickers' supply chains and circuit behaviors. Human trafficking, both locally and globally, is exacerbated by public and private supply chains, which necessarily involve various industries and businesses. Although not all trafficking takes place across national borders, it is nonetheless the case that, as infrastructure developments, global forces, and improved technologies have amplified worldwide trade and economic prosperity, they have simultaneously facilitated traffickers' ability to move illicitly sourced goods and services across a wider domain. Trafficking networks are complex, interconnected entities, sometimes under centralized control but with decentralized information sharing. As such, a holistic, system-focused approach is needed in order to understand the operations and dynamics of human trafficking supply networks, and I/O psychology's inherent engagement with both organizations and broader industries can be useful in this regard.

A typical supply chain works under the "source-make-deliver" principle (Association for Supply Chain Management, 2022). Trafficking networks are similar such that they work under the "acquisition-movement-exploitation" triangle (Kara, 2017). The *acquisition* of trafficking victims (labor- or sex-related) primarily occurs in one (or more) of five ways: deceit, sale by family, abduction, seduction, or recruitment by another currently or formerly trafficked individual (Kara, 2017). Importantly, from a societal angle, risk factors increase as a result of poverty, the attraction of perceived higher standards of living elsewhere, lack of employment, lack of worker rights, organized crime, conflict, natural disasters, and the like. Subsequently, the *movement* of trafficked individuals refers to their transportation from point of origin (acquisition) to destination(s) of exploitation. Such movement is often fraught with neglectful and/or abusive treatment intended to break the victims emotionally and/or physically. This is also an important part of how legitimate employees can be trained to identify and respond to incidents of trafficking (e.g., physical injury or neglect of the trafficking victim as warning signs). Finally, *exploitation* refers to the coercion of unpaid services for the benefit of the trafficker, though, in essence, exploitation begins the moment the individual is acquired (Kara, 2017). Certainly, I/O psychology is beneficial at each of these corners of the triangle, particularly the latter two, as traffickers rely upon certain industries and types of businesses through which to "move" and exploit their victims.

Understanding the circuit behavior common in trafficking networks offers valuable insight into what industries are most appropriate targets for implementing trafficking-related interventions and programming and how so. In line with the humanitarian work psychology arm of I/O psychology, some nongovernmental organizations (NGOs) have been created to help understand the circuits inherent in labor trafficking in particular. For example, the Workers' Rights Consortium (WRC) is an independent labor rights monitoring organization whose main focus is ensuring that collegiate apparel be produced in factories that protect workers from labor abuses and offer a living wage. With 153 university and college affiliates in the United States and Canada, the WRC conducts investigations of factories around the globe and issues public reports on labor rights violations to facilitate supply chain transparency. On the consumer side, the NGO Free2Work folds in the related field of marketing by providing consumers with information about the extent to which their potential purchases are affiliated with forced labor practices. Free2Work's mobile app allows customers to scan the barcodes of their potential purchases to learn about companies' ties to forced and child labor in their supply chains, with the goal of creating more socially responsible purchases—and thus indirectly rewarding companies that steer clear of such practices. The app also evaluates a supply chain's level of forced labor risk based on the overarching industry as well as the countries in the chain.

Regarding sex trafficking, these traffickers likewise tend to operate in a set of locations that are visited in a cyclical pattern, or circuit. This frequent movement is driven by market demand and the desire to avoid local law enforcement. For example, traffickers may run operations in location A for several days before relocating to a nearby location B before law enforcement agents in location A can detect operations and coordinate a response. As this circuit movement often takes place along highways, the organization Truckers Against Trafficking (TAT) was developed with the goal of educating, equipping, and empowering members of the trucking, bus, and energy industries to play a role in proactively combating human trafficking. Transportation professionals are in a unique position to encounter and identify traffickers, given the latter's reliance on the transportation industry in acquiring, moving, and relocating their victims. As such, TAT's professional trainings have resulted in a significant increase in truck drivers reporting potential trafficking cases to the national hotline, ultimately leading to victim recoveries and criminal arrests. The organization also offers best practices to organizations to promote a safe work culture, and has numerous corporate sponsors that require their employees to be trained in trafficking recognition. More broadly, several U.S. states also now require human trafficking training in order for truck drivers to renew their licenses or to acquire new licenses (Wickenhauser, 2019).

FURTHER COMPLICATING FACTORS AND GRAY AREAS

While a variety of challenges are inherent in both labor and sex trafficking, some are especially acute in regard to labor trafficking. Unlike sex trafficking, industry progress in responding to labor trafficking has been more mixed and tentative. While some key industries are willing to take necessary steps to increase employee awareness of sex trafficking, labor trafficking is often a more difficult problem to identify and effectively confront. According to some estimates, labor trafficking is the most prevalent form of modern slavery (International Labour Organization [ILO], 2017). Multiple national and international statutes either encourage or mandate the avoidance of trafficked labor, including the 2015 UK Modern Slavery Act and the UN Global Compact. Further, a panoply of organizations, including the ILO as well as antitrafficking NGOs and labor groups, monitor labor conditions worldwide. Yet, from a corporate perspective, responding to labor trafficking can be much more challenging than responding to sex trafficking.

There are multiple reasons for this dilemma. Foundationally, the definition of labor trafficking itself is "challenged and contested" (Gutierrez-Huerter et al., 2021), as it can be difficult to differentiate labor trafficking from related forms of coerced labor, such as debt bondage, as well as more limited infringements of worker rights, such as unsafe working conditions or unfair wages. In many cases, the workplace situation is ambiguous; for example, it is not uncommon for trafficked workers to receive a marginal wage and to be told that they can leave once their debt is paid, even though their wages are far below market rates, and they face coercion in the workplace. Thus, there is often an unclear demarcation between free and unfree labor, so much so that some have identified it as a "continuum including both what can clearly be identified as forced labor and other forms of labor exploitation and abuse" (ILO, 2009, pp. 8–9; see also Barrientos et al., 2013). For their part, traffickers can readily exploit these gray areas in dealing with inspectors or other labor law enforcement personnel. Nevertheless, while these challenges are exacerbated in relation to labor trafficking, sex trafficking can likewise be complex to identify in some instances. For example, the distinction between sex trafficking and noncoercive commercial sex is not always immediately evident or obvious. Given such ambiguities, even well-intentioned corporations may "struggle to make sense of this phenomenon" (Monciardini et al., 2021, p. 288), though it is nevertheless important that companies do not shy away from antitrafficking efforts as a result of these complexities.

Yet, fortunately, responding to sex trafficking in particular imposes comparatively minimal costs on many legitimate businesses. In fact, in many cases the only direct expense is that of training. Moreover, the most obvious aspects of sex trafficking often occur outside of the primary corporate environment, as opposed to with the employees or subcontractors of the organization itself. By contrast, labor trafficking can more directly involve corporate practices and supply chains, including the potential for subcontracted workers themselves to be trafficked laborers. While there are several high-profile examples of corporate malfeasance in this area, the more common situation is for trafficked labor to be discovered in the production or processing of goods that are ultimately sold in the licit marketplace, including agricultural products and seafood (McDowell et al., 2015). In other words, it is comparatively uncommon for corporations to be directly confronted with a labor trafficking situation; rather, illicit and licit supply chains commonly intermingle, and it is often difficult to discern which parts of the chain rely on trafficked labor. Moreover, responding to labor trafficking can impose potentially substantial costs to industries—costs that often do not align with the surface-level economic goals brought about by the dynamics of corporate power and profit (LeBaron, 2021). In addition to devoting the requisite resources to monitor their own operations to ensure slavery-free supply chains and operations, organizations must be willing to face the potential costs of disrupted supply chains or increased costs of productions if labor trafficking is uncovered—and should have a backup supplier or delivery or service supplier in case of such an instance.

Despite these difficulties, there is some evidence that corporations are giving increasing consideration to the importance of maintaining slavery-free supply chains, an area of particular relevance to the humanitarian work psychology arm of I/O psychology (Carr et al., 2012). For example, the 2015 UK Modern Slavery Act (as well as a similar law in California) requires corporations to publish yearly transparency in supply chains statements that outline their "efforts to eradicate slavery and human trafficking from their supply chains" (State of California, 2021). Although such statements are certainly a step in the right direction, they also represent a "light touch" (Flynn & Walker, 2021, p. 312) regulation, as they require only a disclosure of actions (if any) rather than implementing actual measures—an important distinction.

While parts of this section likely raise more questions than they answer, there are some notable observations to be made. Namely, substantial progress against labor trafficking cannot be made without two things. First, firms need to establish substantial partnerships with other key stakeholders, including labor organizations and antitrafficking NGOs, as well as the countries in which the firm is doing business. Intentions (or even corporate actions) aside, the ability of firms to improve labor conditions is ultimately limited; for example, corporate measures to prevent the use of forced labor may have difficulty taking root in countries without a robust system of labor rights protections (Locke, 2013). Second, at the industry level, an effective response to labor trafficking requires, at all levels of the organization, a genuine commitment to and an enacted organizational culture that is staunchly dedicated to working within ethical bounds—and that such a value holds true for both visible aspects of the company as well as less visible ones. That is, even if organizations themselves are acting ethically internally, they cannot be willing to turn a blind eye to indiscretions in their supply chains. Rather, corporations must commit to making substantial efforts to get labor trafficking out of their supply chains—even when doing so may be counter to their short-term economic interests. I/O psychology offers critical supports underpinning these practices—attesting to the importance of alignment between an organization's espoused and enacted values (organizational value congruence), as well as the long-term bottom-line benefits that often accompany ethical organizational action and decision making.

Ultimately, it is ethically incumbent upon organizational leaders to make an effort to better understand the realities of trafficking in their organizations and broader supply chains. Fortunately, a number of readily available websites (e.g., https://www.slaveryfootprint.org, https://www.responsiblesourcingtool. org) provide information and downloadable templates that can serve as an important initial starting point to help companies raise awareness of potential trafficking in their supply chains. That said, while there is substantial research surrounding legal supply chain networks, knowledge of illicit supply networks is still extremely limited. To this end, researchers—including I/O psychologists—can contribute to mapping human trafficking networks, characterizing their components, and understanding geospatial data patterns. These analyses require substantial amounts of data, yet it is often the case that data are scarce or highly fragmented (Konrad et al., 2017). Moreover, due to its clandestine nature, it is often difficult even to gather statistics on human trafficking crimes, though, as we address next, some limited data sources do exist. I/O psychology's inroads with organizations and industries, as well as its vast data analytic potential, enable it to play an important role in the data collection, dissemination, and analyses that help in the fight against human trafficking.

USING DATA FOR PREDICTION AND PREVENTION

A central service offered by I/O psychology and its practitioners is the ability to curate, analyze, and interpret data in a way that is meaningful to organizations, industries, and, ultimately, the individuals affiliated with them. While many I/O psychologists strategically design and launch targeted data collections internally within an organization or industry, there is also great potential for I/O psychologists to use preexisting or externally available data to further understand problems and to inform solutions. In the case of trafficking, multiple sources of such data exist and can be used for the following purposes.

Online Advertisement Marketplaces as Sources of Trafficking-Related Data

It is well known that the internet has attracted many players from illicit enterprises, and its ubiquity and breadth offer a good example of the many unique nuances inherent in data collection and analyses for trafficking-related data. That is, while there has been considerable attention paid to the role of the internet in human trafficking, in many ways "the Internet-trafficking nexus remains unclear" (Volodko et al., 2020, p. 7). Labor trafficking, for instance, is perpetuated through the internet and online advertisement marketplaces via both formal and informal channels, including common social media sites such as Facebook (Latonero et al., 2015). Research has found, however, that a vast majority of reviewed job advertisements contained at least one indicator of trafficking, suggesting that the utility of such indicators for identifying trafficking may be somewhat limited. Specifically, exclusive or primary reliance on supposed indicators may result in an overwhelming number of "false positives" requiring additional information in order to identify actual trafficking-related job advertisements with improved precision (Volodko et al., 2020). Moreover, despite efforts to monitor recruitment agencies and identify illegal and abusive practices (e.g., those undertaken by the Philippines Overseas Employment Administration), many online advertisements go unmonitored, leaving the responsibility for verification of the job posting in the hands of the job seeker. Further exacerbating this problem is the finding that job seekers are more inclined to trust the opinions of others on familiar social media sites than they are to trust expert sources such as trafficking coalitions and national agencies—a widespread problem with dangerous ramifications (Latonero et al., 2015).

Similarly to labor trafficking's advertisements on common recruitment and social media sites, sex trafficking also leaves traces in public areas of the internet, including commercial sex and escort sites. Indeed, in April 2018, the U.S. Department of Justice seized the dominant online commercial sex marketplace Backpage (Savage & Williams, 2018). Five days later, the Stop Enabling Sex Traffickers Act and the Allow States and Victims to Fight Online Sex Trafficking Act were signed. These events dramatically changed the online distribution layer serving the underground commercial sex economy in the United States, thus impacting sex trafficking as a notable subset of that economy. Since those events, the online distribution channel has been fragmented across dozens of websites (Whitcomb, 2019). There are several challenges in trying to monitor, track, and interdict trafficking activities within this environment.

First, advertisers use social networking, dating, chat, and community websites, with more proficient traffickers frequently altering their online presence to elude identification. Some initial research assumed the phone numbers used by a provider stay the same over time and recommended group data on the basis of phone numbers (Whitcomb, 2019). However, recent technological changes make it easier for individuals to change phone numbers or have multiple numbers. To respond to these challenges, pictures posted in the advertisements are used to group similar posts (Freeman et al., 2022; Keskin et al., 2021). For online trafficking activities, similar activities to identify and uncover human trafficking circuits requires interdisciplinary research drawing on specialties beyond I/O psychology to also include the disciplines of computer science, information systems, operations research, and criminal justice.

Second, counter to best practice recommendations within industrial psychology, labor traffickers may intentionally write job ads in vague terms, with little job description, terms, or conditions of employment specified. Similarly, ads may use coded emojis rather than words (Whitney et al., 2018). For instance, sex traffickers may use an umbrella emoji to signify condom use or a crown to illustrate services managed by a pimp. Other obfuscation methods include constructing letters and numbers from character symbols or interspersing text within a phone number. These obfuscation techniques make it difficult for a computer to interpret and monitor advertisements while still allowing human readers to understand the intent of the posting. Some research exists on using machine learning to detect instances of human trafficking in escort advertisements, as well as social network analysis to detect human trafficking entities and networks in general.

Third, with multiple sites posting ads and promoting activities, the sheer volume of the data generated on these websites makes it challenging for law enforcement to trace, track, and interdict activities. The annual volume of posts from only a handful of popular websites can easily exceed 20 million records (Freeman et al., 2022). Even storing and manipulating this volume of data requires computational resources and expertise that, again, often calls for an interdisciplinary approach.

Finally, a significant amount of the content posted on these sites is a scam. In labor trafficking, job seekers may be scammed into paying a "fee" for recruitment, visa processing, or accommodations for jobs that do not exist. Beyond defrauding job seekers, such scams may also result in individuals finding themselves in conditions of forced labor if the fees are not paid. A similar situation can happen in sex trafficking, whereby a scammer may post an ad with the intent of having potential consumers pay an electronic deposit. While the potential consumer believes an encounter will follow, the scammer collects the deposit, and the interaction is terminated. In this case, the scammed individual essentially has no recourse, since the activity for which the deposit was made is generally illegal. Observing the same or very similar ads targeting multiple, geographically disparate regions is a strong indicator that an ad is a scam and does not represent a legitimate provider. Hence, searching for real networks within the voluminous data is similar to looking for a needle in a haystack. Combining anomaly detection procedures from the graph theory literature with machine learning and natural language processing is an active area of research that can help with this task.

Cell Phones as Sources of Trafficking-Related Data

Like the internet, applications on mobile devices collect massive amounts of data regarding individuals' habits and way of life—data that can be of great importance to I/O psychologists and other social scientists studying the behavior of individuals and organizations. Some data categories include core location data, spatial hierarchy metadata, place traffic data, and more. The availability of these data provides opportunities for legitimate businesses to innovate products and services, and a number of companies specialize in analyzing and optimizing this data. A secondary benefit of such data tracking is the ability to track and determine anomalies compared to regular patterns, which can be instrumental in flagging potential criminal activity. One company that curates such data is SafeGraph (https://www.safegraph.com). Some of the information SafeGraph makes available for academic purposes include place, traffic, and demographic aggregations that answer questions such as how often people visit a particular place, how long they stay, where they came from, and where else they go. Having access to these data points for particular locales, businesses, or transit routes has the potential to yield important information for not only law enforcement and researchers but also for organizations and industries as they attempt to better understand how their particular company or industry may be used by traffickers. With their expertise in data analysis, I/O psychologists can play an important role in analyzing, optimizing, and providing this information to organizations and industries and in advising leaders regarding appropriate organizational responses to what the data reveal.

Organizational Data as a Means of Prevention

Of course, companies in the industries most likely to encounter cases of human trafficking (e.g., hospitality, transportation, health care [sex trafficking]; agriculture, domestic work, garment industry [labor trafficking]) should be especially mindful of the roles they play in preventing trafficking. Beyond the more public sources of data addressed previously, many organizations themselves are also in possession of a vast amount of data, much of which often goes untouched but can be enormously informative in the hands of I/O psychologists. It is imperative that organizations lean on I/O psychologists and other data analysts to ensure they are optimizing their data and using data-driven measures to prevent trafficking to the best of their ability.

Although extensive and complex manufacturing channels can make it difficult for companies to monitor their supply chains for forced labor, new technology developments have made it easier for companies to better understand the ethics of their supply chains. Specifically, Forced Labor Risk Determination & Mitigation (FRDM), a software developed by the nonprofit organization Made in a Free World, uses machine learning to measure forced labor risks, in real time, at each level of production. Using an algorithm, FRDM predicts the likelihood that a certain product was made via forced labor and allows companies to compare themselves against industry norms.

More broadly, organizations should—at a minimum—become more aware of trafficking in their geographical area and industry, including keeping up-to-date on statewide reports (e.g., Polaris, Health and Human Services). Organizations can also seek out local trafficking taskforces and coalitions, and may find it beneficial to partner with such organizations for mutually beneficial outcomes—an undertaking that could be effectively facilitated by an I/O psychologist. In so doing, however, they should also engage with local populations that may have been negatively affected by antitrafficking interventions, including migrants and those engaging in commercial sex. That is, trafficking experts can provide information to organizations on how to prevent and respond to trafficking and can offer guidance for collecting and managing trafficking-relevant data in a way that it is useful for antitrafficking task forces but does not yield unintentionally harmful consequences. In a similar vein, organizations in industries that have greater potential to interact with trafficking victims (e.g., airlines, hospitals) may find it helpful to receive feedback from experts about the wording of questions or the development of data collection tools to ensure the appropriateness and reliability of the resulting data.

Not surprisingly, gaining reliable data has proven to be one of the biggest challenges in antitrafficking research, and there have been continuous calls for increased data collection, more reliable data, and a plan for data sharing (Laczko, 2007). Organizations in possession of data that could potentially inform trafficking trends should consult with trafficking coalitions and taskforces to find the best way to share the data (within the appropriate laws and policies). There are national databases (e.g., the Counter-Trafficking Data Collaborative led by Polaris and the United Nations' International Organization for Migration, the Human Trafficking Reporting System led by the Department of Justice) that aim to compile data used to predict and prevent trafficking. In 2017, IBM partnered with trafficking coalitions and financial institutions to develop and launch the Traffik Analysis Hub (TA Hub; https://www.traffikanalysis.org), an international data sharing and analytics platform for organizations aimed to disrupt human trafficking. Today, nonprofits, law enforcement, and financial institutions alike are using the TA Hub to share trafficking data and analyze trends and hotspots. Given that trafficking prevention relies on coordinated, community-based, data-driven approaches across multiple agencies and institutions, collecting and sharing data in such a manner is of the utmost importance.

CIVIC RESPONSIBILITY OF ORGANIZATIONS

Taking a step back, all of these considerations also bring into question the civic and societal responsibility of organizations. That is, to what extent do organizations have a responsibility to serve the larger community by investing corporate resources into addressing a societal problem? When, however, does an organization overstep? We take the position that, due to its broad societal relevance, the workscape (Mills et al., 2018) has a moral responsibility to work within its scope to proactively prevent any relevant underlying structural, societal, or individual vulnerabilities that might increase the likelihood of trafficking. This includes ensuring that all workers are paid a living wage (Carr et al., 2016; Jolluck, 2017). This is also relevant to ongoing discussions in I/O psychology about the potentiality of universal basic income initiatives (Hüffmeier & Zacher, 2021; Mills, 2021), which would enable individuals to be financially solvent as baseline, thus lessening their likelihood of falling victim to dangerous, illegal, or exploitative practices such as trafficking.

More specifically, we likewise take the position that organizations, while certainly justified in serving their own needs as an income-generating and sustainable entity, also bear some responsibility to, if not ensure that their organization is entirely divorced from any untoward activity (which is not always possible or realistic), at least take reasonable measures to reduce the likelihood that their organization can be used in a way so as to knowingly or unknowingly facilitate illicit activities that contribute to broader societal ills (e.g., International Organization for Standardization, 2018). That is, the organization has an ethical and moral responsibility to take reasonable steps within its power to combat such activity, to the extent possible. For individual organizations in relevant industries, this means training employees on how to identify trafficking indicators and to respond accordingly without fear of repercussions. For the overarching industries more broadly, this means being proactive and forthright with information about supply chains and labor sourcing, and collecting and analyzing industry-wide data that can be used to predict and, eventually, reduce or prevent human trafficking in the industry.

CONCLUSION

As the fight against human trafficking continues, I/O psychology has the potential to play an important role in informing, guiding, and optimizing how organizations can disrupt trafficking through proactivity, prediction, and prevention. Despite the known challenges inherent in tackling such an intentionally clandestine issue as human trafficking, organizations in trafficking-adjacent industries should heed the advice and undertake the actions recommended herein, working within the identified constraints to limit how and the extent to which traffickers can continue to rely on certain industries to enable their networks of human exploitation.

REFERENCES

Association for Supply Chain Management. (2022). *Introduction to processes*. https://scor.ascm.org/processes/introduction

Barrientos, S., Kothari, U., & Phillips, N. (2013). Dynamics of unfree labor in the contemporary global economy. *The Journal of Development Studies, 49*(8), 1037–1041. https://doi.org/10.1080/00220388.2013.780043

Bates, R. (2004). A critical analysis of evaluation practice: The Kirkpatrick model and the principle of beneficence. *Evaluation and Program Planning, 27*(3), 341–347. https://doi.org/10.1016/j.evalprogplan.2004.04.011

Brandenburg, D. C., & Ellinger, A. D. (2003). The future: Just-in-time learning expectations and potential implications for human resource development. *Advances in Developing Human Resources, 5*(3), 308–320. https://doi.org/10.1177/1523422303254629

Burke, L. A., & Hutchins, H. M. (2007). Training transfer: An integrative literature review. *Human Resource Development Review, 6*(3), 263–296. https://doi.org/10.1177/1534484307303035

Carr, S. C., MacLachlan, M., & Furnham, A. (Eds.). (2012). *Humanitarian work psychology*. Palgrave Macmillan. https://doi.org/10.1057/9781137015228

Carr, S. C., Parker, P. J., Arrowsmith, J., & Watters, P. A. (2016). The living wage: Theoretical integration and an applied research agenda. *International Labour Review, 155*(1), 1–24. https://doi.org/10.1111/j.1564-913X.2015.00029.x

Cockbain, E., & Bowers, K. (2019). Human trafficking for sex, labour and domestic servitude: How do key trafficking types compare and what are their predictors? *Crime, Law, and Social Change, 72*(1), 9–34. https://doi.org/10.1007/s10611-019-09836-7

ECPAT-USA. (2019). *Unpacking human trafficking: A survey of state laws targeting human trafficking in the hospitality industry*. https://static1.squarespace.com/static/594970e91b631b3571be12e2/t/5cc46d4dee6eb01fc10ed662/1556376919721/Unpacking+Human+Trafficking-v4.pdf

Flynn, A., & Walker, H. (2021). Corporate responses to modern slavery risks: An institutional theory perspective. *European Business Review, 33*(2), 295–315. https://doi.org/10.1108/EBR-05-2019-0092

Freedom United. (n.d.). *Survivor Alliance pledge to interact ethically with survivors*. https://www.freedomunited.org/advocate/survivor-alliance-pledge/

Freeman, N. K., Keskin, B. B., & Bott, G. J. (2022). Collaborating with local and federal law enforcement for disrupting sex trafficking networks. *INFORMS Journal of Applied Analytics, 52*(5), 446–459.

Fukushima, A. I., Hill, A., & Suchland, J. (2021). Editorial: Anti-trafficking education: Sites of care, knowledge, and power. *Anti-Trafficking Review, 17*(17), 1–18. https://doi.org/10.14197/atr.201221171

Furnham, A. (2016). The difficulties of applied research: A challenge for humanitarian work psychology and the Millennium Development Goals. In I. McWha-Hermann, D. C. Maynard, & M. O'Neill Berry (Eds.), *Humanitarian work psychology and the global development agenda* (pp. 176–180). Routledge.

Grossman, R., & Salas, E. (2011). The transfer of training: What really matters. *International Journal of Training and Development, 15*(2), 103–120. https://doi.org/10.1111/j.1468-2419.2011.00373.x

Gutierrez-Huerter, O. G., Gold, S., & Trautrims, A. (2021). Change in rhetoric but not in action? Framing of the ethical issue of modern slavery in a UK sector at high risk of labor exploitation. *Journal of Business Ethics, 182*(1), 35–58.

Hüffmeier, J., & Zacher, H. (2021). The basic income: Initiating the needed discussion in industrial, work, and organizational psychology. *Industrial and Organizational Psychology: Perspectives on Science and Practice, 14*(4), 531–562. https://doi.org/10.1017/iop.2021.91

Ibanez, M., & Gazan, R. (2016). *Detecting sex trafficking circuits in the U.S. through analysis of online escort advertisements.* IEEE/ACM International Conference on Advances in Social Networks Analysis and Mining (ASONAM), 892–895.

International Labour Organisation. (2009). *The cost of coercion.* International Labour Conference, Geneva, Switzerland. https://www.ilo.org/wcmsp5/groups/public/---ed_norm/---declaration/documents/publication/wcms_106

International Labour Organisation. (2017). *Global estimates of modern slavery.* https://www.ilo.org/wcmsp5/groups/public/@dgreports/@dcomm/documents/publication/wcms_575479.pdf

International Organization for Standardization. (2018). *Discovering ISO 26000.* https://www.iso.org/files/live/sites/isoorg/files/store/en/PUB100258.pdf

Jolluck, K. R. (2017). The future of work: A living wage and freedom for today's slaves. *Pacific Standard.* https://psmag.com/economics/the-future-of-work-a-living-wage-and-freedom-for-todays-slaves

Kahn, W. A. (1990). Psychological conditions of personal engagement and disengagement at work. *Academy of Management Journal, 33*(4), 692–724. https://doi.org/10.2307/256287

Kara, S. (2017). *Sex trafficking: Inside the business of modern slavery.* Columbia University Press. https://doi.org/10.7312/kara18033

Keskin, B. B., Bott, G. J., & Freeman, N. K. (2021). Cracking sex trafficking: Data analysis, pattern recognition, and path prediction. *Production and Operations Management, 30*(4), 1110–1135.

Kirkpatrick, D. L. (1976). Evaluation of training. In R. L. Craig (Ed.), *Training and development handbook: A guide to human resource development* (pp. 301–319). McGraw Hill.

Konrad, R. A., Trapp, A. C., Palmbach, T. M., & Blom, J. S. (2017). Overcoming human trafficking via operations research and analytics: Opportunities for methods, models, and applications. *European Journal of Operational Research, 259*(2), 733–745. https://doi.org/10.1016/j.ejor.2016.10.049

Laczko, F. (2007). Enhancing data collection and research on trafficking in persons. In E. U. Savona & S. Stefanizzi (Eds.), *Measuring human trafficking complexities and pitfalls* (pp. 37–44). Springer. https://doi.org/10.1007/0-387-68044-6_5

Latonero, M., Wex, B., & Dank, M. (2015). Technology and labor trafficking in a network society: General overview, emerging innovations, and Philippines case study.

https://cpb-us-e1.wpmucdn.com/sites.usc.edu/dist/2/672/files/2015/10/USC_Tech-and-Labor-Trafficking_Feb2015.pdf

LeBaron, G. (2021). *Combatting modern slavery: Why labor governance is failing and what we can do about it* [PowerPoint presentation]. Max Planck Institute for the Study of Societies. https://vimeo.com/520892117

Locke, R. (2013). *The promise and limits of private power.* Cambridge University Press. https://doi.org/10.1017/CBO9781139381840

Marriott International. (2021). *Marriot International modern slavery statement.* http://serve360.marriott.com/wp-content/uploads/2021/08/Modern_Slavery_Statement_2020.pdf

McDowell, R., Mason, M., & Mendoza, M. (2015, March 25). *AP investigation: Are slaves catching the fish you buy?* Associated Press. https://2016.sopawards.com/wp-content/uploads/2016/05/Seafood-From-Slaves.pdf

Miller, C., Greenbaum, J., Napolitano, K., Rajaram, S., Cox, J., Bachrach, L., Baldwin, S. B., & Stoklosa, H. (2019). *Health care provider human trafficking education: Assessment tool.* Laboratory to Combat Human Trafficking and HEAL Trafficking. https://www.dignityhealth.org/content/dam/dignity-health/pdfs/sacramento/msh-lcht-heal-assessment-survey.pdf

Miller, Q. C., Todorovic, K., Perez, C. O., Capparelli, A. L., & London, K. (2021). Lay-people's knowledge and misconceptions of sex trafficking influenced by training formats. *Journal of Human Trafficking, 9*(1), 94–118.

Mills, M. J. (2021). For the love of it: The overjustification effect and motivation crowding theory as the missing pieces in discussions of basic income's (a)motivating potential. *Industrial and Organizational Psychology: Perspectives on Science and Practice, 14*(4), 586–589. https://doi.org/10.1017/iop.2021.102

Mills, M. J., Pervez, A., & Mandeville, A. M. (2018). We're not there yet: Gender and the work-family interface in the modern workscape. In J. Nicklin (Ed.), *Work-life balance in the 21st century: Perspectives, practices, and challenges* (pp. 17–54). Nova Science Publishers.

Mills, M. J., Tortez, L. M., & Blanton, R. (2019). Moving beyond employees: Anti-trafficking training as facilitating social change. *Industrial and Organizational Psychology: Perspectives on Science and Practice, 12*(1), 34–38. https://doi.org/10.1017/iop.2019.4

Mills, M. J., Tortez, L. M., & Blanton, R. (2020). *Be the eyes: Training employees to recognize industry-relevant indicators of sex trafficking* [White paper]. Society for Industrial and Organizational Psychology. www.siop.org/Portals/84/docs/White%20Papers/trafficking.pdf?ver=2020-05-07-085835-860

Monciardini, D., Bernaz, N., & Andhov, A. (2021). The organizational dynamics of compliance with the UK Modern Slavery Act in the food and tobacco sector. *Business & Society, 60*(2), 288–340. https://doi.org/10.1177/0007650319898195

Newman, A., Donohue, R., & Eva, N. (2017). Psychological safety: A systematic review of the literature. *Human Resource Management Review, 27*(3), 521–535. https://doi.org/10.1016/j.hrmr.2017.01.001

Peck, J. L. (2021). A train-the-trainer programme to deliver high quality education for healthcare providers. *Anti-Trafficking Review, 17*(17), 140–147. https://doi.org/10.14197/atr.201221179

Pourmokhtari, N. (2015). Global human trafficking unmasked: A feminist rights-based approach. *Journal of Human Trafficking, 1*(2), 156–166. https://doi.org/10.1080/23322705.2014.1000078

Powell, C., Dickins, K., & Stoklosa, H. (2017). Training US health care professionals on human trafficking: Where do we go from here? *Medical Education Online, 22*(1), 1267980. https://doi.org/10.1080/10872981.2017.1267980

Ryff, C. D. (2018). Well-being with soul: Science in pursuit of human potential. *Perspectives on Psychological Science, 13*(2), 242–248. https://doi.org/10.1177/1745691617699836

Savage, C., & Williams, T. (2018, April 7). U.S. seizes backpage.com, a site accused of enabling prostitution. *The New York Times*. https://www.nytimes.com/2018/04/07/us/politics/backpage-prostitution-classified.html

Schreter, L. D., Jewers, M. M., & Sastrawidjaja, S. (2007). *The danger of conflating trafficking and sex work: A position paper of the Sex Workers Project at the Urban Justice Center*. Urban Justice Center. https://sexworkersproject.org/media-toolkit/downloads/20070330-BriefingPaperOnConflationOfTraffickingAndSexWork.pdf

State of California. (2021). The California Transparency in Supply Chains Act. https://oag.ca.gov/SB657

Stoklosa, H., Lyman, M., Bohnert, C., & Mittel, O. (2017). Medical education and human trafficking: Using simulation. *Medical Education Online, 22*(1), 1412746. https://doi.org/10.1080/10872981.2017.1412746

United States Department of Health and Human Services. (n.d.). *HHS competency framework*. https://humancapital.learning.hhs.gov/competency/framework.asp

Volodko, A., Cockbain, E., & Kleinberg, B. (2020). "Spotting the signs" of trafficking recruitment online: Exploring the characteristics of advertisements targeted at migrant job-seekers. *Trends in Organized Crime, 23*(1), 7–35. https://doi.org/10.1007/s12117-019-09376-5

Whitcomb, D. (2019). *Report gives a glimpse into the murky world of U.S. prostitution in post-Backpage-era*. Reuters. https://www.reuters.com/article/us-usa-prostitution-internet-exclusive-idUSKCN1RN13E

Whitney, J., Jennex, M., Elkins, A., & Frost, E. (2018). Don't want to get caught? Don't say it: The use of emojis in online human sex trafficking ads. In T. X. Bui (Ed.), *Proceedings of the 51st Hawaii International Conference on System Sciences* (pp. 4273–4282). HICSS Conference Office. https://scholarspace.manoa.hawaii.edu/server/api/core/bitstreams/4795f6bc-41a2-4924-a7da-9519beaef62a/content

Wickenhauser, D. (2019). *More states signing on to enlist truckers against human trafficking*. Trucking Truth. https://www.truckingtruth.com/news/Article-87/truckers-against-trafficking

Wilkens, C. (2018). Using drones to fight slavery in the fields: An examination of the practicality and constitutionality of applying 21st century technology to a 21st century problem. *Hastings Environmental Law Journal, 24*(1), 157–178.

Yale Global Health Justice Partnership. (2020, June). *Sex work vs trafficking: How they are different and why it matters*. https://law.yale.edu/sites/default/files/area/center/ghjp/documents/issue_brief_sex_work_vs_trafficking_v2.pdf

8 THE PSYCHOLOGICAL IMPACTS OF LABOR AND SEX TRAFFICKING

ELIZABETH K. HOPPER AND KELLY KINNISH

Human trafficking impacts survivors in complex ways. Experiences while being trafficked, as well as conditions of vulnerability prior to trafficking, although quite heterogeneous, often involve high rates of trauma and result in significant psychological harm. Conditions of coercive control, compounded by violence and emotional and relational harm, can lead to significant posttraumatic stress symptoms, depression, anxiety, substance use problems, suicidal ideation, self-injury, and other deleterious mental health outcomes. This chapter explores clinical psychological perspectives on the traumatic nature of human trafficking and related impacts on survivors' biological, emotional, cognitive, behavioral, and relational functioning.

TRAFFICKING EXPERIENCES

Experiences within trafficking can be quite disparate, including variability in the relationship of the victim to the perpetrator, elements of coercion, types of activities that are coerced, length of trafficking, and level of trauma exposure. Trauma exposure may include violence and abuse, harm to others, and nonphysical means of coercive control.

https://doi.org/10.1037/0000379-009
Psychological Perspectives on Human Trafficking: Theory, Research, Prevention, and Intervention, L. Dryjanska, E. K. Hopper, and H. Stoklosa (Editors)

Violence and Abuse

Trafficking survivors experience a range of traumatic and harmful experiences while being trafficked (Curtis et al., 2008; Hopper, 2017a; Kiss, Pocock, et al., 2015; Kiss, Yun, et al., 2015; Lederer & Wetzel, 2014; Nodzenski et al., 2020; O'Callaghan et al., 2013; Ottisova et al., 2018; Sprang & Cole, 2018; Swaner et al., 2016; Turner-Moss et al., 2014; Twis et al., 2020; Zimmerman et al., 2006). Physical assault and injury are commonly experienced by victims of both labor and sex trafficking (Curtis et al., 2008; Moore et al., 2021; Reid, 2016; Stöckl et al., 2021; Turner-Moss et al., 2014). A study of sexually exploited youth found that close to half of survivors (47%) reported being hit, pushed, slapped, or beaten as a means of control (Hopper, 2017a). Physical harm may also stem from trafficking conditions; for instance, the lack of personal protective equipment and safety regulations increases the risk of injuries and other physical health impacts in labor trafficking survivors (De Vries & Farrell, 2018). Sex trafficking typically involves multiple experiences of coerced or forced sex acts, in some cases, including violent sexual assaults, that may last anywhere from hours to years (Curtis et al., 2008; Hopper, 2017a; Lederer & Wetzel, 2014). Although sex trafficking is marked by sexual violence, sexual assault can also be an element of coercive control and abuse in situations of labor trafficking (Hopper & Gonzalez, 2018).

In a recent study involving the largest global dataset of trafficking survivors to date, with the majority (69.7%) being survivors of labor trafficking, around half of the sample reported physical and sexual violence, with higher rates reported among women and girls, and among victims of sexual exploitation (Stöckl et al., 2021). Similarly, in a sample of over 1,000 men, women, and children in Southeast Asia who experienced labor and/or sex trafficking (Kiss, Pocock, et al., 2015), 38% reported physical violence (49% men, 41% women, 43% boys, 20% girls), and 20% reported sexual violence (1% men, 44% women, 2% boys, 26% girls), with 22% sustaining a serious injury. Although physical violence and sexual violence are frequently found in situations of human trafficking, notably, around half or more of the participants in these studies did not report physical or sexual violence as a method of coercion, which highlights the role of other coercive tactics common to conditions of sex and labor trafficking (Stöckl et al., 2021).

Harm to Others

Trafficking victims are sometimes forced to witness or participate in violence against others (McMullen et al., 2013; Kiss, Yun, et al., 2015; Hopper, 2017a; Reid, 2016). Kiss, Yun, et al. (2015) reported that 17% of a sample of labor and sex trafficked children in Southeast Asia witnessed the trafficker beat or intentionally hurt someone else. Migrants aboard Thai fishing vessels have reported witnessing beatings, torture, and even the murder of fellow crew members (Lagon, 2014; United Nations Inter-Agency Project on Human Trafficking, 2009). In a group of former child soldiers, having to personally kill or torture other people was identified as the worst thing that had happened during the war by 32% of boys (McMullen et al., 2013).

Coercive Control

Beyond direct violence and forced witnessing or infliction of harm to others, traffickers may maintain control through psychological means such as threats (to the survivor, survivor's family, and others), isolation and alienation from other sources of support, deprivation of basic needs, and emotional abuse in the form of verbal aggression, belittling, and humiliation; these psychological forms of coercion are often purposely employed to facilitate dependence and maintain control (Baldwin et al., 2015; Casassa et al., 2022; Curtis et al., 2008; Hopper, 2017a; Iglesias-Rios et al., 2019a; Moore et al., 2021; Reid, 2016). Close to half (47%) of survivors in a cross-sectional study in Southeast Asia experienced threats of harm to themselves or someone they cared about while being trafficked (Kiss, Pocock, et al., 2015). A large study involving primarily survivors of labor trafficking identified a range of methods of coercive control, including: excessive work hours and withholding of wages (82%), deception (80%), denial of movement, food, or medical attention (76%), threats to self or family (60%), documents confiscated (60%), debt bondage (35%), and being given alcohol and/or drugs (4%; Stöckl et al., 2021). Similar forms of violence and exploitation were found in a study of sexually exploited youth, with nearly all participants (97%) describing some means by which they were monitored and controlled by their trafficker. Beyond physical and sexual violence, youth reported experiencing social isolation (91%), resource deprivation (78%), and psychological coercion in the form of threats, verbal abuse, and the instillation of fear (84%; Hopper, 2017a).

MENTAL HEALTH AND PSYCHOLOGICAL IMPACTS OF TRAFFICKING

As a result of these often extreme experiences of coercive control, physical assault and injury, and sexual violation, survivors of trafficking may have complex mental health needs. Emerging research on labor trafficking indicates that dangerous, physically harmful work tasks and excessive work hours result in physical, psychological, social/relational and educational harms to survivors (De Vries & Farrell, 2018; Ibrahim et al., 2019; Murphy, 2017; Owens et al., 2014; Turner-Moss et al., 2014; Whetten et al., 2011). Sex trafficking is associated with more extensive developmental impacts, including greater severity of symptoms, higher risk behaviors, more comorbid mental health diagnoses, and greater functional impairment than other forms of trauma exposure (Chapple & Crawford, 2019; Cole et al., 2016; M. C. Cook et al., 2018; Lanctôt et al., 2020; Palines et al., 2020). Numerous studies document high rates of psychiatric disorders among trafficking survivors, especially posttraumatic stress disorder (PTSD), depression, and anxiety, as well as comorbid conditions such as psychotic disorders, bipolar disorder, conduct disorder, and attention-deficit/hyperactivity disorder (Abas et al., 2013; Basson et al., 2012; Beksinska et al., 2021; Choi et al., 2009; Cole et al., 2016; Hossain et al., 2010; Institute of Medicine & National Research Council, 2013; Le et al., 2018; Lederer & Wetzel, 2014; Oram et al., 2016; Ottisova et al., 2016; Ottisova et al., 2018; Palines et al., 2020).

Pretrafficking trauma and adversity contribute to trafficking vulnerability (see Chapter 1, this volume), and trafficking compounds the impacts of earlier trauma. Findings from multiple studies indicate that more significant mental health symptoms posttrafficking are associated with higher levels of trauma and abuse prior to the trafficking experience(s) (Abas et al., 2013; Beksinska et al., 2021; Choi et al., 2009; Hopper, 2017a; Ottisova et al., 2016). Additionally, there are specific dimensions of trafficking experiences that are associated with greater mental health symptoms and diagnoses, including the level of coercion, threats, sexual violence, physical violence, and serious injury; the length of time being trafficked; perceived restrictions to freedom; and poor living and work conditions (Hossain et al., 2010; Iglesias-Rios et al., 2019a; Kiss et al., 2015; Ottisova et al., 2016).

Posttraumatic Stress and Complex Trauma Symptoms

Given the extent of trauma exposure during trafficking and the high rates of pretrafficking trauma exposure (e.g., child physical and sexual abuse, traumatic loss and separation, intimate partner violence and community violence; Basson et al., 2012; Greenbaum et al., 2022; Hopper, 2017a; Landers et al., 2017), it is not surprising that traumatic stress impacts are especially prominent among trafficking survivors (Oram et al., 2016; Ottisova et al., 2016; Stoltz et al., 2007; Turner-Moss et al., 2014; Wilson & Butler, 2014). Numerous studies document very high rates of posttraumatic stress (PTS) symptoms and PTSD diagnosis (Abas et al., 2013; Basson et al., 2012; Cole et al., 2016; Hossain et al., 2010; Kiss, Pocock, et al., 2015; Kiss, Yun, et al., 2015; Lederer & Wetzel, 2014; Oram et al., 2016; Ottisova et al., 2018; Palines et al., 2020; Turner-Moss et al., 2014). Among a sample of labor-trafficked and exploited adults in the United Kingdom, over half reported PTSD symptoms (Turner-Moss et al., 2014).

PTS symptoms associated with trafficking may be more severe than that of other traumas. Cole et al. (2016) compared service seeking youth who had experienced sexual abuse and commercial sexual exploitation (CSEC) with a matched sample of youth who experienced sexual abuse but not commercial sexual exploitation. The CSEC group endorsed significantly greater overall PTSD symptoms, as well as greater avoidance and hyperarousal subdomain symptoms. Other research demonstrates the compounded impacts of multiple traumas experienced by trafficking survivors on PTS symptom presentation (Iglesias-Rios et al., 2019b; Self-Brown et al., 2021). Self-Brown et al. (2021) found that sex-trafficked youth who reported a history of multiple trauma types were significantly more likely to meet PTSD criteria and endorse higher rates of emotional distress than youth who had not experienced multiple types of trauma. Trauma exposure in multiple categories was a better predictor of mental health symptoms than individual categories, consistent with polyvictimization research with other populations (Finkelhor et al., 2007; Holt et al., 2007; Turner et al., 2010; Vranceanu et al., 2007).

Posttrauma symptoms are likely to be more extensive if the trauma is repeated or chronic, begins early in development, and involves interpersonal trauma that is severe or pervasive (Herman, 1992), conditions that characterize the pretrafficking and/or trafficking experiences of many people (Hopper, 2017a; Zimmerman et al., 2006). *Complex trauma* is a term that refers both to these experiences of multiple or chronic trauma and to their widespread impacts across various domains of development and functioning, including attachment and relationships, affect regulation, behavior, self-concept, attention and cognition, and biology and health (A. Cook et al., 2005; Courtois, 2008; Herman, 1992). Complex posttraumatic stress disorder (C-PTSD) is a new diagnostic category included in the *International Statistical Classification of Diseases and Related Health Problems (ICD-11)* that describes these more complex reactions related to exposure to early and/or chronic trauma.[1]

---

[1]Beyond the core PTSD symptoms of reexperiencing, avoidance, and hyperarousal, C-PTSD includes three additional "disturbances in self-organization," including severe and persistent difficulties with affect regulation (e.g., emotional volatility), negative self-concept (e.g., beliefs about oneself as worthless, accompanied by feelings of shame), and relationship difficulties (e.g., challenges in feeling close to others and sustaining relationships; World Health Organization, 2019).

Complex trauma presentations have been identified in survivors of both labor and sex trafficking (Evans, 2020; Hopper & Gonzalez, 2018; Jowett et al., 2021; Ottisova et al., 2018). In fact, two thirds of a sample of adult survivors of labor and/or sex trafficking had symptoms in multiple complex trauma domains, including affect dysregulation and impulsivity, alterations in attention and consciousness, changes in interpersonal relationships, revictimization, somatic dysregulation, and alterations in self-perception (Hopper & Gonzalez, 2018). A study of Yaziki women who were held in prolonged captivity and experienced sexual slavery by Islamic State forces found that half of the survivors (50.9%) had probable C-PTSD, while 20% had probable PTSD (Hoffman et al., 2018). In a sample of over 100 asylum-seeking adults from 37 countries, including survivors of torture, human trafficking, and other forms of interpersonal violence, 66% met full C-PTSD diagnostic criteria (Jowett et al., 2021). A systemic review of the prevalence of complex trauma in survivors of human trafficking found that an average of 44% of survivors of human trafficking in the reviewed studies had C-PTSD (Evans et al., 2022).

Researchers are similarly beginning to examine complex trauma in trafficked youth. A qualitative study of youth who had experienced sex trafficking as minors found that over half (56%) of them showed symptoms from multiple symptoms domains of C-PTSD (Hopper, 2017a). Boys and girls trafficked for sex and labor in the United Kingdom had greater rates of complex trauma than matched, nontrafficked controls, with symptoms being particularly notable in the case of multiple trauma exposure (Ottisova et al., 2018). Complex trauma domains of impact among trafficking survivors are further described below.

Attachment and Relationships
Trauma related to human trafficking and exploitation is inherently interpersonal and may compound earlier experiences of the world as unsafe and others as untrustworthy (Cecchet & Thoburn, 2014; Ravi et al., 2017). Trauma-coerced attachment to the trafficker can result in minimization or denial of the coercion and abuse and a sense of loyalty to the perpetrator, which leaves victims more likely to return to their exploiter (Chambers et al., 2022). Even after exiting, trauma-related impacts often lead to subsequent difficulties for survivors in forming and maintaining relationships, ranging from mistrust and avoidance of close relationships to rapid engagement in new relationships without self-protective boundaries, increasing vulnerability to revictimization. Relational challenges were endorsed by 91% of participants in a qualitative study of youth who experienced sex trafficking,

including feelings of alienation, social avoidance, difficulty setting bound-aries, posttrafficking involvement in unhealthy and/or abusive relationships, high-risk sexual practices, and revictimization (Hopper, 2017a). Similarly, in a qualitative study of adult female survivors of sex trafficking, Mumey et al. (2021) noted three types of trafficking-related relational impacts among survivors: alterations in closeness to preexisting social networks, difficulty trusting others, and difficulty maintaining lasting intimate relationships. Dif-ficulty establishing trust in relationships was also noted among labor traf-ficking survivors (Owens et al., 2014). Survivors may experience a sense of alienation from family or community after exiting the trafficking situation. In Kiss, Yun, et al. (2015), 54% of trafficked youth worried about how they would be treated upon their return home. Survivors' concerns about social ostracization and maltreatment by others in their community of origin have been linked to more negative mental health outcomes (e.g., PTSD, depres-sion, anxiety; Ibrahim et al., 2018; Kiss, Yun, et al., 2015; Nabunya et al., 2021). In a study of asylum seekers and trafficking survivors, participants with C-PTSD presented with significantly higher relationship-related needs compared with those with PTSD (Jowett et al., 2021).

Self-Concept

Poor self-concept is recognized as both a risk factor and impact of trafficking (Reid, 2011). Negative cognitive appraisals (changes in views of the self, the world, and the future), especially low self-esteem and shame, are com-monly found in survivors of trafficking (Contreras et al., 2017; Nodzenski et al., 2020; Perry et al., 2022; Ravi et al., 2017). This reaction is exacer-bated for survivors who live within social contexts that blame victims for the acts of offenders. Human trafficking creates subcultures in which a victim's personal worth is equated with the ability to bring financial benefit to the trafficker(s). Moreover, traffickers may utilize emotional abuse to further manipulate and coerce victims, strategically undermining self-concept; for example, an exploiter may tell their victim that they are "dirty" or "worth-less" and that no one else loves them or will ever want them, positioning themselves as the sole potential source of affection and support. In Hopper (2017a), 91% of youth described negative impacts of trafficking on their sense of self. Specifically, the youth described being blamed for early sexual abuse and labeled "promiscuous," "bad," and "damaged." In Kiss, Yun, et al. (2015), 56% of trafficked youth reported feelings of guilt or shame, and 5% said they had no hopes for the future. When every effort to change or get out of the trafficking situation has been thwarted, victims may experience "learned helplessness," a conditioned sense of powerlessness that prevents victims from seeing any potential different future for themselves (Peterson et al., 1993). These experiences can lead trafficking survivors to perceive efforts to create positive change as futile and to view the world as a meaningless place. (See also Chapter 6, this volume, for a social psychological exploration of the intersection of self-concept and trafficking.)

Emotions and Regulatory Capacity
Difficulty with emotion identification, expression, and modulation is a hallmark of complex trauma. Trafficking survivors may internalize their stress reactions, leading to increased incidence of depression, anxiety, and shame. Others experience more explosive emotional reactions and have difficulty calming down. Hopper (2017a) found impairments in emotion regulation and impulse control in 88% of a sample of youth who had experienced sex trafficking. Basson et al. (2012) similarly noted mental health needs related to anger control (58%) and affect regulation (43%) in a sample of over 200 girls who experienced CSEC. In interviews of over 200 adult and adolescent women from 14 countries who had been sex trafficked or sexually assaulted while being exploited for labor, survivors reported high rates of irritability (83%), temper outbursts (67%), frequent arguments (57%), urges to injure others (36%), and urges to break things (29%; Zimmerman et al., 2006). Because emotional regulation and expression is so foundational to interpersonal interactions and individual functioning, these impacts can have broad effects on relationships, learning, work life, and many other aspects of personal growth and development.

Behavior
Emotional dysregulation can interfere with reflective decision making and lead to impulsive, risky, or destructive behavior. Because of these trauma-related impacts, trafficking survivors may act in ways that appear defensive, volatile, oppositional, and extreme. They may engage in hazardous behaviors such as self-harm, unsafe sexual practices, harmful alcohol and substance use, running away, excessive risk-taking, and illegal activities such as stealing or assaulting others (Basson et al., 2012, 2018; Cole et al., 2016; Hopper, 2017a). At other times, they may be overcontrolled and rigid or excessively compliant. Cole et al. (2016) found that commercially sexually exploited youth struggle with more emotional and behavioral problems than peers who experienced sexual abuse only, including truancy, running away, conduct disorder, sexualized behaviors, and substance abuse. High-risk behavior and trauma impacts often compound and escalate vulnerabilities. For example, pretrafficking physical or sexual violence is linked to an increased risk of self-harm in sex and labor-trafficked children (Kiss, Yun et al., 2015); self-harm

is often coupled with feelings of guilt or shame (Reid, 2011), cyclically contributing to further unsafe behavior. High-risk behavior such as running away or substance use increases the risk of revictimization through retrafficking or exposure to other forms of interpersonal abuse such as sexual assault or intimate partner violence. Early research suggests that rates of revictimization for youth who have experienced CSEC are extremely high (69–90%; Reid & Piquero, 2014).

Although there has been limited research on behavioral concerns related to labor trafficking, there is evidence that child labor exposes children to abuse, which is associated with several adverse mental health outcomes. In a systematic review of studies of child labor trafficking impact, Ibrahim et al. (2019) found that child labor was associated with emotional and behavioral disorders, including issues with peers and conduct problems, and decreased coping efficacy.

Attention and Cognition

Mobilization of the body's stress response system is associated with activation of areas of the brain associated with more primitive emotional responses (e.g., the locus coeruleus and the amygdala) and impaired function of areas implicated in executive functioning (e.g., the prefrontal cortex), leading to difficulty thinking clearly, reasoning, or problem solving (Arnsten et al., 2015). During or after traumatic events, survivors might find it difficult to anticipate and plan for the future, sustain attention in order to learn new information, and calmly think through a problem and consider alternatives before responding. Research has identified significant attentional and impulse control concerns in youth who experienced commercial sexual exploitation (Basson et al., 2012; Hopper, 2017a). Such challenges in attention and cognition may exacerbate preexisting conditions (e.g., intellectual or developmental disabilities; Reid, 2018) and can impact a person's ability to learn in school, develop new skills, and perform successfully in a work setting.

Dissociation is another trauma-related form of altered attention and consciousness that involves detachment from one's body or mental processes (e.g., thoughts, feelings, memories, or sense of identity) to protect against exposure to intense trauma and overwhelming emotion (Putnam, 1997). Trafficking survivors may experience transient dissociative reactions during extreme or repeated episodes of threat or violence, sometimes termed "peritraumatic dissociation." This can lead trafficking survivors to experience memory loss or difficulty in recalling significant events (Salami et al., 2018). Episodes of dissociation may continue even after exiting the trafficking situation and can lead to a fractured sense of time and of identity. A study of trafficked youth found dissociation and dysregulation in consciousness in the majority (81%) of participants (Hopper, 2017a); people who were initially commercially sexually exploited as minors may be particularly vulnerable to experiencing dissociative symptoms (e.g., depersonalization, out of body experiences, derealization, and psychic numbing) due to the developmental impacts of trauma (Roe-Sepowitz, 2012). However, as in other areas of mental health impact, trafficking may have a unique contribution to dissociative symptoms. Commercially sexually exploited minors show more dissociation than sexually abused peers who have not experienced trafficking, perhaps due to the extent of trauma exposure and/or to societal responses to the victimization (Cole et al., 2016; Kenny et al., 2020). In Kenny et al.'s (2020) study, 20% of commercially sexually exploited girls met criteria for PTSD dissociative subtype, while only 7.7% of a comparison group of at-risk youth did. Dissociation impacts multiple domains of well-being and functioning, including physical and psychological safety, learning, relationships, and identity.

Biology and Health

Researchers have documented a range of somatic symptoms and physical health impacts commonly reported by survivors of labor and sex trafficking (Crawford & Kaufman, 2008; Ibrahim et al., 2019; Lederer & Wetzel, 2014; Turner-Moss et al., 2014; Volgin et al., 2019). Although some such impacts result directly from malnourishment, lack of medical and dental care, unsafe working conditions, and physical and sexual violence during trafficking (Ottisova et al., 2016), trafficking survivors may also experience impacts related to chronic exposure to stress and trauma including fatigue, headaches, insomnia, pain, dizziness, and memory problems (Grossman et al., 2019; Kiss, Pocock, et al., 2015; Lederer & Wetzel, 2014; Oram et al., 2016; Ottisova et al., 2016; Turner-Moss et al., 2014).

Chronic activation of the body's survival system may lead to some of these short and long-term biological responses and somatic impacts in trafficking survivors. Results from the Adverse Childhood Experiences study have highlighted the long-term impact of multiple early adverse or traumatic experiences on later health (Felitti et al., 1998). Stress and trauma activate the central nervous system and sensitize the hypothalamus–pituitary–adrenal axis, impacting release of glucocorticoids such as the stress hormone cortisol (Godoy et al., 2018). Repeated or chronic activation of the body's stress response may lead to physiological impacts through various pathways, such as ongoing muscular tension that gives rise to physical complaints like headaches, repeated epinephrine surges that lead to long-term outcomes such as high blood pressure, and chronic activation of the body's stress hormones and systemic inflammatory responses that contribute to fatigue, weight gain, and other health risks such as cardiovascular disease (De Bellis & Zisk, 2014; Godoy et al., 2018; Zarse et al., 2019). More research is needed to explore the impact of chronic stress and trauma on long-term health for survivors of labor and sex trafficking.

Depression, Anxiety, and Suicidal Ideation

In addition to PTS and complex trauma symptoms, symptoms of depression and anxiety are frequently experienced by trafficking survivors (Basson et al., 2012; Kiss, Pocock, et al., 2015; Kiss, Yun et al., 2015; Lederer & Wetzel, 2014; Oram et al., 2016; Ottisova et al., 2016). In Basson et al. (2012), 75% of a sample of sexually exploited and trafficked youth in the United States experienced depression, and 55% experienced anxiety. Kiss, Pocock, et al. (2015) reported that 61% of a large sample of men, women, and children trafficked for labor and sex in Southeast Asia met criteria for probable depression and 43% for anxiety. In an associated study focused on children, more than half of participants had depression, with higher rates in girls than boys, and about one third suffered from anxiety (Kiss, Yun, et al., 2015).

Rates of suicidal ideation and suicide attempts are reportedly also very high among trafficking survivors (Basson et al., 2012; Kiss, Yun, et al. 2015; Lederer & Wetzel, 2014; Ottisova et al., 2018; Sprang & Cole, 2018). A study of survivors who sought posttrafficking services in England found that over half of the women, and 13.5% of men, endorsed suicidal ideation (Oram et al., 2016). In Hopper's (2017a) study, 59% of the youth endorsed experiencing suicidal ideation, and 38% acknowledged a history of suicide attempts. Half of a sample of familial sex-trafficked children in the United States reported having attempted suicide (Sprang & Cole, 2018). Of 51 labor- and sex-trafficked children from 21 countries receiving services in the United Kingdom, 27% reported having attempted suicide (Ottisova et al., 2018). Among children who experienced labor or sex trafficking, greater suicidal ideation was associated with early experiences of physical and sexual violence, as well as with particular experiences during trafficking, including excessive work hours, threats, adverse living conditions, restricted freedom, severe physical violence, and sexual violence (Kiss, Yun, et al., 2015).

Substance Use and Substance Use Disorder

Problematic substance use is an area of concern for many trafficking survivors (Basson et al., 2012; Bath et al., 2020; Cole et al., 2016; M. C. Cook et al., 2018; Hopper, 2017b; Landers et al., 2017; Lederer & Wetzel, 2014; Moore et al., 2021; Reid & Piquero, 2014; Varma et al., 2015). In some cases, substance use precedes trafficking and may be related to earlier trauma and adversity, while in others, the trafficking experience is a precursor of any substance use. Traffickers may use substances as a tool to facilitate recruitment and grooming of potential victims, including targeting individuals with pre-existing substance use disorders or introducing new substances (Hopper, 2017b). In a study of youth who experienced sex trafficking, 47% described the use of alcohol or drugs during their trafficking initiation process (Hopper, 2017a). Substance use may be a method for coping with extreme trauma exposure during the trafficking experiences; in some cases, the use of substances is facilitated by traffickers throughout the trafficking experience in order to maintain control over those being exploited. Posttrafficking, substance use may continue to be a strategy for coping specifically with upsetting memories of trafficking experiences and with trauma and dysregulation more broadly (Hopper, 2017b; Ravi et al., 2017).

There is a growing body of literature on the intersection between human trafficking and substance use, underscoring compounding vulnerabilities and impacts. A review of cases from a hospital-based antihuman trafficking program in the United States identified a particularly strong link between familial trafficking and substance use, including substance use among family members, as well as patients who experienced trafficking (White et al., 2023). Commercial sexual exploitation itself appears to be a unique risk factor for substance use, above the contribution of other forms of sexual abuse. In one study, 68% of service-seeking youth who had experienced sex trafficking had problematic substance use, as compared with only 26% of sexually abused peers who had not experienced trafficking (Cole et al., 2016). A study of youth in a trafficking-specific specialty court found that 88% of juvenile justice-involved youth impacted by commercial sexual exploitation reported substance use, including marijuana (87%), alcohol (54%), and methamphetamine (33%) use (Bath et al., 2020). A history of child abuse and co-occurring mental health problems was associated with greater substance use problems among these young people; in fact, youth with a mood disorder were five times more likely to report substance use than those without one (Bath et al., 2020).

There are little data available on problematic substance use in some populations, such as survivors of labor trafficking, particularly those from immigrant communities. Results from a large dataset involving primarily survivors of labor trafficking found a relatively low overall frequency of the use of drugs and alcohol as a coercive element, particularly for males (3.3%, versus 8.9% for females; Stöckl et al., 2021). Similarly, providers in the

Midwest who served both foreign-born and domestic-born survivors of trafficking reported some substance use among the labor trafficking survivors that they served, particularly as a posttrafficking coping mechanism, but did not endorse concerns that rose to the level of a substance use disorder. In contrast, they noted problematic substance use among survivors of sex trafficking, including frequent use of alcohol and marijuana, polysubstance use, significant use of opioids, and increased use of stimulants (Koegler et al., 2022). More research is needed to identify whether confounding variables such as immigration-related concerns, cultural perspectives on substance use, and/or lack of access to health care may be interfering with the identification of needs related to substance use for survivors of labor trafficking.

Psychological Impacts by Trafficking Type

As highlighted earlier, there is a growing research base on the psychological effects of sex trafficking, with more limited literature describing the mental health impacts of labor trafficking. In particular, there is a lack of research that directly compares mental health outcomes of labor trafficking with those of sex trafficking. A scoping review of labor trafficking of children found that it shares common risk factors with sex trafficking, such as prior child maltreatment and out of home placement; however, labor-trafficked children had less prior child welfare involvement than children who experienced sex trafficking and showed demographic differences (e.g., more likely to be younger, male, Black or nonwhite, and Hispanic; Greenbaum et al., 2022). In one of the few studies comparing sex and labor trafficking impacts (Hopper & Gonzalez, 2018), sex trafficking survivors reported more severe posttrauma reactions than labor trafficking survivors, including more PTSD and C-PTSD symptoms. Sex trafficking survivors also had higher prevalence rates of pretrafficking child abuse and a higher incidence of physical and sexual violence during trafficking than those who had experienced labor trafficking. In a study of female trafficking survivors in Nepal, although there were higher rates of depression and PTSD among women who had been trafficked for sexual exploitation, women who were trafficked for other forms of labor had a very high prevalence of mental health impacts, most notably, anxiety (87.5%) and depression (81.8%; Tsutsumi et al., 2008).

Further research is needed to explore variation in psychological impacts across various forms of trafficking, including elucidation of differences among different forms of labor trafficking. For instance, Rose et al. (2021) conducted a cross-sectional study that compared survivors of domestic servitude, survivors of other forms of labor trafficking, and survivors of sexual exploitation in the United Kingdom. They found that those exploited for domestic servitude reported more experiences of violence and restriction than survivors of other forms of labor trafficking and endorsed higher levels of mental health problems. Although these results may have been confounded by gender, the authors highlighted the importance of research that separates findings across types of exploitation, including highly disparate experiences of labor trafficking.

CONCLUSION AND RECOMMENDATIONS

Extensive psychological impacts have been found in survivors of human trafficking, most notably, symptoms of PTSD; anxiety, depression, and suicidal ideation; and related conditions such as substance use disorders, self-injury, and other high-risk behaviors. The evidence base regarding impacts of labor trafficking specifically is more limited but shows a similar range of adverse mental health outcomes, including PTSD, depression, suicidal ideation, and impaired coping. Because of common experiences of developmental trauma, polyvictimization, and severe traumatic stress exposure, researchers are beginning to explore complex trauma presentations and C-PTSD diagnosis in trafficking survivors, documenting impacts in affect regulation, self-concept, relationships, and other related domains of development and functioning.

Additional research is needed to develop a more advanced and nuanced understanding of the psychological impacts of trafficking. In particular, there is a paucity of research that focuses specifically on the psychological impacts of labor trafficking, including subtypes of labor trafficking, and that compares labor and sex trafficking experiences and outcomes. Further research is needed to identify contributors to variation in trafficking-related symptomatology, including characteristics of the trafficking experience, relationship with the perpetrator, pretrafficking trauma exposure, intersectionality, and other potential contributors. Given the strong link between trauma, substance use, and human trafficking, additional research is also needed to increase understanding of substance use in survivors of trafficking. Another underexplored but potentially fruitful area of research is the identification and exploration of resiliency factors (e.g., internal characteristics such as self-efficacy and external factors such as the quality of the support network) that influence the psychological impact of human trafficking (see Chapter 10, this volume, on positive psychology).

Given the extensive trauma exposure and posttrafficking psychological symptoms and risk behaviors that may be found in survivors of sex or labor trafficking, psychology has a key role in many areas within the antitrafficking field. Psychologists, social workers, and other mental or behavioral health professionals can contribute through research that furthers the understanding of psychological impacts of sex or labor trafficking; education and consultation that disseminates awareness of these impacts; advocacy that utilizes this awareness to influence public policy, laws, budgets, and systems that are relevant for people who have been affected by trafficking; and service delivery that is responsive to the unique needs of different groups of trafficking survivors.

REFERENCES

Abas, M., Ostrovschi, N. V., Prince, M., Gorceag, V. I., Trigub, C., & Oram, S. (2013). Risk factors for mental disorders in women survivors of human trafficking: A historical cohort study. *BMC Psychiatry*, *13*(1), 204. https://doi.org/10.1186/1471-244X-13-204

Arnsten, A. F. T., Raskind, M. A., Taylor, F. B., & Connor, D. F. (2015). The effects of stress exposure on prefrontal cortex: Translating basic research into successful treatments for post-traumatic stress disorder. *Neurobiology of Stress*, *1*, 89–99. https://doi.org/10.1016/j.ynstr.2014.10.002

Baldwin, S. B., Fehrenbacher, A. E., & Eisenman, D. P. (2015). Psychological coercion in human trafficking: An application of Biderman's framework. *Qualitative Health Research*, *25*(9), 1171–1181. https://doi.org/10.1177/1049732314557087

Basson, D., Langs, J., Acker, K., Katz, S., Desai, N., & Ford, J. (2018). *Psychotherapy for commercially sexually exploited children: A guide for community-based behavioral health practitioners and agencies*. West Coast Children's Clinic. https://www.westcoastcc.org/wp-content/uploads/2018/10/MH_Treatment_Guide_CSEC.pdf

Basson, D., Rosenblatt, E., & Haley, H. (2012). *Research to action: Sexually exploited minors needs and strengths*. West Coast Children's Clinic. https://www.westcoastcc.org/WCC_SEM_Needs-and-Strengths_FINAL.pdf

Bath, E., Barnert, E., Godoy, S., Hammond, I., Mondals, S., Farabee, D., & Grella, C. (2020). Substance use, mental health, and child welfare profiles of juvenile justice-involved commercially sexually exploited youth. *Journal of Child and Adolescent Psychopharmacology*, *30*(6), 389–397. https://doi.org/10.1089/cap.2019.0057

Beksinska, A., Jama, Z., Kabuti, R., Kungu, M., Babu, H., Nyariki, E., Shah, P., Nyabuto, C., Okumu, M., Mahero, A., Ngurukiri, P., Irungu, E., Adhiambo, W., Muthoga, P., Kaul, R., Seeley, J., Beattie, T. S., Weiss, H. A., Kimani, J., & the Maisha Fiti Study Champions. (2021). Prevalence and correlates of common mental health problems and recent suicidal thoughts and behaviours among female sex workers in Nairobi, Kenya. *BMC Psychiatry*, *21*(1), 503. https://doi.org/10.1186/s12888-021-03515-5

Casassa, K., Knight, L., & Mengo, C. (2022). Trauma bonding perspectives from service providers and survivors of sex trafficking: A scoping review. *Trauma, Violence & Abuse*, *23*(3), 969–984.

Cecchet, S. J., & Thoburn, J. (2014). The psychological experience of child and adolescent sex trafficking in the United States: Trauma and resilience in survivors.

Psychological Trauma: Theory, Research, Practice, and Policy, 6(5), 482–493. https://doi.org/10.1037/a0035763

Chambers, R., Gibson, M., Chaffin, S., Takagi, T., Nguyen, N., & Mears-Clark, T. (2022). Trauma-coerced attachment and complex PTSD: Informed care for survivors of human trafficking. *Journal of Human Trafficking*, 1–10. https://doi.org/10.1080/23322705.2021.2012386

Chapple, C., & Crawford, B. (2019). Mental health diagnoses of youth commercial sex exploitation victims: An analysis within an adjudicated delinquent sample. *Journal of Family Violence, 34*(8), 723–732. https://doi.org/10.1007/s10896-019-00065-z

Choi, H., Klein, C., Shin, M. S., & Lee, H. J. (2009). Posttraumatic stress disorder (PTSD) and disorders of extreme stress (DESNOS) symptoms following prostitution and childhood abuse. *Violence Against Women, 15*(8), 933–951. https://doi.org/10.1177/1077801209335493

Cole, J., Sprang, G., Lee, R., & Cohen, J. (2016). The trauma of commercial sexual exploitation of youth: A comparison of CSE victims to sexual abuse victims in a clinical sample. *Journal of Interpersonal Violence, 31*(1), 122–146. https://doi.org/10.1177/0886260514555133

Contreras, P. M., Kallivayalil, D., & Herman, J. L. (2017). Psychotherapy in the aftermath of human trafficking: Working through the consequences of psychological coercion. *Women & Therapy, 40*(1–2), 31–54. https://doi.org/10.1080/02703149.2016.1205908

Cook, A., Spinazzola, J., Ford, J., Lanktree, C., Blaustein, M., Cloitre, M., DeRosa, R., Hubbard, R., Kagan, R., Liautaud, J., Mallah, K., Olafson, E., & van der Kolk, B. (2005). Complex trauma in children and adolescents. *Psychiatric Annals, 35*(5), 390–398. https://doi.org/10.3928/00485713-20050501-05

Cook, M. C., Barnert, E., Ijadi-Maghsoodi, R., Ports, K., & Bath, E. (2018). Exploring mental health and substance use treatment needs of commercially sexually exploited youth participating in a specialty juvenile court. *Behavioral Medicine, 44*(3), 242–249. https://doi.org/10.1080/08964289.2018.1432552

Courtois, C. (2008). Complex trauma, complex reactions: Assessment and treatment. *Psychological Trauma: Theory, Research, Practice, and Policy, S*(1), 86–100. https://doi.org/10.1037/1942-9681.S.1.86

Crawford, M., & Kaufman, M. R. (2008). Sex trafficking in Nepal: Survivor characteristics and long-term outcomes. *Violence Against Women, 14*(8), 905–916. https://doi.org/10.1177/1077801208320906

Curtis, R., Terry, K., Dank, M., Dombrowski, K., & Khan, B. (2008). *The commercial sexual exploitation of children in New York City: Vol. 1. The CSEC population in New York City: Size, characteristics, and needs.* Office of Justice Programs. https://www.ojp.gov/pdffiles1/nij/grants/225083.pdf

De Bellis, M. D., & Zisk, A. (2014). The biological effects of childhood trauma. *Child and Adolescent Psychiatric Clinics of North America, 23*(2), 185–222. https://doi.org/10.1016/j.chc.2014.01.002

De Vries, I., & Farrell, A. (2018). Labor trafficking victimizations: Repeat victimization and polyvictimization. *Psychology of Violence, 8*(5), 630–638. https://doi.org/10.1037/vio0000149

Evans, H. (2020). The integral role of relationships in experiences of complex trauma in sex trafficking survivors. *International Journal of Human Rights in Healthcare*, *13*(2), 109–123. https://doi.org/10.1108/IJHRH-07-2019-0054

Evans, H., Sadhwani, S., Singh, N., Robjant, K., & Katona, P. C. (2022). Prevalence of complex post-traumatic stress disorder in survivors of human trafficking and modern slavery: A systematic review. *European Journal of Psychiatry*, *36*(2), 94–105. https://doi.org/10.1016/j.ejpsy.2022.01.005

Felitti, V. J., Anda, R. F., Nordenberg, D., Williamson, D. F., Spitz, A. M., Edwards, V., Koss, M. P., & Marks, J. S. (1998). Relationship of childhood abuse and household dysfunction to many of the leading causes of death in adults: The adverse childhood experiences (ACE) study. *American Journal of Preventive Medicine*, *14*(4), 245–258. https://doi.org/10.1016/S0749-3797(98)00017-8

Finkelhor, D., Ormrod, R. K., & Turner, H. A. (2007). Poly-victimization: A neglected component in child victimization. *Child Abuse & Neglect*, *31*(1), 7–26. https://doi.org/10.1016/j.chiabu.2006.06.008

Godoy, L. D., Rossignoli, M. T., Delfino-Pereira, P., Garcia-Cairasco, N., & de Lima Umeoka, E. H. (2018). A comprehensive overview on stress neurobiology: Basic concepts and clinical implications. *Frontiers in Behavioral Neuroscience*, *12*, 127. https://doi.org/10.3389/fnbeh.2018.00127

Greenbaum, J., Sprang, G., Recknor, F., Harper, N. S., & Titchen, K. (2022). Labor trafficking of children and youth in the United States: A scoping review. *Child Abuse & Neglect*, *131*, 105694. https://doi.org/10.1016/j.chiabu.2022.105694

Grossman, E. S., Hoffman, Y. S. G., Shrira, A., Kedar, M., Ben-Ezra, M., Dinnayi, M., & Zivotofsky, A. Z. (2019). Preliminary evidence linking complex-PTSD to insomnia in a sample of Yazidi genocide survivors. *Psychiatry Research*, *271*, 161–166. https://doi.org/10.1016/j.psychres.2018.11.044

Herman, J. L. (1992). Complex PTSD: A syndrome in survivors of prolonged and repeated trauma. *Journal of Traumatic Stress*, *5*(3), 377–391. https://doi.org/10.1002/jts.2490050305

Hoffman, Y. S. G., Grossman, E. S., Shrira, A., Kedar, M., Ben-Ezra, M., Dinnayi, M., Koren, L., Bayan, R., Palgi, Y., & Zivotofsky, A. Z. (2018). Complex PTSD and its correlates amongst female Yazidi victims of sexual slavery living in post-ISIS camps. *World Psychiatry*, *17*(1), 112–113. https://doi.org/10.1002/wps.20475

Holt, M. K., Finkelhor, D., & Kantor, G. K. (2007). Multiple victimization experiences of urban elementary school students: Associations with psychosocial functioning and academic performance. *Child Abuse & Neglect*, *31*(5), 503–515. https://doi.org/10.1016/j.chiabu.2006.12.006

Hopper, E. K. (2017a). Polyvictimization and developmental trauma adaptations in sex trafficked youth. *Journal of Child & Adolescent Trauma*, *10*(2), 161–173. https://doi.org/10.1007/s40653-016-0114-z

Hopper, E. K. (2017b). Trauma-informed treatment of substance use disorders in trafficking survivors. In M. Chisolm-Straker & H. Stoklosa (Eds.), *Human trafficking is a public health issue* (pp. 211–230). Springer. https://doi.org/10.1007/978-3-319-47824-1_12

Hopper, E. K., & Gonzalez, L. D. (2018). A comparison of psychological symptoms in survivors of sex and labor trafficking. *Behavioral Medicine*, *44*(3), 177–188. https://doi.org/10.1080/08964289.2018.1432551

Hossain, M., Zimmerman, C., Abas, M., Light, M., & Watts, C. (2010). The relationship of trauma to mental disorders among trafficked and sexually exploited girls and women. *American Journal of Public Health*, *100*(12), 2442–2449. https://doi.org/10.2105/AJPH.2009.173229

Ibrahim, A., Abdalla, S. M., Jafer, M., Abdelgadir, J., & de Vries, N. (2019). Child labor and health: A systematic literature review of the impacts of child labor on child's health in low- and middle-income countries. *Journal of Public Health*, *41*(1), 18–26. https://doi.org/10.1093/pubmed/fdy018

Ibrahim, H., Ertl, V., Catani, C., Ismail, A. A., & Neuner, F. (2018, September 13). Trauma and perceived social rejection among Yazidi women and girls who survived enslavement and genocide. *BMC Medicine*, *16*(1), 154. https://doi.org/10.1186/s12916-018-1140-5

Iglesias-Rios, L., Harlow, S. D., Burgard, S. A., Kiss, L., & Zimmerman, C. (2019). Gender differences in the association of living and working conditions and the mental health of trafficking survivors. *International Journal of Public Health*, *64*(7), 1015–1024. https://doi.org/10.1007/s00038-019-01269-2

Iglesias-Rios, L., Harlow, S. D., Burgard, S. A., West, B., Kiss, L., & Zimmerman, C. (2019). Patterns of violence and coercion with mental health among female and male trafficking survivors: A latent class analysis with mixture models. *Epidemiology and Psychiatric Sciences*, *29*, e38. https://doi.org/10.1017/S2045796019000295

Institute of Medicine and National Research Council. (2013). *Confronting commercial sexual exploitation and sex trafficking of minors in the United States*. The National Academies Press.

Jowett, S., Argyriou, A., Scherrer, O., Karatzias, T., & Katona, C. (2021). Complex posttraumatic stress disorder in asylum seekers and victims of trafficking: Treatment considerations. *BJPsych Open*, *7*(6), e181. https://doi.org/10.1192/bjo.2021.1007

Kenny, M. C., Helpingstine, C., Long, H., & Harrington, M. C. (2020). Assessment of commercially sexually exploited girls upon entry to treatment: Confirmed vs. at risk victims. *Child Abuse & Neglect*, *100*, 104040. https://doi.org/10.1016/j.chiabu.2019.104040

Kiss, L., Pocock, N. S., Naisanguansri, V., Suos, S., Dickson, B., Thuy, D., Koehler, J., Sirisup, K., Pongrungsee, N., Nguyen, V. A., Borland, R., Dhavan, P., & Zimmerman, C. (2015). Health of men, women, and children in post-trafficking services in Cambodia, Thailand, and Vietnam: An observational cross-sectional study. *The Lancet. Global Health*, *3*(3), e154–e161. https://doi.org/10.1016/S2214-109X(15)70016-1

Kiss, L., Yun, K., Pocock, N., & Zimmerman, C. (2015). Exploitation, violence, and suicide risk among child and adolescent survivors of human trafficking in the Greater Mekong Subregion. *JAMA Pediatrics*, *169*(9), e152278. https://doi.org/10.1001/jamapediatrics.2015.2278

Koegler, E., Wood, C. A., Johnson, S. D., & Bahlinger, L. (2022). Service providers' perspectives on substance use and treatment needs among human trafficking survivors. *Journal of Substance Abuse Treatment*, *143*, 108897. https://doi.org/10.1016/j.jsat.2022.108897

Lagon, M. P. (2014, February 12). *Netting people: Treaties reducing illicit fishing and human trafficking*. Council on Foreign Relations. https://www.cfr.org/sites/default/files/pdf/2014/02/Lagon%20SFRC%20Testimony%20on%20Fisheries%20Treaties%2002-12-2014%20C.pdf

Lanctôt, N., Reid, J. A., & Laurier, C. (2020). Nightmares and flashbacks: The impact of commercial sexual exploitation of children among female adolescents placed in residential care. *Child Abuse & Neglect, 100*, 104195. https://doi.org/10.1016/j.chiabu.2019.104195

Landers, M., McGrath, K., Johnson, M. H., Armstrong, M. I., & Dollard, N. (2017). Baseline characteristics of dependent youth who have been commercially sexually exploited: Findings from a specialized treatment program. *Journal of Child Sexual Abuse, 26*(6), 692–709. https://doi.org/10.1080/10538712.2017.1323814

Le, P. D., Ryan, N., Rosenstock, Y., & Goldmann, E. (2018). Health issues associated with commercial sexual exploitation and sex trafficking of children in the United States: A systematic review. *Behavioral Medicine, 44*(3), 219–233. https://doi.org/10.1080/08964289.2018.1432554

Lederer, L., & Wetzel, C. (2014). The health consequences of sex trafficking and their implications for identifying victims in healthcare facilities. *Annals of Health Law, 23*(1), 61–91.

McMullen, J., O'Callaghan, P., Shannon, C., Black, A., & Eakin, J. (2013). Group trauma-focused cognitive-behavioural therapy with former child soldiers and other war-affected boys in the DR Congo: A randomised controlled trial. *Journal of Child Psychology and Psychiatry, and Allied Disciplines, 54*(11), 1231–1241. https://doi.org/10.1111/jcpp.12094

Moore, J. L., Goldberg, A. P., & Barron, C. (2021). Substance use in a domestic minor sex trafficking patient population. *Pediatric Emergency Care, 37*(4), e159–e162. https://doi.org/10.1097/PEC.0000000000001749

Mumey, A., Sardana, S., Richardson-Vejlgaard, R., & Akinsulure-Smith, A. M. (2021). Mental health needs of sex trafficking survivors in New York City: Reflections on exploitation, coping, and recovery. *Psychological Trauma: Theory, Research, Practice, and Policy, 13*(2), 185–192. https://doi.org/10.1037/tra0000603

Murphy, L. (2017). *Labor and sex trafficking among homeless youth—A ten-city study: Full report.* Modern Slavery Research Project. https://oag.ca.gov/sites/all/files/agweb/pdfs/ht/murphy-labor-sex-trafficking-homeless-youth.pdf

Nabunya, P., Byansi, W., Damulira, C., Bahar, O. S., Jennings Mayo-Wilson, L., Tozan, Y., Kiyingi, J., Nabayinda, J., Braithwaite, R., Witte, S. S., & Ssewamala, F. M. (2021). Predictors of depressive symptoms and post traumatic stress disorder among women engaged in commercial sex work in southern Uganda. *Psychiatry Research, 298*, 113817. https://doi.org/10.1016/j.psychres.2021.113817

Nodzenski, M., Kiss, L., Pocock, N. S., Stoeckl, H., Zimmerman, C., & Buller, A. M. (2020). Post-trafficking stressors: The influence of hopes, fears and expectations on the mental health of young trafficking survivors in the Greater Mekong Sub-region. *Child Abuse & Neglect, 100*, 104067. https://doi.org/10.1016/j.chiabu.2019.104067

O'Callaghan, P., McMullen, J., Shannon, C., Rafferty, H., & Black, A. (2013). A randomized controlled trial of trauma-focused cognitive behavioral therapy for sexually exploited, war-affected Congolese girls. *Journal of the American Academy of Child & Adolescent Psychiatry, 52*(4), 359–369. https://doi.org/10.1016/j.jaac.2013.01.013

Oram, S., Abas, M., Bick, D., Boyle, A., French, R., Jakobowitz, S., Khondoker, M., Stanley, N., Trevillion, K., Howard, L., & Zimmerman, C. (2016). Human trafficking and health: A survey of male and female survivors in England. *American Journal of Public Health, 106*(6), 1073–1078. https://doi.org/10.2105/AJPH.2016.303095

Ottisova, L., Hemmings, S., Howard, L. M., Zimmerman, C., & Oram, S. (2016). Prevalence and risk of violence and the mental, physical and sexual health problems associated with human trafficking: An updated systematic review. *Epidemiology and Psychiatric Sciences*, *25*(4), 317–341. https://doi.org/10.1017/S2045796016000135

Ottisova, L., Smith, P., & Oram, S. (2018). Psychological consequences of human trafficking: Complex posttraumatic stress disorder in trafficked children. *Behavioral Medicine*, *44*(3), 234–241. https://doi.org/10.1080/08964289.2018.1432555

Owens, C., Dank, M., Breaux, J., Bañuelos, I., Farrell, A., Pfeffer, R., & McDevitt, J. (2014). *Understanding the organization, operation, and victimization process of labor trafficking in the United States*. Urban Institute. https://www.immigrationresearch.org/system/files/413249-Labor-Trafficking-in-the-United-States.pdf

Palines, P. A., Rabbitt, A. L., Pan, A. Y., Nugent, M. L., & Ehrman, W. G. (2020). Comparing mental health disorders among sex trafficked children and three groups of youth at high-risk for trafficking: A dual retrospective cohort and scoping review. *Child Abuse & Neglect*, *100*, 104196. https://doi.org/10.1016/j.chiabu.2019.104196

Perry, E. W., Osborne, M. C., Lee, N., Kinnish, K., & Self-Brown, S. R. (2022). Posttraumatic cognitions and posttraumatic stress symptoms among young people who have experienced commercial sexual exploitation and trafficking. *Public Health Reports*, *137*(Suppl. 1), 91S–101S.

Peterson, C., Maier, S. F., & Seligman, M. E. P. (1993). *Learned helplessness: A theory for the age of personal control*. Oxford University Press.

Putnam, F. W. (1997). *Dissociation in children and adolescents: A developmental perspective*. Guilford Press.

Ravi, A., Pfeiffer, M. R., Rosner, Z., & Shea, J. A. (2017, December). Trafficking and trauma: Insight and advice for the healthcare system from sex-trafficked women incarcerated on Rikers Island. *Medical Care*, *55*(12), 1017–1022. https://doi.org/10.1097/MLR.0000000000000820

Reid, J. A. (2011). An exploratory model of girls' vulnerability to commercial sexual exploitation in prostitution. *Child Maltreatment*, *16*(2), 146–157. https://doi.org/10.1177/1077559511404700

Reid, J. A. (2016). Entrapment and enmeshment schemes used by sex traffickers. *Sexual Abuse*, *28*(6), 491–511. https://doi.org/10.1177/1079063214544334

Reid, J. A. (2018). Sex trafficking of girls with intellectual disabilities: An exploratory mixed methods study. *Sexual Abuse*, *30*(2), 107–131. https://doi.org/10.1177/1079063216630981

Reid, J. A., & Piquero, A. R. (2014). On the relationships between commercial sexual exploitation/prostitution, substance dependency, and delinquency in youthful offenders. *Child Maltreatment*, *19*(3–4), 247–260. https://doi.org/10.1177/1077559514539752

Roe-Sepowitz, D. E. (2012). Juvenile entry into prostitution: The role of emotional abuse. *Violence Against Women*, *18*(5), 562–579. https://doi.org/10.1177/1077801212453140

Rose, A. L., Howard, L. M., Zimmerman, C., & Oram, S. (2021). A cross-sectional comparison of the mental health of people trafficked to the UK for domestic servitude, for sexual exploitation and for labor exploitation. *Journal of Human Trafficking*, *7*(3), 258–267. https://doi.org/10.1080/23322705.2020.1728495

Salami, T., Gordon, M., Coverdale, J., & Nguyen, P. T. (2018). What therapies are favored in the treatment of the psychological sequelae of trauma in human trafficking victims? *Journal of Psychiatric Practice, 24*(2), 87–96. https://doi.org/10.1097/PRA.0000000000000288

Self-Brown, S. R., Osborne, M. C., Lee, N., Perry, E. W., & Kinnish, K. (2021). Exploring the impact of trauma history on the mental health presentations of youth who have experienced commercial sexual exploitation and trafficking. *Behavioral Medicine, 48*(4), 261–272.

Sprang, G., & Cole, J. (2018). Familial sex trafficking of minors: Trafficking conditions, clinical presentation, and system involvement. *Journal of Family Violence, 33*(3), 185–195. https://doi.org/10.1007/s10896-018-9950-y

Stöckl, H., Fabbri, C., Cook, H., Galez-Davis, C., Grant, N., Lo, Y., Kiss, L., & Zimmerman, C. (2021). Human trafficking and violence: Findings from the largest global dataset of trafficking survivors. *Journal of Migration and Health, 4,* 100073. https://doi.org/10.1016/j.jmh.2021.100073

Stoltz, J. A., Shannon, K., Kerr, T., Zhang, R., Montaner, J. S., & Wood, E. (2007). Associations between childhood maltreatment and sex work in a cohort of drug-using youth. *Social Science & Medicine, 65*(6), 1214–1221. https://doi.org/10.1016/j.socscimed.2007.05.005

Swaner, R., Labriola, M., Rempel, M., Walker, A., & Spadafore, J. (2016). *Youth involvement in the sex trade: A national study.* Center for Court Innovation. https://www.ojp.gov/pdffiles1/ojjdp/grants/249952.pdf

Tsutsumi, A., Izutsu, T., Poudyal, A. K., Kata, S., Marui, E. (2008). Mental health of female survivors of human trafficking in Nepal. *Social Science & Medicine, 66,* 1841–1847.

Turner, H. A., Finkelhor, D., & Ormrod, R. (2010). Poly-victimization in a national sample of children and youth. *American Journal of Preventive Medicine, 38*(3), 323–330. https://doi.org/10.1016/j.amepre.2009.11.012

Turner-Moss, E., Zimmerman, C., Howard, L. M., & Oram, S. (2014). Labour exploitation and health: A case series of men and women seeking post-trafficking services. *Journal of Immigrant and Minority Health, 16*(3), 473–480. https://doi.org/10.1007/s10903-013-9832-6

Twis, M. K., Gillespie, L., & Greenwood, D. (2020). An analysis of romantic partnership dynamics in domestic minor sex trafficking case files. *Journal of Interpersonal Violence, 37*(7–8), NP5394–NP5418.

United Nations Inter-Agency Project on Human Trafficking. (2009). *Exploitation of Cambodian men at sea.* https://www.ilo.org/wcmsp5/groups/public/---ed_norm/---declaration/documents/publication/wcms_143251.pdf

Varma, S., Gillespie, S., McCracken, C., & Greenbaum, V. J. (2015). Characteristics of child commercial sexual exploitation and sex trafficking victims presenting for medical care in the United States. *Child Abuse & Neglect, 44,* 98–105.

Volgin, R. N., Shakespeare-Finch, J., & Shochet, I. M. (2019). Posttraumatic distress, hope, and growth in survivors of commercial sexual exploitation in Nepal. *Traumatology, 25*(3), 181–188. https://doi.org/10.1037/trm0000174

Vranceanu, A. M., Hobfoll, S. E., & Johnson, R. J. (2007). Child multi-type maltreatment and associated depression and PTSD symptoms: The role of social support and stress. *Child Abuse & Neglect, 31*(1), 71–84. https://doi.org/10.1016/j.chiabu.2006.04.010

Whetten, R., Messer, L., Ostermann, J., Whetten, K., Pence, B. W., Buckner, M., Thielman, N., O'Donnell, K., & the Positive Outcomes for Orphans Research Team. (2011). Child work and labour among orphaned and abandoned children in five low and middle income countries. *BMC International Health and Human Rights, 11*(1), 1. https://doi.org/10.1186/1472-698X-11-1

White, C. N., Robichaux, K., Huang, A., & Luo, C. (2023). When families become perpetrators: A case series on familial trafficking. *Journal of Family Violence.* Advance online publication. https://doi.org/10.1007/s10896-023-00522-w

Wilson, B., & Butler, L. D. (2014). Running a gauntlet: A review of victimization and violence in the pre-entry, post-entry, and peri-/post-exit periods of commercial sexual exploitation. *Psychological Trauma: Theory, Research, Practice, and Policy, 6*(5), 494–504. https://doi.org/10.1037/a0032977

World Health Organization. (2019). *ICD-11: International classification of diseases* (11th rev.). https://icd.who.int/

Zarse, E. M., Neff, M. R., Yoder, R., Hulvershorn, L., Chambers, J. E., & Chambers, R. A. (2019). The adverse childhood experiences questionnaire: Two decades of research on childhood trauma as a primary cause of adult mental illness, addiction, and medical diseases. *Cogent Medicine, 6*(1), 1581447. https://doi.org/10.1080/2331205X.2019.1581447

Zimmerman, C., Hossain, M., Yun, K., Roche, B., Morison, L. A., & Watts, C. (2006). *Stolen Smiles: The physical and psychological health consequences of women and adolescents trafficked in Europe.* The London School of Hygiene & Tropical Medicine. https://researchonline.lshtm.ac.uk/id/eprint/3732/1/StolenSmiles_Full_Report.pdf

9

TRAUMA-INFORMED INTERVENTION WITH SURVIVORS OF HUMAN TRAFFICKING

KELLY KINNISH AND ELIZABETH K. HOPPER

As a result of the complex and often severe psychological impacts of sex and labor trafficking (see Chapter 8, this volume), mental health intervention is a significant need for survivors. Current approaches to clinical intervention with trafficking survivors include utilization of evidence-based treatments (EBTs) targeting the primary mental health impacts of trafficking (e.g., posttraumatic stress disorder [PTSD], complex posttraumatic stress disorder [C-PTSD], depression, anxiety, substance use problems, suicidal ideation, and self-harm) and other evidence-informed or promising practices, often augmented by a range of adjunctive treatments and strategies to best meet client needs. Unfortunately, treatment outcome research with trafficking survivors is sparse (O'Brien et al., 2022; although see O'Callaghan et al., 2013; Robjant et al., 2017), especially with regard to labor trafficking.

A growing body of research suggests that engagement and completion of treatment with survivors of trafficking, regardless of treatment approach or type of trafficking experienced, may be especially challenging (Albright et al., 2020; Barnert et al., 2019; Bath et al., 2020; Ijadi-Maghsoodi et al., 2018; Mumey et al., 2021; Robitz et al., 2020); thus, survivors are less likely to receive the very services needed to ameliorate the impacts of trafficking

https://doi.org/10.1037/0000379-010
Psychological Perspectives on Human Trafficking: Theory, Research, Prevention, and Intervention, L. Dryjanska, E. K. Hopper, and H. Stoklosa (Editors)

and other forms of trauma. To achieve effective engagement with trafficking survivors, excellence in core clinical skills, utilization of engagement and motivational enhancement strategies, and adherence to principles of trauma-informed care are essential. Moreover, the complexity of the client history and clinical presentation amplifies the importance of skilled trauma- and trafficking-informed psychological assessment to guide case conceptual-ization and treatment planning (Hopper, 2018; Lurie et al., 2020). Finally, effective treatments that target primary mental health impacts of trafficking and are tailored to the unique needs of trafficking survivors are foundational to meaningful trafficking intervention. This chapter reviews engagement, assessment, and treatment approaches and highlight recommendations for further development in trauma-informed intervention with survivors of human trafficking.

ENGAGEMENT AND THE THERAPEUTIC ALLIANCE

Engagement of a client in services and the establishment of a therapeutic alli-ance are among the first goals of mental health treatment (Horvath & Greenberg, 1994). Numerous studies conducted with trafficking survivors and mental health providers have identified an array of challenges and barriers to achiev-ing these goals.[1] Survivor shame, stigma regarding mental health care, fear of judgment, and cultural barriers feature especially prominently, as well as fears of a range of other potential negative and harmful impacts such as reprisals from traffickers and consequences of mandated reporting (e.g., criminal justice and child welfare involvement, involuntary hospitalization, or deportation; Aberdein & Zimmerman, 2015; Albright et al., 2020; Contreras et al., 2017; Ijadi-Maghsoodi et al., 2018; Mumey et al., 2021; Powell et al., 2018). Immi-grants who have experienced trafficking may face unique challenges in access and engagement with mental health services, including linguistic barriers, stigma and misunderstanding of mental health services, lack of provider knowledge related to the individual's and family's cultural beliefs and prac-tices, disparate worldviews between the individual, their family members, and

---

[1] There are many "concrete" logistical or practical barriers (transportation, funding, child care, interpretation or translation services) that are not the focus of this chapter. However, it is often critically important that mental health providers collaborate with other professionals (e.g., case managers, navigators) to ensure a comprehensive needs assessment is conducted and collaborative case management services are provided to address these barriers (e.g., Gibbs et al., 2015; Hopper, 2017a, 2018). See also Chapter 11 of this volume regarding multidisciplinary approaches.

mental health practitioners, and prioritization of stressors related to resettlement (Albright et al., 2020; Ellis et al., 2020). Male survivors may encounter gender-related stigma and stereotypes regarding emotional expression, sexual orientation, acknowledgement of "victimization," and acceptance of help seeking, while the lack of tailored services creates further barriers to access and engagement (National Human Trafficking Training and Technical Assistance Center, n.d.).

Many challenges to engagement in mental health care are related to the survivor's trafficking experiences, past interpersonal experiences, and, perhaps most powerfully, current and past negative experiences with mental health providers and formal service systems (Barnert et al., 2019; Bath et al., 2020; Contreras et al., 2017; Ijadi-Maghsoodi et al., 2018; Powell et al., 2018). In a qualitative interview study with youth who had experienced commercial sexual exploitation, Ijadi-Maghsoodi et al. (2018) identified fear of judgment or feeling judged as a primary barrier for youth engagement in mental health treatment, as well as perceptions and experiences of generally low-quality mental health care (see also Mumey et al., 2021). In a systematic review of facilitators and barriers to services, Albright et al. (2020) noted that one of the most commonly identified barriers to service was "providers' poor interactional approach with patients (e.g., judgmental, insensitive, dismissive, not trauma-informed)" (p. 18). Distrust of mental health providers is further grounded in past experiences of deception, manipulation, and violation by traffickers and others (caregivers, systems professionals), as well as prior negative experiences specifically with mental health providers such as delays breaches of confidentiality or unexpected and sometimes unexplained termination of the therapeutic relationship (Albright et al., 2020; Barnert et al., 2019, Bath et al., 2020; Contreras et al., 2017).

Beyond identifying barriers, many of these studies also highlight factors that may facilitate engagement, including approaches that emphasize collaboration, power sharing and autonomy granting, honoring survival, and rejection of victim labeling in service delivery. Research into the perspectives on health care of commercially sexually exploited girls and young women identified a core theme of "fierce autonomy," noting that participants' past experiences of coercion and lack of control led them to strongly value autonomy regarding health care decision making (Barnert et al., 2019; Godoy et al., 2020). Sahl and Knoepke (2018) specifically drew from applications of shared-decision-making models in other health contexts, incorporating it into service delivery with youth who have experienced commercial sexual exploitation in order to promote agency, support the therapeutic alliance, respect individual preference and competence, and encourage development of autonomy.

The role of provider knowledge of trafficking and culture- and gender-responsive care in facilitating survivor engagement in services has been highlighted (Batley et al., 2021; Powell et al., 2018). The importance of cultural humility and linguistically and culturally responsive care is especially amplified in service engagement of survivors of labor trafficking (Owens et al., 2014). This may include acknowledging different non-Western perspectives and worldviews, utilization of language consistent with the person's identity (gender, sexual orientation, other aspects of identity relevant to the person), consideration of utilization of cultural brokers to enhance communication and understanding, and recognizing multiple and intersecting dimensions of identity. Especially pivotal to engagement of survivors of human trafficking in treatment is the establishment of a collaborative working relationship or therapeutic alliance. This involves factors such as empathetic communication, trust and connection between client and practitioner, agreement about the goals and tasks of therapy, and hope and positive expectations about treatment. Research suggests that common factors (characteristics shared across psychotherapies, also referred to as nonspecific factors) such as the therapeutic alliance have a greater influence over outcomes than any particular therapy technique (Kidd et al., 2017; Wampold, 2015), underscoring the primacy of these skills in delivering effective services with trafficking survivors. Clinician self-awareness and self-care lay an important foundation for the prospect of a stable therapeutic relationship (Corbett-Hone & Johnson, 2022). In addition, there are a number of conceptual models and treatment approaches that can help support the development of a strong therapeutic alliance and encourage self-determination with survivors of trafficking. These include principles of trauma-informed care, the transtheoretical model of behavior change (also known as "stages of change"), harm reduction, and motivational interviewing (MI).

Trauma-Informed Care

Survivor experiences of trauma and adversity are often at the heart of both the need for mental health treatment and the common reluctance or inability to engage in treatment. Meaningful strategies necessary to overcome these obstacles are captured especially succinctly by the principles of trauma-informed care, a service delivery approach that focuses on an understanding of, and responsiveness to, trauma-related impacts (Substance Abuse and Mental Health Services Administration, 2014). Specifically, survivor experiences of physical and emotional threat, fear, and harm (prior to, while being, and after trafficking) are the foundation for the first principle of trauma-informed care, establishing physical and psychological *safety*. Experiences of deception and profound violations of trust, by traffickers but also more broadly by others who had responsibilities of care and support, elevate the importance of *trustworthiness and transparency*. The multiple and often highly complex strategies of coercion and control prior to and while being trafficked accentuate the essentiality of *empowerment, voice, and choice* and *collaboration and mutuality* as principles of care. Additionally, incorporation of *peer support* serves as a powerful instrument against stigma and isolation experienced by survivors. Finally, the complex sociocultural and historical factors, especially the multiple and intersecting vulnerabilities of gender, sexual orientation, race/ethnicity in trafficking vulnerability, mental health impacts, and mental health service access, amplify the importance of *cultural, historical, and gender issues* in trauma-informed mental health care with trafficking survivors.

The Transtheoretical Model of Behavior Change

The transtheoretical model of behavioral change (Prochaska & Norcross, 2002), also known as the "stages of change" model, can be a beneficial framework for practitioners in understanding change as a complex process and in supporting clinician regulation and attunement to the client. It may be especially helpful for clinicians who struggle with feelings of frustration, worry, and helplessness when engaging with clients who are not ready to exit a trafficking situation, who relapse with substance use or other high-risk behaviors, or who return to their exploiter multiple times. This approach is responsive to survivors in all stages in the change process represented in the model, including precontemplation (not considering change), contemplation (considering change), preparation (getting ready for action), action (active movement toward change), and maintenance (sustaining behavioral changes); and it acknowledges relapse as an expected part of the change process for many risk behaviors (Lloyd, 2018). This model is grounded in the notion that working with a person at their current stage of readiness for change will increase engagement and receptiveness to intervention and may also enhance outcomes.

Safety and Harm Reduction

Many people impacted by trafficking face significant ongoing threats to safety and risk of harm, such as engaging in unsafe sexual practices or working in unsafe work environments, using substances that are directly harmful or that result in risky or dangerous behavior, leaving placements ("running away"), and experiencing revictimization (e.g., returning to the identified exploiter; engaging in commercial sex to meet basic needs; or being targeted by other exploiters due to ongoing risk factors such as homelessness, lack of a supportive caregiving system and environment, immigration-related vulnerabilities, mental health symptoms, or substance use disorders). Harm reduction is an evidence-based approach that proactively works to reduce negative personal and public health impacts of risk behaviors (Logan & Marlatt, 2010; Marlatt, 1996). Harm reduction was originally designed to address the negative individual and community impacts of alcohol and other substance use. One of the key principles of harm reduction in public health is a nonjudgmental approach, in which providers acknowledge that high-risk behaviors may continue and should not be an impediment to the provision of services. Instead, providers offer options for decreasing harms and protecting the safety of others (e.g., condoms, needle exchanges, safety planning) and provide information and support when ready to change. Consistent with the transtheoretical model of behavior change, harm reduction incorporates a range of strategies that meet people "where they are" in their change process, potentially creating a pathway to prevention, treatment, and recovery services. Harm reduction approaches may be beneficial to reduce detriments associated with ongoing sex or labor trafficking and other risk behaviors (e.g., substance use, self-injury; Hickle & Hallett, 2016; Pierce, 2012; Preble, 2018).

Motivational Interviewing

MI (W. R. Miller & Rollnick, 2013) is an evidence-based intervention that is highly regarded and widely recommended for work with trafficking survivors (e.g., Gerassi & Esbensen, 2021; Knott et al., 2021). A particular strength of MI in working with trafficking survivors is the set of principles ("spirit") that values autonomy and self-determination. Instead of applying pressure or using other coercive methods to induce change, this collaborative, person-centered approach works to identify and explore ambivalence, eliciting and strengthening a person's motivation for change in ways that are consistent with their values, beliefs, and wishes. This is important in countering the loss of power often experienced in conditions of human trafficking. Its utility is recognized on several fronts: ambivalence regarding engagement in services, broadly, engagement in mental health treatment, specifically, ambivalence regarding leaving a relationship with an identified exploiter, and/or cessation of engagement in commercial sex (leaving "the life") or exploitative labor conditions in general, especially in partnership with the "stages of change" conceptualization of trafficking described previously (Lloyd, 2018).

MI has been utilized extensively in substance abuse and addiction treatment and, therefore, also has benefit in addressing substance use with trafficking survivors.[2]

TRAUMA-INFORMED PSYCHOLOGICAL ASSESSMENT AND TREATMENT PLANNING

A hallmark of quality clinical intervention is skilled psychological assessment and case conceptualization that drives treatment planning and execution. Consistent with a trauma-informed approach, psychological assessment and treatment planning with trafficking survivors should be strengths based, collaborative, culturally responsive, and led with an emphasis on establishing physical and psychological safety (Hopper, 2018).

Unfortunately, survivors often have assessment and treatment planning experiences that are not aligned with the principles of trauma-informed care. Survivors may be engaged in multiple systems (e.g., criminal justice or juvenile justice, immigration, child welfare, health care, and behavioral health and psychiatry) with proscriptive practices, contributing to a sense of disempowerment and mistrust. For instance, a young person may be scheduled for multiple assessments, taken to different treatment providers, and moved from placement to placement, without having a say in the treatment planning process. This can lead to treatment noncompliance or refusal, leaving placement, relapse, and revictimization. Likewise, early emphasis on extensive paperwork can be alienating. Instead, early interactions should be focused on engagement, identification of internal and external resources, and collaboration that enables the person who has experienced trafficking to receive some immediate benefit, whether it be information, connection, the experience of being heard, a sense of hope, symptom relief, or concrete resources (Hopper, 2018; Kerig, 2013). In particular, survivors should be involved in setting goals and making decisions about their own treatment to the extent possible. Even addressing safety (including legal mandates and ethical obligations) should be approached with consideration of relational impacts, utilizing trauma-informed safety assessment and planning strategies that best preserve and even enhance engagement. A social-ecological framework is beneficial in assessment and treatment planning because of

---

[2]A note of caution: The parallels of the utility of "stages of change" harm reduction and MI with substance use do not extend to conceptualization of engagement in commercial sex as a form of "sex addiction." Such a mischaracterization is potentially quite harmful to survivors.

its emphasis on the person in context, leading to recommendations for the individual and also addressing relationships with peers, families, and communities (Hopper, 2017a).

Core components of psychological assessment with trafficking survivors include rapport building and informed consent, a clinical interview with the survivor (and caregiver, if the survivor is a minor and there is an identified supportive caregiver available) and standardized measures to obtain a full picture of client history and vulnerability factors, trauma history, and trafficking experiences (including elements of force, fraud, and coercion), as well as an understanding of basic needs and safety, psychological symptoms and diagnoses, and client strengths and coping. Because of the breadth and complexity of emotional and behavioral impacts, standardized broadband and trauma-specific instruments are especially important in psychological assessment. In addition, screening and assessment of substance use, suicidal ideation, and self-injury are also crucial given the strong presence of these concerns among survivors (Hopper, 2018; Moore et al., 2020). Assessment of cognitive-developmental functioning may also be beneficial, due to the associated exploitation risk (Nichols & Heil, 2022; Reid, 2018; Reid et al., 2018) and relevance for treatment planning.

Beyond its primary function of information gathering, psychological assessment conducted by a skilled clinician can facilitate client engagement and alliance building. A positive experience of talking with someone about their experiences and emotions can relieve the burden of secrecy, decrease shame, and instill hope. Survivors may then be less fearful of mental health care and more open to further intervention. Opportunistic incorporation of psychoeducation (deriving from the survivor's focus, needs, and interests) transfers knowledge to the survivor and demonstrates possible utility of mental health treatment. As part of the assessment process, education about trauma can normalize and destigmatize many mental health "symptoms," framing these as psychological, biological, and behavioral coping responses to repeated or chronic trauma (Herman, 1997; van der Kolk, 1994). Opportunities to build regulatory capacities may also be incorporated, including education about regulation and teaching and practice of basic regulatory skills (Hopper, 2018). Careful attention to pacing, drawing on therapist attunement and coregulation skills, is important throughout the assessment.

As articulated previously, it is essential that the assessment is appropriately paced, with engagement and relational impacts prioritized over assessment completion objectives. A completed assessment is of no benefit if the client disengages from treatment or continues to attend but no longer trusts the therapist or believes treatment can be of benefit. As much as organizational requirements will allow, it is often helpful to conduct assessment over multiple sessions with strategies embedded to enhance the therapeutic relationship and build regulatory capacities, titrating assessment tasks with careful attunement to client regulation and the strength of the therapeutic relationship.

TREATMENT APPROACHES WITH SURVIVORS OF TRAFFICKING

The American Psychological Association Presidential Task Force on Evidence-Based Practice (2006) defined *evidence-based practice* as "the integration of the best available research with clinical expertise in the context of patient characteristics, culture and preferences." This amplifies the importance of research, clinician's skills, as well as individualized culturally responsive care and client empowerment, voice, and choice, consistent with principles of trauma-informed care, in treatment delivery. An *evidence-based treatment* is an intervention proven in a field of research as effective in treating a particular disorder, symptom, or problem in a specific population and is generally considered the gold standard of clinical care. Trafficking survivors are deserving of the best care available, utilizing treatment approaches with the strongest evidence of their effectiveness at ameliorating the specific symptoms and difficulties that survivors experience. Unfortunately, there is a limited body of empirical treatment outcome research conducted with trafficking survivors. There are, however, EBTs for analogous or overlapping populations (e.g., sexual abuse and domestic violence survivors) that address common psychological impacts and mental health concerns experienced by trafficking survivors. These are potentially important intervention tools for people impacted by trafficking and exploitation (O'Brien et al., 2022; Salami et al., 2018). In addition, an array of "promising practices" and adjunctive interventions may also offer benefit to survivors. Due to the prevalence of traumatic experiences and high rates of PTSD, C-PTSD, and other trauma-related impacts, trauma-focused treatments are especially prioritized in trafficking response (Powell et al., 2018), and trauma treatments with an evidence base, specifically with trafficking survivors, are described first here.

Trauma-Focused Treatments

Trauma-focused treatments address the effects of traumatic experiences and have as their goal the amelioration of trauma-related symptoms. They typically involve some combination of establishing physical and psychological safety, building regulatory capacities, learning about trauma, addressing relational impacts, and direct processing of the traumatic experiences through cognitive, exposure-based, and/or narrative strategies.

Trauma-Focused EBTs With Trafficking-Related Outcome Research

Trauma-focused cognitive behavioral therapy (TF-CBT; Cohen et al., 2017) is an EBT for children and adolescents impacted by trauma. It uses a phase-based approach that includes safety, psychoeducation, coping skills, cognitive processing, and gradual exposure in a trauma narration phase, as well as a strong emphasis on caregiving and support (for parents and/or other supportive adults). TF-CBT has been used with trafficked children in an array of settings globally. In a randomized controlled trial (O'Callaghan et al., 2013), 52 girls recovered from a brothel in the Democratic Republic of Congo were assigned to TF-CBT or a waitlist control group. The TF-CBT treatment was delivered in a 15-session culturally modified group format by nonclinical lay facilitators. There was a significant reduction in posttraumatic stress (PTS) symptom scores for youth in TF-CBT treatment compared with the waitlist control group. There were also significant improvements in symptoms of depression, anxiety, conduct problems, and prosocial behavior in the TF-CBT group. In a contemporaneous study with former child soldiers in the Democratic Republic of Congo (McMullen et al., 2013), boys in the TF-CBT group treatment similarly reported significant reductions in PTS symptoms compared with the waitlist control group, as well as improvements in depression, anxiety, conduct problems, psychosocial distress, and prosocial behavior. In both studies, effects were sustained at 3-month follow-up. TF-CBT has also been successfully implemented with trafficked girls in Cambodia (Bass et al., 2011), Haiti (Wang et al., 2016), and the United States (Kinnish et al., 2020). TF-CBT treatment applications have been developed specifically for minors who have experienced commercial sexual exploitation, with specialized training and an implementation guide available for clinicians certified in TF-CBT (Kinnish et al., 2020, 2021).

Narrative exposure therapy (NET; Schauer et al., 2011) is a trauma-focused EBT that has been found to be effective at reducing trauma symptoms in both adult and minor survivors of human trafficking (Brady et al., 2021; Ertl et al., 2011; Robjant et al., 2017, 2019). NET is a short-term EBT developed specifically for individuals who have experienced multiple traumas, often in complex sociopolitical and cultural contexts. It involves development of a life narrative with a focus on traumatic experiences and associated thoughts, feelings, and sensory experiences, actively guided by a therapist toward reprocessing and integration. In a study of child soldiers in Uganda, children were randomly assigned to NET, an academic catch-up program, or waitlist control. Those receiving NET experienced reduced trauma symptoms compared with the other conditions (Ertl et al., 2011). Robjant et al. (2017) reported significant improvement in PTS symptoms pre- and posttreatment, which were sustained at 3-month follow-up, in a small sample ($N = 10$) of sex-trafficked women. All participants reported clinically meaningful change, with symptom scores in the severe range pretest and in the mild or moderate range posttest and at follow-up. In a more recent randomized clinical trial feasibility study, Brady et al. (2021) similarly reported significant reductions in PTS symptoms or PTSD, depression, and anxiety in a mixed sample of survivors of sex and labor trafficking.

Cognitive processing therapy (CPT; Resick et al., 2016) is an EBT for adults and youth that aids clients in identifying beliefs and thought processes that interfere with posttraumatic recovery. Clients learn to identify their "stuck points" (negative thoughts created to deal with trauma) and consider more balanced perspectives. A feasibility study was conducted of modified group CPT with 10 adolescent survivors of commercial sexual exploitation in Cambodia. Participants in the pilot study reported high satisfaction and attendance, as well as reductions in PTS and depression symptoms posttreatment and at 3-month follow-up, with no incidents of suicidal behavior or nonsuicidal self-injury during the group or at follow-up (Clemans et al., 2021).

Trauma-Focused EBTs for PTSD

Current gold standard treatments for adults with PTSD include CPT (Resick et al., 2016), cognitive therapy (Beck, 2005), eye movement desensitization and reprocessing (EMDR; Shapiro, 2018), individual cognitive behavioral therapy (CBT) with a trauma focus (Monson & Shnaider, 2014), and prolonged exposure (PE; Foa et al., 2007; International Society for Traumatic Stress Studies, 2018c). The most strongly recommended EBTs for children and adolescents with PTSD are CBT with a trauma focus (with caregiver and child or with child alone) and EMDR (International Society for Traumatic Stress Studies, 2018c). These approaches all have a substantial evidence base and have been utilized effectively with adults and youth in a range of treatment settings and locales and with individuals with an array of trauma experiences, including trauma exposures that may overlap with the experiences of trafficking survivors (e.g., Edmond, 2018; Foa et al., 2013; LoSavio et al., 2021; Rodenburg et al., 2009); however, outcome research specifically with trafficking survivors is lacking for these approaches. Their value and specific cautions in implementation with trafficking survivors have been thoughtfully reviewed elsewhere (Salami et al., 2018; see also O'Brien et al., 2022). Specific concerns identified include the limitations of exposure-based interventions to address stigma and shame, potential poorer retention of PE compared with CPT, and impacts of low literacy for CPT (ameliorated by the omission of a written trauma account in CPT-C [cognitive therapy only]). Challenges of impaired recall and concerns regarding dissociative responses when exposure is not preceded by skillful preparation (including grounding, mindfulness, or other coping and regulation skills) were also identified. If exposure is not sufficiently supported, modulated, or titrated, there may also be risk of harm associated with unsafe behaviors (e.g., substance use, running away) that are attempts to cope with dysregulation elicited by trauma reminders.

Dialectical behavioral therapy (DBT; Linehan, 1993) is another EBT that may be especially helpful in treatment with trafficking survivors. DBT is a cognitive behavioral therapy originally developed to address suicidal ideation in individuals diagnosed with borderline personality disorder, and not designed as a trauma-focused treatment; however, protocols have been developed to address trauma (see DBT-PTSD [Bohus et al., 2013] and DBT-PE [Harned, 2022]). DBT has also been adapted to be more developmentally appropriate for adolescents who struggle with emotional dysregulation and self-harm (A. L. Miller et al., 2007). It is of high potential value with trafficking survivors due to its effectiveness in reducing suicidal ideation and self-harm, and enhancing coping, regulation, and interpersonal effectiveness (McCauley et al., 2018), all of which are prioritized concerns with trafficking survivors.

C-PTSD Treatments

As described in the previous chapter, early research has identified a high incidence of C-PTSD symptoms in survivors of human trafficking. Based on evidence supporting the *International Classification of Diseases 11th Revision (ICD-11*; World Health Organization, n.d.) distinction between PTSD and C-PTSD (Brewin et al., 2017; see Chapter 8, this volume), there are limitations to the direct application of existing outcome literature on PTSD to trauma survivors with C-PTSD (Karatzias et al., 2019), including trafficking survivors who have C-PTSD. A key feature of C-PTSD treatment is a phase-based approach that includes a sequence of stabilization and skills building, followed by trauma processing, and concluding with consolidation of treatment gains and integration into everyday life (Cloitre et al., 2012). Trafficking survivors with C-PTSD may benefit from multicomponent treatments delivered in a phased approach that directly address the core impacts of C-PTSD, including affect dysregulation, negative self-concept, and disturbances in relationships (Hopper, 2017a). Early emphasis in treatment on development of coping and regulation skills is likely to be especially important for trafficking survivors, many of whom continue to live under conditions of chronic stress even after exiting trafficking. Treatment for C-PTSD is also likely to be lengthier than for PTSD due to the need for stabilization work involving the development of safety, a strong treatment alliance, and emotional regulation skills, as well as the need to address a greater number of trauma experiences and symptoms (International Society for Traumatic Stress Studies, 2018a, 2018b). In fact, the need for greater length and/or frequency of treatment with trafficking survivors is commonly noted in the literature (Cohen, Mannarino, & Kinnish, 2017; Judge et al., 2018; Kinnish et al., 2020; Ottisova et al., 2018). In a study comparing the electronic health records of trafficked compared with nontrafficked youth in mental health services in England, treatment length was 56% greater for youth who had experienced trafficking (Ottisova et al., 2018).

Evidence-informed treatments targeting C-PTSD are of significant potential benefit to this population. For instance, treatment outcome studies on interventions such as skills training in affective and interpersonal regulation/narrative therapy (STAIR-NT; Cloitre et al., 2002) have included both participants with PTSD and C-PTSD. STAIR actively targets C-PTSD impacts, including affective regulation skills, interpersonal functioning, and self-efficacy and can be combined with trauma processing interventions (narrative therapy or others) that target the core symptoms of PTSD. Narrative exposure therapy (described previously) has been utilized with trauma survivors with poly-traumatization and has protocols for dissociation, a common C-PTSD symptom (Chessell et al., 2019).

Regarding C-PTSD approaches with children and adolescents, the attachment, regulation, and competency (ARC) framework (Blaustein & Kinniburgh, 2018) has shown significant reductions in social, emotional, and behavioral outcomes for complex trauma-impacted youth in community-based (Fehrenbach et al., 2021) and residential (Hodgdon et al., 2013) settings. Preliminary outcome data on the integrative treatment of complex trauma for adolescents approach have likewise shown promising impacts on socially marginalized, multiply traumatized children and adolescents (Briere & Lanktree, 2013). Systematic efforts to tailor these models and evaluate their effectiveness with trafficking survivors are a clear priority.

Although TF-CBT (described earlier) was not initially developed as a treatment targeting C-PTSD, C-PTSD applications have been developed for TF-CBT that incorporate the identified core features of C-PTSD intervention, specifically a phased-based approach prioritizing safety, stabilization and skills building and greater length of treatment, among other enhancements (Cohen et al., 2012; Kliethermes & Wamser, 2012). In a study utilizing these C-PTSD modifications, youth in foster care and at high risk of placement disruption showed significantly greater improvement in emotional and behavioral problems and PTSD symptoms as well as less placement disruption and running away compared with treatment as usual (Weiner et al., 2009). Even unmodified TF-CBT has demonstrated effectiveness addressing core symptoms of reexperiencing, avoidance, and sense of threat with youth diagnosed with C-PTSD comparable to its impacts with PTSD-diagnosed youth, as well improvements in emotional regulation, self-concept, and interpersonal problems (Sachser et al., 2017).

Adjunctive Interventions

Many existing therapeutic programs for trafficking survivors integrate a range of adjunctive treatments, including practices as varied as mindfulness, yoga, and expressive arts interventions. A growing body of literature suggests the value of experiential therapies to build and promote better regulatory capacities, emotional expression and communication, increased self-awareness, and improved self-concept with survivors of trafficking (Hopper et al., 2018; Namy et al., 2022; Sanar Wellness Institute and Polaris Project, 2015).

Mind–body interventions (e.g., meditation, visualization/guided imagery, breathing techniques, and body-based therapies) have been found to impact trauma-related symptoms (Gene-Cos et al., 2016; Gordon et al., 2008; Wahbeh et al., 2014; Warner et al., 2014) and should be further explored as adjunctive treatments for trafficking survivors. For instance, mindfulness (e.g., mindfulness-based stress reduction) has been shown to decrease symptoms of PTS and depression in survivors of interpersonal violence (Boyd et al., 2018; Follette et al., 2015; Kelly & Garland, 2016; Ortiz & Sibinga, 2017) and has been explored for trafficking survivors (McCaw, 2019). Yoga has gained increasing attention as an intervention for trauma (van der Kolk et al., 2014), and a pilot study of yoga with adult women who had experienced sex trafficking in Uganda showed reductions in symptoms of depression and improvements in self-rated emotional and physical health. This method was suggested as viable within low-resource settings such as shelters (Namy et al., 2022). Mind–body interventions may be utilized independently or incorporated into EBTs to facilitate development of coping and regulation skills.

Expressive arts interventions (e.g., visual arts, music, journaling and poetry, dance or movement) are commonly used with trafficking survivors. Current evidence regarding application of these approaches for trafficking survivors primarily involves case studies and small qualitative investigations (Schrader & Wendland, 2012; Tan, 2012). A qualitative study of therapists incorporating expressive arts interventions with adult survivors of commercial sexual exploitation found that these modalities allow a strengths-based, client-centered approach with a range of benefits, including establishment of the therapeutic alliance, installation of hope, connection to others, trauma exploration, release of emotions, and development of identity and self (Lee, 2019). Hopper et al. (2018) described the positive impacts of an experiential group intervention that incorporated theater games or expressive arts activities to address C-PTSD in a sample of sex-trafficked women and girls. In qualitative analyses, participants reported impacts of the group in the areas of trust and relationships, regulation, self-awareness, and future orientation. Trauma-focused or trauma-informed experiential interventions are of significant potential benefit, especially as braided or sequenced with EBTs.

Treatment for Substance Use Problems and Other Comorbid Conditions

Due to the high rates of substance use and intersecting trauma among trafficking survivors, integrated trauma and substance use treatments are essential in trafficking response. Unfortunately, there are few EBTs that target trauma and substance abuse and no outcome studies conducted with trafficking survivors. Seeking safety (Najavits, 2002) is especially highly regarded for its evidence base and concurrent focus on trauma and substance use (National Human Trafficking Training and Technical Assistance Center, 2021). It has both adult and youth applications, can be delivered in individual and group formats, uses professional and lay facilitators, and is flexible and adaptive, with 25 possible modules that can be delivered in any order. Risk reduction through family therapy (RRFT; Danielson et al., 2010, 2020) is a model of particular relevance for intervention with adolescents in that it addresses both trauma and substance use and includes components to address family communication, risky sexual behaviors, cognitive coping and trauma-specific cognitive processing, all of which are prioritized needs of trafficked youth. These interventions may be used in conjunction with other treatment modalities targeting substance use, including other cognitive behavioral interventions, 12-step programming, and medication-assisted therapy (Hopper, 2017b). It is noted that, in addition to the treatment engagement challenges previously outlined, there are specific barriers related to substance use intervention, especially requirements of complete abstinence from substance use in order to access services (Gerassi, 2018).

Although EBTs for trauma broadly target associated symptoms such as trauma-related anxiety and depression, trafficking survivors may have primary diagnoses other than PTSD or comorbid conditions that require additional treatment (Cary et al., 2016; Oram et al., 2015; Stoklosa et al., 2017).

Given the range, heterogeneity, and comorbidity among trafficking survivors, common elements and transdiagnostic approaches may have particular value. For example, modular approaches to therapy for children with anxiety, depression, trauma, and conduct problems (MATCH-ADTC; Chorpita & Weisz, 2009) may have utility with trafficked youth. The common elements treatment approach (CETA) likewise targets the common impacts of PTSD, depression, anxiety, and substance use and has the added advantage of application in low-resource settings and successful utilization with non-professionals (Murray et al., 2014, 2018).

Serious mental illness includes primary depressive disorders that persist following trauma treatment, bipolar disorder, or disorders that produce psychotic symptoms such as schizophrenia or schizoaffective disorder. For trafficking survivors whose symptom picture is further complicated by serious mental illness, treatment planning should also include interventions specific to these conditions, including therapy as well as consideration of psychopharmacological intervention (Cary et al., 2016; Oram et al., 2015).

Group Interventions

At least in part because of the shame, stigma, and isolation they often experience, group treatments may be especially beneficial for trafficking survivors (McMullen et al., 2013; O'Callaghan et al., 2013; Usacheva et al., 2022). Groups may serve psychoeducational, psychotherapeutic, and support functions and may create a motivating factor to remain in treatment and prevent return to the trafficker (Countryman-Roswurm & Bolin, 2014; Hickle & Roe-Sepowitz, 2014; Kenny et al., 2018). Ending the Game™ is a group intervention that targets shame, isolation, regulation of emotion and behavior, maladaptive cognitions, identity disturbance, and dissociation and has demonstrated positive trends in improving regulation, relational capacity, sense of self, and future orientation (Usacheva et al., 2022). The STARS experiential group (previously described) was similarly developed specifically for trafficking survivors, targeting complex trauma impacts and utilizing experiential strategies (Hopper et al., 2018). EBTs may also be delivered in a group format. For instance, the TF-CBT treatment in the previously described RCTs (McMullen et al., 2013; O'Callaghan et al., 2013) were delivered in a group setting. Moreover, the skills training component of DBT is often, and perhaps preferentially with trafficking survivors, delivered in a group setting. Group treatments may also address resource challenges in low-resource settings.

Relationship Development and Community Reintegration

Interpersonal connections are often central to the recovery of human trafficking survivors. Intervention should incorporate opportunities to establish or reestablish healthy supportive relationships and connection with family, close relationships, and community, if and when it is safe to do so (Brunovskis & Surtees, 2013).

Family Engagement and Intervention

As previously discussed, many trafficking survivors come from complex family environments marked by financial stress, violence, abuse, or neglect, substance use, and/or chronic stress which may have directly contributed to trafficking victimization. Therefore, family attitudes regarding the victimization vary widely. Responses may range from active support of the survivor to lack of awareness of the exploitation, disengagement or helplessness to intervene, blaming the survivor, or even active support of, or direct involvement in, the trafficking. Family and caregiver perspectives that may contribute to shame and stigma are especially important considerations for this population (Cohen, Mannarino, & Kinnish, 2017; Kiss et al., 2015).

For trafficked youth, involvement of a safe and supportive caregiver can be particularly pivotal. Engagement of caregivers is highly individualized and considers survivors' pre-trafficking circumstances, features of the relationship that contributed to trafficking vulnerability, specific trafficking experiences, as well as, and perhaps most importantly, the caregiver(s) current functioning. When considering family engagement, it is important to note that "caregivers" may include members of the family of origin, a new caregiving relationship, a close mentoring relationship, or adults within formal caregiving systems (foster parents, congregate care staff). Intervention can include caregiver education and support, individual counseling for caregivers, and dyadic or family therapy. Many of the therapies described earlier include one or more of these elements (e.g., TF-CBT, ARC, RRFT).

Parenting Support

Trauma-related impacts on survivors' parenting of their own children can include lack of confidence in parenting abilities, overprotective parenting and avoidance of socialization with other children or adults, and emotional disconnection from children when the caregiver is struggling with chronic stress and/or mental health symptoms (Marti Castaner et al., 2021). Thus, parent–child interventions (e.g., child–parent psychotherapy, parent–child interaction therapy, ARC-based parenting support) or family therapy (e.g., ecologically based family therapy; Murnan et al., 2018) may be important therapeutic modalities for some trafficking survivors. Research is needed on applications of these models for families affected by trafficking.

Survivor Mentoring and Community Supports

Peer support and mentoring, especially connection to a survivor mentor, can be beneficial in building safe, supportive relationships and reducing shame and stigma (Ijadi-Maghsoodi et al., 2018; National Human Trafficking Training and Technical Assistance Center, 2021; Rothman et al., 2020). Community supports, including case management services, may mitigate some of the negative long-term impacts of human trafficking. Successful community integration has been shown to indirectly ameliorate PTSD symptoms through an influence on perceived social support (Okech et al., 2018). Especially promising are comprehensive service models that establish levels of care based on individualized needs and incorporate significant case management and survivor mentoring or coaching. For example, the CHANCE (Citrus Helping Adolescents Negatively impacted by Commercial Exploitation) program (Landers et al., 2017) provides individual and group therapy for trafficked youth and their caregivers to reduce shame and isolation and teach practical skills, individual TF-CBT treatment to address trauma impacts, specialized placement, life coaches with lived experiences of commercial sexual exploitation, intensive case management, and 24/7 youth and caregiver support access. Other helpful programs provide training or opportunities for advancement in leadership and advocacy and scaffolded development of autonomy, confidence, and leadership (e.g., Elevate Academy, My Life My Choice Youth Leadership Corps).

CONCLUSION AND RECOMMENDATIONS

The complex interplay of vulnerabilities and experiences prior to and while being trafficked often result in significant mental health effects for survivors. Effective mental health intervention requires trauma- and trafficking-informed application of a full continuum of intervention skills. It begins with engagement and establishment of a quality therapeutic alliance that especially prioritizes safety, trust, empowerment, and collaboration, to counter the trafficking survivor's previous experiences of threat, harm, coercion, manipulation, and deception. Trauma-informed psychological assessment with trafficking survivors utilizes conventional approaches and tools to better understand a client's current functioning and to guide treatment planning, as well as enhances client engagement and promotes self-awareness and effective copings. Treatment with trafficking survivors should be trauma-informed, culturally responsive, developmentally adapted, collaborative, and responsive to individual client needs and preferences, while being informed by the best available research to guide treatment decision making. This includes evidence regarding the effectiveness of specific treatment approaches with trafficking survivors as well as the effectiveness of interventions addressing primary mental health impacts (e.g., PTSD symptoms and other trauma-related impacts) with related populations.

The development, application, adaptation, and evaluation of interventions to address complex human problems and support positive change is perhaps clinical psychology's greatest potential contribution to the trafficking field. There are a number of mental health interventions with an emerging evidence base with survivors of trafficking and many treatment models and intervention strategies that show promise in addressing the needs of this population. However, more work is needed in the development of effective interventions, and more outcome research is needed on existing treatment approaches. This includes more outcome research utilizing EBTs specifically with survivors of trafficking, greater study of trafficking-specific adaptations of these approaches, and more refined approaches to identifying factors that contribute to better outcomes to inform treatment decision making. Interventions addressing the person in context, including treatments addressing relationships and interventions focusing on community reintegration, as well emerging strategies that incorporate mental health treatment into a broad array of services and supports, are also important and warrant further study.

Finally, additional research is needed that focuses on intervention with underserved populations, including those who have experienced labor trafficking, men and boys, persons who identify as LGBTQ+, especially transgender, survivors, individuals with substance use disorders, people from different racial and ethnic groups (Native American, Alaska Native, Black, Hispanic and Latino, Asian, and Pacific Islander survivors), immigrant, refugee, or forcibly displaced persons, individuals with disabilities, and those with comorbid severe mental illness, among others. As noted elsewhere in this volume, much less is known about the experiences of labor trafficking survivors compared with survivors of sex trafficking. This is perhaps especially true of their mental health treatment needs, experiences, and outcomes. There are multiple common features across various forms of trafficking, including commodification, coercive control, shame, and experiences of trauma prior to, during, and subsequent to trafficking; therefore, there are significant overlapping treatment needs between survivors of labor and sex trafficking. This is especially true regarding trauma impacts and treatment addressing these impacts, which is a primary focus of this chapter. However, research is needed to affirm these commonalities and to identify and articulate areas of divergence within and across trafficking experiences, highlighting unique treatment needs. Policy changes are needed to increase funding to support development and evaluation of effective treatment approaches for all survivors of human trafficking.

REFERENCES

Aberdein, C., & Zimmerman, C. (2015). Access to mental health and psychosocial services in Cambodia by survivors of trafficking and exploitation: A qualitative study. *International Journal of Mental Health Systems, 9*(1), 1–13. https://doi.org/10.1186/s13033-015-0008-8

Albright, K., Greenbaum, J., Edwards, S. A., & Tsai, C. (2020). Systematic review of facilitators of, barriers to, and recommendations for healthcare services for child survivors of human trafficking globally. *Child Abuse & Neglect, 100*, 104289. https://doi.org/10.1016/j.chiabu.2019.104289

American Psychological Association Presidential Task Force on Evidence-Based Practice. (2006). Evidence-based practice in psychology. *American Psychologist, 61*(4), 271–285. https://doi.org/10.1037/0003-066X.61.4.271

Barnert, E., Kelly, M., Godoy, S., Abrams, L. S., Rasch, M., & Bath, E. (2019). Understanding commercially sexually exploited young women's access to, utilization of, and engagement in health care: "Work around what I need." *Women's Health Issues, 29*(4), 315–324. https://doi.org/10.1016/j.whi.2019.02.002

Bass, J., Bearup, L., Bolton, P., Murray, L., & Skavenski, S. (2011). *Implementing trauma focused cognitive behavioral therapy (TF-CBT) among formerly trafficked-sexually exploited and sexually abused girls in Cambodia: A feasibility study.* World Vision. https://doi.org/10.1037/e533652013-111

Bath, E., Barnert, E., Godoy, S., Hammond, I., Mondals, S., Farabee, D., & Grella, C. (2020). Substance use, mental health, and child welfare profiles of juvenile justice-involved commercially sexually exploited youth. *Journal of Child and Adolescent Psychopharmacology, 30*(6), 389–397. https://doi.org/10.1089/cap.2019.0057

Batley, C., Chon, K., Garrett, A., Greenbaum, J., Hopper, E., Murphy, L., Peck, J., Pfenning, E., Robitz, R., & Stoklosa, H. (2021). *Core competencies for human trafficking response in health care and behavioral health systems.* National Human Trafficking Training and Technical Assistance Center, Department of Health and Human Services. https://nhttac.acf.hhs.gov/sites/default/files/2021-02/Core%20Competencies%20Report%20%282%29.pdf

Beck, A. T. (2005). The current state of cognitive therapy: A 40-year retrospective. *Archives of General Psychiatry, 62*(9), 953–959. https://doi.org/10.1001/archpsyc.62.9.953

Blaustein, M., & Kinniburgh, K. (2018). *Treating traumatic stress in children and adolescents: How to foster resilience through attachment, self-regulation, and competency* (2nd ed.). Guilford Press.

Bohus, M., Dyer, A. S., Priebe, K., Krüger, A., Kleindienst, N., Schmahl, C., Niedtfeld, I., & Steil, R. (2013). Dialectical behaviour therapy for post-traumatic stress disorder after childhood sexual abuse in patients with and without borderline personality disorder: A randomised controlled trial. *Psychotherapy and Psychosomatics, 82*(4), 221–233. https://doi.org/10.1159/000348451

Boyd, J. E., Lanius, R. A., & McKinnon, M. C. (2018). Mindfulness-based treatments for posttraumatic stress disorder: A review of the treatment literature and neurobiological evidence. *Journal of Psychiatry & Neuroscience, 43*(1), 7–25. https://doi.org/10.1503/jpn.170021

Brady, F., Chisholm, A., Walsh, E., Ottisova, L., Bevilacqua, L., Mason, C., von Werthern, M., Cannon, T., Curry, C., Komolafe, K., Robert, R. E., Robjant, K., & Katona, C. (2021). Narrative exposure therapy for survivors of human trafficking: Feasibility randomised controlled trial. *BJPsych Open, 7*(6), e196. https://doi.org/10.1192/bjo.2021.1029

Brewin, C. R., Cloitre, M., Hyland, P., Shevlin, M., Maercker, A., Bryant, R. A., Humayun, A., Jones, L. M., Kagee, A., Rousseau, C., Somasundaram, D., Suzuki, Y., Wessely, S., van Ommeren, M., & Reed, G. M. (2017). A review of current evidence regarding the ICD-11 proposals for diagnosing PTSD and complex PTSD. *Clinical Psychology Review, 58*, 1–15. https://doi.org/10.1016/j.cpr.2017.09.001

Briere, J., & Lanktree, C. B. (2013). *Integrative treatment of complex trauma for adolescents (ITCT-A): A guide for the treatment of multiple-traumatized youth* (2nd ed.). University of Southern California-Adolescent Trauma Training Center, National Child Traumatic Stress Network, U.S. Department of Substance Abuse and Mental Health Services Administration. https://keck.usc.edu/adolescent-trauma-training-center/wp-content/uploads/sites/169/2016/06/ITCT-A-TreatmentGuide-2ndEdition-rev20131106.pdf

Brunovskis, A., & Surtees, R. (2013). Coming home: Challenges in family reintegration for trafficked women. *Qualitative Social Work: Research and Practice, 12*(4), 454–472. https://doi.org/10.1177/1473325011435257

Cary, M., Oram, S., Howard, L. M., Trevillion, K., & Byford, S. (2016). Human trafficking and severe mental illness: An economic analysis of survivors' use of psychiatric services. *BMC Health Services Research, 16*(1), 284. https://doi.org/10.1186/s12913-016-1541-0

Chessell, Z. J., Brady, F., Akbar, S., Stevens, A., & Young, K. (2019). A protocol for managing dissociative symptoms in refugee populations. *Cognitive Behaviour Therapist, 12*, e27. Advance online publication. https://doi.org/10.1017/S1754470X19000114

Chorpita, B. F., & Weisz, J. R. (2009). *Modular approach to therapy for children with anxiety, depression, trauma, or conduct problems (MATCH-ADTC)*. PracticeWise.

Clemans, T. A., White, K. L., Fuessel-Herrmann, D., Bryan, C. J., & Resick, P. A. (2021). Acceptability, feasibility, and preliminary effectiveness of group cognitive processing therapy with female adolescent survivors of commercial sexual exploitation in Cambodia. *Journal of Child & Adolescent Trauma, 14*(4), 571–583. https://doi.org/10.1007/s40653-021-00405-6

Cloitre, M., Courtois, C. A., Ford, J. D., Green, B. L., Alexander, P., Briere, J., Herman, J. L., Lanius, R., Stolbach, B. C., Spinazzola, J., Van der Kolk, B. A., & Van der Hart, O. (2012). *The ISTSS expert consensus treatment guidelines for complex PTSD in adults.*

https://istss.org/ISTSS_Main/media/Documents/ISTSS-Expert-Concesnsus-Guidelines-for-Complex-PTSD-Updated-060315.pdf

Cloitre, M., Koenen, K. C., Cohen, L. R., & Han, H. (2002). Skills training in affective and interpersonal regulation followed by exposure: A phase-based treatment for PTSD related to childhood abuse. *Journal of Consulting and Clinical Psychology, 70*(5), 1067–1074. https://doi.org/10.1037/0022-006X.70.5.1067

Cohen, J. A., Mannarino, A. P., & Deblinger, E. (2017). *Treating trauma and traumatic grief* (2nd ed.). Guilford Press.

Cohen, J. A., Mannarino, A. P., & Kinnish, K. (2017). Trauma-focused cognitive behavioral therapy for commercially sexually exploited youth. *Journal of Child & Adolescent Trauma, 10*(2), 175–185. https://doi.org/10.1007/s40653-015-0073-9

Cohen, J. A., Mannarino, A. P., Kliethermes, M., & Murray, L. A. (2012). Trauma-focused CBT for youth with complex trauma. *Child Abuse & Neglect, 36*(6), 528–541. https://doi.org/10.1016/j.chiabu.2012.03.007

Contreras, P. M., Kallivayalil, D., & Herman, J. L. (2017). Psychotherapy in the aftermath of human trafficking: Working through the consequences of psychological coercion. *Women & Therapy, 40*(1–2), 31–54. https://doi.org/10.1080/02703149.2016.1205908

Corbett-Hone, M., & Johnson, N. L. (2022). Psychosocial correlates of mental health work with human trafficking survivors: Risk and resilience. *Psychological Services, 19*(Suppl. 1), 84–94. https://doi.org/10.1037/ser0000615

Countryman-Roswurm, K., & Bolin, B. (2014). Domestic minor sex trafficking: Assessing and reducing risk. *Child & Adolescent Social Work Journal, 31*(6), 521–538. https://doi.org/10.1007/s10560-014-0336-6

Danielson, C. K., Adams, Z., McCart, M. R., Chapman, J. E., Sheidow, A. J., Walker, J., Smalling, A., & de Arellano, M. A. (2020). Safety and efficacy of exposure-based risk reduction through family therapy for co-occurring substance use problems and posttraumatic stress disorder symptoms among adolescents: A randomized clinical trial. *JAMA Psychiatry, 77*(6), 574–586. https://doi.org/10.1001/jamapsychiatry.2019.4803

Danielson, C. K., McCart, M. R., de Arellano, M. A., Macdonald, A., Doherty, L. S., & Resnick, H. S. (2010). Risk reduction for substance use and trauma-related psychopathology in adolescent sexual assault victims: Findings from an open trial. *Child Maltreatment, 15*(3), 261–268. https://doi.org/10.1177/1077559510367939

Edmond, T. (2018). Evidence-based trauma treatments for survivors of sex trafficking and commercial sexual exploitation. In A. Nichols, T. Edmond, & E. Heil (Eds.), *Social work practice with survivors of sex trafficking and commercial sexual exploitation* (pp. 70–96). Columbia University Press. https://doi.org/10.7312/nich18092-006

Ellis, B. H., Abdi, S. M., & Winer, J. P. (2020). *Mental health practice with immigrant and refugee youth: A socioecological framework*. American Psychological Association. https://doi.org/10.1037/0000163-000

Ertl, V., Pfeiffer, A., Schauer, E., Elbert, T., & Neuner, F. (2011). Community-implemented trauma therapy for former child soldiers in Northern Uganda: A randomized controlled trial. *JAMA, 306*(5), 503–512. https://doi.org/10.1001/jama.2011.1060

Fehrenbach, T., Sax, R. M., Urban, T. H., Simon-Roper, L., Novacek, J., Aaby, D. A., & Hodgdon, H. B. (2021). Trauma treatment for youth in community-based settings:

Implementing the Attachment, Regulation, and Competency (ARC) framework. *Journal of Child and Family Studies*. Advance online publication.

Foa, E. B., Hembree, E., & Rothbaum, B. (2007). *Prolonged exposure therapy for PTSD: Emotional processing of traumatic experiences.* Oxford University Press.

Foa, E. B., McLean, C. P., Capaldi, S., & Rosenfield, D. (2013). Prolonged exposure vs supportive counseling for sexual abuse-related PTSD in adolescent girls: A randomized clinical trial. *JAMA, 310*(24), 2650–2657. https://doi.org/10.1001/jama.2013.282829

Follette, V. M., Briere, J., Rozelle, D., Hopper, J. W., & Rome, D. I. (2015). *Mindfulness-oriented interventions for trauma: Integrating contemplative practices.* Guilford Press.

Gene-Cos, N., Fisher, J., Ogden, P., & Cantrell, A. (2016). Sensorimotor psychotherapy group therapy in the treatment of complex PTSD. *Annals of Psychiatry and Mental Health, 4*(6), 1080.

Gerassi, L. B. (2018). Barriers to accessing detox facilities, substance use treatment, and residential services among women impacted by commercial sexual exploitation and trafficking. *Behavioral Medicine, 44*(3), 199–208. https://doi.org/10.1080/08964289.2017.1384360

Gerassi, L. B., & Esbensen, K. (2021). Motivational interviewing with individuals at risk of sex trafficking. *Journal of Social Work, 21*(4), 676–695. https://doi.org/10.1177/1468017320919856

Gibbs, D. A., Hardison Walters, J. L., Lutnick, A., Miller, S., & Kluckman, M. (2015). Services to domestic minor victims of sex trafficking: Opportunities for engagement and support. *Children and Youth Services Review, 54*, 1–7. https://doi.org/10.1016/j.childyouth.2015.04.003

Godoy, S. M., Abrams, L. S., Barnert, E. S., Kelly, M. A., & Bath, E. P. (2020). Fierce autonomy: How girls and young women impacted by commercial sexual exploitation perceive health and exercise agency in health care decision-making. *Qualitative Health Research, 30*(9), 1326–1337. https://doi.org/10.1177/1049732320913857 https://doi.org/10.1177/1049732320913857

Gordon, J. S., Staples, J. K., Blyta, A., Bytyqi, M., & Wilson, A. T. (2008). Treatment of posttraumatic stress disorder in postwar Kosovar adolescents using mind-body skills groups: A randomized controlled trial. *The Journal of Clinical Psychiatry, 69*(9), 1469–1476. https://doi.org/10.4088/JCP.v69n0915

Harned, M. S. (2022). *Treating trauma in dialectical behavior therapy: The DBT prolonged exposure protocol (DBT-PE).* Guilford Press.

Herman, J. L. (1997). *Trauma and recovery: The aftermath of violence—From domestic abuse to political terror.* Basic Books.

Hickle, K., & Hallett, S. (2016). Mitigating harm: Considering harm reduction principles in work with sexually exploited young people. *Children & Society, 30*(4), 302–313. https://doi.org/10.1111/chso.12145

Hickle, K., & Roe-Sepowitz, D. (2014). Putting the pieces back together: A group intervention for sexually exploited adolescent girls. *Social Work with Groups, 37*(2), 99–113. https://doi.org/10.1080/01609513.2013.823838

Hodgdon, H. B., Kinniburgh, K., Gabowitz, D., Blaustein, M. E., & Spinazzola, J. (2013). Development and implementation of trauma-informed programming in youth residential treatment centers using the ARC framework. *Journal of Family Violence, 28*(7), 679–692. https://doi.org/10.1007/s10896-013-9531-z

Hopper, E. K. (2017a). The multimodal social ecological (MSE) approach: A trauma-informed framework for supporting trafficking survivors' psychosocial health. In M. Chisolm-Straker & H. Stocklosa (Eds.), *Human trafficking is a public health issue: A paradigm expansion in the United States* (pp. 153–183). Springer International Publishing. https://doi.org/10.1007/978-3-319-47824-1_10

Hopper, E. K. (2017b). Trauma-informed treatment of substance use disorders in trafficking survivors. In M. Chisolm-Straker & H. Stocklosa (Eds.), *Human trafficking is a public health issue: A paradigm expansion in the United States* (pp. 211–230). Springer International Publishing. https://doi.org/10.1007/978-3-319-47824-1_12

Hopper, E. K. (2018). Trauma-informed psychological assessment of human trafficking survivors. In N. M. Sidun & D. L. Hume (Eds.), *A feminist perspective on human trafficking of women and girls: Characteristics, commonalities and complexities.* (pp. 6–24). Routledge/Taylor & Francis Group.

Hopper, E. K., Azar, N., Bhattacharyya, S., Malebranche, D. A., & Brennan, K. L. (2018). STARS experiential group intervention: A complex trauma treatment approach for survivors of human trafficking. *Journal of Evidence-Informed Social Work, 15*(2), 215–241. https://doi.org/10.1080/23761407.2018.1455616

Horvath, A. O., & Greenberg, L. S. (Eds.). (1994). *The working alliance: Theory, research, and practice.* John Wiley & Sons.

Ijadi-Maghsoodi, R., Bath, E., Cook, M., Textor, L., & Barnert, E. (2018). Commercially sexually exploited youths' health care experiences, barriers, and recommendations: A qualitative analysis. *Child Abuse & Neglect, 76*, 334–341. https://doi.org/10.1016/j.chiabu.2017.11.002

International Society for Traumatic Stress Studies. (2018a). *ISTSS guidelines position paper on complex PTSD in adults.* https://istss.org/getattachment/Treating-Trauma/New-ISTSS-Prevention-and-Treatment-Guidelines/ISTSS_CPTSD-Position-Paper-(Adults)_FNL.pdf.aspx

International Society for Traumatic Stress Studies. (2018b). *ISTSS guidelines position paper on complex PTSD in children and adolescents.* https://istss.org/getattachment/Treating-Trauma/New-ISTSS-Prevention-and-Treatment-Guidelines/ISTSS_CPTSD-Position-Paper-(Child_Adol)_FNL.pdf.aspx

International Society for Traumatic Stress Studies. (2018c). *ISTSS prevention and treatment guidelines.* https://istss.org/getattachment/Treating-Trauma/New-ISTSS-Prevention-and-Treatment-Guidelines/ISTSS_PreventionTreatmentGuidelines_FNL.pdf.aspx

Judge, A. M., Murphy, J. A., Hidalgo, J., & Macias-Konstantopoulos, W. (2018). Engaging survivors of human trafficking: Complex health care needs and scarce resources. *Annals of Internal Medicine, 168*(9), 658–663. https://doi.org/10.7326/M17-2605

Karatzias, T., Murphy, P., Cloitre, M., Bisson, J., Roberts, N., Shevlin, M., Hyland, P., Maercker, A., Ben-Ezra, M., Coventry, P., Mason-Roberts, S., Bradley, A., & Hutton, P. (2019). Psychological interventions for ICD-11 complex PTSD symptoms: Systematic review and meta-analysis. *Psychological Medicine, 49*(11), 1761–1775. https://doi.org/10.1017/S0033291719000436

Kelly, A., & Garland, E. L. (2016). Trauma-informed mindfulness-based stress reduction for female survivors of interpersonal violence: Results from a stage I RCT. *Journal of Clinical Psychology, 72*(4), 311–328. https://doi.org/10.1002/jclp.22273

Kenny, M. C., Helpingstine, C. E., Harrington, M. C., & McEachern, A. G. (2018). A comprehensive group approach for commercially sexually exploited girls. *Journal for Specialists in Group Work, 43*(4), 376–398. https://doi.org/10.1080/01933922.2018.1484540

Kerig, P. K. (2013). *Trauma-informed assessment and intervention*. National Child Traumatic Stress Network. https://www.nctsn.org/sites/default/files/resources/trauma_informed_assessment_intervention.pdf

Kidd, S. A., Davidson, L., & McKenzie, K. (2017). Common factors in community mental health intervention: A scoping review. *Community Mental Health Journal, 53*(6), 627–637. https://doi.org/10.1007/s10597-017-0117-8

Kinnish, K., Cohen, J. A., Mannarino, A., Kliethermes, M., Rubiales, R., & Wozniak, J. (2021). *TF-CBT for the commercial sexual exploitation of children: An implementation manual*. Allegheny General Hospital. https://tfcbt.org/wp-content/uploads/2022/05/CSEC-Imp-Manual-Final.pdf

Kinnish, K., McCarty, C., Tiwari, A., Osborne, M., Glasheen, T., Franchot, K. K., Kramer, C., & Self-Brown, S. (2020). Featured counter-trafficking program: Project intersect. *Child Abuse & Neglect, 100*, 104132. https://doi.org/10.1016/j.chiabu.2019.104132

Kiss, L., Yun, K., Pocock, N., & Zimmerman, C. (2015). Exploitation, violence, and suicide risk among child and adolescent survivors of human trafficking in the Greater Mekong Subregion. *JAMA Pediatrics, 169*(9), e152278. https://doi.org/10.1001/jamapediatrics.2015.2278

Kliethermes, M., & Wamser, R. (2012). Adolescents with complex trauma. In J. A. Cohen, A. P. Mannarino, & E. Deblinger (Eds.), *Trauma focused CBT for children and adolescents: Treatment applications* (pp. 175–198). Guilford Press.

Knott, L. E., Salami, T., Gordon, M. R., Torres, M. I., Coverdale, J. H., & Nguyen, P. T. (2021). Motivational interviewing as a therapeutic strategy for trafficked persons. *Journal of Cognitive Psychotherapy, 35*(2), 104–115. https://doi.org/10.1891/JCPSY-D-20-00028

Landers, M., McGrath, K., Johnson, M. H., Armstrong, M. I., & Dollard, N. (2017). Baseline characteristics of dependent youth who have been commercially sexually exploited: Findings from a specialized treatment program. *Journal of Child Sexual Abuse, 26*(6), 692–709. https://doi.org/10.1080/10538712.2017.1323814

Lee, R. K. (2019). *Expressive arts as a treatment for survivors of sexual trauma: Studying the phenomenon and efficacy of expressive arts use with adult survivors* of commercial sexual exploitation [Doctoral dissertation, Pepperdine University]. Pepperdine Digital Commons. https://digitalcommons.pepperdine.edu/etd/1061/

Linehan, M. M. (1993). *Cognitive-behavioral treatment of borderline personality disorder*. Guilford Press.

Lloyd, R. (2018). Change is a process: Using the transtheoretical model with commercially sexually exploited and trafficked youth and adults. In A. Nichols, T. Edmond, & E. Heil (Eds.), *Social work practice with survivors of sex trafficking and commercial sexual exploitation* (pp. 51–69). Columbia University Press. https://doi.org/10.7312/nich18092-005

Logan, D. E., & Marlatt, G. A. (2010). Harm reduction therapy: A practice-friendly review of research. *Journal of Clinical Psychology, 66*(2), 201–214. https://doi.org/10.1002/jclp.20669

LoSavio, S. T., Murphy, R. A., & Resick, P. A. (2021). Treatment outcomes for adolescents versus adults receiving cognitive processing therapy for posttraumatic stress disorder during community training. *Journal of Traumatic Stress, 34*(4), 757–763. https://doi.org/10.1002/jts.22668

Lurie, I., Cohn, E., & Slobodin, O. (2020). Cultural aspects in the assessment and management of trafficked persons. In J. H. Coverdale, M. R. Gordon, & P. T. Nguyen, (Eds), *Human trafficking: A treatment guide for mental health professionals* (pp. 193–212). American Psychiatric Association.

Marlatt, G. A. (1996). Harm reduction: Come as you are. *Addictive Behaviors, 21*(6), 779–788. https://doi.org/10.1016/0306-4603(96)00042-1

Marti Castaner, M., Fowler, R., Landers, C., Cohen, L., & Orjuela, M. (2021). How trauma related to sex trafficking challenges parenting: Insights from Mexican and Central American survivors in the US. *PLOS ONE, 16*(6), e0252606. https://doi.org/10.1371/journal.pone.0252606

McCauley, E., Berk, M. S., Asarnow, J. R., Adrian, M., Cohen, J., Korslund, K., Avina, C., Hughes, J., Harned, M., Gallop, R., & Linehan, M. M. (2018). Efficacy of dialectical behavior therapy for adolescents at high risk for suicide: A randomized clinical trial. *JAMA Psychiatry, 75*(8), 777–785. https://doi.org/10.1001/jamapsychiatry.2018.1109

McCaw, A. (2019). *Use of mindfulness to treat mental health symptoms of individuals subjected to human sex trafficking and prostitution* [Doctoral dissertation, National Louis University]. Digital Commons at NLU. https://digitalcommons.nl.edu/diss/370

McMullen, J., O'Callaghan, P., Shannon, C., Black, A., & Eakin, J. (2013). Group trauma-focused cognitive-behavioural therapy with former child soldiers and other war-affected boys in the DR Congo: A randomised controlled trial. *Journal of Child Psychology and Psychiatry, and Allied Disciplines, 54*(11), 1231–1241. https://doi.org/10.1111/jcpp.12094

Miller, A. L., Rathus, J. H., & Linehan, M. M. (2007). *Dialectical behavior therapy with suicidal adolescents*. Guilford Press.

Miller, W. R., & Rollnick, S. (2013). *Motivational interviewing: Helping people change* (3rd ed.). Guilford Press.

Monson, C. M., & Shnaider, P. (2014). *Treating PTSD with cognitive-behavioral therapies: Interventions that work*. American Psychological Association. https://doi.org/10.1037/14372-000

Moore, J. L., Houck, C., Hirway, P., Barron, C. E., & Goldberg, A. P. (2020). Trafficking experiences and psychosocial features of domestic minor sex trafficking Victims. *Journal of Interpersonal Violence, 35*(15–16), 3148–3163. https://doi.org/10.1177/0886260517703373

Mumey, A., Sardana, S., Richardson-Vejlgaard, R., & Akinsulure-Smith, A. M. (2021). Mental health needs of sex trafficking survivors in New York City: Reflections on exploitation, coping, and recovery. *Psychological Trauma: Theory, Research, Practice, and Policy, 13*(2), 185–192. https://doi.org/10.1037/tra0000603

Murnan, A., Wu, Q., & Slesnick, N. (2018). Effects of ecologically-based family therapy with substance-using, prostituting mothers. *Journal of Family Therapy, 40*(4), 557–583. https://doi.org/10.1111/1467-6427.12187

Murray, L. K., Dorsey, S., Haroz, E., Lee, C., Alsiary, M. M., Haydary, A., Weiss, W. M., & Bolton, P. (2014). A common elements treatment approach for adult mental health problems in low- and middle-income countries. *Cognitive and Behavioral Practice, 21*(2), 111–123. https://doi.org/10.1016/j.cbpra.2013.06.005

Murray, L. K., Hall, B. J., Dorsey, S., Ugueto, A. M., Puffer, E. S., Sim, A., Ismael, A., Bass, J., Akiba, C., Lucid, L., Harrison, J., Erikson, A., & Bolton, P. A. (2018). An evaluation of a common elements treatment approach for youth in Somali refugee camps. *Global Mental Health, 5*, e16. https://doi.org/10.1017/gmh.2018.7

Najavits, L. M. (2002). *Seeking safety: A treatment manual for PTSD and substance abuse.* Guilford Press.

Namy, S., Carlson, C., Morgan, K., Nkwanzi, V., & Neese, J. (2022). Healing and resilience after trauma (HaRT) yoga: Programming with survivors of human trafficking in Uganda. *Journal of Social Work Practice, 36*(1), 87–100. https://doi.org/10.1080/02650533.2021.1934819

National Human Trafficking Training and Technical Assistance Center. (n.d.). *How to improve services for males experiencing trafficking.* https://nhttac.acf.hhs.gov/sites/default/files/2022-02/How%20to%20Improve%20Services%20for%20Males%20Experiencing%20Trafficking_508_Final_02.10.22.pdf

National Human Trafficking Training and Technical Assistance Center. (2021). *Core competencies for human trafficking response in health care and behavioral health systems.* https://nhttac.acf.hhs.gov/sites/default/files/2021-02/Core%20Competencies%20Report%20%282%29.pdf

Nichols, A., & Heil, E. (2022). Human trafficking of people with a disability: An analysis of state and federal cases. *Dignity: A Journal of Analysis of Exploitation and Violence, 7*(1), 1–21. https://doi.org/10.23860/dignity.2022.07.01.01

O'Brien, J., Finkelhor, D., & Jones, L. (2022). Improving services for youth survivors of commercial sexual exploitation: Insights from interventions with other high-risk youth. *Children and Youth Services Review, 132*, 106313. Advance online publication. https://doi.org/10.1016/j.childyouth.2021.106313

O'Callaghan, P., McMullen, J., Shannon, C., Rafferty, H., & Black, A. (2013). A randomized controlled trial of trauma-focused cognitive behavioral therapy for sexually exploited, war-affected Congolese girls. *Journal of the American Academy of Child & Adolescent Psychiatry, 52*(4), 359–369. https://doi.org/10.1016/j.jaac.2013.01.013

Okech, D., Hansen, N., Howard, W., Anarfi, J. K., & Burns, A. C. (2018). Social support, dysfunctional coping, and community reintegration as predictors of PTSD among human trafficking survivors. *Behavioral Medicine, 44*(3), 209–218. https://doi.org/10.1080/08964289.2018.1432553

Oram, S., Khondoker, M., Abas, M., Broadbent, M., & Howard, L. M. (2015). Characteristics of trafficked adults and children with severe mental illness: A historical cohort study. *The Lancet. Psychiatry, 2*(12), 1084–1091. https://doi.org/10.1016/S2215-0366(15)00290-4

Ortiz, R., & Sibinga, E. M. (2017). The role of mindfulness in reducing the adverse effects of childhood stress and trauma. *Children, 4*(3), 16. https://doi.org/10.3390/children4030016

Ottisova, L., Smith, P., & Oram, S. (2018). Psychological consequences of human trafficking: Complex posttraumatic stress disorder in trafficked children. *Behavioral Medicine, 44*(3), 234–241. https://doi.org/10.1080/08964289.2018.1432555

Owens, C., Dank, M., Breaux, J., Banuelos, I., Farrell, A., Pfeffer, R., Bright, K., Heitsmith, R., & McDevitt, J. (2014). *Understanding the organization, operation, and victimization process of labor trafficking in the United States.* The Urban Institute. https://www.urban.org/sites/default/files/publication/33821/413249-Understanding-the-Organization-Operation-and-Victimization-Process-of-Labor-Trafficking-in-the-United-States.PDF

Pierce, A. S. (2012). American Indian adolescent girls: Vulnerability to sex trafficking, intervention strategies. *American Indian and Alaska Native Mental Health Research, 19*(1), 37–56. https://doi.org/10.5820/aian.1901.2012.37

Powell, C., Asbill, M., Louis, E., & Stoklosa, H. (2018). Identifying gaps in human trafficking mental health service provision. *Journal of Human Trafficking, 4*(3), 256–269. https://doi.org/10.1080/23322705.2017.1362936

Preble, K. (2018). 6. Client-centered harm reduction, commercial sex, and trafficking: Implications for rights-based social work practice. In A. Nichols, T. Edmond, & E. Heil (Eds.), *Social work practice with survivors of sex trafficking and commercial sexual exploitation* (pp. 97–116). Columbia University Press. https://doi.org/10.7312/nich18092-007

Prochaska, J. O., & Norcross, J. C. (2002). Stages of change. In J. C. Norcross (Ed.), *Psychotherapy relationships that work: Therapist contributions and responsiveness to patients* (pp. 303–313). Oxford University Press.

Reid, J. A. (2018). Sex trafficking of girls with intellectual disabilities: An exploratory mixed methods study. *Sexual Abuse, 30*(2), 107–131. https://doi.org/10.1177/1079063216630981

Reid, J. A., Strauss, J., & Haskell, R. A. (2018). Clinical practice with commercially sexually exploited girls with intellectual disabilities. In A. J. Nichols, T. Edmond, & E. C. Heil (Eds.), *Social work practice with survivors of sex trafficking and commercial sexual exploitation* (pp. 218–238). Columbia University Press. https://doi.org/10.7312/nich18092-012

Resick, P. A., Monson, C. M., & Chard, K. M. (2016). *Cognitive processing therapy for PTSD: A comprehensive manual.* Guilford Press.

Robitz, R., Ulloa, E. C., Salazar, M., & Ulibarri, M. D. (2020). Mental health service needs of commercially sexually exploited youth: Voices of survivors and stakeholders. *Violence and Victims, 35*(3), 354–362. https://doi.org/10.1891/VV-D-18-00213

Robjant, K., Koebach, A., Schmitt, S., Chibashimba, A., Carleial, S., & Elbert, T. (2019). The treatment of posttraumatic stress symptoms and aggression in female former child soldiers using adapted Narrative Exposure therapy—A RCT in Eastern Democratic Republic of Congo. *Behaviour Research and Therapy, 123*, 103482. https://doi.org/10.1016/j.brat.2019.103482

Robjant, K., Roberts, J., & Katona, C. (2017). Treating posttraumatic stress disorder in female victims of trafficking using narrative exposure therapy: A retrospective audit. *Frontiers in Psychiatry, 8*, 63.

Rodenburg, R., Benjamin, A., de Roos, C., Meijer, A. M., & Stams, G. J. (2009). Efficacy of EMDR in children: A meta-analysis. *Clinical Psychology Review, 29*(7), 599–606. https://doi.org/10.1016/j.cpr.2009.06.008

Rothman, E. F., Preis, S. R., Bright, K., Paruk, J., Bair-Merritt, M., & Farrell, A. (2020). A longitudinal evaluation of a survivor-mentor program for child survivors of sex trafficking in the United States. *Child Abuse & Neglect, 100*, 104083. https://doi.org/10.1016/j.chiabu.2019.104083

Sachser, C., Keller, F., & Goldbeck, L. (2017). Complex PTSD as proposed for ICD-11: Validation of a new disorder in children and adolescents and their response to trauma-focused cognitive behavioral therapy. *Journal of Child Psychology and Psychiatry, and Allied Disciplines, 58*(2), 160–168. https://doi.org/10.1111/jcpp.12640

Sahl, S., & Knoepke, C. (2018). Using shared decision making to empower sexually exploited youth. *Journal of the American Academy of Child & Adolescent Psychiatry, 57*(11), 809–812. https://doi.org/10.1016/j.jaac.2018.07.873

Salami, T., Gordon, M., Coverdale, J., & Nguyen, P. T. (2018). What therapies are favored in the treatment of the psychological sequelae of trauma in human trafficking victims? *Journal of Psychiatric Practice, 24*(2), 87–96. https://doi.org/10.1097/PRA.0000000000000288

Sanar Wellness Institute and Polaris Project. (2015). *Promising practices: An overview of trauma-informed therapeutic support for survivors of human trafficking.* https://polarisproject.org/resources/promising-practices-an-overview-of-trauma-informed-therapeutic-support-for-survivors-of-human-trafficking/

Schauer, M., Neuner, F., & Elbert, T. (2011). *Narrative exposure therapy: A short-term treatment for traumatic stress disorders* (2nd ed.). Hogrefe Publishing.

Schrader, E. M., & Wendland, J. M. (2012). Music therapy programming at an aftercare center in Cambodia for survivors of child sexual exploitation and rape and their caregivers. *Social Work & Christianity, 39*(4), 390–406.

Shapiro, F. (2018). *Eye movement desensitization and reprocessing (EMDR) therapy: Basic principles, protocols, and procedures* (3rd ed.). Guilford Press.

Stoklosa, H., MacGibbon, M., & Stoklosa, J. (2017). Human trafficking, mental illness, and addiction: Avoiding diagnostic overshadowing. *AMA Journal of Ethics, 19*(1), 23–34. https://doi.org/10.1001/journalofethics.2017.19.1.ecas3-1701

Substance Abuse and Mental Health Services Administration. (2014). *SAMHSA's concept of trauma and guidance for a trauma-informed approach.* https://ncsacw.samhsa.gov/userfiles/files/SAMHSA_Trauma.pdf

Tan, L. A. (2012). Art therapy with trafficked women. *Therapy Today, 23*(5), 26–31.

Usacheva, M., Smalley, C., Hafer, N., & Brooks, S. (2022). Ending the Game®: A new psychoeducational curriculum for victims of commercial sexual exploitation. *Women & Criminal Justice, 32*(3), 1–20. https://doi.org/10.1080/08974454.2021.1885568

van der Kolk, B. A. (1994). The body keeps the score: Memory and the evolving psychobiology of posttraumatic stress. *Harvard Review of Psychiatry, 1*(5), 253–265. https://doi.org/10.3109/10673229409017088

van der Kolk, B. A., Stone, L., West, J., Rhodes, A., Emerson, D., Suvak, M., & Spinazzola, J. (2014). Yoga as an adjunctive treatment for posttraumatic stress disorder: A randomized controlled trial. *The Journal of Clinical Psychiatry, 75*(6), e559–e565. https://doi.org/10.4088/JCP.13m08561

Wahbeh, H., Senders, A., Neuendorf, R., & Cayton, J. (2014). Complementary and alternative medicine for posttraumatic stress disorder symptoms: A systematic review. *Journal of Evidence-Based Complementary & Alternative Medicine, 19*(3), 161–175. https://doi.org/10.1177/2156587214525403

Wampold, B. E. (2015). How important are the common factors in psychotherapy? An update. *World Psychiatry, 14*(3), 270–277. https://doi.org/10.1002/wps.20238

Wang, D. C., Aten, J. D., Boan, D., Jean-Charles, W., Griff, K. P., Valcin, V. C., Davis, E. B., Hook, J. N., Davis, D. E., Van Tongeren, D. R., Abouezzeddine, T., Sklar, Q., & Wang, A. (2016). Culturally adapted spiritually oriented trauma-focused cognitive–behavioral therapy for child survivors of restavek. *Spirituality in Clinical Practice*, *3*(4), 224–236. https://doi.org/10.1037/scp0000101

Warner, E., Spinazzola, J., Westcott, A., Gunn, C., & Hodgdon, H. (2014). The body can change the score: Empirical support for somatic regulation in the treatment of traumatized adolescents. *Journal of Child & Adolescent Trauma*, *7*(4), 237–246. https://doi.org/10.1007/s40653-014-0030-z

Weiner, D. A., Schneider, A., & Lyons, J. S. (2009). Evidence-based treatments for trauma among culturally diverse foster care youth: Treatment retention and outcomes. *Children and Youth Services Review*, *31*(11), 1199–1205. https://doi.org/10.1016/j.childyouth.2009.08.013

World Health Organization. (n.d.). *ICD-11: International classification of diseases 11th revision.* https://icd.who.int/

10

USING A POSITIVE PSYCHOLOGY FRAMEWORK TO EMPOWER SURVIVORS OF HUMAN TRAFFICKING

JESSA DILLOW CRISP AND BECCA C. JOHNSON

The founding father of positive psychology, Martin Seligman (2018), first started the process of researching optimism through seeing test animals experience permanent helplessness after encountering multiple sessions of "inescapable shock" (p. 101). After noticing that these test animals were not able to recover, Seligman discovered that when some individuals experience inescapable trauma and/or ongoing stressful situations, they, too, give up control. Seligman defined this process of giving up control as *learned help-lessness*, leading to symptomatology of pessimism and depression. He also noted that some people who experience trauma end up growing "stronger and wiser rather than deteriorating" (p. 208), leading him to question why this is the case. What makes some individuals stronger than others? Why do some people who experience traumatic events recover and appear to have greater resilience than those who experience hardship and end up in a state of extreme powerlessness? Why do traditional therapeutic approaches focus on the things that are wrong or negative with clients when one could focus on hope, good, and positive elements of their strengths? And how can greater resilience and posttraumatic growth be fostered in an individual's

https://doi.org/10.1037/0000379-011
Psychological Perspectives on Human Trafficking: Theory, Research, Prevention, and Intervention, L. Dryjanska, E. K. Hopper, and H. Stoklosa (Editors)

life (Rashid & Seligman, 2018)? Through the process of wrestling with these questions, Seligman founded and launched positive psychology in 1999.

Positive psychology has been defined as an umbrella term used to stimulate and organize research, application, and scholarship on strengths, virtues, excellence, thriving, flourishing, hope, resilience, flow, and optimal functioning (Donaldson & Ko, 2010; Rashid & Seligman, 2018). The focus on strengths, solutions, and meaning making can be viewed as crucial and complementary to traditional problem-focused practice. One may argue that positive psychology has been instrumental in guiding this shift in conceptualizing psychotherapeutic intervention away from client deficits toward a focus on client assets.

The process of integrating a positive psychology framework into the work that one does with survivors of trafficking looks like focusing on strengths versus symptoms, resources instead of risks, and hope instead of regrets, to bring somatic, relational, emotional, and spiritual balance (Rashid & Seligman, 2018). Hopper (2017) indicated that utilizing an empowerment approach may increase access to services for trafficking survivors, reiterating that complex trauma treatment emphasizes the development of competencies not solely on symptom reduction. Johnson (2012) wrote that both breadth of knowledge and sensitivity are needed in the provision of aftercare services for those exiting a life of victimization, further advocating for the inclusion of a strengths-focused perspective. In a study on resilience and personal growth in sex trafficking survivors, Sobon (2014) encouraged service providers to identify every potential strength and to view these courageous individuals as possessing skills and assets useful for their future.

Ultimately, psychologists and individuals on multidisciplinary teams that utilize positive psychology believe that even when hard things happen, it is through understanding strengths and positive pursuit of regulation with self and others, that one can experience meaning, resilience, and posttraumatic growth. Providers must understand the complex trauma and psychological growth development associated with trafficking and use this knowledge to help survivors build self-esteem, empowerment, and reconnection with themselves and society (Clawson et al., 2008; Hopper, 2017). In an effort to assimilate positive psychology as it relates to all typologies of trafficking and how it can be integrated into the diversity of survivors, this chapter identifies the theoretical tenets of positive psychology, ways to integrate a positive psychology framework into one's work with survivors of human trafficking, as well as how positive psychology is essential when helping survivors move into a place where they are not just defined by their victimization but empowered into their potential.

THEORETICAL TENETS OF POSITIVE PSYCHOLOGY

Built on the three pillars of positive experiences, positive traits, and positive social institutions (Seligman, 2021), positive psychology is a scientific study that looks at the traits that make "life worth living" (Seligman & Csikszentmihalyi, 2014, p. 280). Within the first pillar, *positive experiences,* happiness and subjective well-being can be both changed and measured through flow, which is a psychological term describing a state of optimal experience emerging from enjoyable pursuits (American Psychological Association [APA], 2020a; Csikszentmihalyi et al., 2014). When one experiences flow, they are highly focused on the here and now, absorbed in pleasurable activities (APA, 2020a; Csikszentmihalyi et al., 2014; Nakamura & Csikszentmihalyi, 2009). Positive experiences, like flow, create agency for one to feel pleasurable emotions and make choices. Seligman (2021) indicated that exercising the freedom of choice empowers individuals to find "contentment with the past, happiness in the present, and hope for the future," even when life is hard (para. 3). The next pillar, *positive traits,* includes looking at individual strengths, values, resilience, wisdom, gratitude, compassion, and creativity; the pillar of *positive social institutions* looks at the role of connection with others, social justice, fostering and engaging in healthy communities and teamwork, the experience of meaning and purpose, and growing as a leader (Perry & Winfrey, 2021; Rashid & Seligman, 2018; Seligman, 2021). These three tenets create the theoretical assumption that all humans, including survivors of human trafficking, hold inherent capacity for growth. Even though these tenets may be hard for a survivor of trafficking to implement by themselves, clinicians need to see that the strengths survivors present are just as important to look at as their symptoms. No matter what one has experienced in the past, healing power can be found within therapeutic connection (Herman, 1997; Rashid & Seligman, 2018).

Shifting a Focus Onto Positive Psychology in the Antitrafficking Movement

After a survivor of trafficking is able to experience freedom from their exploitation, they will often receive multiple mental health diagnoses and feel a range of both negative and positive emotions: "I am so glad I am no longer being raped every night by strangers, and I miss the attention I received from my *boyfriend*" or "Even though I was taken advantage of when I was labor trafficked, I want to stay in this country. Yet, the immigration process makes me so anxious." In response to the dichotomy of feelings, depth of questions, and grief that most survivors carry, many clinicians try to jump into trauma processing without determining if a client has the capacity and both the external and internal resources to do trauma processing. Positive psychology does not take the place of processing traumatic memories, nor does it mean a survivor should suppress or feel ashamed of negative emotions, but it can be used to help build resilience and strength, while fostering greater external and internal stability. Facilitating space where the survivor might eventually be able to process the traumatic events they have experienced.

Using positive psychology in antitrafficking work is not only for mental health providers, but it is also essential for other organizations, including multidisciplinary team members, law enforcement, medical professionals, and media outlets. Those whose programs and services touch trafficking victims must shift their focus from sensationalized elements of trafficking to the positive strengths survivors carry in their healing process (Crisp, 2018). Negative elements that are often the focus include the idiosyncratic experiences of exploitation, challenging symptomatology related to relational wounding, details about traumatic encounters, comorbid mental health struggles, and the lack of finances and housing. While these elements are realities, the negative aspects of what happens during trafficking should not become the sole focus of those working with survivors. With a focus on sensationalized experiences of exploitation, it is easy to jump into trauma processing before a client is ready and misrepresent the realities that many survivors of exploitation and trafficking face. Creating difficulty in recognizing the diversity of victims and typologies of exploitation taking place within their culture (Crisp, 2018). For example, many men, boys, and sexual and gender minorities are not identified as victims of trafficking because they do not look like what is seen in the media. Similarly, labor trafficking, familial trafficking, and domestic servitude are often not recognized because of the sensationalized narratives of pimp-controlled sex trafficking (Crisp, 2018; Henderson, 2022; Hogan & Roe-Sepowitz, 2023; Office of the Special Representative and Co-ordinator for Combating Trafficking in Human Beings, 2021).

Recently, Ari,[1] a queer survivor of gang-controlled trafficking was doing an interview with a well-known magazine. When it came time for Ari to submit photos for publication, the photo editor indicated that the pictures they provided were too happy and did not resemble someone who had been trafficked. The reality is that although horrible things happen during exploitation, a person who has experienced trafficking is not excluded from experiencing happiness. While processing this experience in therapy, Ari said, "It is so frustrating and hurts. During my

---

[1]All names and identifying details within this chapter have been deidentified, and these examples have been used with consent.

trafficking, I was not seen as a victim due to the fake smiles I was made to wear and now I am genuinely smiling in these pictures and I am not sad enough to be a survivor." Ari then went on to say, "What if it is through the depth of pain I have experienced, that I have the ability to feel even greater happiness and joy? I want to be seen as me."

Tiffany, a cis female survivor of familial trafficking and labor trafficking, who is now a mental health professional and PhD student, was asked to speak at an antitrafficking event about complex trauma. When she arrived, Tiffany gave the event coordinator a copy of her bio and instructions on how she wanted to be introduced. Yet, when the event coordinator introduced Tiffany, she stated, "We are honored to have a survivor of trafficking speak to us today." Tiffany afterward expressed how frustrated she felt. "At this event, I did not plan to share my story because I have worked so hard to not be defined by the trauma I have experienced. Yet, no matter the professional job titles, licensures, and degrees I carry, people can only see me for the trauma I have endured. What will it take for people to see me for who I am today, versus for my victimization?"

Those engaging with survivors of trafficking should intentionally create an environment where happiness can thrive, and recovery is highlighted more than traumatic experiences. What would the future look like if survivors of trafficking could be seen as more than their victimization? What if positive psychology was used to help survivors gain the capacity to do trauma processing? And how would experiencing optimism change the way survivors engage with other people and the world? Survivors encourage providers to focus on positivity and to value their strengths—ultimately, promoting resilience and posttraumatic growth.

Fostering an Environment for Positive Psychology

As a survivor of labor trafficking in an agricultural setting, Sabin indicated to his doctor that he has no hope and does not believe that life can get better. Since he does not have a professional background, not only is it hard to find a job that will pay a living wage in his city, but also his lungs are damaged from all the years of using fertilizer containing large amounts of ammonia without proper training and protection. In the midst of their last conversation, Sabin's doctor stated, "It is okay if you do not feel hope right now; you can borrow some of mine. I have hope that you will medically get to a place where you will have strength and energy to do things you would like." Sabin started to cry, "This is the first time anyone has told me that they have hope for me. Maybe it is possible to experience joy again!"

It takes both trauma-informed intentionality and cultural humility to create an environment where survivors of trafficking are seen through the lens of positive psychology. Mental health providers may find it hard to see survivors through their strengths, especially when the impact of trauma impedes survivor functioning, when trauma memories are triggered, when relapse occurs, or when maladaptive coping mechanisms are enacted. A positive psychology perspective takes a step back and acknowledges, "I choose to see the good in you [the survivor]." Positive psychology does not disregard the trauma or negate the overwhelming and accompanying emotions survivors may feel. Rather, it provides empathy, while also communicating value, future orientation, and optimism to the survivor.

An environment that incorporates positive psychology tenets, creates space for trafficking survivors to explore meaning and purpose beyond their past and present trauma. The process of exploring self-concept, meaning, and purpose outside of one's trafficking often takes place through having a safe space to experience healthy relationships, building generativity and altruism, social activism, and experiences with education, career, or spirituality (Rashid & Seligman, 2018). Clinicians using this framework would focus on validating emotions, normalizing diagnoses and the impact of trauma, providing opportunities for clients to read other survivor stories to stimulate hope, and asking for feedback if there is anything they would like to add or change in the office to make it feel welcoming and calm.

Tangibly, when working with survivors of trafficking, it is essential to intentionally welcome the range of emotions one might feel. Fredrickson (2001) and Seligman (2017) indicate that the process of creating space for emotions can look like facilitating experiences of joy through exposure to fun activities and opportunities that foster authentic laughter, expressing gratefulness, and giving permission to grieve the traumas that have happened.

> Due to familial trafficking, Duncan had never been to school, and thoughts of trying to get a GED brought him debilitating fear. Yet, after a social worker told him that she believed he could do well in school, Duncan started his educational process. Several years later, he completed his GED and was accepted into a college program. Currently, Duncan is finishing a graduate degree and attributes his success to "someone who believed that my past does not define my future—someone who helped me see beyond what I was currently experiencing. I never thought I could do anything but sex work, but I am now working toward my goals."

One psychologist integrates positive psychology into their work with teen survivors of trafficking by intentionally asking them to share funny TikTok videos at the end of each session. By engaging in a culturally relevant activity that also helps them laugh, these survivors are able to experience a spectrum of emotions, and laughter also helps in regulating them after processing deep pain. Another mental health provider invites trafficking survivors to do a collage of magazine pictures that make them smile, which is often both hard and freeing.

When traumatic events happen, most people seek out social support as a means of comfort (Rashid & Seligman, 2018). Due to the way that many traffickers condition victims not to trust people, the very process of seeking help and connection for survivors is often filled with terror, betrayal, or abandonment. Therefore, survivors might experience internal distress regarding sharing their experiences, fearful of the consequences or possible judgment. Many survivors watch body language to see if they are believed and still accepted. In response, mental health providers must make sure their body language and facial expressions are inviting and safe. This welcoming warmth may include sitting in silence, asking survivors questions about positive or negative memories, interests, dreams, and regrets.

Just as communication and connectedness are vital in creating an affirming environment, meaningful and positive relationships are also essential in facilitating a place for survivors of trauma to recover (Herman, 1997; Perry & Winfrey, 2021). Cozolino (2006) stated, "Adults who thrive despite childhood neglect and abuse often describe life-affirming experiences with others who made them feel cared for and worthwhile" (p. 314).

Hilary, a survivor of labor trafficking, finds meaningful relationships with other survivors in the weekly support group she attends. She finds it helpful to listen to other survivors disclose their process of finding meaning in the pain and take steps towards their dreams. Hilary also shares of experiencing kindness, support, and celebration within the group, which is giving her power to see a future for herself. She once stated that she never thought that she would live beyond 24 years of age. Thinking about and planning for her future are things she never thought possible.

Similarly, survivors who are now professionals often highlight that at least one person (like a mentor, professor, victim advocate, therapist, family member, or friend) loved them through the ups and downs of their recovery process. This relational investment in their lives gave them strength to keep pushing on during hard days. Rashid and Seligman (2018) described positive relationships as allowing one to grow from another's strengths and resources enabling the building of individual competencies, skills, and capacity. On a neurobiological level, positive relationships also provide opportunities for individuals to learn how to coregulate, learn self-regulation skills, and engage with society (Dana, 2020).

Due to triggers and potential harm, engaging in relationships is a risk that can be hard for many survivors of exploitation (Gable & Maisel, 2021). Yet, fighting for relational connection is important in helping survivors experience quality of life, wellness, and resilience (Gable & Maisel, 2021). Some ways to build therapeutic alliance with survivors is to reiterate confidentiality, maintain professional boundaries, create ongoing consent, invite sharing of concerns, and ask if they have questions. Additionally, Gable and Maisel (2021) indicated that "when people experience positive emotions together, such as amusement and excitement, these shared experiences can result in potentially long-lasting social bonds" (p. 602). For nongovernmental organizations, this might look like staff and program participants doing fun, laugh-provoking activities like a dance party in the rain, watching a funny movie, going for a gondola ride, visiting a zoo, going for a scenic hike, or swimming under a waterfall. While, for clinicians, this process might look like reading a picture book together and talking about the story, coloring, going for a walk, or talking about a favorite movie.

Change Created by Positive Psychology

Timothy, a transgender man, first began thinking about exiting the commercial sex trade after he ended up in the hospital after a bad trick (customer). Yet, after being released, he went back to the trade. It took 2 more years to eventually leave the life. Taking this courageous step was incredibly hard for Timothy, but after he was able to leave, he expressed, "I am working with an organization providing transitional housing to homeless young adults. For the first time, I am receiving gender affirming medical and mental health care. Through the respect I am receiving, my self-esteem is growing, and I am pursuing my dreams. For the first time, I am excited about the future."

For survivors of human trafficking and commercial sexual exploitation, change can be measured through relapses, therapeutic growth, precontemplation, contemplation, planning and taking action, as well as microscopic movement toward goals (Johnson et al., 2021). Since positive psychology focuses on one's positive character qualities and builds upon the agency they already possess, positive psychology can be seen to broaden "cognitive and behavioral repertoire" (Seligman, 2018, p. 238), building on strengths leading to change. For instance, this approach can be likened to a row of dominos, where change in one area of a person's life can lead to change in other areas, which, for survivors, can appear as an increase in positive emotions, self-esteem, optimism toward the future, and heightened awareness surrounding "attentional-resources" (Rashid & Seligman, 2018, p. 53). Consequently, it is via mental health providers modeling attachment and building on strengths that survivors can grow in capacity to face challenges leading to developing resilience and, ultimately, posttraumatic growth (Dagan & Yager, 2019).

Overall, positive psychology encourages an emphasis on strengths rather than weaknesses, potential, possibilities and problem solving rather than just the problems themselves. Under this framework, an examination of contributing areas of study includes strengths-based approaches, embracing values, the role of spirituality, resilience, posttraumatic growth, learned optimism, and hope.

Strength-Based Approach

An important aspect of positive psychology is the strengths-based perspective. This approach views individuals as resourceful, resilient, and as possessing useful strengths when challenges arise (Laursen, 2003; McCashen, 2005; Stoerkel, 2019). Here, the goal is to identify what is going well, how to do more of it, and how to build on it—fostering empowerment and hope (Barwick, 2004). For instance, research shows that students often feel more empowered and motivated to strive for social and emotional health when their strengths are acknowledged (Epstein et al., 2001; LeBuffe & Shapiro, 2004). Other studies have indicated that using a strengths-based approach with individuals and communities helps provide culturally relevant processes and improves personal outcomes, such as quality of life, employment, and health (Barwick, 2004; España et al., 2023; Krabbenborg et al., 2013).

When using a strength-based approach with survivors, psychologists and individuals on multidisciplinary teams are intentional to *not* focus on the trauma, diagnoses, and symptoms but rather on identifying and capitalizing on one's internal or external resources and personal strengths. Overall, the aim of engaging these resources and helping one connect to their strengths is to identify possibilities and abilities rather than failures and flaws, while also not minimizing or negating the challenges one faces. The process of empathetically acknowledging the hard but also seeing the good is often a balancing act. If empathy is lacking, one will struggle to have agency to face challenges, creating a downward spiral of negativity and helplessness (Jones, 2017); but if one feels supported and empowered, they will have greater agency and capacity to engage their strengths and engage in future orientation. For many survivors, it is an empowering process for them to realize they are not broken or lost, but they possess resilience and strengths to help them tackle current and future challenges, facilitating a shift from victim and survivor to a thriver.

> *Susan, a young woman at a residential recovery home for victims of sexual exploitation, approached one of the therapists after a group session and asked to talk. "You are the doppelganger of my trafficker. You look and talk like her and have some of the same mannerisms. You are a big trigger for me." Surprised, the therapist responded, "Then you are quite an amazing person. You are brave to have sat next to me during the group meeting. And you shared some insightful ideas. You are remarkable that you could contribute and listen with me in the room. You are amazing!" The young woman, shocked by this response, replied,*

"I'm glad I shared." This therapist used a strengths-based response, not focusing on the negative triggers but on Susan's coping skills, which ultimately led the survivor to experience greater agency.

A strengths perspective goes beyond individual practice to encompass social and community networks, including case management, education, community development, and working within the juvenile justice system (Cowger, 1994; Nissen, 2006). Foot and Hopkins (2010) found that communities with local associations that are supportive and utilize a strength-based attitude in their community engagement can empower their residents. Further, when people's achievements are praised or when they are encouraged to be proud of their contributions, their confidence increases (Foot & Hopkins, 2010). On a communal level, a strengths-based approach may contribute to destigmatization and an increase in social acceptance, understanding, and empowerment (Cowger, 1994).

Embracing Values

Values are "fundamental attitudes guiding our mental processes and behavior" (Vyskocilova et al., 2015, p. 41). According to Rashid and Seligman (2018), personal strengths and values are similar in the ways that they can help create future-oriented goals. Values are often seen as prescriptive, guiding the path one takes, while strengths give a foundation for how those values might play out in their life (Rashid & Seligman, 2018). For many survivors of trafficking, knowing what they value gives them a roadmap that can be referenced when they are in the decision-making process: "Does the longing to go out on a drug binge tonight line up with your [survivor] desire to do well on a school exam tomorrow?" or "Although it is scary, will speaking to law enforcement about the recent sexual assault experienced support your [survivor] value of justice?"

After survivors of trafficking exit their situation, common therapeutic themes include feelings of guilt for the things that they were made to do to survive, as well as grief over the things that were taken or lost during their exploitation. The latter includes their identity, relationships with loved ones, opportunities to do typical age-appropriate things, feelings of safety, physical health, celebrating traditions and cultures, being able to work without triggers, the capability to trust other people, and the ability to choose sexual encounters. Here, survivors might benefit from exploring who they are, their likes and dislikes, what they value, and the ways these characteristics fit into the person they were before their exploitation, during their trafficking, today, as well as the person that they want to become in the future. During a therapy session where values were discussed, one survivor, Lisa, stated that although the "bad things happened, my values haven't changed and I am still me. My [trafficker] wasn't able to take away my passion for fairness, harmony, curiosity, and peace."

The Role of Spirituality

As researchers, clinicians and social service providers focus on the positive, helpful aspects of growth after trauma, the role of spirituality and faith must be included. Although spirituality is defined differently per individual, it is often viewed as engagement in a religious practice such as meditation, prayer, or going to a mosque, temple, or church; belief in a higher power; or deep connection with self, others, or nature (Delagran, 2016). Regardless of how spirituality is incorporated into one's life, research shows that it is a way to grow in connection, optimism, resilience, and posttraumatic growth (APA, 2020b; Cadell et al., 2003; O'Rourke et al., 2008). In a study Laufer and Solomon (2006) did with Israeli adolescents exposed to terrorist attacks, those with stronger religious beliefs experienced higher levels of growth and well-being. Additionally, O'Rourke et al. (2008) and Ross (1990) indicated that those who are exposed to trauma might engage in spiritual practices as a means of coping with emotional anguish, leading to lower levels of psychological distress.

Conversely, although spirituality is described as a factor in the recovery and development of well-being in the lives of some trafficking survivors, anecdotally, other survivors of trafficking have reported spiritual abuse at the hands of their traffickers and caregivers and nongovernmental organizations (Hodge, 2021; Nguyen et al., 2014). The delicate balance between integrating spirituality into the care given to survivors of trafficking needs to adhere to ethical standards of recognizing and honoring individual beliefs (including the absence of beliefs), culture, and diversity (Association for Spiritual, Ethical, and Religious Values in Counseling, 2022).

Developing Resilience

Masten (2001), defined *resilience* as "as a class of phenomena characterized by *good outcomes in spite of serious threats to adaptation or development*" (p. 228). When thinking about the development of resilience, and/or why one person may be more resilient than others, it is essential to consider that resilience is not abnormal; rather, it is "a common phenomenon arising from ordinary human adaptive processes" (p. 234). Since resilience is a normal adaptive response to traumatic circumstances, it can be stated that the ability to respond and recover from injury is a marker of "well-being and depends on the actions of the autonomic nervous system" (Dana, 2020, p. 1).

Using this neurobiological perspective, resilience can be developed through helping individuals feel safe, fostering attachment, as well as assisting one to expand and stay in their window of tolerance through coregulation and self-regulation (Dana, 2020; Kain & Terrell, 2018). As Porges (2016) stated, "A history of successful and predictable co-regulation tunes the nervous system to be sufficiently resilient to function during periods of separation" (p. 6), which can then be correlated to the process of helping people find more adaptive ways of getting through stressful times.

Many trafficking survivors have experienced trauma-coerced attachment (Chambers et al., 2022), which means that mental health providers will need to focus on attunement and creating safety so that these attachment wounds can begin to heal (Baruch & Higgins, 2020). As attachment develops, coregulation naturally ensues. This might look like labeling emotions that are being expressed, normalizing the process of recovery, modeling self-calming activities, inviting the use of animal assisted interventions like therapy dogs or other animals that might provide comfort, asking if they would like a support person to be present during appointments, and creating clear and concise boundaries (Cozolino, 2006; Dana, 2020; Kain & Terrell, 2018; Perry & Winfrey, 2021).

Experiencing Posttraumatic Growth

The term *posttraumatic growth* was coined in the mid-1990s by the University of North Carolina researchers Tedeschi and Calhoun (2004), who found that people who develop posttraumatic growth flourish in life and exhibit more resilience. In his book *Flourish*, Seligman (2011) made the case for increasing public knowledge of posttraumatic growth in the same way that the public recognizes posttraumatic stress disorder (PTSD). Seligman indicated that many more people know the concept and term "PTSD," which focuses on symptoms, than "posttraumatic growth," which focuses on future possibility. Other terms used to describe posttrauma growth include thriving, stress-related growth, benefit finding, perceived benefits, positive life change, and adversarial growth (Park, 2009).

Davis and Porter (2021) defined *posttraumatic growth* as the process of making meaning out of the pain through "cognitively rebuilding, restoring, or reconciling what has been lost in such a way that it allows one to look back at the loss or trauma experience with equanimity" (p. 919). Although it is common for people who have experienced hard or traumatic circumstances to see the world as a dangerous place where vulnerabilities are exploited (Calhoun & Tedeschi, 2006), not everyone responds to hardship and loss in this manner (Calhoun & Tedeschi, 2006; Tedeschi & Calhoun,

2004). Rather, some individuals who endure traumatic things experience "an increased sense that one has been tested . . . and found to be a person who has survived the worst" (Calhoun & Tedeschi, 2006, p. 5). This positive change can be seen in individuals holding the tension between "I am more vulnerable than I thought, but much stronger than I ever imagined" (p. 5), as well as in the process of creating new goals to match the limitations the trauma has perpetrated (Davis & Porter, 2021).

Some view posttraumatic growth as empowering insight that comes after an emotional distress while others might depict it as finding meaning in emotional pain, resulting in intrapersonal growth. This change is viewed as beneficial self-growth rather than harmful self-absorption. Interestingly, Tedeschi and Calhoun (2004) reported that as many as 89% of trauma survivors disclosed at least one aspect of posttraumatic growth, such as a renewed appreciation for life after distress. Park and Helgeson's (2006) study showed a positive correlation between posttraumatic growth, psychological development, and physical well-being. Survivors who engage in personal development after trauma show an increase in empathy and the ability to relate to others' struggles (Tedeschi & Calhoun, 1996, 2004).

Although people who undergo posttraumatic growth flourish in life with a greater appreciation and more resilience (Tedeschi & Calhoun, 2004), posttraumatic growth is different from resilience in the sense that it represents the new growth and positive transformation that can develop after a traumatic event, the tension of vulnerability *and* strength. People can be resilient and not experience posttraumatic growth, while people who have posttraumatic growth are always resilient. While resiliency is a desired trait, posttraumatic growth seeks evolutionary progress beyond resilience and looks for positive traits in one's relationship to others, personal capacity and strength, appreciation of life, new possibilities, and spirituality (Tedeschi & Calhoun, 1996). For example, some survivors may be content with treatment focused on coping skills and not on the existential reconstruction of negative schemas, while others might want to look at the ways the trauma has impacted their lives and the person that they are today (Sobon, 2014).

Overall, survivors of trafficking who engage in posttraumatic growth leading to an increase of hope will more likely view their past experiences, psychological barriers, and lack of resources as challenges to overcome rather than through the process of *giving up* (Snyder, 1994). Through posttraumatic growth, some survivors identify as a *survivor leader* or *lived experience expert* to fight systems that created pain in their lives, providing a model of hope and inspiration for other trafficking survivors. Anecdotally, many survivors of trafficking indicate that they experience deep meaning and strength when they see another survivor reach out for help or do something that is triggering and hard.

Despite the strength survivors of trafficking have and the benefits of posttraumatic growth, it is vital that clinicians and multidisciplinary teams be sensitive to the capacity and goals of individual clients rather than push for deeper meaning to the trauma. Providers can, however, be intentional in identifying small areas of growth within the individuals whom they are working with. For one survivor of trafficking, success might be showing up to therapy. For another, it might be the growth and curiosity shown in their willingness to ask and to answer hard questions. The posttraumatic growth process must be seen as both an individualistic and variable process. Those working with survivors in victim recovery must always be culturally sensitive and person centered (Johnson, 2012; Sobon, 2014).

> One survivor leader who cofounded a gender-inclusive nonprofit stated, "Recently, I was told that a survivor was able to escape their trafficker after hearing me share my story. Although I wouldn't wish anyone to experience the horrible experiences I have survived, I wouldn't change my past. For the first time, my pain has purpose and has helped another person."

For posttraumatic stress to become posttraumatic growth, Sobon (2014) encouraged providers to give survivors of sex trafficking the opportunity to "describe their process of courage and growing through incredibly disempowering, objectifying, and terrifying experiences" (p. 50). Other recommendations to increase positive growth and decrease the likelihood of developing trauma-spectrum and mood disorders include the development of self-regulation skills (Shuwiekh et al., 2018) and spiritual practices (O'Rourke et al., 2008).

From practice and observation, the amount of posttraumatic growth a survivor of human trafficking experiences appears to be related to the amount of time removed from the exploitive situation as well as to the individual's ability to critically process, evaluate, and reflect on the traumas. In situations of trauma bonding and coercive attachment, common in sexual exploitation, time is needed for the victim to disengage from their trafficker. Once the survivor realizes the extent of their exploitation, they are better able to encounter posttraumatic growth.

Fostering Learned Optimism and Hope

As the opposite of learned helplessness, *learned optimism* can be defined as "the process of adapting one's explanatory style toward a more optimistic orientation" (Fineburg, 2009, p. 574). This process can be seen in people seeking ways to change their thought processes from negative to positive and choosing to move from despair to hope (Cherry, 2021). Hope may be viewed as an individual's desire accompanied by a belief or an expectation that they can achieve their goals (Fineburg, 2009; Snyder, 2002).

Hope has a positive correlation with positive psychological health and is found to be decisive predictors of psychological well-being, satisfaction of life, and resilience (Cheavens et al., 2005; Cramer & Dyrkacz, 1998; Kwon, 2002; Laranjeira & Querido, 2022). Furthermore, hope leads to greater self-efficacy (Bailey et al., 2007), positive affect (Cramer & Dyrkacz, 1998; Shorey et al., 2005), and personal fulfillment (Bailey et al., 2007). Therefore, hope and resilience are considered to be key factors in understanding how victims and survivors cope with trauma, adapt, and experience recovery (Masten & Narayan, 2012).

To reach a goal, one must possess both desire and opportunity (Fineburg, 2009; Snyder, 2002). The combination of desire and opportunity creates the hope seen in the *ability to plan* steps to the wanted goals and the intersection of *belief in one's capability* to attain them, which is learned optimism. Here, most people lack intentionality in thinking about how they were able to experience their accomplishments; rather, they simply experience the positive emotions of happiness and relief (Fineburg, 2009). When one experiences something positive but unexpected, these outcomes might facilitate "contemplation, which then lead[s] to developing action plans when the situation returns" (Fineburg, 2009, p. 575). This contemplation facilitates opportunities for one to recognize their strengths, and it initiates hope that they can similarly experience other good and positive things in the future. Similarly, optimism creates agency and evidence that one can dispute the "unrealistic catastrophic thoughts" that are holding them back from moving toward their goals (Seligman, 2018, p. 281). Tong et al. (2010) indicated that the very possibility of a desired outcome can create hope, even if it is outside of a person's control, while some people might need external support.

Tangibly, this external support might look like helping survivors identify educational and vocational opportunities that can aid them towards their goals. For example, a survivor shared, "I have no skills or work experience except prostitution, so it is pointless to even think about a future." What this survivor expressed is similar to what many other survivors of all typologies of trafficking have indicated—after exploitation, it can be extremely hard to get a job due to the lack of work history, and it can be almost impossible to find a job that pays a living wage. Numerous trafficking survivors share how their first paycheck can be difficult and triggering. Discouragement sets in as they reflect upon their ability to make more than $1,000 per day while being exploited versus a minimum-wage paycheck. It is important to prepare survivors for these possible struggles during the job-search process. Similarly, it is vital to include discussion on money making, money triggers, budgeting, and the temptation toward relapse. It can be helpful to remind the survivor that although a large amount of money was made during their trafficking, it was not at their disposal but given to their trafficker. These preemptive discussions address the reality of the situation and also prepare the individual for possible negative reactions they might feel. Additionally, it may be helpful to use a positive psychology lens in helping survivors change their focus from a deficit of job skills to transferable skills desired by employers. Examples of transferable skills survivors of trafficking often possess include the ability to read people and situations, customer service and satisfaction, experience working long hours, hardworking attitude, and proficiency in problem solving.

A POSITIVE PSYCHOLOGY FRAMEWORK

The five elements of Seligman's (2011) theory of well-being are "positive emotion, engagement, positive relationships, meaning, and accomplishments (PERMA)" (p. 25). Although some people use PERMA as a framework for incorporating positive psychology into all areas of their work, when working with survivors of trafficking, PERMA is often not enough. Instead, since survivors of trafficking have engaged with familial, societal, and environmental systems during their exploitation and recovery process, the authors of this chapter would like to propose that positive psychology needs to be intentionally combined with other frameworks that examine these socioecological systems. For instance, just as Jaffe et al. (2020) used Bronfenbrenner's (1979) socioecological model to describe primary prevention of trafficking, an adapted framework can intersect Bronfenbrenner's model and PERMA. Overall, this multidimensional framework helps providers understand the unique challenges survivors of trafficking face, behaviors they might present, and the way different systems engage—ultimately, impacting a recovery process.

Within this positive psychology framework, PERMA is intentionally used by clinicians, service providers, and multidisciplinary teams to formulate an understanding of the survivor, as well as the micro-, meso-, exo-, and macro- systems within which they are engaging. Before this framework is synthesized, however, providers need to assimilate the complex ecology of development in the life of a trafficking survivor. For instance, from a socio-ecological model, individual development and functioning does not take place in isolation, but, rather, it takes place in relation to the environment, time, and other organisms (Magnusson, 1995). By integrating this perspective into work with survivors of trafficking, providers intentionally seek to understand the chaotic and cyclical trauma survivors of trafficking experience and how it may intersect with other systems over the course of their life.

As one understands these synergistic interconnections and proximal processes, unique themes will arise that need to be addressed. These themes assist survivors as they move through their healing process and contextually integrate into society (e.g., processing feelings related to betrayal within a system, learning how to create a community of choice, realizing not all people in society are bad). Clinicians and other service providers need to be aware that the process of healing from past trauma can be extremely difficult emotionally, physically, spiritually, relationally, and psychologically. Many survivors find it incredibly challenging to learn new ways of functioning and reengage with the systems that systemically contributed to their victimization or environment exploitation.

> William, a cis man, grew up in a family where domestic violence was experienced on a daily basis. During this time, an older boy in the neighborhood built a relationship with him, eventually leading to a violent sexual assault and sexual exploitation, where he was made to have sex with other men. In an effort to cope, William used drugs to numb the emotional pain. One day, William punched another kid at school who was making fun of him for being a rent boy. Law enforcement was called and charged him with assault and possession of illegal substances. Sadly, due to the lack of trauma-informed care and understanding of trafficking among boys, William was not identified as a victim of commercial sexual exploitation and domestic violence. The inability to recognize the root of William's symptomatology as a minor led him to experience further trauma in the judicial system, a juvenile record, as well as a lack of appropriate mental health care and help. As an adult, William struggles to regulate his emotions, engage in interpersonal relationships, trust authorities, and make a living wage due to the complex trauma he experienced.

As a result, within this framework, positive elements of the survivor's micro-, meso-, exo-, and macrosystems are highlighted, and behavior is understood as personal, contextual, and interactional (Cook, 2012).

- *Individual/survivor:* Engaging in altruistic behaviors, embracing strengths, finding meaning, learning what one values and how they define justice, celebrating small wins, and exploring identity and how self is construed.

- *Microsystem:* Exploring positive and healthy relationships, taking care of medical and mental health needs with trauma-informed and multicultural mental health providers, learning parenting skills (if needed), and finding a place of belonging.

- *Mesosystem:* Due to the ways many survivors of trafficking survived during their victimization, even when they leave their trafficking, they often compartmentalize relationships as a means of control. This positive psychology framework encourages survivors to foster positive relationships between the microsystem and exosystem, like having a survivor's court advocate meet a mentor from a resourcing organization.

- *Exosystem:* Empowering policies and media representation to be survivor centered, finding supportive organizations to assist in recovery process and areas of need, engaging with educational and career affirming opportunities, and building relationships with communities (e.g., neighborhood, recovery groups, and religious congregations) that foster individual meaning and purpose.

- *Macrosystem:* Acknowledging both the historical and cultural traumas survivors might face within our community, as well as the challenges of being able to find economic success in the current climate, recognizing the stigmas and biases society holds toward individuals coming out of exploitation, empowering survivors to have a voice with political leaders by voting, participating in policy-driven advocacy through lived experience networks and task forces, engaging legislatively to create laws that are trauma informed and survivor centered, and understanding the vastness of the world and how one belongs and finds meaning as a small part of the whole.

This positive psychology framework is centered on the culturally diverse needs survivors embody as they try to find their place in the world and make meaning of their exploitation. It also serves to help survivors find balance between the ongoing challenges experienced and support that is available (Cook, 2012). Through more research, differences might arise in how this positive psychology framework can be implemented when working with minors versus adults, including the possible points of intervention within each of the systems that might help create opportunities for recovery and prevent recidivism.

IMPLICATIONS

Since survivors of trafficking come from variable backgrounds, experiences, and life circumstances, the way this framework is integrated into each system and situation needs to be fluid and variable. Positive psychology has been used effectively as a primary tool in helping survivors gain the ability to take bold steps into their future and connect to their strengths, values, resources, and hope (Bintliff et al., 2018; Sharma & Choudhary, 2013). For some survivors, this process has looked like pursuing social justice through suing their traffickers or choosing to wake up each day to fight their internal battles all over again. Other survivors, like Laurie, seek volunteer opportunities in order to spend time connecting to animals. Any growth in positive psychology's three central pillars (experiences, traits, and social institutions) is indicative of the power of positive psychology in someone's life and them engaging in learned optimism.

As positive psychology is integrated into socioecological systems, clinicians, multidisciplinary teams, and other providers need to provide cultural sensitivity and inclusive services to survivors who have experienced different typologies of trafficking and are different genders, races, and sexualities. Part of this nonbinary process includes acknowledging and addressing power differentials, including privilege and biases, as well as advocating for collaborative responsibility in creating equity and equality within systems (Bintliff et al., 2018).

Success is defined as movement toward survivor empowerment, which acknowledges and allows survivors to define what that represents. It is vital to view survivors as part of socioecological systems and have conversations surrounding ways to build safety and positive relationships within these systems. This can be accomplished through individual and group counseling, mentorship programs, survivor-led support groups, educational opportunities, and other relationships (Knight et al., 2021). PERMA is used to support growth, agency, and well-being across a survivor's lifespan and within the systems that they engage.

CONCLUSION

Proponents of research and practice in positive psychology agree that in the past, therapeutic interventions have primarily focused on the negative outcomes of trauma, overlooking resilience and the potential for posttraumatic growth (Sobon, 2014). Positive psychology believes that attention should be given to both the trauma reactions, as well as courage and strength, including those who have survived human trafficking. Here, the authors urge mental health practitioners, multidisciplinary teams, and providers to utilize and advocate for a strengths-based perspective within all socioecological systems to foster positive, resilient, and growth-oriented outcomes with individuals who have been victimized and exploited. In this framework, survivors are not expected to ignore, minimize, or feel shame for negative emotions and reactions; rather, practitioners need to allow for the fluctuations survivors feel, negative and positive, hopeless and hopeful. For clients, this dynamic process may cyclical and move between processing negative emotions and events to identifying strengths, growth, and competencies.

Without positive psychology, mental health providers may remain focused on identifying, assessing, and reprocessing trauma, omitting survivor strengths and resilience. Implementing a positive psychology framework invites therapist and other service providers to engage survivors with a positive rather than pathological approach. The resilience, hope, posttraumatic growth approach fostered systemically in this framework are essential in helping survivors of human trafficking move beyond victimization to a place of surviving and thriving (Bintliff et al., 2018), facilitating an environment for survivors to accomplish goals and grow into the person that they want to become (Morse & Doberneck, 1995; Snyder, 1994).

REFERENCES

American Psychological Association. (2020a). *Flow*. APA Dictionary of Psychology. https://dictionary.apa.org/flow

American Psychological Association. (2020b, February 1). *Building your resilience*. http://www.apa.org/topics/resilience

Association for Spiritual, Ethical, and Religious Values in Counseling. (2022). *Spiritual and religious competencies*. https://aservic.org/spiritual-and-religious-competencies/

Bailey, T. C., Eng, W., Frisch, M. B., & Snyder, C. R. (2007). Hope and optimism as related to life satisfaction. *The Journal of Positive Psychology, 2*(3), 168–175. https://doi.org/10.1080/17439760701409546

Baruch, A., & Higgins, A. (2020, Oct 29). *Healing attachment wounds by being cared for and caring for others*. Counseling Today. https://ct.counseling.org/2020/10/healing-attachment-wounds-by-being-cared-for-and-caring-for-others/

Barwick, H. (2004). *Young males: Strength-based and male-focused approaches: A review of the research and best evidence*. Ministry of Youth Development. https://www.myd.govt.nz/documents/resources-and-reports/publications/young-males/young-males-strengths-based-and-male-focused-approaches.pdf

Bintliff, A. V., Stark, C., Brown, L. D., & Alonso, A. (2018). Lifelong wellbeing for survivors of sex trafficking: Collaborative perspectives from survivors, researchers, and service providers. *Dignity: A Journal of Analysis of Exploitation and Violence, 3*(3), 1–50.

Bronfenbrenner, U. (1979). *The ecology of human development: Experiments by nature and design*. Harvard University Press.

Cadell, S., Regehr, C., & Hemsworth, D. (2003). Factors contributing to posttraumatic growth: A proposed structural equation model. *American Journal of Orthopsychiatry, 73*(3), 279–287. https://doi.org/10.1037/0002-9432.73.3.279

Calhoun, L. G., & Tedeschi, R. G. (2006). The foundations of posttraumatic growth: An expanded framework. In L. G. Calhoun & R. G. Tedeschi (Eds.), *Handbook of posttraumatic growth: Research & practice* (pp. 3–23). Lawrence Erlbaum Associates Publishers.

Chambers, R., Gibson, M., Chaffin, S., Takagi, T., Nguyen, N., & Mears-Clark, T. (2022). Trauma-coerced attachment and complex PTSD: Informed care for survivors of human trafficking. *Journal of Human Trafficking*, 1–10. Advance online publication. https://doi.org/10.1080/23322705.2021.2012386

Cheavens, J. S., Michael, S. T., & Snyder, C. R. (2005). The correlates of hope: Psychological and physiological benefits. In J. Elliot (Ed.), *Interdisciplinary perspectives on hope* (pp. 101–118). Nova Science.

Cherry, K. (2021, June 28). *Using learned optimism in your life*. Verywell Mind. https://www.verywellmind.com/learned-optimism-4174101

Clawson, H. J., Salomon, A., & Grace, L. G. (2008). *Treating the hidden wounds: Trauma treatment and mental health recovery for victims of human trafficking*. ASPE Office of the Assistant Secretary for Planning and Evaluation. https://aspe.hhs.gov/reports/treating-hidden-wounds-trauma-treatment-mental-health-recovery-victims-human-trafficking-0

Cook, E. (2012). *Understanding people in context: The ecological perspective in counseling*. American Counseling Association.

Cowger, C. D. (1994). Assessing client strengths: Clinical assessment for client empowerment. *Social Work*, *39*(3), 262–268.

Cozolino, L. (2006). *The neuroscience of human relationships: Attachment and the developing social brain*. Norton.

Cramer, K. M., & Dyrkacz, L. (1998). Differential prediction of maladjustment scores with the Snyder Hope subscales. *Psychological Reports*, *83*(3), 1035–1042. https://doi.org/10.2466/pr0.1998.83.3.1035

Crisp, J. D. (2018, March 19). *Images of human trafficking: Moving beyond sensationalism in journalism*. The Irina Project. http://www.theirinaproject.org/blogs-and-news/images-of-human-trafficking-moving-beyond-sensationalism-in-journalism

Csikszentmihalyi, M., Abuhamdeh, S., & Nakamura, J. (2014). Flow. In M. Csikszentmihalyi (Ed.), *Flow and the foundations of positive psychology: The collected works of Mihaly Czikszentmihalyi* (pp. 227–236). Springer. https://doi.org/10.1007/978-94-017-9088-8_15

Dagan, Y., & Yager, J. (2019). Posttraumatic growth in complex PTSD. *Psychiatry: Interpersonal & Biological Processes*, *82*(4), 329–344. https://doi.org/10.1080/00332747.2019.1639242

Dana, D. (2020). *Polyvagal exercises for safety and connection: 50 client-centered practices*. W. W. Norton.

Davis, C. G., & Porter, J. E. (2021). Pathways to growth following trauma and loss. In C. R. Snyder, S. J. Lopez, L. M. Edwards, & S. C. Marques (Eds.), *The Oxford handbook of positive psychology* (3rd ed., pp. 919–927). Oxford University Press.

Delagran, L. (2016). *What is spirituality?* University of Minnesota. https://www.takingcharge.csh.umn.edu/what-spirituality

Donaldson, S. I., & Ko, I. (2010). Positive organizational psychology, behavior, and scholarship: A review of the emerging literature and evidence base. *The Journal of Positive Psychology*, *5*(3), 177–191. https://doi.org/10.1080/17439761003790930

Epstein, M. H., Hertzog, M. A., & Reid, R. (2001). The behavioral and emotional rating scale: Long-term test-retest reliability. *Behavioral Disorders*, *26*(4), 314–320. https://doi.org/10.1177/019874290102600403

España, M., Karandikar, S., McCloskey, R., & Reno, R. (2023). The journey through sex trafficking, motherhood, and building resilience: A qualitative study among women living in Kamathipura red-light area. *Journal of Human Trafficking, 9*(2), 229–241.

Fineburg, A. C. (2009). Learned optimism. In Shane J. Lopez (Ed.), *The encyclopedia of positive psychology* (pp. 574–578). Hoboken, NJ: Wiley-Blackwell.

Foot, J., & Hopkins, T. (2010). *A glass half full: How an asset approach can improve community health and wellbeing.* Improvement and Development Agency. https://www.local.gov.uk/sites/default/files/documents/glass-half-full-how-asset-3db.pdf

Fredrickson, B. L. (2001). The role of positive emotions in positive psychology. The broaden-and-build theory of positive emotions. *American Psychologist, 56*(3), 218–226. https://doi.org/10.1037/0003-066X.56.3.218

Gable, S. L., & Maisel, N. C. (2021). Positive processes in close relationships. In C. R. Snyder, S. J. Lopez, L. M. Edwards, & S. C. Marques (Eds.), *The Oxford handbook of positive psychology* (3rd ed., pp. 599–610). Oxford University Press.

Henderson, M. F. (2022). Human trafficking by families. *UNC School of Government: Public Management Bulletin, 24,* 1–17. https://www.sog.unc.edu/sites/default/files/reports/PMB%2024_Henderson.pdf

Herman, J. (1997). *Trauma and recovery: The aftermath of violence—From domestic abuse to political terror.* Basic Books.

Hodge, D. R. (2021). How do trafficking survivors cope? Identifying the general and spiritual coping strategies of men trafficked into the United States. *Journal of Social Service Research, 47*(2), 155–166. https://doi.org/10.1080/01488376.2020.1729925

Hogan, K. A., & Roe-Sepowitz, D. (2023). LGBTQ+ homeless young adults and sex trafficking vulnerability. *Journal of Human Trafficking, 9*(1), 63–78. https://doi.org/10.1080/23322705.2020.1841985

Hopper, E. K. (2017). Trauma-informed psychological assessment of human trafficking survivors. *Women & Therapy, 40*(1–2), 12–30. https://doi.org/10.1080/02703149.2016.1205905

Jaffe, G., Kimbrough-Melton, R., McLeigh, J. D., Sullivan, M., Boberiene, L., Crisp, J. D., Janus, N., Landers, M., Larson, J., & Recknor, F. (2020). *Primary prevention framework for child trafficking: A white paper* [White paper]. Global Alliance for Behavioral Health and Social Justice. https://gla.memberclicks.net/assets/Policy/White%20Paper-%20Primary%20Prevention%20Framework%20September%202020.pdf

Johnson, B. C. (2012). Aftercare for survivors of human trafficking. *Social Work & Christianity, 39*(4), 370–389.

Johnson, B. C., Crisp, J. D., & Johnson, K. C. (2021). *Leaving the life: Embracing freedom from exploitation.* BridgeHope.

Jones, J. (2017). *The two problems with the strengths-based approach.* http://drjasonjones.com/characterstrengthsapproach/

Kain, K. L., & Terrell, S. J. (2018). *Nurturing resilience: Helping clients move forward from developmental trauma.* North Atlantic Books.

Knight, L., Xin, Y., & Mengo, C. (2021). A scoping review of resilience in survivors of human trafficking. *Trauma, Violence & Abuse, 23*(4), 1048–1062. https://doi.org/10.1177/1524838020985561

Krabbenborg, M. A., Boersma, S. N., & Wolf, J. R. (2013). A strengths based method for homeless youth: Effectiveness and fidelity of Houvast. *BMC Public Health*, *13*(1), 359–369. https://doi.org/10.1186/1471-2458-13-359

Kwon, P. (2002). Hope, defense mechanisms, and adjustment: Implications for false hope and defensive hopelessness. *Journal of Personality*, *70*(2), 207–231. https://doi.org/10.1111/1467-6494.05003

Laranjeira, C. A., & Querido, A. I. F. (2022). The multidimensional model of hope as a recovery-focused practice in mental health nursing. *Revista Brasileira de Enfermagem*, *75*(75, Suppl. 3), e20210474. https://doi.org/10.1590/0034-7167-2021-0474

Laufer, A., & Solomon, Z. (2006). Posttraumatic symptoms and posttraumatic growth among Israeli youth exposed to terror incidents. *Journal of Social and Clinical Psychology*, *25*(4), 429–447. https://doi.org/10.1521/jscp.2006.25.4.429

Laursen, E. K. (2003). Frontiers in strength-based treatment. *Reclaiming Children and Youth: The Journal of Strength-Based Interventions*, *12*(1), 12–17.

LeBuffe, P. A., & Shapiro, V. B. (2004). Leading "strength" to the assessment of pre-school social-emotional health. *California School Psychologist*, *9*(1), 51–61. https://doi.org/10.1007/BF03340907

Magnusson, D. (1995). Individual development: A holistic, integrated model. In P. Moen, G. H. Elder, Jr., & K. Lüscher (Eds.), *Examining lives in context: Perspectives on the ecology of human development* (pp. 19–60). American Psychological Association. https://doi.org/10.1037/10176-001

Masten, A. S. (2001). Ordinary magic: Resilience processes in development. *American Psychologist*, *56*(3), 227–238. https://doi.org/10.1037/0003-066X.56.3.227

Masten, A. S., & Narayan, A. J. (2012). Child development in the context of disaster, war, and terrorism: Pathways of risk and resilience. *Annual Review of Psychology*, *63*(1), 227–257. https://doi.org/10.1146/annurev-psych-120710-100356

McCashen, W. (2005). *The strengths approach*. St. Lukes Innovative Resources.

Morse, J. M., & Doberneck, B. (1995). Delineating the concept of hope. *Image—the Journal of Nursing Scholarship*, *27*(4), 277–285. https://doi.org/10.1111/j.1547-5069.1995.tb00888.x

Nakamura, J., & Csikszentmihalyi, M. (2009). Flow theory and research. In C. R. Snyder & S. J. Lopez (Eds.), *Oxford handbook of positive psychology* (pp. 195–206). Oxford University Press.

Nguyen, T.-T. Bellehumeur, C. R., & Malette, J. (2014). Women survivors of sex trafficking: a trauma and recovery model integrating spirituality. *Counseling et Spiritualité*, *33*(1), 111–133. https://doi-org.denverseminary.idm.oclc.org/10.2143/CS.33.1.3044833

Nissen, L. (2006). Bringing strength-based philosophy to life in juvenile justice. *Reclaiming Children and Youth*, *15*(1), 40–46.

Office of the Special Representative and Co-ordinator for Combating Trafficking in Human Beings. (2021). *Applying gender-sensitive approaches in combating trafficking in human beings*. Organization for Security and Co-operation in Europe. https://www.osce.org/files/f/documents/7/4/486700_1.pdf?fbclid=IwAR14pBTI4G19cJnHyB0SuXuxlIAbotmW-gnzHDrA2h_Rm4I_EQJ7B5iqI1I

O'Rourke, J. J. F., Tallman, B. A., & Altmaier, E. M. (2008). Measuring post-traumatic changes in spirituality/religiosity. *Mental Health, Religion & Culture*, *11*(7), 719–728. https://doi.org/10.1080/13674670801993336

Park, C. L. (2009). Overview in theoretical perspectives. In C. L. Park, S. C. Lechner, M. H. Antoni, & A. L. Stanton (Eds.), *Medical illness and positive life change: Can crisis lead to personal transformation?* (pp. 11–30). American Psychological Association. https://doi.org/10.1037/11854-001

Park, C. L., & Helgeson, V. S. (2006). Introduction to the special section: Growth following highly stressful life events—Current status and future directions. *Journal of Consulting and Clinical Psychology, 74*(5), 791–796. https://doi.org/10.1037/0022-006X.74.5.791

Perry, B. D., & Winfrey, O. (2021). *What happened to you? Conversations on trauma, resilience, and healing.* Flatiron Books.

Porges, S. W. (2016). *Mindfulness & co-regulation.* Active Pause. https://activepause.com/zug/transcripts/Porges-2016-09.pdf

Rashid, T., & Seligman, M. (2018). *Positive psychotherapy: Clinician manual.* Oxford University Press.

Ross, C. E. (1990). Religion and psychological distress. *Journal for the Scientific Study of Religion, 29*(2), 236–245. https://doi.org/10.2307/1387431

Seligman, M. E. P. (2011). *Flourish: A new understanding of happiness and wellbeing— And how to achieve them.* Nicholas Brealey Publishing.

Seligman, M. E. P. (2017). *Authentic happiness: Using the new positive psychology to realize your potential for lasting fulfillment.* Nicholas Brealey Publishing.

Seligman, M. E. P. (2018). *The hope circuit: A psychologist's journey from helplessness to optimism.* Public Affairs.

Seligman, M. E. P. (2021). *Positive psychology center: Our mission.* University of Pennsylvania. https://ppc.sas.upenn.edu/our-mission

Seligman, M. E. P., & Csikszentmihalyi, M. (2014). Positive psychology: An introduction. In M. Csikszentmihalyi (Ed.), *Flow and the foundations of positive psychology: The collected works of Mihaly Czikszentmihalyi* (pp. 279–296). Springer. https://doi.org/10.1007/978-94-017-9088-8_18

Sharma, C., & Choudhary, A. (2013). Positive psychology: An approach to rehabilitation of trafficked victims. *International Journal of Scientific and Research Publications, 3*(8), 1–5. http://www.ijsrp.org/research-paper-0813/ijsrp-p2070.pdf

Shorey, H. S., Snyder, C. R., Yang, X., & Lewin, M. R. (2005). The role of hope as mediator in recollected parenting, adult attachment, and mental health. *Journal of Social and Clinical Psychology, 22*(6), 685–715. https://doi.org/10.1521/jscp.22.6.685.22938

Shuwiekh, H., Kira, I. A., & Ashby, J. S. (2018). What are the personality and trauma dynamics that contribute to posttraumatic growth? *International Journal of Stress Management, 25*(2), 181–194.

Snyder, C. R. (1994). *The psychology of hope: You can get there from here.* Free Press.

Snyder, C. R. (2002). Hope theory: Rainbows in the mind. *Psychological Inquiry, 13*(4), 249–275. https://doi.org/10.1207/S15327965PLI1304_01

Sobon, M. (2014). *A preliminary perspective for identifying resilience and promoting growth among survivors of sex trafficking* [Doctoral dissertation, Wright State University]. CORE Scholar. https://corescholar.libraries.wright.edu/cgi/viewcontent.cgi?article=2472&context=etd_all

Stoerkel, E. (2019, Mar 12). Strengths and virtues: *What is a strength-based approach?* Positive Psychology. https://positivepsychology.com/strengths-based-interventions/

Tedeschi, R. G., & Calhoun, L. G. (1996). The posttraumatic growth inventory: Measuring the positive legacy of trauma. *Journal of Traumatic Stress, 9*(3), 455–471. https://doi.org/10.1002/jts.2490090305

Tedeschi, R. G., & Calhoun, L. G. (2004). Posttraumatic growth: Conceptual foundations and empirical evidence. *Psychological Inquiry, 15*(1), 1–18. https://doi.org/10.1207/s15327965pli1501_01

Tong, E. W., Fredrickson, B. L., Weining, C., & Zi Xing, L. (2010). Re-examining hope: The roles of agency thinking and pathways thinking. *Cognition and Emotion, 24*(7), 1207–1215. https://doi.org/10.1080/02699930903138865

Vyskocilova, J., Prasko, J., Ociskova, M., Sedlackova, Z., & Mozny, P. (2015). Values and values work in cognitive behavior therapy. *Activitas Nervosa Superior Rediviva, 57*(1–2), 40–48. http://rediviva.sav.sk/57i1/40.pdf

11

A MULTIDISCIPLINARY COLLABORATIVE APPROACH TO HUMAN TRAFFICKING

JESSICA WOZNIAK AND DEIDRE HUSSEY

As evidenced in the prior chapters of this volume, human trafficking for labor and commercial sex is complex, with many interrelated causal factors and circumstances that need to be considered when developing effective strategies to combat and prevent human trafficking. Best practices suggest that a robust and diverse set of team members is key to this work. A collaborative response is critical because narrow, singular efforts will likely not meet the diverse needs of individuals who have been trafficked. Psychologists can play a crucial role across, within, and leading these multidisciplinary efforts.

The term "multidisciplinary" is frequently used across professional settings, particularly in health care. However, it can be defined quite differently depending on the type of collaboration. Generally, multidisciplinary teams are individuals from different disciplines working together with a common goal or providing care to a particular population. Teams that focus on an issue related to public health generally focus on more efficacious outcomes for patients, clients, and families (Andreatta, 2010). Community uniqueness will lead to varied development and function of multidisciplinary teams from one community to another and may impact the role psychologists play in these settings.

https://doi.org/10.1037/0000379-012
Psychological Perspectives on Human Trafficking: Theory, Research, Prevention, and Intervention, L. Dryjanska, E. K. Hopper, and H. Stoklosa (Editors)

Is it important to take a multidisciplinary approach to supporting and treating survivors of human trafficking due to the fact that human trafficking is a public health issue that impacts all individuals and communities across generations and must be addressed at all levels of the social–ecological model (American Psychological Association [APA], 2014; U.S. Department of Health & Human Services, 2020). This model focuses on individual, relationship, community, and societal factors and the interaction between them in order to prevent and protect individuals from victimization such as human trafficking (Dahlberg & Krug, 2002). A *multidisciplinary team* (MDT) for trafficking victims refers to a group of professionals and potentially trafficking survivors that come from different disciplines, to provide different services or support to the victim. In their role, psychologists can help improve identification methods, promote the development and utilization of evidence-based services and programs for persons who have been impacted by human trafficking through practice, consultation, providing training and education, conducting research and program evaluation, and policy and prevention promotion (Greenbaum, Bodrick, et al., 2017; Lederer, 2017).

A MULTIDISCIPLINARY TEAM APPROACH TO HUMAN TRAFFICKING

The U.S. Department of State (n.d.) reported that "coordinated federal efforts that incorporate state, local, and tribal entities; the private sector; civil society; survivors; religious communities; and academia are essential to an integrated response to human trafficking" (para. 1); thus, a multidisciplinary public health approach to trafficking requires input from a diverse sector of professionals. As part of this team, psychologists can play a critical role in promoting this coordinated and trauma-informed response to human trafficking survivors.

MDTs serving individuals who have experienced human trafficking can take many forms including task forces, coalitions, and immediate response teams. Others may be discipline driven such as law enforcement or medical. However, successful MDTs have key components such as a shared mission and decision making on services and support for victims, which guide the process and protocol that all team members follow and promote within the community. This coordinated approach leads to shared definitions of human trafficking and a consistent approach to training, prevention, and treatment. The most effective teams are made up of a diverse group of professionals including, but not limited to, medical and health care providers, law enforcement, attorneys, victim advocates, schools, faith-based groups, and child welfare and state and federal agencies. Psychologists and mental health professionals have important roles within the multidisciplinary team approach to human trafficking, as well as specific consultative roles with each of these professional groups. The individual members of task forces may have varied goals depending on discipline; however, the team approach can be critical to success in these individual goals due to the complexity of human trafficking and no one discipline having the capacity to serve a victim's broad spectrum of needs.

There are many reasons that an MDT approach is crucial to serving persons who have been impacted by human trafficking. It can be overly burdensome, particularly for those with unmet mental health needs, to have to navigate multiple systems to help get their needs met; thus, the comprehensive approach of MDTs will ensure that each survivor's individual needs are met in a coordinated fashion at the state, federal, regional, local, and tribal levels (Powell et al., 2018). Partnerships among community stakeholders can develop a coordinated response to ensure efficiency and referrals across disciplines (Macias-Konstantopoulos et al., 2013). An interdisciplinary approach with professionals from varying fields also allows for more immediate assistance and support for human trafficking survivors. Thus, immediate needs are met, and referrals are provided to appropriate MDT collaborators (Awerbuch et al., 2020). Psychologists are well suited to lead and coordinate these teams based on their understanding of the complexities of human behavior and how it is impacted by social, political, and economic issues (APA, 2014).

There are numerous structural (i.e., lack of coordination among providers) and organizational barriers (i.e., funding, training) that impact the response and treatment for human trafficking survivors (Vollinger & Campbell, 2022). Further, human trafficking survivors may avoid seeking help due to a mistrust of systems (Awerbuch et al., 2020). When providers and agencies work in tandem, there is a more efficient use of resources, better identification of gap areas, and a reduction of service duplication. Thus, a multidisciplinary approach can streamline communication and may improve positive outcomes for survivors related to services and support. From firsthand experience, collaboration among the MDT members prioritizes survivor needs, empowers their voices, and improves their comfort engaging with professionals. Case management and service coordination are also crucial components to help create a safety net for victims and minimize revictimization risk. Assistance in care coordination between providers and across systems is imperative to truly support persons who have been impacted by human trafficking (Macias-Konstantopoulos & Bar-Halpern, 2016). APA's Task Force on Trafficking of

Women and Girls (2014) recommended that psychologists "advocate for survivor-centered, survivor-informed, and survivor-led efforts guiding policy-making, protocol development, research design, methodology, and clinical approaches" (p. 7). Further, incorporating survivors in the development of education and training is crucial to ensure their voice is included. Integrating the survivor perspective in this process allows for education and theory to be applicable to the actual practices and programs (Miller et al., 2020).

An MDT response to human trafficking can also help with barriers such as data sharing. Formal and consistent communication through memorandums of understanding and sharing data, protocols, policies, and procedures can improve the efficiency and collaboration in the work being done across the various providers working with human trafficking survivors (Clawson et al., 2006). One study found that service programs for youth human trafficking survivors sought out support from local task forces to help with the struggles they faced addressing the complex needs of survivors due to restrictions on information sharing (Vollinger & Campbell, 2022). The increased need for connection further highlights the importance of a coordinated approach for human trafficking survivors and the associated service organizations that make up the MDT.

Specific to child victims of trafficking, research suggests heightened vulnerabilities and potential health, emotional, and behavioral consequences of human trafficking led children to interface with several child-serving systems, all using different frameworks to assess and treat them. However, these providers may have varying levels of education, training, and understanding, which can potentially lead to retraumatization. This idea provides more support for the need to adopt a common comprehensive framework such as the one used in human trafficking MDTs (Macias-Konstantopoulos & Bar-Halpern, 2016). Psychologists can often serve as the lead in supporting this approach and promoting MDT practices that are trauma-responsive.

The following example highlights success and benefit of an MDT response and the key role the psychologist can play.[1] A psychologist in a large hospital system is working a consultative shift in the emergency department. She notices a young woman (18 years old) has been admitted to the adult behavioral health pod. The psychologist recognizes the name from her three recent prior emergency department admissions to the child division and repeated requests for pregnancy and sexually transmitted disease testing. Knowing these items can be a red flag for sex trafficking, the psychologist meets with

---

[1]All case information in this chapter is fictional.

the young woman and asks a series for trauma-informed screening questions that lead to the woman disclosing that she had been a repeated victim of sexual assault and had, at times, exchanged sex for items of value or to have her basic needs meet; however, she emphasized that she was "not a prostitute." She went on to describe significant and repeated sexual traumas and physical assaults, many at the hands of the man that would be considered her exploiter. For the next 30 minutes, the psychologist used a series of nonjudgmental engagement strategies that led the woman to agree to a sexual assault exam and consider trauma-focused mental health treatment. Additionally, she consented to allow the psychologist to connect her with the county case coordinator for survivors of human trafficking. The psychologist briefed the emergency department team regarding the information she learned and provided guidance on best practice for conducting the medical exam in a way that was responsive to the woman's trauma history. She also emphasized the importance of use of language, as the woman did not see herself as a trafficking victim or a "prostitute." Ultimately, the woman was admitted to inpatient psychiatric treatment due to suicidal intent. In the week that followed, the psychologist made the connection to the case coordinator, who was able to enter the inpatient unit to explain trauma-informed treatment opportunities, the rights she had as a victim of sexual violence, and safe living arrangements. Based on this discussion, the coordinator connected with local and federal law enforcement, as some crimes took place out of the country the young woman resided in. She ensured law enforcement and the prosecutor's office were aware of the sexual assault exam being conducted and made a referral to trauma-focused therapy services. The same consulting psychologist was also a member of the county MDT team, so, when the team met, she was able to provide insight to the team on this young woman's needs, her current stage of change, and suggestions on helpful engagement strategies.

ROLE OF PSYCHOLOGISTS IN MDTs

Psychologists are well positioned to address human trafficking in collaboration with MDTs. Practice, consultation, education and training, research and program evaluation, awareness and prevention, and policy and advocacy are all critical areas in the field of psychology that provide unique opportunities to address human trafficking. Human trafficking must be examined from the social-ecological perspective, from individual protective and risk factors to societal and policy factors (APA, 2014), which makes the role of the psychologist key in this approach. Based on their training and experience, psychologists participate in various aspects of the MDT, outlined in the following subsections.

Practice

Human trafficking experiences can often lead to significant emotional and mental health effects; thus, psychologists and mental health providers are a necessary and fundamental part of every MDT. Clinical psychologists and other allied mental health professionals can ensure there is a coordinated response that addresses the broad spectrum of needs, with specific attention to psychological concepts that interplay in human trafficking. Psychologists can ensure human trafficking survivors receive an evidence-based, trauma-informed response across all encounters with professionals (APA, 2014). Further, psychological theory can inform clinical practices and treatment. Taking into account the psychological dynamics of power, control, and coercion that make it difficult for survivors to leave human trafficking and trust psychotherapy will increase providers' knowledge and ability to meet survivors where they are at. Within psychotherapy, providers can work directly with survivors to explore their specific experiences with human trafficking and what basic or emotional needs may have been met during their trafficking experience. Further, they can provide psychoeducation on mental health symptoms to validate and normalize experiences to build comfort for survivors to process their experiences.

In addition, psychologists can promote the integration of behavioral health services in settings where trafficking survivors reside and receive services, including schools, victim services, communities, foster and residential care, juvenile justice, criminal justice, and health care. As members of the MDT team, psychologists can identify, promote, and provide effective therapeutic techniques and programs specifically created to support human trafficking survivors across the lifespan (APA, 2014).

Psychologists with training in psychological assessment can evaluate across cognitive, academic, personality, and other functioning domains to provide specific recommendations for treatment and follow-up. Psychological assessment can serve as a means to identify and normalize symptoms and experiences, as well as provide trauma-informed recommendations around treatment and support that can empower survivors (Hopper, 2017). Psychologists can also provide assessments in civil, criminal, and family courts.

Psychologists who work directly within the school and educational settings can play a robust role in service provision, and prevention and training efforts as schools and educational systems are multidisciplinary partners who can help identify and connect victims to services (U.S. Department of

Education, Office of Safe and Supportive Schools, 2021). For example, social skill groups and creative arts programs to support youth identified as high risk may lead to prevention of trafficking. School psychologists can create psychoeducational material regarding warning signs of trafficking and provide educational opportunities for parents and caregivers that can then lead to having conversations about trafficking with their children (Rojas, 2020). For example, school psychologists can host parent or caregiver nights with educational material on identification signs or internet and other safety methods. Further, efforts tailored to train school personnel and develop prevention efforts can also be done by school psychologists (APA, 2014).

Consultation

Within MDTs, psychologists often play a consultative role not only with the team as a whole but also with each specific discipline that makes up the team. Psychologists can serve as coordinators and mobilizers to create and lead coalitions and multidisciplinary teams, which ensures a comprehensive approach that incorporates the impact of human behavior (APA, 2014). Another key role is advocating for the development and implementation of evidence-based, developmentally and culturally appropriate trauma-informed services for survivors of human trafficking (APA, 2014). Within the MDT, psychologists can inform and provide recommendations for effective therapeutic treatments, as well as support the mental health referral process.

Psychologists can work in collaboration with medical providers who treat human trafficking victims. Medical providers may provide specific services to human trafficking survivors such as sexual assault exams or child sexual abuse exams provided through the children's advocacy center (CAC) model, or they may treat survivors in general primary care or emergency settings. Mental health providers can offer consultations to medical providers to increase identification of victims in general medical practice and how to provide a trauma-informed approach to care. Mental health professionals can also provide an integrated behavioral health approach during, pre-, or postexamination (Gordon et al., 2018; Iqbal et al., 2021).

When working with child victims of human trafficking, there may be other collaborators who are important to include in an MDT. For example, child welfare or child protection professionals will play a key role, particularly in states where child trafficking is considered child abuse and thus falls under mandated reporting laws. However, even in states where laws have not yet changed, including child welfare professionals on these teams is key to raising awareness and perhaps moving the state toward recognizing trafficking as a form of child abuse. The CAC model was developed through merging a social service and a medical model for addressing child abuse, thus making CACs and psychologists or mental health providers who work within them well positioned to serve child trafficking victims (Starcher et al., 2021). As a requirement for national accreditation, this type of MDT must include mental health providers to provide evidence-based therapy to survivors and many also include mental health support during medical exams and forensic interviews.

Psychologists also play an important consultative role in the law enforcement and prosecution sectors of the MDT. Collaboration with prosecutors in the district and U.S. attorneys offices, attorneys general and their victim advocate teams, detention centers, and parole and probation systems can also be a valuable resource to the MDT collaboration. Psychologists can collaborate as legal experts to provide expert testimony on trafficking dynamics, and forensic psychologists can assist with interviews and evaluations of victims (APA, 2014). Psychologists have the ability to provide psychoeducation and testimony on the psychological coercion and nuances of complex trauma and its impact on survivors' cognition and behavior within the realm of human trafficking, as well as their willingness to work with law enforcement and participate in treatment (APA, 2014). Mental health providers can provide consultation to ensure that victims are treated with this trauma lens and that a trauma-informed approach is being taken throughout the legal process even when there is an overlap between the criminal element and victim support (National District Attorneys Association, 2020). Psychologists may be particularly critical in speaking to victim–offender intersectionality and the complex psychological dynamics at play (Shared Hope International & Villanova Law Institute to Address Commercial Sexual Exploitation, 2020).

Further, psychologists can also collaborate with religious and spiritual community members as part of the MDT. As we explore practices to support recovery and healing, psychologists can provide referrals and connections for survivors who identify religion or spirituality as important to their journey. Research has found that religion and religious leaders can play a key role in a victim's recovery (Barrows, 2017; National Human Trafficking Resource Center, 2016). For example, for survivors present within health care settings that have spiritual service departments, potential opportunities for spiritual service consults and connections could be beneficial to offer when available and in line with the survivor's wishes.

Training and Education

Since human trafficking is a public health concern, it is essential to provide education and training to all individuals and communities to increase awareness of prevalence, risk factors, identification, and the response to human trafficking. However, many training curriculum lack an evidence-based, trauma-informed, survivor-informed approach (Miller et al., 2020). Thus, there is a need for training and education by experts in human trafficking who are also knowledgeable in the most up to date research (Miller et al., 2020), which places psychologists in a key position as trainers in this realm with their expertise in psychological theory, and research and the dynamics that perpetuates violence. Requiring this training across disciplines is intended to reduce vulnerability of trafficking but also will lead to early victim identification and hopefully intervention (APA, 2014). Psychologists play an integral role based on their specific skill set in conducting presentations and their ability to share knowledge to MDTs on psychological concepts that intersect with human trafficking such as coercion, readiness for change, human development and behavior, and the psychological or emotional impact on all multidisciplinary professionals who work with survivors. Psychologists can also inform these training curricula to incorporate misconceptions of victim behavior and symptom presentation, thus leading to earlier and more accurate detection, as well as allowing for more prevention and intervention opportunities. Training targeted at MDTs can improve collaboration and communication across professionals (Clawson & Dutch, 2008).

Regarding education, psychologists can incorporate issues related to human trafficking into curricula across undergraduate, graduate, and postdoctoral education (APA, 2014). Psychologists and mental health professionals involved in teaching at higher education levels should consider integrating topics related to human trafficking into their courses and lectures to equip future mental health professionals in meeting the needs of individuals who have been trafficked (APA, 2014). Education and awareness that starts in the classroom can improve the development of professionals' skills in screening, assessment, and treatment of human trafficking survivors, as well as provide early multidisciplinary professionals a solid foundational understanding of human trafficking. To increase antitrafficking efforts among professionals, education on human trafficking in all health-related curriculums and clinical training programs may allow for better engagement among future professionals in the field (Macias-Konstantopoulos et al., 2013).

Awareness and Prevention

Awareness campaigns and outreach efforts that increase the general public's understanding of risk and identification of human trafficking are often developed by trafficking MDTs and leading such initiatives are in line with the psychologist's role. For professionals, the first critical step is increasing one's own awareness of the scope, nature, and dynamics of human trafficking. According to the APA's Task Force on Trafficking of Women and Girls (2014), psychological theory and research can be used to develop awareness campaigns and training curricula to maximize learning among multiple sectors that interface with trafficked persons or are involved in prevention efforts. More specifically, community and social psychologists can play a vital role in creating programs and campaigns targeted toward specific audiences while research psychologists have training in the interpretation of research findings which they can make more accessible to the general public to increase awareness of human trafficking (APA, 2014). Because psychologists have a comprehensive understanding of risk factors that can increase vulnerability to human trafficking, they are positioned to help create public awareness campaigns and prevention programs that incorporate how exposure to prior trauma, substance use, and mental health disorders can increase risk and vulnerability to human trafficking (APA, 2014). MDT professionals, particularly psychologists, can promote and build awareness and prevention efforts that incorporate strengths and protective factors for children, families, and communities. Psychologists can create prevention programs that are sensitive to the nuances that impact marginalized and more vulnerable populations to human trafficking such as survivors of labor trafficking and those who identify as LGBTQ+.

Research and Program Evaluation

Research and program evaluation are essential from a public health perspective to address human trafficking. Psychologists can conduct empirically based research that helps examine risk factors that are culture and gender inclusive, develop screening methods, provide more accurate prevalence data, increase awareness of risk factors that place children and other vulnerable populations at increased danger, assess the physical and emotional health impacts, increase the understanding of complex trauma and long-term impacts, and evaluate the effectiveness of the various programs, services, and interventions for survivors (Greenbaum, Bodrick, et al., 2017). Research psychologists also "have a critical role to play in conceptualizing, designing, conducting, analyzing, and publishing investigations related to human trafficking" (APA, 2014, p. 53). For example, they can conduct efficacy studies on existing trauma-informed evidence-based therapies to see if they have the same efficacy with trafficking survivors. Additionally, the evaluation of educational and treatment programs is necessary to ensure that the identified programs are effective, of high quality, and built on the most up-to-date research. As they become more aware of effective programs and treatment, psychologists work closely with the MDT to share referrals and vet services and programs that are being provided in their county, state, or elsewhere.

Through research and the creation of programs, psychologists can also explore aspects of human trafficking that get less attention, such as labor trafficking (APA, 2014). There still remains limited research on and understanding of the complexities around labor trafficking, and psychologists must make this a part of their research to bring attention to the issue, which will further the development of programs and treatment specific for this population. Psychological research can also address how religion and spirituality can serve as risk and protective factors in the realm of human trafficking (APA, 2014).

Policy and Advocacy

Empirical research is needed on the nuances of human trafficking to inform the development of national and international policies (Martinho et al., 2020). Psychologists can use their expertise to support policy efforts related to trafficking in governmental and nonprofit organizations. Psychologists inform policy on a social level and can be involved in decision making around resource allocation (APA, 2014). Throughout the years, interests related to advocacy and policy have been critical in the development of antiviolence and sustainable programs (Macias-Konstantopoulos et al., 2013). This can occur at local, state, national, and international levels to help advocate for primary prevention needs and to address vulnerabilities. Greenbaum, Bodrick, et al. (2017) recommended that health care providers, such as psychologists, support specific legislation and policies for primary prevention efforts that involve the education of children and caregivers about human trafficking risks, recruitment practices, and its negative impacts. Additionally, providers can support legislation and policy across all levels, including those that impact access to direct services for survivors, increased collaboration among agency providers, awareness of and work to address the social determinants of health, and improved screening and other practices related to immigration (Greenbaum, Bodrick, et al., 2017).

Psychologists have an essential role in advocacy around policy review and reform related to immigration, work visa programs, and human rights protections to ensure the elimination of abusive labor practices and conditions and support worker rights and interests (APA, 2014). Helping law and policy makers understand social issues, such as human trafficking and the consequences of trafficking on individuals and communities is critical to advocate for evidence-based, culturally appropriate, trauma-informed education and training, practices, programs, research, protocols, and procedures (APA, 2014).

CONCLUSION

As a public health issue, human trafficking is best approached from a multidisciplinary perspective. Psychologists have varying roles across the different subfields of psychology, and depending on the area of specialty, psychologists have unique and critical roles across, within, and leading these multidisciplinary efforts.

Psychologists can help improve identification methods, promote the development of evidence-based services and programs for persons who have been impacted by human trafficking by conducting research and program evaluation, and are in a key position to ensure effective, culturally appropriate, trauma-informed services (Greenbaum, Bodrick, et al., 2017; Lederer, 2017). As evidenced throughout this chapter, psychologists are an important part of the larger MDT due to their role in practice, consultation, education and training, awareness and prevention, research and program evaluation, and policy and advocacy.

REFERENCES

American Psychological Association. (2014). *Report of the Task Force on Trafficking of Women and Girls.* http://www.apa.org/pi/women/programs/trafficking/report.aspx

Andreatta, P. B. (2010). A typology for health care teams. *Health Care Management Review, 35*(4), 345–354. https://doi.org/10.1097/HMR.0b013e3181e9fceb

Awerbuch, A., Gunaratne, N., Jain, J., & Caralis, P. (2020). Raising awareness of human trafficking in key professional fields in a multidisciplinary educational approach. *International Journal of Human Rights in Healthcare, 13*(2), 159–169. https://doi.org/10.1108/IJHRH-07-2019-0053

Barrows, J. (2017). The role of faith-based organizations in the U.S. anti-trafficking movement. In M. Chisolm-Straker & H. Stoklosa (Eds.), *Human trafficking is a public health issue* (pp. 277–291). Springer. https://doi.org/10.1007/978-3-319-47824-1_16

Clawson, H. J., & Dutch, N. (2008). *Identifying victims of human trafficking: Inherent challenges and promising strategies from the field.* United States Department of Health and Human Services. https://aspe.hhs.gov/sites/default/files/migrated_legacy_files//42671/ib.pdf

Clawson, H. J., Dutch, N., & Cummings, M. (2006). *Law enforcement response to human trafficking and implications for victims: Current practices and lessons learned* [Final report]. Caliber. https://www.ncjrs.gov/pdffiles1/nij/grants/216547.pdf

Dahlberg, L. L., & Krug, E. G. (2002). Violence: A global public health problem. In E. G. Krug, L. L. Dahlberg, J. A. Mercy, A. B. Zwi, & R. Lozano (Eds.), *World report on violence and health* (pp. 1–21). World Health Organization.

Gordon, M., Salami, T., Coverdale, J., & Nguyen, P. T. (2018). Psychiatry's role in the management of human trafficking victims: An integrated care approach. *Journal of Psychiatric Practice, 24*(2), 79–86. https://doi.org/10.1097/PRA.0000000000000287

Greenbaum, J., Bodrick, N., the Committee on Child Abuse and Neglect, the Section on International Child Health, Flaherty, E. G., Idzerda, S. M., Laskey, A., Legano, L. A., Leventhal, J. M., Gavril, A. R., Suchdev, P. S., Chan, K. J., Howard, C. R., McGann, P. T., St. Clair, N. E., & Yun, K. (2017). Global human trafficking and child victimization. *Pediatrics, 140*(6), e20173138. https://doi.org/10.1542/peds.2017-3138

Hopper, E. (2017). Trauma-informed psychological assessment of human trafficking survivors. *Women & Therapy, 40*(1–2), 12–30. https://doi.org/10.1080/02703149.2016.1205905

Iqbal, S. Z., Salami, T., Reissinger, M. C., Masood, M. H., Ukrani, K., & Shah, A. A. (2021). The mental health clinician's role in advocacy for survivors of human trafficking: Treatment and management. *Psychiatric Annals, 51*(8), 373–377. https://doi.org/10.3928/00485713-20210707-02

Lederer, L. J. (2017). Combating modern bondage: The development of a multidisciplinary approach to human trafficking. In M. Chisolm-Straker & H. Stoklosa (Eds.), *Human trafficking is a public health issue* (pp. 401–413). Springer. https://doi.org/10.1007/978-3-319-47824-1_23

Macias-Konstantopoulos, W., Ahn, R., Alpert, E. J., Cafferty, E., McGahan, A., Williams, T. P., Castor, J. P., Wolferstan, N., Purcell, G., & Burke, T. F. (2013). An international comparative public health analysis of sex trafficking of women and girls in eight cities: Achieving a more effective health sector response. *Journal of Urban Health, 90*(6), 1194–1204. https://doi.org/10.1007/s11524-013-9837-4

Macias-Konstantopoulos, W., & Bar-Halpern, M. (2016). Commercially sexually exploited and trafficked minors: Our hidden and forgotten children. In R. Parekh & E. W. Childs (Eds.), *Stigma and prejudice: Touchstones in understanding diversity in healthcare* (pp. 183–202). Humana Press/Springer Nature.

Martinho, G., Goncalves, M., & Matos, M. (2020). Child trafficking, comprehensive needs and professional practices: A systematic review. *Children and Youth Services Review, 119*, 105674. https://doi.org/10.1016/j.childyouth.2020.105674

Miller, C. L., Chisholm-Straker, M., Duke, G., & Stoklosa, H. (2020). A framework for the development of healthcare provider education programs on human trafficking part three: Recommendations. *Journal of Human Trafficking, 6*(4), 425–434. https://doi.org/10.1080/23322705.2019.1635342

National District Attorneys Association, Women Prosecutors Section. (2020). *National human trafficking prosecution: Best practices guide* [White paper]. https://ndaa.org/wp-content/uploads/Human-Trafficking-White-Paper-Jan-2020.pdf

National Human Trafficking Resource Center. (2016). *Faith-based partnerships to combat human trafficking.* https://humantraffickinghotline.org/sites/default/files/Faith-Based%20Partnerships%20to%20Combat%20Human%20Trafficking.pdf

Powell, C., Asbill, M., Louis, E., & Stoklosa, H. (2018). Identifying gaps in human trafficking mental health service provision. *Journal of Human Trafficking, 4*(3), 256–269. https://doi.org/10.1080/23322705.2017.1362936

Rojas, M. E. (2020). *Fighting child trafficking in Texas: Equipping schools with awareness tools for parents* [Master's thesis, Texas State University]. University Scholarship. https://digital.library.txstate.edu/handle/10877/9865

Shared Hope International & Villanova Law Institute to Address Commercial Sexual Exploitation. (2020). *Responding to sex trafficking victim-offender intersectionality: A guide for criminal justice stakeholders.* https://sharedhope.org/wp-content/uploads/2020/01/SH_Responding-to-Sex-Trafficking-Victim-Offender-Intersectionality2020_FINAL.pdf

Starcher, D. L., Anderson, V. R., Kulig, T. C., & Sullivan, C. J. (2021). Human trafficking cases presenting within child advocacy centers. *Journal of Child Sexual Abuse, 30*(6), 637–652. https://doi.org/10.1080/10538712.2021.1955791

United States Department of Education, Office of Safe and Supportive Schools. (2021). *Human trafficking in America's schools: What schools can do to prevent, respond, and help students to recover from human trafficking* (2nd ed.). https://safesupportivelearning.ed.gov/human-trafficking-americas-schools

United States Department of Health & Human Services. (2020). *What is human trafficking?* https://www.acf.hhs.gov/otip/about/what-human-trafficking

United States Department of State. (n.d.). *Federal response on human trafficking.* https://www.state.gov/humantrafficking/

Vollinger, L., & Campbell, R. (2022). Youth service provision and coordination among members of a regional human trafficking task force. *Journal of Interpersonal Violence, 37*(7–8), NP5669–NP5692.

Index

A

Ability to plan, 243
Abolitionist psychology, 56, 64–68
Abuse. *See also* Substance use and abuse
  child, 22–23, 108, 189, 261
  developmental pace of children with history of, 103–104
  emotional, 22–23, 179, 183
  news coverage linking trafficking and, 121, 122
  physical, 22–23
  as risk factor, 180
  sexual, 22–23, 183, 184, 186
  spiritual, 239
  in trafficking experience, 3, 17, 20–24, 35–36, 75, 77, 7–91, 100, 102–103, 105–109, 119, 121–122, 126, 137, 146, 177–191, 215
Academics, as frame sponsors, 125–126
ACEs. *See* Adverse childhood experiences
"Acquisition-movement-exploitation" principle, 162–163
Action stage, 203
Actor–observer bias, 141–144
Actual self, 138
Acute symptoms of mental illness, 83
Acute traumatic injuries, 83
Addiction, 12, 205. *See also* Substance use and abuse
Adjunctive treatments, trauma-informed, 212–213
Adolescents. *See also* Youth
  CHANCE program for, 216
  cognitive development for, 105
  C-PTSD approaches with, 211–212
  developmental trajectory for, 103

  educational opportunities for, 33
  emotional regulation for adolescent survivors, 184
  risk reduction through family therapy with, 213
  safety assessments for, 86
  spirituality and resilience for, 239
  trauma-focused EBTs for, 208–210
Advantageous childhood experiences (counter-ACEs), 35
Adverse childhood experiences (ACEs), 10, 35, 99–100, 103, 186
Advocacy, 65–67, 80, 91, 261, 265–266
After the training phase, in antitrafficking training, 160–161
Agency, 231, 237–238
Agenda setting, 115
Aggression, 12, 18
Agricultural workers (farmworkers)
  during COVID-19 pandemic, 87
  effects of labor trafficking for, 79
  participants in trafficking of, 12
  protecting rights of, 30
  stereotypes about, 148
  whistleblower protections for, 162
  workers rights/protections for, 80
Albright, K., 201
Alienation, 23, 25, 179, 183
Allow States and Victims to Fight Online Sex Trafficking Act, 168
American Hospital Association, 89
American Psychological Association (APA)
  call to raise public awareness from, 121
  on deportation of unaccompanied minors, 122–123

About the Editors

Laura Dryjanska, PhD, is a psychology professor at Asbury University in Wilmore, Kentucky, United States, and Cardinal Stefan Wyszyński University in Warsaw, Poland. Since 2009, she has been active on the Shadow Children Committee in Italy, which is dedicated to raising funds for shelters for "street children" in different countries and organizing conferences on this topic. In addition to publishing articles and book chapters on the topic of sex trafficking, objectification, and dehumanization, she has implemented a number of human trafficking awareness-raising initiatives at Biola University and in service organizations in Italy and Southern California. Dr. Dryjanska has presented on human trafficking during scientific and advocacy-oriented events, including the European Association of Social Psychology meeting in Trento (Italy) in 2015, the American Psychological Association (APA) Convention in Toronto in 2015, the APA Annual Convention in Washington, DC, in 2017, the APA Convention in San Francisco in 2018, and the APA Convention in San Diego in 2020, as well as networked with other scientists and activists during the Freedom From Slavery Forum in Palo Alto in 2017 and regular meetings of the Orange County Human Trafficking Task Force. She has developed two courses on human trafficking for psychology undergraduate and graduate students as well as an online lifelong learning course.

Elizabeth K. Hopper, PhD, is a licensed clinical psychologist with a focus on human trafficking and traumatic stress. She is codirector of the National Center on Child Trafficking (NCCT), a federally funded program focused on improving care for trafficked and commercially sexually exploited children and their families. Dr. Hopper is also project director of the Metropolitan Boston Complex Trauma Treatment Initiative, a mobile service network delivering evidence-based trauma interventions to high-risk and underserved complex trauma-exposed children and youth and families. She was previously the director of Project REACH, a national antitrafficking direct services and training and technical assistance (T/TA) program, and director of the New England Coalition Against Trafficking. Dr. Hopper serves as an expert consultant for nonprofits and federal agencies, including the Department of Health and Human Services (National Human Trafficking Training and Technical Assistance Center) and the Department of Justice (The Office for Victims of Crime Training and Technical Assistance Center), and she has collaborated with multiple agencies and organizations in developing trauma-informed care systems. She is coauthor of *Treating Adult Survivors of Childhood Emotional Abuse and Neglect: Component-Based Psychotherapy* and *Overcoming Trauma Through Yoga: Reclaiming Your Body* and has written numerous scholarly articles and book chapters on developmental trauma, trauma-informed care, and human trafficking.

Hanni Stoklosa, MD, MPH, is the CMO and cofounder of HEAL Trafficking and an emergency physician at Brigham and Women's Hospital with appointments at Harvard Medical School and the Harvard Humanitarian Initiative. Dr. Stoklosa is an internationally recognized expert, advocate, researcher, and speaker on the well-being of trafficking survivors in the United States and internationally, using a public health lens. She has advised the United Nations, International Organization for Migration, U.S. Department of Health and Human Services, U.S. Department of Labor, U.S. Department of State, and the National Academy of Medicine on issues of human trafficking and has testified as an expert witness multiple times before the U.S. Congress. Moreover, she has conducted research on trafficking and persons facing the most significant social, economic, and health challenges in a diversity of settings, including Australia, China, Egypt, Guatemala, India, Liberia, Nepal, Kazakhstan, the Philippines, South Sudan, Taiwan, and Thailand. Among other accolades, Dr. Stoklosa has been honored with the U.S. Department of Health and Human Services Office of Women's Health Emerging Leader award, the Harvard Medical School Dean's Faculty Community Service award, and has been named as an Aspen Health Innovator and National Academy of Medicine Emerging Leader. Her antitrafficking work has been featured by CNN, *The New York Times*, NPR, *Fortune*, *Glamour*, the Canadian Broadcasting Corporation, STAT News, and *Marketplace*. Dr. Stoklosa published the first textbook addressing the public health response to trafficking, *Human Trafficking Is a Public Health Issue: A Paradigm Expansion in the United States*.